A

BOOK

The Philip E. Lilienthal imprint
honors special books
in commemoration of a man whose work
at the University of California Press from 1954 to 1979
was marked by dedication to young authors
and to high standards in the field of Asian Studies.
Friends, family, authors, and foundations have together endowed the
Lilienthal Fund, which enables the Press
to publish under this imprint selected books
in a way that reflects the taste and judgment
of a great and beloved editor.

The publisher gratefully acknowledges the generous contribution to this book provided by the Philip E. Lilienthal Asian Studies Endowment Fund of the University of California Press Associates, which is supported by a major gift from Sally Lilienthal.

築地

TSUKIJI

魚河岸

CALIFORNIA STUDIES IN FOOD AND CULTURE

Darra Goldstein, Editor

THEODORE C. BESTOR

TSUKIJI

THE FISH MARKET AT THE CENTER OF THE WORLD

UNIVERSITY OF CALIFORNIA PRESS

Berkeley   Los Angeles   London

Half-title page: the Japanese inscription reads "Tsukiji *uogashi,*" the Tsukiji fish quay or fish market

Title page: the crest is Tsukiji's *uogashi* logo

University of California Press
Berkeley and Los Angeles, California

University of California Press, Ltd.
London, England

© 2004 by the Regents of the University of California

Unless otherwise credited, all photographs were taken by the author,
© Theodore C. Bestor. Tōkyō Uoichiba Oroshi Kyōdō Kumiai has kindly
given permission for the reproduction of sketches from Mori Kazan's
Mori Kazan Gashū: Nihonbashi Uogashi (1977), which appear in figures
26, 27, 48, 62, and 67.

Library of Congress Cataloging-in-Publication Data

Bestor, Theodore C.
  Tsukiji : the fish market at the center of the world / Theodore C.
Bestor.
    p.   cm.—(California studies in food and culture; 11)
  Includes bibliographical references and index.
  ISBN 978-0-520-22024-9 (pbk. : alk. paper)
    1. Tōkyō-to Chūō Oroshiuri Shijō—History.   2. Markets—Japan—
Tokyo—History.   3. Seafood industry—Japan—Tokyo—History.
4. Tokyo (Japan)—Social life and customs.   I. Title.   II. Series.
HF5475.J3T653 2004
381'.437'0952135—dc22   2003022763

Manufactured in the United States of America

16   15   14   13   12   11   10
12   11   10   9   8   7   6

The paper used in this publication meets the minimum requirements of
ANSI/NISO Z39.48−1992 (R 1997) *(Permanence of Paper).*

For Vic,
for being here through the raw and the cooked

Contents

Illustrations

Tables

Preface

Economic theorists, like French chefs in regard to food, have
developed stylized models whose ingredients are limited by
some unwritten rules. Just as traditional French cooking does
not use seaweed or raw fish, so neoclassical models do not make
assumptions derived from psychology, anthropology, or sociology.
I disagree with any rules that limit the nature of the ingredients
in economic models.

George A. Akerlof, *An Economic Theorist's Book of Tales* (1984)

During the boom years, books about Japanese markets became commonplace:
market access, market secrets, market barriers. Then, market meltdowns.

Even in the wake of Japan's sustained economic downturn since the early
1990s—or perhaps especially in that wake—there is much to be learned
from Japanese markets: about how Japanese economic life is organized, how
markets are formed out of the cultural and social stuff of everyday life in this
or any other society, how economic activity is embedded in social institutions.

This is another book about a Japanese market. I cover the waterfront,
exploring currents of collusion, favoritism, and inefficiency; close relationships between trade cartels and government bureaucracies; patterns of
insider trading; and asymmetrical flows of information around which
keiretsu—vertical combines—are organized. I describe trends in marketing
and in the microdifferentiation of consumption as the prosperity of the past
two generations has transformed the lifestyles of most urban Japanese. I
examine the dynamics of employer paternalism, the management of consensus, and the cultural underpinnings of economic and social dynamism,
from techniques that samurai used for managing market behavior to the
twentieth-century expansion of Japanese trade overseas. And with Japanese
political and economic systems now almost endlessly adrift amid scandal,
self-doubt, and stagnation, I discuss how the economic success of the 1980s
has given way to the economic recession and psychological depression of
Japan after the Bubble.

But *this* market study does not herald lessons for foreign businesspeople
to apply in their own organizations. I do not tout any twelve-step programs
to success in one's dealings with Japanese trade partners. Nor is it a tri-
umphal exposé of why Japanese markets don't work, why Japanese eco-

nomic success was short-lived, or why Japan's economic miracle was a sham to begin with. No theory Z; no enigmas of power; no five rings; no free sushi.

Instead, this is an ethnography of trade and economic institutions as they are embedded in and shaped by the cultural and social currents of Japanese life, an ethnography of how economies—how markets—are themselves created by the production and circulation of *cultural* and *social* capital as well as of goods, services, and financial assets.

I focus on a market of singular scale and scope: Tsukiji, the world's largest marketplace for fresh and frozen seafood, which supplies Tokyo's sushi chefs and homemakers alike. Located in the middle of Tokyo, only a few blocks from the Ginza shopping district, the Tsukiji marketplace is a prominent landmark of the city, well known but little understood by most Tokyoites, and also a popular and fascinating destination for foreign tourists. It is a modern market with an enormous volume of trade—roughly ¥544 billion ($4.7 billion) worth of seafood in 2001, about 2.3 million kilograms a day— and it is also a marketplace with a venerable history dating from the early seventeenth century. Tsukiji is closely attuned to the subtleties of Japanese food culture and to the representations of national cultural identity that cloak cuisine, but this is also the market that drives the global fishing industry, from sea urchin divers in Maine to shrimp farmers in Thailand, from Japanese long-liners in the Indian Ocean to Croatian tuna ranchers in the Adriatic.

Tsukiji's vibrant present and colorful past reflect the market's significance along many dimensions—cultural, historical, economic, culinary, institutional, and social—and readers may come to this book curious about quite distinct and widely varying aspects of the marketplace.

Anthropologists and other social scientists who study markets, exchange, and commodification may be most interested in the social structure of economic process and the role of a marketplace as a cultural institution. Professionals in the seafood industry may want to learn about the channels of trade and the culture of cuisine within the world's largest and at times most profitable seafood market. Urban specialists may look for analyses of infrastructure as an important element in the cultural construction of space and place. Academic specialists on Japan may focus on the historical development of the marketplace, its relationship to food culture and consumption, its resonances with the mercantile lifestyles of "downtown" Tokyo, and the interlocking cultural meanings and structural forms that create distinctive modes of economic organization. Trade officials and businesspeople may be interested in questions of market access, the spread of supermarkets, and the structure of distribution channels.

To help readers navigate the pages ahead, I offer here a brief overview of the chapters that follow. The Tsukiji marketplace is complex and any good account of it must necessarily be rich in facts both big and small. Inevitably, I repeat myself from time to time as I try to explain the flow of institutional life and the market's dynamics; the minutiae may strain the attention of some readers while occasional repetitions of explanations, definitions, or crucial events may irritate others. Chapters 1 and 2, in particular, briefly introduce material that I explore in greater depth in later chapters. The devil is, indeed, in the details—particularly for an author—but equally, from those details, I hope, will emerge a clear picture of the fascinating enterprise that is Tsukiji.

In chapter 1, "Tokyo's Pantry," I describe my own introduction to Tsukiji and how my research developed out of an initial interest in the small-scale family-operated businesses so characteristic of Tsukiji and many other sectors of the Japanese economy. I outline my anthropological approach to Tsukiji as an ethnographic study of complex institutional structures attached to and motivated by the dynamics of cultural meaning, a cultural version of institutional economics. This chapter also places Tsukiji in wider cultural, historical, and social contexts: as a central element in Tokyo's infrastructure; as a key site for the transmission and transformation of Japanese food culture; as a crucial link between Japan's domestic fishing industry and the global exploitation of marine resources; and as an exemplar of Japanese distribution channels.

The book's second chapter, "Grooved Channels," walks the reader through Tsukiji's physical layout and its daily rhythms, and discusses the way in which market and place—economic exchange and the spatial and temporal frameworks that order it—are inextricably intertwined. Visitors to the marketplace who want an overview of the market's sights and sounds may find this chapter a good place to begin.

"From Landfill to Marketplace," chapter 3, gives a brief history of the market from the early seventeenth century to the present. I focus primarily on Tsukiji's institutional evolution as Japan's political economy moved from seventeenth-century feudalism to late-twentieth-century bureaucratic capitalism, and discuss the cultural identity that Tsukiji's traders derive from the market's history.

Readers particularly interested in Japanese food culture may want to start with chapter 4, "The Raw and the Cooked." Here, I focus on seafood as a central aspect of Japanese culinary culture and consumption to explain the tricky currents of trade and custom that Tsukiji traders must navigate in their daily business and that shape the social structure of culinary specializations within the marketplace.

The next three chapters examine the social networks and institutions that make the market run. In chapter 5, "Visible Hands," I discuss the structure of auctions; the roles of auction houses, auctioneers, and traders; and the ways in which the institutional structures of trade are linked to patterns of vertical coordination and horizontal cohesion that center on the exchange of contextualized information. "Family Firm," chapter 6, describes the dynamics of family firms, including patterns of inheritance, apprenticeship, and training, as well as various personal affiliations among wholesalers, such as kinship and hometown ties. Chapter 7, "Trading Places," examines the social institutions and relationships that organize traders' activities, including the determination of auction rules and other norms of trade, the institutionalized trade guilds that govern much of the market's activities, the formation of alliances and coalitions among wholesalers, and principles of competition and equalization that run through the traders' institutional lives.

"Full Circle," chapter 8, summarizes my ethnographic conclusions about the institutional structure of trade and the cultural meanings that attach to and motivate the market's social structure, both formal and informal. I place these conclusions in several broader contexts, including interpretations of Japanese economic organization and behavior; anthropological perspectives on markets, exchange, and commodification; and anthropological engagement with the analysis of complex, urban, industrial societies.

The worlds of Japanese cuisine and of wholesale markets have highly specialized vocabularies, so for both traders and food aficionados the glossary may be useful.

Because Tsukiji is a popular attraction, I offer general suggestions for tourists in "Visiting Tsukiji" (appendix 1).

And finally, Tsukiji is a swiftly moving place: for up-to-date information on market trends, trade channels, and environmental issues, "Video, Web, and Statistical Resources" (appendix 2) lists many links related to the marketplace and wider worlds of the fishing industry, including my own Tsukiji research homepage, www.people.fas.harvard.edu/~bestor/tsukiji.

Acknowledgments

An almost endless list of people deserve my deepest thanks for their cooperation and assistance with my research on Tsukiji. To thank them all individually would be impossible and would violate repeated assurances of confidentiality.

Many people at Tsukiji, including dozens whose names I never knew, gave generously of their time and knowledge about the marketplace and made possible my access to it. First and foremost, I cannot say enough to thank the dozens of midlevel wholesalers whom I interviewed—formally and informally—who answered my questions; allowed me to observe their daily work lives; provided me introductions to their own friends, colleagues, and customers; and occasionally sent me home with a kilogram of highgrade tuna in my briefcase.

The officers and staff of the federation of Tsukiji's intermediate wholesalers, Tō-Oroshi (Tōkyō Uoichiba Oroshi Kyōdō Kumiai—the Tokyo Fishmarket Wholesalers' Cooperative Federation), provided me with enormous amounts of information and assistance. The late Matsumoto Hiroshi, then executive director of Tō-Oroshi, spent patient hours answering my questions. And Mr. Koizumi of the Tō-Oroshi staff found the time again and again to dig up documents in answer to my insatiable demand for detailed statistics, histories, and lists. From the many kindnesses of then President Masuda, who encouraged my interest in the market on several early visits, to the giggling help of Ms. Yanase, who adjusted my festival *yukata*, I owe great thanks.

Many officials of the Tokyo Metropolitan Government's market administration also were exceedingly helpful; Naganuma Tomoe, former director of the General Affairs Section of the Bureau of Markets, played an especially important role in opening doors and offering me his own insights into the operation of the marketplace.

The Ginrinkai, an informal reading room and social club located inside the marketplace, often provided me with pleasant company in which to pursue extended discussions of the market both past and present. I was taken under the wing of the Ginrinkai's director, Nishimura Eiko (1923–1996), a woman who presided with earthy cynicism over her corner of Tsukiji (and it was a much larger corner than her crowded rooms would have suggested to a casual observer).

The Iida family has made me feel welcome again and again—in their stall, on the auction floor, in their restaurant, at their home, and in their offices. I have learned enormous amounts from them and from Michiko and Yuji Imai, all of whom have become close friends of mine in the past dozen years.

Tom Asakawa of the Foreign Commercial Section of the U.S. Embassy has repeatedly and unstintingly given me the benefit of his own detailed and extensive knowledge of Japanese fisheries trade. Bill Court, of Transpac Fisheries, generously provided early guidance and introductions, and continuing hospitality.

Officers and staff from several of the major auction houses at Tsukiji— especially Daiichi Suisan, Daito Gyorui, and Tōto Suisan—were very gracious in allowing me access to auction areas and in answering many questions about their business dealings.

Robert Campbell took me under his wing with great patience and good humor as I learned about the American fishing business and observed Tsukiji's overseas reach on docks in New England. Rich Ruais and many members of the East Coast Tuna Association were also very helpful and informative on the U.S.-Japan seafood trade.

My thanks go also to Inomata Hideo, an official of the Ministry of Agriculture, Forestry and Fisheries and a former graduate student at Cornell University, who has been unfailingly helpful in providing information on MAFF documents and policies. And to Matsunobu Yōhei, a dedicated Cornell alumnus (and retired MAFF official), who has over the years provided me with innumerable introductions to individuals and institutions throughout the Japanese food industry.

From the birth of an idea for a book about Tsukiji to the completion of this manuscript, my fieldwork—during research trips and teaching assignments both long and short, between 1989 and 2003—has been generously supported by many organizations at various times and for various phases of the project: the Japan Foundation; the U.S. Department of Education

Fulbright Program; the Joint Committee on Japanese Studies of the American Council of Learned Societies and the Social Science Research Council; the Geirui Kenkyūjō; the National Science Foundation (Grants BNS 90–08696 and its continuation as SBR 94–96163); the Center on Japanese Economy and Business and the Toyota Program of the East Asian Institute, both of Columbia University; the Abe Fellowship Program of the Japan Foundation's Center for Global Partnership; the New York Sea Grant Institute (Grants R/SPD-3 and R/SPD-4); the Korean Studies Program of the Northeast Asia Council of the Association for Asian Studies; the Japanese Ministry of Education (through a collaborative project titled *Model of Global Japan and Globalization,* organized by Harumi Befu, then of Kyoto Bunkyō University [Mombushō Project Number 10041094]); and the Japan Research Fund of Cornell University's East Asia Program. Funds from the Reischauer Institute of Japanese Studies at Harvard University assisted with final manuscript preparation. I am grateful to each of these programs, but of course none of them is responsible in any way for the findings, conclusions, or interpretations presented here.

Many talented and dedicated research assistants aided my research at various times, some for extended periods of time, some more briefly. Kagohashi Hideki, then a student at Sophia University, worked with me at the very beginning of the project in 1989 and accompanied me on research trips to Hokkaidō, Miyagi, and Mie Prefectures. Together we struggled to learn basic vocabularies of fish and markets. Takada Hiroko, then an undergraduate student at Barnard College and later a graduate student at Columbia University, submerged herself in Tsukiji's history and became my bibliographic specialist on historical sources. I am extremely grateful as well for research assistance from many others at various times while in the United States, Japan, and Korea, including Gigi Chang (Cornell), Joo-Hee Chung (Harvard), Neriko Musha Doerr (Cornell), Christine Donis-Keller (Barnard), Evan Frisch (Cornell), Fukatsu Naoko (Barnard), Evan Hanover (Cornell), Horiike Mika (Tokyo Toritsu University), Ishige Naoko (Tokyo Toritsu University), Jiang Guo-ren (Cornell), Kuroda Makoto (Harvard), Sage Nagai (Cornell), Nakamura Yoko (Cornell), Niikawa Shihoko, Ogawa Akihiro (Cornell), Jean Oh (Chicago), Kelly Price (Stanford), Elissa Sato (Harvard), Elizabeth Shea (Cornell), Shiotani Kiki (Columbia), Katrina Stoll (Cornell), Takada Motoko (Keio University), Takeuchi Kaori (Cornell), Michael Wittmer (Cornell), and Lisia Zheng (Harvard). Dawn Grimes-MacLellan (Cornell, now at the University of Illinois) read a complete revision of the manuscript with a superb eye for detail and a diplomatic flair for raising excellent questions.

Obara Yumiko labored with great resourcefulness to track down permissions for many of the illustrations reproduced in this volume, and Matt Thorn was very helpful in providing contacts to Japanese *manga* publishers. The following individuals and organizations generously gave permission to reproduce materials included as illustrations in this book: Hanasaki Akira; Hyōronsha; the Japan Times, Ltd.; the Herbert F. Johnson Museum of Art at Cornell University; Kariya Tetsu; Kōdansha; Mainichi PhotoBank; Maruha Corporation; the Morita Photo Laboratory; Okeguchi Mako; Sawada Shigetaka; Shōgakkan; Terasawa Daisuke; the Tokyo Metropolitan Government, Bureau of Markets and Bureau of Public Health; Tōkyō Tsukiji Uoichiba Ōmono Gyōkai; Tōkyō-to Uoichiba Oroshi Kyōdō Kumiai; Tsukiji 4-chōme Seinenkai; and Jacqueline Wender, for the use of photographs taken by her father, Russell B. Bryan. I am extremely grateful to them all.

Kazuko Sakaguchi of Harvard University's Documentation Center on Contemporary Japan cheerfully provided great assistance in locating statistical sources of information during the final preparation of the manuscript.

One of the immense pleasures of research at Tsukiji is that so many other people find the place fascinating. Victoria Lyon Bestor, Chiba Ayako, Laurel Cornell, Andrew and Megumi Gordon, Peter Gourevitch, G. Cameron Hurst, Peter Katzenstein, Stephen Krasner, Elizabeth MacLachlan, Matsuoka Tomo, Niikawa Shihoko, Jordan Sand, Sheila Smith, and Carolyn Stevens are just a few of the friends and colleagues whose interest in seeing the market has been a boon to my research. Colleen Coyne (of the American Seafood Institute) and Susan Barber (of the Maine Lobster Promotion Council) allowed me to accompany a delegation of American seafood producers that visited Japan and Korea on an export promotion tour in 1995, and I took members of that delegation on several tours of the marketplace as well. And several times I have shown working journalists around the marketplace. Most anthropologists do not get—or want—many opportunities to show off their field sites; in my experience, these chances to guide friends, fellow academics, seafood professionals, and journalists through the complicated scene and to field their own on-the-spot questions coming from many different viewpoints have been immensely helpful in making me question my own assumptions, focus my inquiry, and (I hope) clarify my answers.

Like wholesale markets, scholarly communities are held together by complex forms of exchange, with transactions conducted in varying currencies. An author incurs debts in the intellectual (and political) economy of scholarship as well as in its moral economy. The exchange rates are tricky, as I have found, but moral support is the only hard currency, and in this realm I have racked up enormous debts that I can never fully repay. Without the generosity of time and spirit of many colleagues who gave advice, read drafts, noted errors, encouraged me through moments of despair, suggested other approaches, convinced me that I was not crazy (and pointed out when I was), this book would not have been completed.

James Acheson, Harumi Befu, Muriel Bell, Eyal Ben-Ari, Mattias Böckin, Kasia Cwiertka, Robert Gibbons, Roger Haydon, Roger Janelli, William Kelly, David Koester, Setha Low, Owen Lynch, Richard Nelson, Emiko Ohnuki-Tierney, Ken Oshima, David Plath, Blair Ruble, Roger Sanjek, John Singleton, Henry D. Smith III, Robert J. Smith, Sheila A. Smith, R. Kenji Tierney, William Tsutsui, and Merry I. White have all given me excellent suggestions, in some cases pointing me toward valuable data and in other cases helping me clarify the structure of my arguments, in part or in whole.

Ikeda Keiko, a good friend and colleague at Barnard, now at Doshisha University, has on many occasions lent her critical eye to improving the idiomatic style of my Japanese translations, and has also given me the benefit of her own anthropological insights into both American and Japanese culture.

Several former colleagues at Columbia deserve extraordinary thanks for immeasurable support in difficult times, including Paul Anderer, Myron Cohen, the late Libbet Crandon-Malamud, Carol Gluck, Hugh Patrick, Henry D. Smith II, and Madeleine Zelin.

My deepest appreciation as well to Laurie Damiani, David Holmberg, Steve Sangren, and Robert J. Smith, my close colleagues at Cornell, for their moral support.

Special thanks go as well to Setha Low for keeping at me to keep at it. And to Harry Segal for encouragement along the way.

Sheila Levine, of the University of California Press, despaired repeatedly of ever seeing a finished manuscript. Without the skill and patience—and the persuasive application of toughness—that she and others, including Dore Brown and Alice Falk, brought to bear, this book would never have reached its final form; my deep appreciation to them for all their help. Bill Nelson did a fabulous job of creating the maps for the book.

Dorothy Koch Bestor has read and reread many drafts of the book, not only out of maternal interest but also as a skilled and demanding editor. Her innumerable suggestions and unflappable patience have enormously improved the organization and presentation of my material; I owe her an unrepayable debt for this, as for many other things. My father, Arthur

Bestor, did not live to see the completion of the book, nor did Joseph Lyon and Mona Lyon, my parents-in-law, but without their love and encouragement the book would have been impossible.

My son, Nick, has endured visits ("what? another one?") to ports and fish markets beyond all reason; his only reward, a well-developed enthusiasm for expensive kinds of sushi at a young age. I wish that I had been as tolerant of my father's idiosyncrasies as he is of mine.

Victoria Lyon Bestor deserves far, far more than just my thanks for living with this book from the beginning. Most of my previous research in Japan was conducted with her at my side, and this research, much of it conducted as a *tanshin* ("spouse away on business"), has made me even more keenly aware of Vickey's wise counsel and the many contributions—intellectual and commonsensical—that she makes to my research. For all her help when we were in Japan together, and for all her willingness to hold a family and household together when I was in Japan for research on my own, I dedicate this book to her.

In spite of all the good advice I received, where I flounder the fault is entirely my own. I bear sole responsibility for errors, omissions, and interpretations, however fishy they may be.

Words, Dates, Statistics, Money

PRONOUNCING *TSUKIJI*

Many foreigners stumble over the pronunciation of "Tsukiji," the name of both the market and the neighborhood that surrounds it. "Tsukiji" roughly rhymes with "squeegee." The "ts" sound (like "*ts*etse fly" in English) is difficult for many foreigners, and the vowels are elided. Americans often mispronounce the name by applying stress: tsu-KI-ji. But in Japanese, all syllables receive equal emphasis.

PEOPLE'S NAMES

All individuals mentioned in the text of book are identified by pseudonyms, except for public figures and published authors. The names of Japanese individuals are presented in the Japanese fashion: family name first, personal name second.

TERMS

A glossary of Japanese terms, particularly the specialized vocabulary of a wholesale seafood market, appears in the back of the book. The most extensive and detailed English-language glossary of Japanese culinary terms, foodstuffs, and techniques is modestly titled *A Dictionary of Japanese Food*, by Richard Hosking (1996). Other good glossaries can be found in Condon and Ashizawa (1978) and Richie (1985).

Two major sets of actors at Tsukiji are the *nakaoroshi gyōsha* (also sometimes called *nakagai* or *nakagainin*) and the *oroshi gyōsha*. Although these terms are translated in a variety of ways in the seafood industry, I refer to them throughout the book as "intermediate wholesalers" and "auction houses" respectively.

Tokyo was known as Edo until the Meiji Restoration of 1868. Throughout the book I refer to the pre-Meiji city, bay, and castle as Edo.

Abbreviations

I use the following abbreviations in the text and in citations:

MAFF   Ministry of Agriculture, Forestry and Fisheries (Nōrinsuisanshō, in Japanese)

TMG   Tokyo Metropolitan Government (Tōkyō-to, in Japanese)

Transliterations and Translations

Japanese terms commonly used in English—sushi, sashimi, saké—are not italicized, and well-known place-names—Tokyo, Osaka, Kyoto—are written without diacritical markings, unless they appear in a Japanese phrase or as part of a proper name. All other Japanese terms are written with appropriate diacritical markings. Japanese words in the body of the text are italicized only on first use in a chapter, except when the word itself is the subject of discussion. Japanese words are transliterated according to the system used in *Kenkyūsha's New Japanese-English Dictionary* (4th ed.).

All translations from Japanese sources are my own.

DATES

Japanese history is conventionally divided into periods based on dynastic names and individual imperial reigns. Just as Americans use time periods to imprecisely identify social and cultural milieu ("the Roaring Twenties," "the sixties"), Japanese identify events and trends with similar blocks of time, which often do not translate meaningfully into Western historical contexts. Where possible, I provide specific dates in Western terms, but the following era names are also used:

Tokugawa period	1603–1868
Meiji period	1868–1912
Taishō period	1912–1925
Shōwa period	1926–1989
Allied Occupation period	1945–1952
Heisei period	1989 to the present

The "postwar" period in Japanese history is often vaguely defined, sometimes meaning anything after 1945; from the perspective of the beginning of the twenty-first century, the term more appropriately applies to the period of postwar recovery, and I use the term to refer to the late 1940s, 1950s, and early 1960s (arbitrarily ending it with the 1964 Tokyo Olympics).

STATISTICS

Markets change quickly, and nowhere more so than in the statistical yard-sticks by which they are often measured and recorded. I do not attempt to provide complete statistical coverage over the span of my fieldwork from the spring of 1989 through the summer of 2003 (when the final copyediting of this manuscript was completed). The never-ending problem is how to draw statistics on changing conditions to a conclusion.

I have tried whenever possible to provide statistics from the approximate beginning, middle, and end of my fieldwork, to indicate trends rather than rely on stand-alone statistical snapshots. I have also tried to obtain statistics from as close to 2003 as possible, but in many cases the most recent available statistics may reflect conditions in 2000, 2001, or 2002. (Market figures often are reported on the basis of the Japanese fiscal year, which begins April 1 and ends March 31.)

Readers who want even more up-to-date statistics on the market's performance should consult the published sources and websites listed in appendix 2, including my own website, www.people.fas.harvard.edu/~bestor/tsukiji, where I will post selected statistics and other information about Tsukiji.

MONEY AND FOREIGN EXCHANGE

Changes in the exchange rate of the U.S. dollar vis-à-vis the yen make discussion of monetary values tricky. Historically, the yen–dollar exchange rate before World War II was two yen to the dollar. After the war, the exchange rate was pegged at 360 yen to the dollar, which remained the stable rate until what the Japanese refer to as "the Nixon shocks" of the 1970s. Over the course of my research, from 1989 to 2003, the average exchange rate fluctuated dramatically (Nihon Tōkei Kyōkai 2003: 430):

1989	¥130 = $1.00	1996	¥106
1990	¥150	1997	¥120
1991	¥135	1998	¥130
1992	¥130	1999	¥118
1993	¥118	2000	¥106
1994	¥107	2001	¥119
1995	¥93		

In July 2002 and July 2003, the rate stood at about ¥117 and ¥118, respectively.

These annual averages themselves sometimes smooth over rapid fluctuations in exchange rates from month to month. Foreign exchange rates are critical for many aspects of Tsukiji's business, and exchange rate risk can amplify market risk to create extreme volatility in the marketplace. However, since this research is not a price-based economic analysis, I usually report values in unadjusted yen wherever possible, without dollar equivalents unless to give non-Japanese readers a sense of scale.

1   Tokyo's Pantry

Watanabe-san* introduced me to Tsukiji. He ran a small sushi shop in Fukagawa, a venerable neighborhood in the *shitamachi* region, the old merchant districts of downtown Tokyo.[1] In 1975 my wife Victoria and I—just married and in Japan to study the language—found ourselves living in an apartment a couple of blocks from Watanabe's shop. Visiting an unknown sushi shop requires a leap of faith. One worries less about the quality of the food than about prices, which in sushi bars are as notoriously unpredictable as the welcome accorded a newcomer (whether Japanese or foreign). On a limited student budget, we eyed Watanabe's shop with some trepidation. But hungering for sushi one evening, we finally mustered the courage to stick our heads through his *noren:* the long split curtain decorated with bold swirls of calligraphy that restaurants and shops hang in their doorways to display their trade names.

As we entered, a roaring chorus of "Irasshaimase" ("Welcome") arose automatically from the throats of the apprentice chefs behind the counter. As their guttural greetings died away, we heard "Come in, please" from a middle-aged man who wielded his long knife over a block of tuna with the authority that clearly marked him as the master of the house. Watanabe-san, we learned within minutes, had had a varied and almost certainly checkered career during the immediate postwar years. He had acquired a liking for Americans, often expressed in staccato bursts of exuberant if cryptic Chandler-esque slang.

We soon became regulars, sustained in part by the discovery that Watanabe's affection ensured, no matter what we ate (within reason), our

---

*Watanabe-san and all other individuals mentioned in this book are identified by pseudonyms.

bill would come to precisely ¥1,000 apiece. Like many *sushiya*,[2] Watanabe's shop kept track of each customer's bill by tossing colored plastic chips into a small *masu*, a square wooden box used variously as a dry measure for rice or as a vessel for drinking cold saké. Prices were not posted, nor were they discussed with customers. At the end of the meal an apprentice would simply count out the chips and arrive at a total by some semisecret calculus. To preserve the niceties in front of the other customers, Watanabe's apprentice would dutifully count our chits and, with feigned concentration at an abacus, announce that our bill came to ¥2,000.

Usually we sat at the tiny sushi bar: half a dozen stools at an unstained wooden counter against a low glass-fronted refrigerated display case, across which Watanabe and his apprentices stood ready to prepare whatever we requested. A huge map of Japan made of cedar burls set into plaster dominated the back wall, only five or six long steps from the entry. Along the side wall were a couple of tables that could seat only two or three patrons, and upstairs was a small room—only six tatami mats—for private parties. But almost no one ever sat anywhere except at the counter, since the charm of Watanabe's shop lay in selecting one's next tidbit from the glass case and in joking with the apprentices as they prepared take-out orders.

Amulets and talismans dotted the restaurant's walls. The iconography of sushi mementos unfolded for us in visit after visit, as Watanabe explained this decoration or that motif: to pull in customers, a large white plaster "beckoning cat" clutching a gold coin in one paw and waving the other to attract passersby; to pull in profits, a huge bamboo rake ornately decorated with the Seven Gods of Fortune, treasure ships, gold coins, and bales of rice. Watanabe and his apprentices brought these and other charms back from the many festivals and fairs they visited at shrines throughout shitamachi. Other talismans were gifts. Over the counter, a wide wooden frame held narrow vertical plaques, each bearing the name of a person or a shop and a squiggle of calligraphy. We puzzled through the characters, learning in the process that a dozen of his main suppliers gave him the piece as a congratulatory gift when Watanabe last remodeled his shop. The names of his friends and their shop names or trade symbols (*yagō*) visibly testified to his network of personal ties in the seafood trade. The calligraphic swirl after each name read *uogashi*—literally, the "fish quay"—the fish market.

During our visits Watanabe's apprentices amused themselves by carving graceful decorations from folded bamboo leaves, pleased at our surprise when a flurry of delicate cuts with a foot-long knife created a crane in flight framed by a fan, or the silhouette of Mount Fuji partially obscured by clouds. They entertained us with jokes and stories recounted in the complicated style of shitamachi banter—*share*—that depends on wordplay, visual puns, and incongruity. They taught us a repertoire of word games and bar tricks to spring on unsuspecting customers tempted to match wits with apparently witless foreigners: if presented with six matches and the injunction not to break or bend any of them, could we form the character for *aki* (autumn), written with nine bold, straight brush strokes? Yes, it would turn out, after the side bets were made, we could.[3] We earnestly listened as they taught us sushi slang—less a secret trade argot than a modest marker of connoisseurship—in which rice is called *shari*, soy sauce is *murasaki*, and a cup of tea is *agari*, not to be confused with *gari*, the sushi word for pickled ginger.[4]

Watanabe's backstreet shop introduced us to Japan outside the straitlaced spheres of salarymen, to life led without suits in the small-scale entrepreneurial world of shitamachi. As a sushi chef, Watanabe was a self-employed master craftsman with two apprentices and a family whose members—his mother, wife, and son—all played roles in keeping the family business going. Watanabe's customers, mostly from the neighborhood, were taxi drivers, proprietors of mom-and-pop retail shops, machine shop owners, bar hostesses, barbers, and Buddhist priests, along with a few weary salarymen stopping off late at night on their way home from Japan, Inc. In Watanabe's sushi bar we glimpsed an easygoing social milieu where home and workplace often overlapped and where social networks easily cut across household, occupation, and neighborhood.

As we hung out at Watanabe's shop week after week, we began to appreciate the variety of seafood he stocked in his glass display case. Some things he had available every evening—tuna, octopus, shrimp, salmon roe—but other delicacies would appear only occasionally or would be in stock for a few weeks before they vanished: the *kurodai* (black sea bream) of late summer giving way to autumn's shad *(kohada)*, red clams *(akagai)*, and flounder *(hirame)*, then to yellowtail *(buri)* as autumn turned to winter. Gradually we learned a little about the seasonal flow of seafood and the scattered regions of Japan where particular species were harvested at different times, and we discovered—to our surprise—that some of the fresh seafood before our eyes was from the United States, Canada, or Southeast Asia.

Occasionally a regular customer would order something that Watanabe would politely decline to serve, even though we—and they—could see a tray of it glistening in the case. Later, when other customers were not around, Watanabe explained that sometimes he bought lower-grade fish to serve during the lunchtime rush hour, but not to regular evening customers who counted on his expertise to provide only the best. At other times, he

Figure 1. Sushi characters: wrapping paper for take-out sushi. (See facing page for translation.)

wouldn't stock a certain fish at all if he couldn't find the quality he wanted. Every time we visited, the selection was somewhat different, but always fresh and always in minute quantities. Once I asked him where he got his fish, innocently wondering aloud whether he and the fishmonger down the block bought seafood together. His apprentice snorted.

Watanabe patiently explained that retail fishmongers bought fish for housewives, not for sushi chefs. He told us about a vast market—Tsukiji— where he and his apprentices went two or three mornings a week to select their fish. Fishmongers and supermarkets also got seafood there, he explained, but the market was so large that dealers supplied every conceivable grade and variety of seafood for every conceivable kind of restaurateur and retailer. Takahashi, his senior apprentice, broke in with a laugh. "Gaijin dakara, wakaru hazu ga nai'n da. Ichido, tsurete ikō ka?"—"They're foreigners; how would they know what you're talking about? Let's take 'em sometime."

Watanabe shrugged. Doubtful, he emphasized how early he and his apprentices made their shopping expedition. We lied and said we liked to get up early. And so, a few days later on a freezing February morning, we arrived outside his shop at 4:30 A.M. Bundled in our warmest clothes, we piled into the back of his minivan with his two apprentices and roared off into the black dawn along deserted streets and across tiny bridges over the canals that wind through the Sumida River delta between Fukagawa and Tsukiji. During daytime the trip might take forty-five minutes or longer through the dense traffic; at that hour, we made it in about a quarter of an hour.

sake	tako	ayu	kujira	surume	aji	koi	tai
(salmon)	(octopus)	(sweetfish)	(whale)	(dried squid)	(horse mackerel)	(carp)	(sea bream)
masu	namazu	awabi	iwana	sawara	unagi	haze	saba
(trout)	(catfish)	(abalone)	(char)	(Spanish mackerel)	(eel)	(goby)	(mackerel)
ishimochi	haya	funa	ame	kisu	fuka	kochi	nishin
(croaker)	(gudgeon)	(crucian carp)	(Biwa trout)	(whiting)	(shark)	(flathead)	(herring)
ankō	shachi	bora	hatahata	hamo	suzuki	buri	karei
(monkfish)	(killer whale)	(gray mullet)	(sandfish)	(conger eel)	(sea bass)	(yellowtail)	(flounder)
dojō	samé	maguro	konoshiro	hokke	ebi	tara	inada
(loach)	(shark)	(tuna)	(shad)	(Atka mackerel)	(shrimp)	(cod)	(yellowtail)
fugu	sayori	hirame	ugui	ei	katsuo	iwashi	kazunoko
(blowfish)	(halfbeak)	(flounder)	(dace)	(stingray)	(bonito)	(sardine)	(herring roe)

Out to the freezing banks of the Sumida River he led us, to see the rows of tuna laid out for the morning auctions. Blanketed in thick cocoons of frost, solidly frozen tuna the size of tree trunks clinked like brittle chimes as prospective buyers picked out slivers of tail meat for inspection. Crowds of buyers and auctioneers warmed their hands at fires stoked with the broken wooden crates lying about. We watched auctions go by in a split second as Watanabe tried to explain to us the hand signals and staccato chants that indicated bids. He led us through warrens of stalls where he or his chief apprentice would stop for a moment or two to purchase a kilogram of shrimp, or a large cut of tuna, or several legs of octopus, or a tray or two of sea urchin roe, and then thrust the purchase into a rectangular bamboo wicker basket slung over the junior apprentice's shoulder. If money changed hands, I didn't see it. In the fast conversations back and forth I couldn't catch any discussions of prices. Watanabe and his crew knew exactly where they were going, and what they were going to buy when they got there. Though they paused along the way to examine products at many stalls scattered around the marketplace, to my inexperienced eyes the *ikura* (salmon roe) they didn't purchase where they bought the *kamaboko* (fish pâté) looked identical to the salmon roe they did buy at the stall where they ignored the pâté.

Suddenly they were done. Out we darted into a swirling mass of tiny trucks and handcarts and threaded our way across the traffic to a dingy hole-in-the-wall restaurant where Watanabe treated us to the best tempura we had ever eaten. We washed our breakfast down with several beers, strolled to a nearby knife shop where Watanabe ordered some cutlery from the proprietor, evidently an old friend, and then climbed into his van and made our way back to Fukagawa, by now—at 8:30 in the morning—almost an hour's drive away.

Tsukiji was transfixing, but overwhelmingly other, a world seemingly beyond our ability to explore more fully, as intriguing yet as remote as the Fulton Fish Market is for most New Yorkers (if much less menacing). Vickey and I chalked up our visit as a fascinating experience, and went about our rounds of language lessons, English teaching jobs, and explorations of Tokyo. A couple of months later we returned to the United States, and after a few postcards we lost touch with Watanabe. Later visits to Tokyo were filled with other preoccupations. From time to time we would take a visitor to Tsukiji, and I would remember Watanabe.

MOM-AND-POP RETAIL

Our six months in Fukagawa had borne other fruit, however. From that stay I had gained an abiding interest in the shitamachi districts of Tokyo, in workaday neighborhoods where ordinary people lead unremarked-upon lives, and in the small shopkeepers and independent entrepreneurs who make such neighborhoods work. A few years later, in 1979, equipped with Japanese language skills for intensive ethnographic research, I returned to Tokyo to work on a doctoral dissertation about daily life in just this sort of neighborhood, though it wasn't in Fukagawa nor—except in the minds of its residents—even in shitamachi (T. Bestor 1985, 1989, 1990, 1992a, 1992b, 1996; Plath 1992b). After that research (from 1979 to 1981)—on communities, on the nature of tradition as a cultural process, and on the roles that small shopkeepers play in sustaining local tradition and community organizations—I returned to Tokyo again in 1988 to focus more on the small businesses themselves. I wanted to understand the kinds of social ties that bolster family-run enterprises in Tokyo and the ways in which networks of kinship, friendship, political advantage, and personal obligation are the fiber of the commercial distribution system.

Foreign businesspeople, trade negotiators, and economists often argue that the Japanese distribution system is a source of great economic inefficiency, a hindrance to consumers, and a nontariff trade barrier that blocks free access to the Japanese marketplace; these were major issues in the so-called Structural Impediments Initiative (SII) that occupied the attention of American trade negotiators during the height of U.S.-Japanese trade friction in the 1980s and early 1990s (Schoppa 1997). My interest was (and is) to understand the social and cultural contexts in which distribution is embedded, seeing the complexity of distribution channels not simply as an economic phenomenon in its own right but as an effect or product of the social milieu in which small-scale sectors of the Japanese economy flourish. Although analysts generally agree about the shape of Japanese distributional systems, they hotly debate their underlying causes and significance.

Some see Japanese distribution channels largely as the product of government regulatory protection of powerful political interests—small shopkeepers, for example—for whom distributional efficiency matters less than other goals. These include limiting the operations of large-scale retail stores, ensuring the survival of neighborhood shopping districts and the hundreds of thousands of mom-and-pop stores that exist in Japan today, and preserving many of the exclusive and particularistic relationships that link producers, wholesalers, and retailers into complex, multilayered distributional systems.

Other analysts, although they are willing to accept the above description as largely accurate, argue that the Japanese wholesale sector owes its complexity and multilayered character to particular conditions of the urban labor market, including the prevalence of household labor and small-scale entrepreneurship, land costs, the density of trade, and costs of credit, that enable small shops and the distribution networks that supply them to capture substantial functional efficiencies absent from the domestic economies of most other industrial societies.

Debates between these two sides—those who see government regulation and political pressure as root causes and those for whom the peculiarities of the urban Japanese economy are fundamental—became embedded in interpretive dogmas, especially during the Japan-U.S. trade frictions of the 1980s. One school of thought viewed (and views) Japan as an intentionally closed economy, dismissing protestations about the particularities of Japanese social and cultural forms as largely protectionist smokescreens. An opposing point of view regards Japan as a semi-open economy moving toward greater flexibility yet retaining special features of social and cultural life that have sustained its economic growth thus far and that cannot be expected to disappear overnight. Both sides agree that the Japanese economy has peculiarities, and that the structure of Japanese distribution channels gets to the heart of fundamental questions about the character of Japanese social organization, economic behavior, and cultural values (see Flath 1988, 1989a, 1989b, 2000; Ito 1992; Ito and Maruyama 1990; Lincoln 1990, 2001; Schoppa 1997).

I spent the academic year 1988–89 in Tokyo conducting research on these questions at street level, focused in a general way on small family-run shops in the food business (see T. Bestor 1990). Midway through the year, my fieldwork among small shopkeepers and their networks of suppliers led me back to Tsukiji to interview a few wholesalers about their connections with retailers and to ask them some questions about supply and demand and market access. Earlier, I had done research on distribution channels for whale meat, examining the routes along which this now-controversial delicacy travels from small coastal whaling communities to regional markets for local consumers and to metropolitan markets for the restaurant trade.[5] People in the whale business introduced me to a few Tsukiji traders whom I could interview about the structure of the marketplace.

TSUKIJI SNAPS INTO FOCUS

In February 1989, an official I knew at the Tokyo Metropolitan Government (henceforth TMG) sent me to meet a colleague who was a senior administrator at the marketplace. Mr. Shimizu was a career bureaucrat who had rotated through dozens of positions, landing in the marketplace only a year or so before my visit to his office. But as a senior official, supervising a staff of dozens, he had the time to exercise his intellectual curiosity and had read a great deal about the historical background of the marketplace. He turned out to be the perfect person to talk to: a newcomer himself, still fascinated by the world in which he found himself a powerful figure, he was surrounded by people who had been there longer and at lower levels who did not share his enthusiastic sense of discovery—and now, sitting before him in his office, was a younger foreign researcher asking him to explain the market.

What began as background inquiry for my research on shopkeepers along dozens of streets across Tokyo's landscape abruptly shifted—foreground and background transposing themselves irreversibly—as I sat in Shimizu's office, watching with one eye the comings and goings of his staff, listening with one ear to his account of the market. Shimizu outlined for me a brief history of Tsukiji and explained the basic patterns of transactions that ebb and flow among the market's seven large auction houses and its hundreds of small-scale wholesalers, as well as among these small wholesalers and their clients, the fishmongers and sushi chefs scattered across the city who were typical of the shopkeepers I had been studying.

Suddenly, his matter-of-fact recital caught my full attention. Details snapped into place and Tsukiji came into sharp focus. As he talked about the marketplace, its history, and its current squabbles, all at once the dry logic of supply and demand, of consignment and auction, of credit and transaction, of risk and competition, became firmly embedded in a social context. The abstractions of economic models became concrete in his account of the social world of Tsukiji's traders. Tsukiji came alive for me again as it had briefly on a cold February morning thirteen years earlier with Watanabe-san.

What particularly seized my attention was Shimizu's description of the interplay between the auction system and the small-scale wholesalers— *nakaoroshi gyōsha,* a term I translate as "intermediate wholesalers"—and the ways in which the development of market institutions had, over time, affected and modified the balance of power between family enterprises and large corporations. From the outset of my research—as I sat in Shimizu's office, my mind roiling—my point of view has placed the intermediate wholesalers at center stage. Any anthropological research necessarily takes one or another group of actors as the leading characters; another researcher approaching Tsukiji from a different point of view could just as easily focus on the role of day laborers in the marketplace, the structure of the Japanese fishing industry, the political influence of fishing interests in affecting policy making, or the impact of consumers' and environmental movements on food distribution. I touch on all of these, but as the reader will find, my focus is on the market as it appears to those who show up at the auctions each morning with money to spend.

INSTITUTIONS, CULTURE, AND MARKETS

The Tsukiji central wholesale market is the world's largest marketplace for fresh, frozen, and processed seafood, a market where almost 50,000 people come each day to buy and sell seafood that will feed many of the Tokyo region's 22 million residents. Six mornings a week, between four and ten o'clock, Tsukiji is a maelstrom of frenetic motion and industrial-strength noise, high-tech electronics and nearly preindustrial manual labor. Each morning, at dozens of separate auctions for hundreds of distinct varieties of seafood, crowds of traders—most representing small, family-owned firms—bid fiercely against one another in arcane hand gestures and venerable semisecret codes. As the auctions end, workers wielding gaffs and hand-carts haul gigantic tuna carcasses and crates of dried sardines, tubs of sea bream and trays of octopus across the wet cobblestones to the long sheds that house the market's 1,677 stalls. Each is presided over by a counting-house little larger than a telephone booth, where cashiers use abacuses, calculators, and laptop computers to keep abreast of shouted orders from salespeople serving the chefs, retailers, and supermarket buyers who roam the market's crowded aisles.

Seafood of every description cascades from sparkling white Styrofoam boxes and across well-worn cutting boards in the tiny stalls that line the market's aisles. Retail fishmongers and supermarket buyers, sushi chefs and box-lunch makers, hotel caterers and even a few ordinary consumers thread their way through the crowded market to pick out their day's fare from the enormous selection on display. Over the course of a year, merchants at Tsukiji sell perhaps two thousand varieties of seafood, and in any given season several hundred are available, although no single stall stocks more than a few dozen at a time.[6] Eels wriggle in plastic buckets; a flotilla of sea bass stare blankly from their tank; live shrimp and crabs kick tiny showers of sawdust onto stall floors; mussels and clams spill across wide trays as if the tide had just exposed them; tubs of salted fish roe glitter and smooth cross sections of dark red tuna and creamy swordfish glisten in lighted refrigerator cases. The selection is global: slabs of Canadian and Chilean salmon, trays of Thai shrimp, Okhotsk crab, fresh bluefin tuna airfreighted from New York or Istanbul, eels from Hamamatsu, boiled West African octopi, Shikoku sea bream, snapper from China, and sea urchin roe from Maine repackaged in Hokkaidō.

Tsukiji stands at the center of a technologically sophisticated, multi-billion-dollar international fishing industry, and every day the market's auctions match international supply with the traditional demands of Japanese cuisine, made ever more elaborate by Japan's prosperity and the gentrification of culinary tastes. Boosters encourage the homey view that Tsukiji is "Tōkyō no daidokoro"—Tokyo's kitchen or pantry—but in this pantry more than 628 million kilograms of seafood worth $5.7 billion changed hands in 1996. (By way of comparison, in the same year New York's Fulton Fish Market, the largest in North America, handled only 13 percent of the tonnage of Tsukiji's trade, valued at about $1 billion.)[7] Despite its enormous scale, the bulk of Tsukiji's daily trade flows through tiny family businesses: some 900 trading firms are licensed to buy at Tsukiji's morning auctions and to resell their purchases in the market's stalls. Against the backdrop of a putative history dating to the early seventeenth century and a turbulent sequence of administrative reforms in the twentieth century, traders at Tsukiji operate in a complex social and economic framework of individual alliances and overarching institutional arrangements. This framework enfranchises them as traders; coordinates their relations with producers, suppliers, and customers; and regulates their behavior within the Tsukiji trading community.

Much about Tsukiji is singular, at first glance both mundane and esoteric. Beyond the particularities of a market for fresh fish in a nation renowned for sushi, a market of highly perishable products for finicky consumers, it is

Figures 2–6.
(*Top left*) Busy stalls.
(*Top right*) Boiled octopus.
(*Left center*) Mussels.
(*Above*) Loading docks (*chaya*), where trade buyers pick up their purchases. Photograph by Russell B. Bryan, reproduced with permission.
(*Left*) Trade buyers on the subway platform at Tsukiji, going home with their purchases.

also a local market for the harvest of a global fishing industry; a market of personalized face-to-face transactions conducted against a backdrop of jet transport, international faxes, and cellular telephones; and a market where small family businesses, some in their twentieth generation, conduct trade with massive modern transnational corporations.

Yet at the same time, Tsukiji is like all markets: its trade takes place within a complex array of social ties and institutions without which economic activity could not occur. Tsukiji exemplifies the institutional frameworks of Japanese economic behavior and organization more generally, a case study of institutional structure and the social and cultural embeddedness of economic life.

But I have broader purposes as well. I am concerned with the anthropological analysis of institutions more generally: as elements that define and constrain complex societies, not just markets for seafood and not just in Japan. The elaborate institutional infrastructures that frame the operation of a market have precisely—albeit not exclusively—economic purposes. Institutions of this kind are typical of the intricate forms of social, cultural, economic, and political integration and coordination that are key forces in the social organization of complex societies throughout the contemporary world. In recent decades anthropology has begun to focus on such societies, but as yet analyses of their complex institutional structures are few. This study of Tsukiji points toward anthropological engagement with the realities of institutional form and process that profoundly shape all complex urban societies.

Although anthropology stakes a century-old claim to examine the entire array of human cultures and their varied social forms, anthropologists have not focused much on the organization of markets and economic transactions—at least not in advanced industrial, capitalist societies. Anthropological attention to complex social organization has been attuned more to descent groups and dowry payments than to the kinds of economic institutions now central to modern complex societies (T. Bestor 2001a). Clearly, the intellectual division of labor among the social sciences has contributed heavily to the lack of anthropological interest in these topics, and this division of labor is equally salient in the popular consciousness of what anthropologists do or ought to do. Throughout my research I have encountered incredulity when I tell Americans that I study contemporary Japanese economic institutions. After their momentary confusion as they attempt to place my interests alongside those of either Margaret Mead or Indiana Jones—the twin icons of anthropology in popular discourse—my questioners often turn the conversation toward one of two directions: "Yes, I read somewhere that the

Japanese are really very tribal," or "Oh? What can tombs tell you about economics?"

My puzzled interlocutors share with many social scientists (including, alas, some anthropologists) the view that anthropology has little business studying business, despite many notable studies to the contrary (e.g., Rohlen 1974; R. Clark 1979; Janelli with Yim 1993). Yet corporations, cartels, and markets should be of as much interest to anthropologists as communities, clans, and matrilineages. The critical issues of organizing social relations around production, commodification, exchange, and consumption—activities to determine ownership, distribute surpluses, legitimate property rights, and structure access to common resources—are of no less anthropological significance in the study of a market than in the study of a moiety. Indeed, territory often conceded to economists, sociologists, and management specialists can yield profitable results for anthropologists. Anthropological analysis contributes usefully to understanding contemporary economic institutions; and if anthropology is to move the core of its analysis toward understanding modern, complex, urban, industrial societies, then the field must begin to seriously address the issues of institutional structure and coordination that are central to the analysis of complex economic organization among many other things.

These are general claims, but this book is concerned with the specifics of Tsukiji as well. It is, after all, a study of economic institutions in a Japanese market. For many readers—accustomed to regarding "Japan" and "Incorporated" as inevitably joined—a demonstration of the linkage between economic behavior and the anthropological analysis of cultural and social patterns may seem too predictable to be worth the bother. Japanese have been widely reviled as "economic animals," and anthropological analysis of the patterns and institutions of their economy seems almost a form of economic ethology, practiced daily in the popular and business press. The danger of this stereotypical association is twofold: it presumes that there is something peculiarly cultural about a Japanese way of economic life, and it reinforces the false idea that in Western societies, economics stands apart from culture and society.

Make no mistake: the cultural and social details of Tsukiji are central to understanding how the market works. But the fact that Tsukiji is a *Japanese* market makes it no more and no less culturally or socially embedded than any other complex economic institution in any other society. The specifics of Japanese culture that surround and emanate from Tsukiji no more obscure or confound its economic activities than the specifics of American culture interfere with the Chicago Board of Trade or the New York Stock

Exchange. Markets reflect and generate cultural and social life in wider structures of social life.

Mark Granovetter forcefully argues that economic activity is firmly embedded in wider structures of social life (Granovetter 1985; Swedberg and Granovetter 1992). Three simple interrelated propositions frame his perspective: that economic action is a form of social action, that economic action takes place in social contexts, and that economic institutions are socially constructed.

Economic activity—"a type of behavior that has to do with choosing among scarce means that have alternative uses" (Swedberg and Granovetter 1992: 6)—does not occur in a vacuum, unaffected by social motives of compliance, power, sociability, or status. Social influences on economic choices cannot be regarded simply as disruptions or imperfections in otherwise "natural" economic arrangements. Economic action is socially situated, "embedded in ongoing networks of personal relationships rather than being carried out by atomized actors[,] . . . *embedded* because it is expressed in interaction with other people" (1992: 9). Economic life, therefore, is not simply the product of individual self-interest, nor are economic systems merely the aggregation of self-interest into some optimal form of collective rationality that maximizes individual benefits.

In an analysis of the fish market of Marseille, Alan Kirman makes similar points, arguing that "the aggregate behavior of a market may well present clear regularities that can be thought of as representing . . . collective rationality. However, these features should not be thought of as corresponding to individual rationality. . . . [T]he relationship between the behavior of the individual participant and the market as a whole is mediated by the way in which the market is organized" (Kirman 2001: 156).

Individual actors *and* institutions socially construct economic systems out of the slow accretions of social knowledge and practice that over time come to seem timeless, appearing natural, inevitable, and compelling in how they organize people's activities and attitudes (de la Pradelle 1995). Institutions that sustain economic activity are not necessarily themselves functional outcomes of economic process, the most rationally efficient means to achieve specifically economic ends. Historical contingency, path dependency, and the logic of social interaction can explain institutional development and form as fully as (or more fully than) the assumption that economic institutions represent a systemic evolution toward rational efficiency or are devices that come into being to prevent "individual rational actions from having irrational collective results" (Swedberg and Granovetter 1992: 14).

The powerful insights of this approach ring true at every turn at Tsukiji. The transactions that make the market, from the bluntly competitive bidding of morning auctions to the more subtle jockeying that keeps customers returning to the same stalls year after year, all take place as part of a complex social fabric. This social context is a mass of minute details that, if taken separately, seem simply arcane: elaborate rules governing auctions, complex systems of assigning stalls, careful agreements on terms of credit and settlement, subtly tended ties of long-term reciprocation between trading partners, and a thousand and one other understandings, agreements, rules, and alliances that give the economic strategies, maneuvers, and motives of individual participants their form and substance. And for each detail, market participants can offer on-the-spot exegeses ranging from functionalist explanations of the economic efficiency of a particular trading practice, to symbolic structuralist interpretations of the cultural significance of products within the historical traditions of Japanese cuisine, to institutional analyses of path dependency. All the participants know what the market means, though they seldom agree with one another, or even with themselves from day to day. Taken together, the details of the marketplace resolve into a patterned social order entailing, among other things, "typically Japanese" structures of administrative guidance, vertical integration, overt in-group harmony, consensus, and long-term stability of ties. But an explanation of patterned integration cannot rely simply on assertions of either cultural inertia or economic rationality.

My analysis of Tsukiji starts with the simple premise that organizational patterns and institutional arrangements (and the cultural principles that such patterns and arrangements reflect and reproduce) create frameworks for marketplace activity and, in so doing, configure the market—both as a specific set of bounded interactions among real actors and as economic process per se. The institutions of the Tsukiji marketplace arise out of particular functional and technical requirements inherent in the seafood trade and are molded by the general principles of capitalism inherent in the wider Japanese economy; yet Tsukiji's social structure is not merely a by-product of an abstract market mechanism. To be sure, the logic of economic life generates changes in both cultural meanings and institutional frameworks, but those changes themselves alter definitions of the appropriate scope and scale of economic activity. The economic life of Tsukiji, in Granovetter's terms, is embedded in an institutional structure, which in turn is shaped by historical and cultural understandings that the market's participants, both individual and institutional, continually revisit and revise. Without this institutional structure and the received understandings of these institutions that guide participants in the market, systematic economic activity itself—that is, a market—could not exist. Institutions do not simply channel inevitably occurring economic transactions into some particular form; they create the conditions under which exchange can be envisioned and hence realized. Both cultural dispositions and historical legacies, in turn, frame the dimensions of institutions and the legitimate sweep of their authority and action, even as the logic of institutions—"path dependency" or "institutional lock-in"—inspires and channels participants' cultural imaginations to look in particular directions.

The perspective I adopt adds to Granovetter's institutionalism an anthropological view of culture as process or practice in Bourdieu's terms. Rather than regarding culture as a point of origin, a historically remote or pristine cultural configuration, a template of predispositions and inclinations socialized into individuals, or a set of idioms, an inflexible script to be memorized, I view culturally driven preferences for particular kinds of social (and economic) relationships as aspects of the social and cultural order that are continuously produced and reproduced in contemporary life. I am far less concerned with cultural antecedents or templates than with the dynamics of specific contemporary relationships or institutions and the ways in which these social forms and the ideological or symbolic expressions of their significance mutually generate and reinforce one another.

Of course, historically derived cultural orientations help shape contemporary institutions and behavior, but their role is not determinative. In other words, often what is most important about the past is the present-day perception of it. The past becomes relevant to understanding contemporary social life insofar as past practices are evoked or invoked to legitimate (or invalidate) contemporary ones, to create ideological norms that one aspires to emulate (or overthrow), or to craft sets of symbolic meanings and references within (or against) which one can situate one's own contemporary circumstances. Many features of contemporary Japanese life are commonly regarded as cultural-historical legacies: group behavior; consensus; collective decision making; hierarchical structures of domination and subordination; and transactional patterns of long-term obligation and reciprocity. Each is a common template for contemporary organization and behavior, economic and otherwise, at Tsukiji and elsewhere. My analysis does not regard these as cultural or historical givens, but as social forms that reproduce themselves in conformity to normative expectations, even as norms and social patterns create the conditions under which they will be reproduced, reinterpreted, and reapplied in the future.

The cultural embeddedness of economic (and social) behavior is frequently misconstrued, especially in the case of Japan. Here lies largely unexplored ground for analyzing the finely detailed cultural processes that shape the everyday practices of economic life. Not the cultural patterns beloved by pundits, conceived at the level of shame versus guilt, group versus individual, neo-Confucian work ethic versus post-Protestant play ethic. Instead, these are the workaday cultural processes whereby the classificatory rationales of cuisine echo in the logic of auction bidding systems; the locational meanings of the marketplace resonate with the historical legacies of mercantile life; the daily rhythms of the marketplace harmonize half a dozen calendars of traffic, paydays, rituals, seasons, and culinary trends; and the institutional elaborations of special privilege jangle restlessly against codes of economic equalization.

PLACE MATTERS

Many formulations of contemporary anthropological analysis focus on deterritorialization, privileging mass markets, mass media, mass migration, and macroeconomics even as they assume that the constellations of organization and meaning that people construct around place are conceptually passé. Tsukiji is a major node in transnational flows of people, commodities, capital, information, and technology, not a component of the "global factory" that could be reassembled offshore. It is a highly specific place. And place matters because sense of space and place is connected with the creation of boundaries, identities, and affiliations. Tsukiji is a complicated physical work environment set in the geographic center of a complex metropolitan region; the operations of the marketplace cannot be understood apart from its placement. If Tsukiji were located in a warehouse complex surrounded by vast parking lots, built amid fields near the interchange of a major superhighway on the distant fringes of the metropolitan region, the market would inherently *be* a different place.

Tsukiji is an intricate cultural environment where historical memory links the Tokugawa regime of the seventeenth through nineteenth centuries and the social and cultural milieu of preindustrial mercantile culture to the contemporary construction of old-fashioned shitamachi life as the "authentic" version of urban culture. Dealing in fine foodstuffs, Tsukiji's traders are centrally involved in elaborations of cuisine as a significant element of Japanese cultural heritage, with all the overlays of regional identity and sense of place that this implies. And as a key element in the infrastructure of the Tokyo metropolitan region, Tsukiji's location matters in vital ways to planners, traders, politicians, and consumers. Tsukiji as a market cannot be understood apart from Tsukiji as a physical space; meanings are attached to space and place through cultural processes that take careful account of Tsukiji's significance concurrently along many dimensions of cuisine, nostalgia, and infrastructure.

This construction of place connects social structure to the generation of meaning, meaning in which place matters: meanings of identity, tradition, affiliation without which institutional structure would grind to a halt. Elsewhere I have shown how "traditionalism" and sense of place are interconnected in the formation and maintenance of local community in a Tokyo neighborhood (T. Bestor 1989). There, as at Tsukiji, the fixity and authenticity of place as a locus of action and identity (both communal and individual) are not evidence of local isolation and insularity. Rather, place is the product of and mechanism for articulating larger spheres of social and cultural relationships. Place creates the perception of spatial (and social) fixity in the midst of processual fluidity.

Writing about transnational relationships, Arjun Appadurai (1990) describes them as existing along or across "ethnoscapes," "technoscapes," "finanscapes," "mediascapes," and "ideoscapes." Very roughly, these terms refer to the complicated tides and undertows of people(s), of technology, of capital, of media representations, and of political ideologies that concurrently link and divide regions of the globe; this perspective suggests ways in which the processes of transnational linkage between any given set of societies may proceed simultaneously along different dimensions, at different rates, in different directions, and to quite different ends. Although Appadurai's emphasis is on the fluid nature of motion along each dimension, by focusing on the visual imagery of "scapes" his terminology suggests that from the perspective of any given actor or observer, the local view—like a landscape—is not necessarily one of motion and process so much as of stability and coherence in a specific setting or perceptual environment. The idea of "scapes" reminds us that people experience global processes in particular locations, from which they derive their understanding and definitions of the processes themselves.

And a market, regardless of its global reach, is a very particular kind of location. Because its products are perishable, Tsukiji's trade is shaped by transactional technicalities that do not affect other markets. It is a demarcated marketplace in which products are visibly offered for sale to traders who are physically present and socially connected. As a market for foodstuffs, Tsukiji is subject to government regulations that seek to ensure the stability and safety of Tokyo's food supply. At the same time, the affective

TABLE 1. *Wholesale Seafood Trade at Tsukiji, 2002*

	Weight (million kg)	Percentage of total	Value (billion yen)	Percentage of total
Fresh seafood	156.0	24	144.9	27
Live fish	14.7	2	19.5	4
Shellfish	43.3	7	38.7	7
Frozen seafood	184.0	29	164.3	31
Freshwater fish	2.2	>1	2.7	1
Seaweed	8.2	1	3.1	1
Processed products	229.2	36	162.9	30
Total	637.5	100	536.0	100

SOURCE: TMG website, data for the year 2002: "Tōkyō-to Chūō Oroshiuri Shijō, Shijō Torihiki Jōhō" (TMG Central Wholesale Market, Market Transaction Information), www.shijou.metro.tokyo.jp/frame02.html.
NOTE: Totals vary slightly because of rounding.

meanings and culinary symbolism of Japanese food culture, including the varied nutritional, social, ritual, recreational, and calendrical contexts of food consumption, join to enhance Tsukiji traders' perceptions of their market's importance as both a supplier of food and a repository of cultural heritage. This sense of purpose—perhaps of calling—is wrapped in the market's putative history, which extends back to the early seventeenth century, and in the strong cultural and social bonds that many of the market's principals maintain with generations-old mercantile and fishing communities.

Tsukiji is not, however, a quiet backwater for cultural reflection. It is Japan's major market for fresh and frozen fish and sits at the center of an enormous network of domestic and international trade (table 1). Each year, Tsukiji's dealers sell more than 450 major species and varieties of fresh, frozen, and processed seafood. Tsukiji alone handles about 15 percent of the tonnage of fresh and frozen fish and other seafood products that annually pass through Japan's fifty-four central wholesale markets (*chūō oroshiuri shijō*) that deal in seafood. Like all such central wholesale markets, Tsukiji is chartered by national legislation and operates under the supervision of the Ministry of Agriculture, Forestry and Fisheries (MAFF), but is directly regulated and administered by a local government, in this case the TMG.

Tsukiji comprises two divisions, one specializing in fresh fruits and vegetables (*seikamono*) and the other, much larger, specializing in *suisanbutsu,* "marine products" including saltwater as well as freshwater fish, shellfish, seaweed, and other aquatic creatures (a scope of products much wider than implied in the commonplace English meanings of "seafood"). This book focuses on Tsukiji's seafood division *(suisan-bu)*.

A MARKET BY ANY OTHER NAME

The term "market" is inherently ambiguous, implying on the one hand abstract sets of economic phenomena, and, on the other hand, specific social relationships and institutions within which economic transactions occur. I distinguish "market" from "marketplace." The first is, in my usage, an abstract economic institution or process. A marketplace, on the other hand, is both a specific geographical place and a localized set of social institutions, transactions, social actors, organizations, products, trade practices, and cultural meanings motivated by a wide variety of factors including, but not limited to, "purely economic" or "market" forces. Stuart Plattner's distinction (1989a: 171) is useful here: " 'market' [refers to] the social institution of exchanges where prices or exchange equivalencies exist. 'Marketplace' refers to these interactions in a customary time and place. . . . A market can exist without being localized in a marketplace, but it is hard to imagine a marketplace without some sort of institutions governing exchanges."

In the case of Tsukiji, *market* as economic phenomenon and as social framework is situated in a particular location—a market*place*—that is both spatially and legally bounded. And at Tsukiji, market-as-economic-process versus market-as-social-institution is further enfolded in other ambiguities of distinguishing place and marketplace.

Tsukiji is a place-name with a venerable history dating from the seventeenth century. Literally, Tsukiji means "built land." The district was a marshy landfill in the century of Edo's expansion after it became the capital of the Tokugawa shōgunate in 1603. Today, Tsukiji is an administrative district within Chūō Ward, one of the twenty-three wards that make up the core of Tokyo Metropolitan Prefecture (Tōkyō-to). The Tsukiji district extends across several square kilometers of mixed commercial and residential neighborhoods in the heart of central Tokyo, lying along the west bank of the Sumida River near its mouth at the head of Tokyo Bay. Most of Tsukiji 5-chōme (the "fifth administrative subdivision of the Tsukiji district") is occupied by Tokyo's major wholesale seafood market. Accordingly, the market is colloquially known as Tsukiji, a name that is almost universally recognized by Japanese: a shorthand reference or geographical metonym in much the same way that Hollywood or Wall Street immediately conveys images not just of a place, but also of an entire industry and its most important center.

Officially, the marketplace is the Tōkyō-to Chūō Oroshiuri Shijō, Tsukiji Shijō (Tokyo Metropolitan Government Central Wholesale Market, Tsukiji Marketplace). Although the Tsukiji market includes both a seafood division and a produce division, the former far overshadows the latter in tonnage, sales, and sheer physical scale; and so, both in popular image and in trade jargon, Tsukiji is Tokyo's fish market and vice versa. Therefore, throughout this book, "Tsukiji" means the seafood division of the marketplace, unless I specify otherwise.

Tsukiji traders themselves use a number of terms to refer—with varying degrees of ambiguity—to the market and the marketplace. The pair of characters read as *shijō*, 市 and 場, can also be read as *ichiba*, depending on context, and both terms mean "market" or "marketplace." *Shijō* implies the abstract sense of "market" as economists often use the term (and as Plattner uses it above). *Shijō* has a formal, legal, or administrative ring to it, and it can refer either to the economic process of a market (e.g., as in the "labor market") or to the institutions that govern trade in a specific location—that is, as in the official designation "Tsukiji Shijō." *Ichiba*, on the other hand, is more colloquial and generally carries with it a connotation of "marketplace" as a specific place and social setting. Put another way, *shijō* administrators leave their offices to have lunch at a sushi bar in the *ichiba*.

Tsukiji regulars also refer to the marketplace as the *uoichiba*, the fish market (with strong connotations of locale and social setting); or *uogashi*, the fish quay; or simply *gashi*, the quay. The latter two terms are redolent with historical associations to Tokyo's past, as well as to the marketplace as specific place and set of social relationships. Mapped along another dimension, the *shijō* is the everyday place of real work, while the *uoichiba* is a place one can visit on a Saturday afternoon as well as during the height of trading; only Tsukiji habitués (and only older ones at that) stroll the *gashi*, mostly in golden memories.

In addition to the officially designated central wholesale market at Tsukiji, a bazaarlike public marketplace stands just outside the municipal market's gates. This "outer market," which mixes wholesale and retail establishments, restaurants and offices, is also known colloquially as Tsukiji, especially by members of the public at large who rarely enter, let alone attempt to shop, in the inner wholesale market. On the nostalgic map sketched above, casual shoppers and tourists visit the Tsukiji outer market as the *uoichiba*, with the sense that a fleeting glimpse of the *gashi* may be just around the next corner. The *shijō* is forbiddingly remote behind admin-

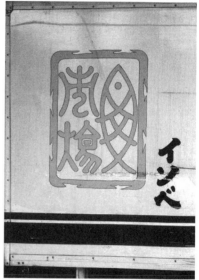

Figure 7. Market logos. (*Left*) *Uogashi* decal on a motorcycle. (*Right*) *Uoichiba* on a delivery truck, with a stylized fish next to the characters for *ichiba*. The company's name is in the lower right-hand corner.

istrative barriers, and most casual visitors to the outer market are only vaguely aware of its operations. Schematic charts presented in guidebooks or distributed to visitors offer the general public only the most rudimentary outlines of this separate world.

Those in the trade use the terms "inner market" (*jōnai shijō*) and "outer market" (*jōgai shijō*) to distinguish between the Tokyo Metropolitan Government's central wholesale market and the unregulated public market outside its gates. *Jōnai shijō* unambiguously names the regulated market environment of the Tsukiji central wholesale market (or of other similar central wholesale markets throughout Japan), but *jōgai shijō*—or simply *jōgai*—broadly refers to transactions and institutions that occur outside regulated central wholesale markets, whether geographically concentrated, as in the Tsukiji outer marketplace, or geographically dispersed and economically abstract, as in "the market for imported tuna." This distinction will become important later, for it is through the parallel existence of "inner" and "outer" markets that producers, traders, and retailers can pursue strategies to bypass the monopolies inherent in the regulated central wholesale markets.

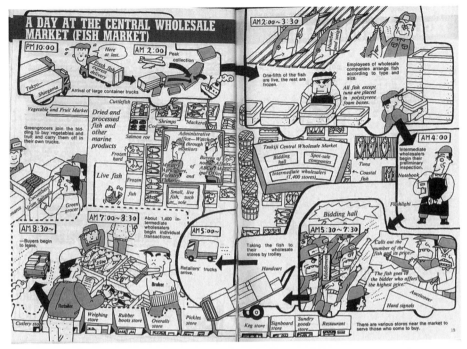

Figure 8. A day at the market. This cartoon-style guide to Tsukiji's many actors and their daily cycles of activities appeared in a popular introduction to the domestic Japanese economy (Rakugakisha 1989: 18–19); English translation reproduced with permission of The Japan Times, Ltd.

WHY TSUKIJI?

At its best—and sometimes, indeed, at its worst—anthropology finds in every facet of social life a microcosm of the whole. In Tsukiji's case the exercise is neither simplistic nor forced. The scale of the marketplace and the complexity of its role in the economic, political, and social life of Tokyo and Japan make the marketplace consequential on many different levels. This book cannot give equal attention to each of these, but several dimensions of Tsukiji's inherent significance bear mention here.

Tsukiji in Tokyo

First, Tsukiji is an urban marketplace, a key institution in the life of Tokyo, with as complicated a relationship—cultural, social, economic, political, linguistic, geographic, even literary and criminal—to its surroundings as those of other major urban marketplaces: Les Halles in Paris, Fulton in New York,

Namdaemun in Seoul, Covent Garden and Billingsgate in London, the great market in Kumasi (G. Clark 1994), Naschmarkt in Vienna (Rotenberg 1992), or Ben Thanh in Ho Chi Minh City (Leshkowich 2000). Tsukiji shares with these markets—as well as with what Timothy Sieber (1992) calls "festival marketplaces" such as Faneuil Hall, Boston; Reading Terminal, Philadelphia; or Pike Place, Seattle—important cultural, social, and spatial roles that define the character of a city for residents and visitors alike. Throughout its history, Tsukiji has been a central pillar in the infrastructure that sustains a massive metropolitan region. For urban engineers, administrators, and legislators it has been and continues to be a planning experiment and political football. But it is not simply a logistical cog serving the needs of the population and drawing on equally mechanical systems of transportation, communication, sewage disposal, or financial settlement.

The long and complex histories of Tsukiji and its predecessor, the Nihonbashi fish market—founded in the early seventeenth century, destroyed in the 1923 Kantō earthquake—nostalgically intertwine with the traditions of the plebeian culture of Edo (as Tokyo was known before 1868). The denizens of the marketplace style themselves heirs to the mercantile traditions of Tokyo's old shitamachi regions. Shitamachi life stereotypically revolves around a "work hard, play hard" attitude toward jobs, leisure, and money; open emotional bonds that link bosses, workers, family members, friends, and customers; and small family firms in which household and workshop are almost inseparable, and women as often as men negotiate the intricate social and economic equilibrium of kinship and production. Tsukiji draws its identity from the lifestyles, cultural pursuits, and commercial customs of the old merchant districts, their historical relations with the old samurai classes and the Tokugawa court, and the late-twentieth-century reinvention of Tokyo's shitamachi region as repository of "authentic" urban culture (T. Bestor 1992b; Kondo 1990). Shitamachi identity is one subaccount in Tsukiji's fund of cultural capital; and if the emotional landscape of old Tokyo has a heartland, Tsukiji's partisans lay claim to a substantial chunk of it. This image is sustained not only in the minds of Tsukiji regulars but also in public perception. Tsukiji occupies a place of distant but relaxed familiarity—built on its traditional imagery—in much media coverage.

Of course, daily newspapers focus on economic matters, usually from the point of view of consumer prices and conditions of supply, especially around the holidays when particular kinds of seafood are in consumers' minds—for example, herring roe *(kazunoko)*, the seasonal delicacy that epitomizes the New Year's holidays. Tsukiji sometimes appears as a footnote to larger economic or political stories, as when the bankruptcy of Tōshoku—one of Japan's major food-processing companies—sent the Nikkei stock average plummeting in December 1997 and shock waves rippled throughout the fishing and food industries. Occasionally something of the inner workings of the market appears in the papers, when a fire or an accident or a brawl among workers garners a few short paragraphs in the back pages of the big Tokyo dailies.

Romantic images of shitamachi life and its connection with Tsukiji are also reinforced. Tsukiji is a staple of television news broadcasts around the New Year's holidays; the year-end and year-opening rituals of the marketplace are rather like the lighting of the Christmas tree at Rockefeller Center in New York, a clear signal that the holiday season is in full swing. Tsukiji is written up from time to time in popular magazines with tips for shopping and dining (in women's magazines) and for simple eating (in men's magazines). Stories inevitably present the marketplace as steeped in history and inhabited by quaint characters—a separate world, fun to explore and a great place for wanna-be connoisseurs to pick up a bit of culinary and cultural lore. Although such articles (as well as guidebooks for shopping, dining, or sightseeing in Tokyo) may explain a bit about the auctions and the structure of trade, the economic details of the marketplace are beside the point. It is presented as a "village," a *mura*, whose habitués tolerate outsiders who respect their customs but also expect them to be grateful at the chance to visit, and then to leave quickly.[8]

For Americans, at least, it is important to point out that news coverage of Tsukiji does not evoke the images of endemic waterfront corruption made familiar by movies like *On the Waterfront* and lurid newspaper exposés of criminal control and violence at New York's Fulton Fish Market. American visitors to Tsukiji almost instinctively expect to find a dark side to the market, certain that beneath the hustle and bustle of the daily fish trade, bosses call the shots, fix prices, rig auctions, and control the marketplace through intimidation, extortion, or worse. Indeed, over the years many Americans have asked me to explain where Tsukiji's underworld hides and how far its tentacles extend. My answer always disappoints them: not since the 1920s has the market been tainted with real scandals of systemic corruption. Tsukiji certainly is not populated entirely by saints, but nothing I have found, nor anyone I have talked to during my research, suggests that market sales are fixed by outside criminals or regularly riddled below the surface by internal networks of corruption.

The market has its share of illegal gambling and loan-sharking; no doubt gangsters are involved in these activities and in recruiting casual day labor for menial jobs in and around the marketplace. In the mid-1980s, Japanese police intercepted a shipment of narcotics packed inside a frozen tuna being unloaded from a Taiwanese vessel in Shizuoka, but no Tsukiji connection was made. The market has occasional fights, sometimes between day laborers and labor bosses (Nakamura 1980, 1990). And one knife dealer gained brief notoriety in the early 1990s when the police discovered that he was selling meter-long tuna knives *(magurobōchō)* to gangsters who used them in illegal sword fights.

To be sure, Tsukiji is part of the rough-and-tumble world of Tokyo's working-class and artisanal shitamachi. The iconography of shitamachi machismo shares the styles affected by wise guys *(chinpira)* and gangsters *(yakuza):* "punch-perm" haircuts of tight ringlets, tinted aviator sunglasses, heavy gold jewelry, and gaudy sports clothes. A flash of elaborate body tattoo commands attention at Tsukiji as elsewhere, but this is surface imagery, not necessarily criminal substance. A man missing a finger would not stand out in the marketplace, and indeed there are yakuza around Tsukiji—I once met the young heir and the widow of the last big boss of the local gang, who told me without conscious irony that the dear departed patriarch was just a man of respect, a man who couldn't help doing favors for people—but gangsters appear only infrequently. They show up at festivals, intrinsically territorial events that traditionally mark turf in shitamachi life. And all this does not taint Tsukiji's public image; it only adds to the luster of Tsukiji's connections with one side of authentic shitamachi life.

Tsukiji and Food Culture

As Tokyo's major wholesale market for perishable food, Tsukiji is in very practical terms a vitally important place in the lives of the city's residents. Earning its self-bestowed title as Tokyo's pantry, Tsukiji every day provides the seafood that millions of cooks—professional chefs and homemakers alike—will prepare. Dealing in foodstuffs, Tsukiji tethers the gruff masculine worlds of fishing and markets to the elegant domains of cuisine and feminine domesticity. But Tsukiji's seafood is not just any foodstuff: fish are central elements of Japanese cuisine, both haute and low, and thus occupy a particularly consequential niche at the center of Japanese conceptions of their culinary culture.

Seafood—with rice, the most "Japanese" of foods—is imbued with all the symbolism of tradition and identity that Japanese so often lavish on their cultural heritage. Japanese interest in all aspects of food is fueled by a never-ending series of popular books and magazine articles that devote loving attention to cuisine, connoisseurship, and consumption as aspects of cultural tradition and identity. Food itself supports genres of Japanese popular culture on a massive scale, well beyond the kitsch of television shows like

The Iron Chef, the hyper- (and hyped) competitive cooking show that originated in Japan in the 1990s and that is now globally popular.

Reminiscences of sushi chefs and tuna dealers are issued by major trade
publishers; examples include *Kanda Tsuruhachi sushibanashi (Sushi Stories
from Kanda Tsuruhachi;* Morooka 1986) and *Maguroya hanjōki (Chronicle
of a Tuna Merchant's Good Times;* Takarai 1991). One Tsukiji tuna dealer
has published both historical sketches, *Nihonbashi monogatari (The Tale of
Nihonbashi;* Omura Kōzaburō 1984), and, under his "poetry name," a volume of haiku about the market, *Kushū: Ichiba-shō—maguro haiku nōto
(Anthology: Market Excerpts—Tuna Haiku Notes;* Omura Bajin 1990).
Travelogues like *Kaitensushi sekai hitomeguri (Rotary Sushi around the
World;* Tamamura 2000) are best-sellers, and more serious monographs like
Sashimi bunka ga sekai o ugokasu (Sashimi Culture Stirs the World; Hori
2001) explore some of the environmental, political, and economic forces
that surround Japanese fishing and seafood consumption. Popular guides to
sushi, of course, are commonplace, such as the December 25, 2001, issue of
the entertainment magazine *Tōkyō Isshūkan (Tokyo One Week),* with the
cover story "Kaiten-zushi dake! 1200-kan!" ("Rotary Sushi Only! 1200
Servings!") introducing hundreds of restaurants all over Tokyo and
Yokohama. And more staid journals of culture devote articles or issues to
Tsukiji and to seafood cuisine; for example, in February 1990 *Taiyō* pub-
lished a special issue titled *Sushi dokuhon (The Sushi Reader),* and similarly
Tōkyōjin in January 2001 offered the special issue *Nenmatsu no Tsukiji
Shijō Annai (Guide to the Tsukiji Market at Year's End).*

Not only Japanese write about Tsukiji. The market itself inspires awe
(e.g., Reid 1995), and the global quest for seafood to supply Tsukiji has sent
many people off to trace connections between the marketplace and distant
shores (e.g., Seabrook 1994; Whynott 1995; T. Bestor 2000, in preparation).

Foreign food people love Tsukiji. Anthony Bourdain calls it "the awe-
inspiring, life-changing mother of all fish markets . . . the smell of limitless
possibilities, countless sensual pleasures" (2001: 139–40). And Japanese cuisine, especially seafood cuisine, is lyrically celebrated by many fine writers,
including Kinjiro Omae and Yuzuru Tachibana (1991), Donald Richie
(1985), and Elizabeth Andoh (1988).

Foreign environmentalists are often of a different mind. Sylvia Earle
writes, "A deft slice with a freshly honed knife exposed dark red flesh and
pale bone near the tail of a struggling silver and blue fish, a young amber-
jack that had been transported alive to the world's largest fish market,
Tsukiji, in Tokyo and was one of more than a million sea creatures offered
for sale there each day" (1995: 167). Viewing the tuna auctions, she muses,

"Fresh or frozen, each of these bluefins . . . is worth a small fortune . . . [but] who, I wondered, notices the cost to the ocean[?]" (183). Carl Safina, a leading American environmentalist, encounters fish imported from his home waters off New York: "Silly, but I am overtaken with a feeling of poignant connection, as though I am visiting comrades taken prisoner of war. I cannot help putting my hand to the glass. The fish, disoriented, crowded, reduced to meat that is still breathing—belaboredly—do not react at all. They are neither curious nor frightened. Their shock, a tender mercy, has them numbed" (1997: 105–6). Sentiment aside, many reports make clear the global dangers of overfishing (e.g., Safina 1995; Kemf, Sutton, and Wilson 1996; Myers and Worm 2003; Hayden 2003), in some cases suggesting that Tsukiji exerts inordinate and pernicious influence over the global fishing industry.

Tsukiji is hardly a marketplace of ideas, but it is not isolated from this flurry of popular interest and press about the place and its products. Widespread concern with cuisine is a major part of Tsukiji's bankroll of cultural capital, investing the market's movements with significance on many complexly related social, economic, and cultural levels. The market's activities are fundamentally shaped by the perceptions, preferences, and ideologies that surround food, its preparation, and its consumption in contemporary Japanese culinary culture. Tsukiji does not simply manipulate abstract market principles when it handles the physical and economic characteristics of perishable commodities; it also delicately calibrates its actions to the cultural significance of the foodstuffs it purveys. The traditions of Japanese culinary culture guide the market's activities; at the same time the market itself is a major agent in creating commodities and transforming seafood into both commercial and culinary objects.

Tsukiji and Fishing

Casual conversations with newly met Japanese acquaintances sometimes stall over elaborate explanations of things Japanese, offered with the formulaic preface, "Japan is a small island country, and therefore . . ." Most foreigners have heard—and disregarded—this line so frequently that they ignore its reality: Japan is indeed an island nation, and hence a maritime culture. Since the earliest times, Japanese culture and society have been shaped by the interaction of human beings with fertile seas. Even today, when Japan has become one of the world's most highly industrialized and heavily urbanized nations, use of the oceans remains a central facet of Japanese society, reflected in everything from the fishing industry and food culture to tourism and Japan's diplomatic standing in the world community. Tsukiji and other wholesale markets, of course, stand at one major intersection of sea and society.

Any Japanese schoolchild can rattle off the facts and figures that underscore the importance of fishing and maritime activity to Japan, both past and present. Japan is an archipelago of four major and 3,000 minor islands; its highly indented coastline stretches roughly 28,000 kilometers (Trewartha 1965: 35). No point on the main island of Honshū is more than about 150 kilometers from the seacoast. Japan's mountainous terrain has clustered its population, now as in the past, into a few relatively narrow plains, almost all coastal, that were historically linked with one another by coastal rather than by overland transportation.

The Japanese archipelago extends roughly 3,000 kilometers from Okinawa to Hokkaidō, from approximately 26 to 46 degrees north latitude— roughly the span of other major world fishing grounds, such as those found between the tip of Baja California and the mouth of the Columbia River, between Miami and Nova Scotia, or between the Canary Islands and Bordeaux. The ocean currents that sweep along Japan's coasts and the climatic diversity of these aquatic environments make these waters among the most productive and varied fishing regions in the world. Japan is surrounded by the Pacific Ocean, the Sea of Okhotsk, the Sea of Japan, and the East China Sea. The Pacific coast is swept by the warm northward flowing Japan Current, also known as the "Black Current" *(Kuroshio)*, which meets the cold southward Okhotsk or Kurile Current (also known as the *Oyashio*) off the Sanriku Coast of northeastern Honshū, creating the fertile mixtures of warm and cold waters that produce great fishing grounds. To the north are the subarctic waters of the North Pacific and the Sea of Okhotsk, much of which falls within Russia's 200-mile Exclusive Economic Zone. To the west is the Sea of Japan, separating Japan and Korea (which demands that the body of water be known internationally as the East Sea). The Tsushima Current, a branch of the warm, northward Kuroshio, flows through the straits between Japan and Korea and sweeps up the western coast of Japan. South and west of Kyūshū is the East China Sea, a shallow, treacherous, semitropical body of water.

The coastal waters of Japan are estimated to contain more than two thousand varieties of fish (approximately 10 percent of all known saltwater species), together with several hundred more species of shellfish. Almost all edible species have played some role in Japanese cuisine.[9] From the earliest ages, marine resources have been widely exploited. Archaeological excavations of shell mounds demonstrate that during the Jōmon period (ca. 10,000–300 B.C.E.) many varieties of fresh- and saltwater fish and shellfish were the mainstay of the diet of the earliest human inhabitants of the Japanese islands; Jōmon people used quite sophisticated techniques for trapping large pelagic species, including dolphins and tuna (Imamura 1996: 8, 73–77).

Japan is today one of the world's leading users of seafood. Japan's seafood supply—roughly 66 kilograms per capita—is far short of Iceland's (91 kg), and is roughly comparable to that of Portugal (58 kg), Malaysia (52 kg), Norway (50 kg), and the Republic of Korea (49 kg). Japan's per capita supply (as of 1999) dwarfs that of Spain (41 kg), France (29 kg), the People's Republic of China (26 kg), the United Kingdom and Canada (22 kg each), the United States (20 kg), and Germany (15 kg) (FAO n.d.). Fish constitute approximately 42 percent of the animal protein consumed by Japanese (Nōrinsuisanshō 1989: 2).

The Japanese fishing industry is among the largest in the world, employing hundreds of thousands of people. Thousands of small fishing ports cluster around the coastal fisheries, which are largely in the hands of small-scale, family-based independent fishing enterprises. Dozens of larger ports are home bases for distant-water fleets deployed to fish in every ocean of the world. The huge corporations that dominate the latter sector of the fishing industry are themselves gigantic, vertically integrated conglomerates with subsidiaries involved in everything from fishing to foreign trade, freezer technology to bioengineering, sausage making to distribution, warehousing to nutritional science.

Tsukiji is a major hub for this industry, itself a large and dynamic sector of the Japanese economy with considerable domestic influence, both social and political. Tsukiji handles about one-sixth of the seafood that passes through Japanese wholesale markets and is the largest single marketplace for fish not only in Japan but in the world. Tsukiji is thus a linchpin in a complex national system of trade that connects thousands of rural communities directly to the social and economic forces of Japan's urban core. The day's trading at Tsukiji affects price, supply, and demand throughout Japan's 800 other wholesale markets for fish. Tsukiji looms large on the horizon— its daily prices signaling success or failure—for the roughly 3,000 Japanese fishing villages and towns where, despite dramatic declines over the past generation, some 278,000 Japanese are employed directly in fisheries production and tens of thousands more are engaged in processing, transporting, and selling seafood.[10]

At the same time, Tsukiji plays an equally central (though by no means exclusive) role linking Japan's domestic fishing and food industries to larger networks in the international economy. Prices set at Tsukiji are faxed to

Figure 9. *The Tuna Flew.* From a children's book, *Maguro ga tonda (The Tuna Flew)*, written and illustrated by Ishiguro Kaoru (1988). Reproduced with permission of the Tōkyō Tsukiji Uoichiba Ōmono Gyōkai.

fishing ports on every continent, and each day tons of fresh fish from around the globe land at Narita International Airport ("Japan's leading fishing port," runs the stale joke at Tsukiji); indeed, in the value of seafood landed, Narita far surpasses all of Japan's more conventional watery ports.

Japan's reliance on imported seafood is enormous (see tables 2 and 3). Imports of fresh, frozen, processed, and live marine products totaled 3.8 billion kilograms in 2001, compared with 6.1 billion kilograms of domestic production (which includes the catches of Japanese distant-water fishing vessels, not just seafood caught in Japanese waters). Imports were valued at over $14 billion in 2001, led by shrimp ($2.5 billion), tuna ($1.8 billion), and salmon ($900 million). The leading exporter of seafood to Japan was the People's Republic of China ($2.3 billion), followed by the United States ($1.4 billion), Thailand ($1.1 billion), and Russia ($1.0 billion) (MAFF 2001: 44–47; Nōrinsuisanshō 2002: 3, 48). Substantial proportions (by value) of many imported seafoods arrive by air freight; given the high cost of such shipping, clearly these are the more expensive, higher-quality products, and much of this import stream flows directly to Tsukiji and other major urban markets. A few examples include eel (*unagi;* 100 percent of imports arrive by air), sea urchin (*uni;* 79 percent), abalone (*awabi;* 73 percent), yellowfin tuna (*kihada;* 55 percent), bluefin tuna (*kuromaguro;* 46 percent), sea

TABLE 2. *Leading Categories of Seafood Imports to Japan, 2001 (ranked by value)*

	Value (billion yen)	Weight (million kg)
Shrimp	302.2	256.2
Tuna and swordfish	226.8	321.7
Salmon	110.1	276.5
Crab	81.6	108.2
Cod roe	72.0	42.7
Eel	66.7	69.4
Processed shrimp products	46.8	39.1
Squid	43.5	82.1
Cod, including surimi products	38.3	177.4
Octopus	37.6	85.7
Sea urchin	29.6	16.6
Mackerel	25.5	174.0

SOURCE: Nōrinsuisanshō 2002: 3.

NOTE: These statistics group fresh, frozen, and in some cases live imports into single categories.

bream (*tai*; 39 percent), swordfish (*kajiki*; 28 percent), southern bluefin tuna (*minami maguro*; 24 percent), big-eye tuna (*mebachi*; 21 percent), salmon (*sake*; 17 percent), and blowfish (*fugu*; 12 percent) (figures for 2001, from Nōrinsuisanshō 2002: 46–47).

Tsukiji stands at the center of a global seafood trade that reaches to virtually every fishing region of the world and handles almost every commercially exploitable seafood product. Situated at a crossroads for both the domestic and international seafood trades, Tsukiji thus both reflects and shapes Japan's position in many of the global economic, environmental, and diplomatic issues in which the nation's fishing industry is entangled, such as the ban on high-seas drift nets, international protests over bluefin tuna fishing, and negotiations over the whaling moratorium.

Maritime issues of every sort permeate Japan's international relations, and many of them directly or indirectly affect seafood markets and hence Tsukiji. For example, the question of control over four small islands in the Kuriles—the so-called Northern Territories—just off the coast of Hokkaidō, held by the Soviets and now the Russians since 1945, continually

TABLE 3. *Origins of Seafood Imported into Japan,*
2001 (ranked by value)

	Value (billion yen)	Weight (million kg)
People's Republic of China	282.1	682.5
United States	175.0	421.2
Thailand	130.2	240.9
Russia	126.6	204.0
Republic of Korea	116.4	183.0
Indonesia	116.4	127.2
Chile	87.6	332.4
Taiwan	82.0	159.7
Norway	71.8	283.7
Australia	58.7	26.8
Vietnam	58.3	80.0
India	54.2	67.9
European Union	46.3	127.6

SOURCE: Nōrinsuisanshō 2002: 48.

bedevils Japanese–Russian relations; as a result, Japan and Russia have not yet signed a treaty to end World War II. Public politics focuses on the islands, the land, but one of the real issues is the sea, in particular the fishing rights to the rich waters of the Sea of Okhotsk. Over the past several decades, there have been innumerable disputes over Japanese vessels in waters claimed by Russians and vice versa, as well as fish poaching by Japanese or Russian or North Korean vessels. In the post-Soviet era of loose borders and even looser black markets, smuggling seafood to Japan from Russian vessels has become an enormously lucrative and violent fact of life.[11] There is no question that a portion of the high-priced seafood, such as crab, that enters Japanese distribution channels in Hokkaidō originates with smugglers or poachers of some stripe.

In the much vaster legitimate waters of the international seafood trade, the Japanese fishing industry operates in a complex and volatile international environment. Over the past two decades the technology and infrastructure of fishing have grown increasingly elaborate and capital-intensive. The international politics of fishing has become much more tense as it has grown more entangled with international maritime law, control over exclusive economic zones, protection of marine species, stability of food supplies, and bilateral trade balances. Japanese fisheries and trading companies are involved in joint ventures throughout the world—with fishing outfits in Spain, the United States, Canada, Thailand, Guinea Bissau, Taiwan, Croatia, Kiribati, China, Korea, Australia, Indonesia, Turkey, Italy, Mexico, and Chile, to mention only a few—to produce, process, and distribute seafood, much but not all of it destined for Japanese markets. The Japanese government is party to dozens of multilateral fisheries conventions that govern international marine resources, as well as many more bilateral fishing agreements that permit full or partial access of Japanese fishing vessels to the waters of other nations. Two of the best known, and most controversial, governing bodies are the International Whaling Commission (IWC) and the International Commission for the Conservation of Atlantic Tuna (ICCAT).

International regulations, trade negotiations, and environmental disputes, some of them with little connection to fishing per se, increasingly encumber the supplies of seafood on which Tsukiji depends. Thus Tsukiji also offers an important vantage point from which to examine the interaction of global and transnational trends with domestic conditions, of emerging international maritime regimes and trade flows with the internal economic, social, cultural, and political dynamics of Japanese society.

From a structural perspective, the global trade in seafood products can be seen as a complex network of "commodity chains" (Gereffi and Korzeniewicz 1994). This perspective, generally applied to the production of manufactured goods through the coordinated activities of far-flung components of the so-called global factory, focuses on the international division of labor into specialized realms. The structure of a commodity chain—the links, stages, phases, and hands through which a particular product passes as it is fabricated, transformed, and distributed between ultimate producers and ultimate consumers—is therefore a highly contingent social formation. It is itself the product of the often minutely calibrated linkages that exist between every pair of hands along the way.

Tsukiji serves as a central node—a command and control center—for this global trade, and the market's activities thus have wide influence both directly and indirectly, both internationally and domestically. Analyzing the emergence of nineteenth-century Chicago as a major market center, the environmental historian William Cronon (1991) examined the reconfiguration of North American agricultural production when Chicago became simultaneously a transportation hub for the American rail system and the production and marketing center for packed meats. These developments not only established the primacy of its markets, bringing vast areas of North

America into direct economic dependence on Chicago, but also redefined the consumption patterns of much of the North American public, with consequent realignments of local systems of production, consumption, and socioeconomic autonomy.

In the latter half of the twentieth century, proliferating technological advances—including highly efficient refrigeration and freezing, the advent of global jet air cargo service, and the proliferation of decentralized telecommunications systems such as fax machines, cellular telephones, and the Internet—have all contributed to a similar reconfiguration of the global fishing industry, with Tsukiji as one of its major hubs. In the late nineteenth century, Chicago became hog butcher for the world; in the late twentieth century, Tsukiji became fishmonger for the seven seas, not only shaping the international fishing industry but also remolding patterns of consumption and distribution across Japan and throughout the world (T. Bestor 2000; 2001b; in preparation).

Tsukiji and Distribution

As a wholesale market, Tsukiji is a critical component in the domestic Japanese distribution system, a feature of Japan's economic and social order that in recent years has become a focus of international attention. Coming under much criticism are the many layers of wholesalers who stand between producers and consumers. These tiers of enterprises include vast numbers of presumably inefficient small-scale (often family-run) wholesale and retail outlets. By the same token, the apparently more efficient large-scale specialty stores, supermarkets, and department stores are relatively few, their development retarded in part by the adamant political opposition of small-scale enterprises (see Kikkawa 1997). Distribution channels themselves are often controlled by vertically integrated combines of firms, known as *keiretsu*, which stifle competition and squeeze out independent operations (Gerlach 1992a, 1992b). And whether directly dominated by keiretsu relationships or not, the distribution sectors of the Japanese economy are generally characterized by close, personalistic ties between suppliers and customers that emphasize long-term stability of relationship over short-term transactional advantage. Taken together, these interrelated traits lead many critics—both foreign businesspeople and domestic consumer advocates—to argue that Japanese distribution channels are economically inefficient, harm the Japanese public, and bar the free entry of foreign goods into the Japanese domestic economy.[12]

Thus, Tsukiji epitomizes the complicated interactions between social context and economic behavior that are at the heart of much debate over Japan's economic structure. And the marketplace embodies many of the features of the Japanese distribution system—small-scale enterprises arrayed in complex, multiple layers and embedded in an almost byzantine social context—that draw so much criticism. At Tsukiji's core are the hundreds of small family-run wholesale firms—some many generations old, most employing the labor of husbands and wives, fathers and sons, aunts and nephews, adopted children and married-in apprentices—that have much more in common with the mom-and-pop retailers that dot Tokyo's commercial landscape than with the huge corporations that more visibly control Japan's economy. Tsukiji's small-scale wholesalers coexist and cooperate with one another in a fast-moving market even as they are locked in subtle but intense struggles to carve out and defend market niches against all comers.

These firms, as mentioned above, are known officially as "intermediate wholesalers" (*nakaoroshi gyōsha*, literally "in-between wholesale traders"). The first character of the term, *naka*—written with two elements: "person" plus "center" or "middle"—neatly signifies the nature of the trade: the person in the middle.[13] An older term, *nakagainin*, puts the business even more clearly: "a person trading in the middle."[14]

Intermediate wholesalers occupy one tier in immensely complicated layers of suppliers and customers, standing at least two stages, sometimes four or five stages, removed from both producers and consumers. Although they are themselves independent entrepreneurs, intermediate wholesalers operate against a backdrop of (and often in competition with) the vertically integrated corporations and keiretsu combines that dominate the domestic fisheries and food industries and directly or indirectly control much of the market's supply: huge fisheries companies, general trading companies (*sōgō shōsha*), and aggressive supermarket chains. Intermediate wholesalers' businesses are hemmed in by deeply rooted sets of personal ties, obligations, feuds, political interests, kinship connections of every variety, and patterns of patronage that are renewed—and hence subtly renegotiated—daily, against a backdrop of decades if not generations of similar calculations. This complicated social world constrains them to temper their economic ties in mutually acceptable ways even as it provides a rich stockpile of opportunities to pursue advantage by manipulating their social capital in ways visible and indeed imaginable only to initiates.

Although Tsukiji is situated in an economic context far different from the third world or from peasant or colonial societies, where most anthropological studies of markets have been done, nonetheless it too is a market that links substantially different sectors of the contemporary economy. In

particular, Tsukiji stands at the border between the large-scale corporations that supply and transport most of Japan's seafood and the small-scale
family-run firms that continue to dominate Tokyo's retail trade in foodstuffs. Upstream from the market, suppliers include enormous Japanese
trading companies and the equally large fishing companies whose activities
span the globe, as well as thousands of small-scale fishing enterprises and
provincial brokers based throughout Japan and overseas as well. From large
and small companies alike, products are funneled through Tsukiji's seven
auction houses, all of them large corporations operating in the midst of tiny
family-run businesses. Downstream, the auction houses sell their products
to the thousands of traders at Tsukiji, whose family-run firms are dwarfed
by the auction houses themselves. Despite the recent inroads made by
supermarkets and chain stores, much of the trade within the marketplace
continues to pass through the hands of relatively small-scale wholesalers
who have much in common with their retailer customers and who draw on
a commercial culture that owes much to precapitalist mercantile traditions.
Tsukiji thus stands between the large- and small-scale sectors of Japan's
domestic economy, bringing into daily contact contrasting versions of economic culture: unself-conscious assumptions of capitalism as a natural economic and social order, jostled on the one hand by the impatient advocates
of continual change, progress and modernization, growth and rationalization, and soothed on the other hand by those who insist that established
economic custom, tradition, and institutional stability rather than transformation are the market's guiding principles. The juxtaposition of large scale
and small, of visions of change and fondness for custom, profoundly structures the activity of the marketplace.

⊞ ⊞ ⊞

Any one of these broadly interrelated perspectives on Tsukiji—as a key
institution of Tokyo's infrastructure; as an important link in Japan's food
chain; as a place where cultural meanings of cuisine, work, gender, and class
identity are formulated; as a node in the Japanese fishing industry; as an
embodiment of Japanese distribution channels; as a border region between
vastly different sectors of the Japanese (and the global) economy—could
easily be the subject of a specialized technical monograph. Writing that
monograph is not my goal.

Instead, what interests me most are those things that link and crosscut
the technical dimensions of the market: the social institutions and cultural

meanings that endow Tsukiji with a sense of place, a social identity, a structural order, and a historical memory, as well as an economic purpose. What I intend is an analysis of the culture of Tsukiji and of the ways in which cultural processes order the social institutions and the economic activity of the marketplace. Economists think of markets, not of places; I am interested in the market*place* and the cultural processes and social institutions that make Tsukiji a world of interest both for its habitués and for an anthropologist. I am, in a sense, less interested in market performance than in performances in the marketplace—the enactments of economic process in a setting richly meaningful in social and cultural terms to its participants.

From one perspective Tsukiji is a freewheeling spot market where one might expect to find competitive, individualistic, short-term profit maximization to be the normal course of events. This book analyzes instead how patterns of trade emerge from and are ordered by the social institutions and cultural patterns in which the marketplace is embedded and without which it could not exist. For the engines of economic activity, culture is not simply a lubricant or a fuel with higher or lower octane ratings. The hand of culture designs the cylinders and camshafts, turns the key, shifts the gears, unfolds the road maps, and writes the traffic tickets. In this study of the Tsukiji marketplace, I hope to make *this* hand more visible.

BUBBLE, BUBBLE, TOIL AND TROUBLE

When I first visited Tsukiji for research in the winter of 1989, Japan was just emerging from the shadows of hushed apprehension and anticipatory mourning during the last lingering illness of the Shōwa Emperor (who died on January 7, 1989). With his death and the announcement of the reign of the new emperor, to be known as Heisei—"Becoming Peace"—the oppressive "self-restraint" *(jishuku)* of the preceding months, which had silenced celebration and consumption alike, lifted. The national mood enlivened and many people assumed that the booming prosperity of the last several decades would immediately resume and carry Japan into the coming "Pacific Century," which, few doubted, would become "Japan's Century." Only gradually did it become clear that the new Heisei era would never match the glitzy economic frenzy of the last decade or so of the Shōwa period. With this realization, the era of the so-called Bubble Economy *(baburu keizai)* was "discovered" after the fact, its end retroactively located sometime around 1990.

My research began, therefore, when people at Tsukiji thought that mourning for the emperor was only a momentary stillness in the midst of an otherwise bustling economy. My fieldwork extended through the growing recognition that the period between 1987 and 1990 had been peak years, not to be repeated anytime soon. And I ended my research in the early twenty-first century in a climate of almost palpable despair, the belief that ruination lay just around the corner. The cumulative numbing impact of disaster after disaster during the 1990s—the Hanshin-Awaji earthquake and the Aum gas attack, both in 1995; the relentless slide of the yen against the dollar; the collapse of savings and loan associations; the *E. coli* outbreak (known in Japan as the O-157 epidemic) that slashed demand for fresh foods, especially sushi, in the summer of 1996; mass layoffs of white-collar workers and the undertow of "restructuring" (*resutora*, the Japanese equivalent of "right-sizing"); and endless political scandals of stock fixing and bank regulators on the take—eroded national confidence across the board.

In their general contours, the trends of Tsukiji's economic condition since the late 1940s mirror the growth, stabilization, and (recent) decline of the Japanese economy as a whole. During the so-called period of high speed economic growth of the 1950s and 1960s, the annual volume of trade in the TMG seafood divisions (all markets combined) grew enormously: 258 million kilograms in 1950, 413 million in 1955, 582 million in 1960, 691 million in 1965, and 826 million in 1970, for an average annual growth rate of about 11 percent.[15] During the period of rising but stable prosperity from about 1970 until the late 1980s, volume leveled off and fluctuated from year to year within a relatively narrow band: 826 million kilograms in 1970, 850 million in 1975, 814 million in 1980, 852 million in 1985, and 847 million in 1990.

Although the "Bubble years" were recognized only in retrospect, several years after the bubble burst, market sales clearly reflect the economic downturn since the late 1980s. In tonnage, the peak year of seafood sales in the TMG market system was 1987 (890 million kilograms), and almost every subsequent year has had a smaller volume than the previous one. Between 1987 and 1998, the annual volume dropped a total of 20 percent: 847 million in 1990, 738 million in 1995, down to 715 million in 1998, and rising slightly to 717 million in 2001. The yen value of seafood handled peaked in 1990, when the market system handled ¥844 billion worth of seafood; in 1996 the market system handled ¥696 billion, and in 2001, only ¥614 billion, a decrease of about 27 percent from 1990.

Figures from the Tsukiji market alone show that its tonnage also peaked in 1987 at 815 million kilograms, declining to 747 million in 1990, 640 million in 1995, and 621 million in 1997, rebounding somewhat to 629 million in 1999 and 632 million in 2001. In terms of value, Tsukiji reached its high point in 1990 when it handled seafood worth ¥755 billion; sales dropped to

¥596 billion in 1995, rose slightly to ¥606 billion in 1997, and dropped again to ¥585 billion in 1999 and ¥545 billion in 2001, a decrease of roughly 28 percent from 1990. Not only did overall tonnage and overall sales drop dramatically, but the average value of products declined as well, from roughly ¥1,010 to ¥860 per kilogram, a drop of about 15 percent between 1990 and 2001.[16]

To hear Tsukiji traders tell it, in the blink of an eye, the best of times had given way to the worst. They, like many other Japanese, were as extreme in their confidence during the Bubble years that things would remain the same, only better, as they were convinced in the wake of the Asian financial collapses of 1997–98 that things could only get worse.

Of course, I knew none of this as I listened to Mr. Shimizu, the marketplace administrator, in February 1989, when details of Tsukiji's history and organization began to align themselves in my mind's eye into sharp but as-yet indecipherable patterns. The feeling of change and of decline, and indeed my understanding of what was pattern and what was not, emerged only gradually through my fieldwork at the marketplace spread over the next dozen years.

FIELDWORK

After my epiphany in Shimizu's office, during the remainder of the winter and spring of 1989, I visited the marketplace several times each week—daily, when possible. From the beginning I cultivated contacts at Tsukiji through every personal connection I could muster, seeking introductions from friends who knew people in the marketplace; through government officials who had colleagues whose work was connected to the marketplace; by way of friends and acquaintances in the fishing industry and in retail business who had professional contacts there; through academic colleagues who knew other researchers who worked on markets; and through journalists, writers, and photographers who were familiar with one or another aspect of the marketplace.

Early on, an aspect of my research strategy was to ask people to whom I was introduced if they would give me a tour of the marketplace. Many people were happy to guide me around, and in the first couple of months of fieldwork I walked the market twice with intermediate wholesalers; three times with officials of auction houses; several times with government officials; twice with restaurant owners; once with a retired sanitation and public health inspector; once with a supermarket buyer; several times with officials of the intermediate wholesalers' federation; and once with the manager of a freezer warehouse. Each tour gave me an individual's perspective on what makes the market tick and how its many pieces and places fit together. And repeated opportunities to walk through the same sites and sights guided by knowledgeable insiders gave me valuable chances to pose similar questions to different escorts and, equally important, to ask entirely different questions about the same things. Of course, after several tours and many explorations on my own, I became quite familiar with the layout and rhythms of Tsukiji (occasionally I had to jog myself to be appropriately astonished when rehearing factoids that I had already jotted down during previous visits). But every guide had his or her own distinct perspective, and from each tour I gained valuable clues about the complexity of the market's organization. Most important, each time I came away with new and as yet unanswered questions that sent me off in search of someone else who could give me some more answers.

By the summer I had completed a reconnaissance of the market as a whole, had acquired a basic understanding of the division of labor and functional organization of the marketplace, and had laid the groundwork for the larger study that has become this book. My early tours had given me the familiarity and confidence to navigate the sprawling marketplace freely and unescorted. In general, I had learned the complicated and topsy-turvy clock of the market, the ebb and flow of its patrons, and the best times to chat casually with merchants. I had also determined that more than enough information was readily available—through observation, through interviews with articulate informants happy to have an appreciative ear, through the masses of statistical reports—to enable full-scale research.

By the time I returned to the United States in August of 1989, I had established a research routine that I would continue during subsequent visits to Tsukiji. Clearly, the illusion of "participant-observation" was not available to me at Tsukiji (T. Bestor 2002b, 2003). Buying or selling or cutting apart a tuna were not things I could do, nor would anyone be foolhardy enough to want me to try it with *their* tuna. Instead, I developed a technique of "inquisitive observation." Most mornings from 5 or 6 or 7 until 10 or 11 A.M. I would roam the marketplace. I hung around, watching the many phases of transactions and following the flow of seafood from hand to hand, from the back of a truck to an auction block to a cutting board to a loading dock. I watched things happen again and again and again. I asked people to explain what a specific technique of handling fish was for, or how a particular kind of bidding system worked, or who that group of men lounging in the corner was, or what this tool was called, or how much that block of ice cost. The next day, I'd ask other people the same questions. Because of the pace of the market, many such interviews were simply a quick question here, a minute or two of conversation there, a few passing comments as someone paused for a cigarette and a cup of instant coffee.

All my fieldwork—both informal encounters of inquisitive observation and formal interviews with market participants—took place in Japanese. My daily exposure to rapid-fire mercantile slang as well as the technical terminology of auctions, the fishing industry, and the seafood business was itself a crash course in market culture as well as an indelible influence on my spoken Japanese. On several occasions early on in my research I took Japanese students along with me as research assistants, but once I realized that I had to translate market language into standard Japanese for them to understand my interviews, I decided to continue solo.

I didn't go to the market every morning before dawn, but at least a couple of times a week I was there to watch the auctions, asking simple questions and storing up more complicated ones for longer interviews later. Several times I spent the night at Tsukiji to watch the marketplace from the arrival of the long-distance trucks to the end of the auctions. Most mornings I was at Tsukiji by seven, prowling the stalls, showing my face, interspersing little questions with my greetings to busy stallholders, and setting up appointments to come back later—the next day or a couple of days afterward in the late morning or early afternoon for a more leisurely yet more focused interview.

During my next major set of visits to Tsukiji—during the fall and winter of 1990–91, when I was able to spend about five months at the marketplace—my contacts at the marketplace had snowballed to the point that people I had met at Tsukiji now introduced me to their colleagues and I no longer had to rely on those I knew "outside" who happened to know someone "inside." I was approaching that happy state (for an anthropologist) where many people didn't quite know where I came from. That is, most of the people I dealt with at Tsukiji no longer exactly remembered (or had never known) from whom my initial introductions had come. Instead, they encountered me as a vaguely inexplicable part of the social landscape. I was just around, and there was usually someone who could vouch for me in an imprecise way if the need ever arose. It never did.[17]

Few people at Tsukiji immediately appreciated the point of anthropological research on a marketplace. They all have very busy lives and jobs, of compelling interest to them and those around them, but it was sometimes perplexing to them that these should also be of interest to me. From their responses, I deduced four or five major notions of who I was and what I was doing. First, if the market was my interest, I must be an economist. Second, if culture was my interest, I must be either a historian or a folklorist. Third, since contemporary trade seemed to be of interest to me, I must be a fisheries marketing specialist. (Occasionally, when Japanese fisheries interests became the momentary subject of international attention, usually for environmental reasons, some people would wonder if I was affiliated with Greenpeace or some similar environmental organization; I was not and am not.) Fourth, my interest in all the fish on display gave rise to the opinion I was some kind of ichthyologist; I once overheard a couple of custodians talking about me as *sakana no sensei,* "the fish professor." And, finally, since I constantly took notes, I must be a journalist, perhaps a novelist. Although most people I talked with could comfortably slot me into one or another of these roles, I tried to avoid being pigeonholed, since labels inevitably become constraints; once, early in my research, after I had explained my interests to a trader in largely economic terms and then had turned my questioning toward kinship and the history of various stalls, I was abruptly called to task for asking "noneconomic" questions. I soon learned to define my interests as broadly as possible and to welcome the ambiguity that accompanied the unaccountable variety of my professional interests.

Since Tsukiji is a busy place, I was always on the run; there is no place to stand still and watch unless you block the entry to someone's business. I became adept at scribbling notes as I walked, always keeping my eyes open for fast-moving carts; I filled dozens of pocket notebooks on the move. I found myself a circuit of hole-in-the-wall coffee shops where I could stop for fifteen or twenty minutes to jot down more detailed notes on conversations and observations. As I began to know some traders personally, I cultivated the habit of dropping by half a dozen stalls during my morning rounds of the marketplace, perching at each for ten or fifteen minutes (if they weren't too busy), to exchange pleasantries, ask some questions, watch the flow of traffic, and get introduced to some of their colleagues and customers. Eventually I discovered places I could sit and talk with people at greater length after I had completed my daily tours. One was the offices of Tō-Oroshi, the federation of intermediate wholesalers. I went there often to consult their extensive files of organizational data, statistical information, and historical material, or to ask officials for introductions to particular people. Sometimes when I dropped by, I would sit next to the managing director's desk that overlooked the entire main office, sipping coffee while chatting with the many traders who dropped by to check on this or that item of business. Sometimes I would be shown to a seat in a large quiet office with eighteen desks reserved for the eighteen wholesalers who sit on the federation's board of directors, each a representative of one of the guilds of wholesalers that organize the activities of distinct trading communities within the marketplace. In solitude I would transcribe statistical reports or leaf through thick institutional histories; if a director drifted into the office to check his mail, more often than not he would ask me what reports I was studying that day and I would try to steer us into a conversation far more lively and illuminating than the documents at hand.

Another perch I located was in the cramped library run by the Ginrinkai (the Silver Scale Society), an organization founded by Tsukiji traders to promote cultural activities. Several times a year it sponsors trips to hot springs; it publishes a magazine of stories, essays, and poetry about the marketplace; and it operates a small reading room jammed with old novels, books about fish, and chronicles of the marketplace. The books were only a minor attraction. Nishimura Eiko[18] presided over the Ginrinkai as her personal salon, and entertained each day a dozen or more traders who came there to eat lunch, change their clothes in the back room, have a beer, and gossip about the day's trading. I spent countless hours at Mrs. Nishimura's cluttered table, asking questions of her and anyone else who joined us, and simply listening to the conversations of traders unwinding after a hard day.

With her death in 1996 Tsukiji lost one of its great raconteurs and repositories of market lore, and I lost one of my best friends in the marketplace. Anthropologists like to think they blend into the background, but as a bearded, bulky, six-foot-tall foreigner, I have few illusions about my invisibility. Nevertheless, sitting in the Ginrinkai library day after day, Mrs. Nishimura allowed me to become enough of a fixture that people took me for granted, even the visiting saleswoman who would stop by every few weeks to try to tempt Mrs. Nishimura to buy lingerie for her daughters.

Through Tō-Oroshi and the Ginrinkai, I acquired those most valuable of assets for an anthropologist: networks of acquaintances who knew me as a relatively normal part of the scene, someone whose presence was tied to something familiar. However unaccountable my being there might be in one scheme of things, at least I was encountered in normal places, talking knowingly about normal topics, vouchsafed by normal people rather than outsiders. I do not mean to suggest that I was not—am not—clearly a foreigner, an outsider, a babe in the marketplace, nor that those facts were or are ever far from the minds of the Tsukiji traders with whom I interact; indeed, my otherness goes a long way toward allowing me to ask questions that I suspect a Japanese outsider would be hesitant to ask and an insider would not answer for another Japanese. But at the same time, it is a distinct advantage to be a familiar foreign outsider; after a while no one quite remembered when I first showed up, who first introduced me, or who (or what) I thought I already knew.

After my initial fieldwork at Tsukiji between February and July 1989, I returned to the marketplace repeatedly over the next several years, for several periods of intensive interviewing and observation. These visits ranged from a few weeks to a few months long: in January, July, and September–November 1990; May–June 1991; the New Year's season spanning December 1991 and January 1992; May–June 1994; and June–July 1995. During the academic year 1997–98, I was a visiting professor at the Kyoto Center for Japanese Studies and made half a dozen trips to Tokyo, lasting from a few days to a couple of weeks—to visit old friends at the market, recheck details of marketplace organization, and update statistical data. Further brief visits to Tokyo in the summer of 1999, the fall of 2000, and in January and July 2003 enabled me to clarify a few final details.

This study focuses directly on the Tsukiji marketplace, but my perspectives on Tsukiji have also been shaped by research at many other markets, in Japan and overseas. Between 1988 and 1999, I visited fifteen markets throughout Japan, including dockside markets in small fishing ports, regional wholesale markets, major urban wholesale markets, and retail public markets.[19]

In 1995 and 1998 I visited major Korean wholesale markets for seafood in Seoul—Garak and Noryangjin—and Busan, as well as open-air, retail seafood markets, such as Namdaemun and Gyeong-dong (both in Seoul) and Jagalchi (in Busan). These Korean markets resemble Japanese ones in some significant respects. Japanese and Korean food culture regarding seafood is similar, and the Japanese colonial occupation of Korea (from 1910 to 1945) strongly influenced both Korean foodways and the organization of markets. Many present-day Korean markets were first established under Japanese colonial laws with institutions similar to those that governed Tsukiji at that time. In 1998 and 1999, visits to Hong Kong, Guangzhou, and Ho Chi Minh City enabled me to trace out further connections between Japanese markets and other Asian centers of production and distribution. During the summer of 1999, a month of fieldwork in Spain—focused particularly on Spanish tuna farms that produce fish for export exclusively for Japanese consumption—also helped me understand the global networks of seafood trade that organize themselves around Japanese consumption patterns.[20]

In the United States, I visited and interviewed participants in various markets, fishing ports, government agencies, and processing centers concerned with seafood destined for Japan, during several dozen research trips between 1994 and 1999. Interviews, observations, and collection of trade data took place in Boston, Chatham, Gloucester, Hyannis, New Bedford, and Newburyport, Massachusetts; Boothbay Harbor, Spruce Head, and West Point, Maine; Portsmouth and Seabrook, New Hampshire; East Hampton and Montauk, Long Island, and the Fulton Fish Market in New York City; Beaufort and Moorehead City, North Carolina; Honolulu, Hawai'i; Silver Spring, Maryland; and Washington, D.C. This research provided me with ethnographically contextualized perspectives on how supplies reach the Tsukiji market and some of the ways in which foreign producers interact with (and regard) Japanese markets. Through my research in the United States, I also gained valuable insights into the many intersecting and competing interests that shape national and international regulations, environmental concerns, and the politics of the commercial fishing industry as they structure the day-to-day and year-to-year activities of the international seafood trade.

During my research at Tsukiji many curious friends—both Japanese and foreign—asked me to take them to the marketplace. I was always happy to do so, because guiding them through the complicated scene and answering their questions was an immensely helpful method for questioning my own assumptions and clarifying my answers. Over the years I have guided groups through the marketplace a dozen or more times, including Japanese and American college students, Japanese friends who are lifelong residents of Tokyo but who had never visited the market, American and British journalists, American academic specialists in Japanese studies, visiting American specialists in international economic issues, and American college professors on cultural familiarization tours of Japan.

One particularly illuminating chance to take visitors through the market came in June 1995, when I accompanied a delegation of American seafood exporters on a two-week promotion tour through Japan and Korea. During their stay in Tokyo I repeatedly guided individuals and small groups of exporters through the marketplace. Viewing Tsukiji from the vantage point of lobstermen from Maine, oyster producers from Long Island Sound, tuna wholesalers from Massachusetts, Rhode Island, and New York, and abalone divers from Los Angeles broadened my understanding of the market in many ways (Bestor 1995). The delegation members were most directly concerned with how to do business at Tsukiji, and from their questions I learned a great deal about the competition, constraints, confusion, and complaints of

American businesses hoping to enter this market. On a more fundamental level, because they were all experts in their own realms of the fisheries trade, their questions, both pointed and general, on such diverse matters as shipping schedules, holding tanks for live seafood, packaging materials, consumer preferences for various species of imported seafood, the color symbolism of lobsters, or public health certification for oysters all helped me sort out what is salient about fish markets to those who know them well.

Just as the tours of Tsukiji I received at the start of my fieldwork oriented me toward the physical layout, the institutional structure, and the cultural complexity of the marketplace, the informal tours I led for others once I had thought I had mastered the place were valuable in pointing out the gaps in my understanding. The tours became my ethnographic reality checks.

CIRCLING BACK

A couple of weeks before I was to leave Japan in 1991, having completed a longish stint of fieldwork at Tsukiji, I spent a hot Sunday rambling around Tokyo in the tow of friends from Tsukiji—Mrs. Nishimura's daughter, Makiko, and her husband, Akira. We visited several tuna dealers at their homes, scattered across Tokyo. As we drove from here to there and back again through the clogged traffic, I kept up my side of the conversation by pointing out neighborhoods where I had lived—a few months here, a half year there, a couple of years in yet a third place—during my visits to Tokyo over the years. On the final leg of the day's journey, we crossed the Sumida River on our way to a Korean barbecue restaurant deep in the heart of shitamachi where we were to meet still more Tsukiji traders for dinner and an evening of barhopping.

The car negotiated several bridges and suddenly I realized we were in Fukagawa. I idly commented that I had once lived here, too. Akira laughed and said they came to the neighborhood often, to have sushi at a little out-of-the-way place run by an old crony who used to buy fish at a stall in Tsukiji where Makiko had once worked as a cashier.

I turned and stared. "What's the owner's name?" I asked, already sensing the answer.

"Watanabe," they replied. "Why?"

I told them about Watanabe's friendship when I had been a language student in Tokyo sixteen years before, and about a freezing morning tour of Tsukiji.

It was their turn to stare.

I told them how Tsukiji had fascinated me that first morning and how I had often wondered about Watanabe in the couple of years since I had redis-covered my interest in the marketplace. And I told them how I had been unable to find the nerve to go back to Watanabe's on my own after all these years.

The outcome was inevitable. Makiko and Akira were delighted at the prospect of pulling off a tremendous surprise. I wasn't so sure, but agreed nonetheless. They called and made reservations for the following Friday, mentioning only that they would bring a guest.

The appointed night came, and with some trepidation I readied myself for explaining where I had been and what I had been doing for the past decade and a half. At the same time, I prepared myself for the likelihood that Watanabe wouldn't remember me at all. Our friendship years ago, I rea-soned, could not have been as vivid for him as it was for Vickey and me.

The cab dropped us off a couple of blocks from Watanabe's shop. I showed Makiko and Akira where our apartment had been and I led them around the corner to the tiny *Inari* shrine that Vickey and I had last visited on our final day in the neighborhood sixteen years before. I thanked Inari-sama for bringing me back and tossed five yen into the collection box: five yen *(go-en)* is a homonym for good luck and for connection. I took a deep breath. We walked another block and there was Watanabe's shop.

My friends went in first, giggling delightedly at the surprise they were expecting to create, cameras poised to capture Watanabe's face. Akira pulled me through the curtain. The shop had changed a little—but only a little—over the years. The boisterous apprentices were gone, replaced by a power-ful young man in his late twenties whom I had last seen as a junior high school boy. A beckoning cat stood atop the pay telephone at the back of the shop. The shop was painted a different color. The large bamboo rake was gone. But the wall still held the map of Japan made from whole cedar burls; Kyūshū was still puzzling because the root had created the island in mirror image. Amulets from shitamachi festivals still covered the walls. The counter was the same.

Watanabe walked slowly from the kitchen to see why Makiko and Akira were making such a fuss. He still wore his hair in the crew cut that made him look like a gangster. He still wore a tightly rolled *hachimaki,* a head-band, tied with the élan of the true denizen of shitamachi. The years had changed his appearance far less than my own.

He peered at me. I bowed deeply and apologized formulaically for the time that had passed since my last visit. He stared, as Akira excitedly asked if he remembered me.

His stare cracked into a grin. He asked something that sounded sort of like "wherethehellyabeen." Then he turned to the back room and roared to his wife:

"Oi! Ano henna gaijin ga kaette kita zo!"—"Hey! That strange foreigner came back!"

2　Grooved Channels

Nowadays central Tokyo faces landward, focused on train lines, subways, and superhighways. Most of its old canals have been filled in, covered with roads, or abandoned. The few remaining stretches of working waterfront are largely out of sight, and for many residents of the city, places like the Tsukiji marketplace are out of mind as well. During most of Tokyo's ordinary working hours, the marketplace is quiet. It comes to life about the time the nearby Ginza bars close down. When the market's day is done and Tsukiji traders drain cold beers to wash down their sushi, it is barely noon. But when the marketplace is in full swing, Tsukiji is the center of the world for the fifty thousand people who do business there each day, and for fishers and food traders around the globe. Every trading day, more than 2.3 million kilograms, ¥2.1 billion (approximately $19.4 million) worth of fresh fish, frozen fish, live fish, processed fish, salted fish, fish pâté, fish cakes, pickled fish, smoked fish, shellfish, dried fish, and fish eggs change hands, often several times within a very few minutes, before chefs and fishmongers carry them out through the market's gates.[1]

Of course, the business of the Tsukiji marketplace is a twenty-four-hour-a-day operation, and when day begins or ends depends on your point of view. Outsiders find the topsy-turvy time clock of Tsukiji, where restaurants open at midnight and close by two in the afternoon and where heavy traffic flows at 3 A.M., endlessly fascinating. But Tsukiji regulars know that their "merchant's time" and the rhythms of the marketplace are delicately governed by the logic of the human stomach, culturally interpreted and economically transmitted through the daily shopping behavior of millions of cooks. Many Japanese homemakers shop almost every day for fresh food—deciding on the spot what they will serve for dinner—and their peak shopping hours are between 3 and 6 P.M.[2] Those in the restaurant trade make their decisions earlier, in time for the lunchtime rush. The business of the marketplace is simple: to get fresh food into stores and restaurants before noon. So trucks from provincial harbors arrive between 10 P.M. and midnight, auctioneers and their assistants begin to arrange seafood around 2 A.M., between 3 or 4 A.M. buyers start to inspect merchandise,[3] the opening bells for the morning auctions ring shortly before 6, and by 11 at the latest, stall keepers wind up their day's business.

Reflecting on the ebb and flow of the marketplace, one old trader commented to me, "Tsukiji is not some big machine stamping out products clunk, clunk, clunk. It's an *arabesuku* (arabesque)." His delicate imagery evokes the precise and intricate footwork of Tsukiji traders as they negotiate the market's "grooved channels" (Geertz 1978) that lead them again and again through familiar settings to regular partners in accustomed arenas of trade. To follow traders along these grooved channels—to make sense of the marketplace—one must first understand who's who, what everybody does, and where and when they do it. This requires a clear picture of the physical settings and the rhythms of activity within the marketplace.

The marketplace consists of a complex institutional hierarchy of actors, occupying at least a dozen distinct layers of regulators, shippers, auctioneers, traders, brokers, and buyers. The marketplace is not an economic institution of disembodied paper and electronic transactions; it's neither the Chicago Mercantile Exchange nor Lloyd's of London. Rather, with each transaction, tangible products—perishable seafood—pass from hand to hand, from location to location. The actors' parts on each tier and the ebb and flow of each twenty-four-hour cycle of trade are physically ordered by the internal layout of the marketplace, and in turn the layout is structured by the actors' varied crafts and cadences (table 4). But the marketplace is also constructed by an external logic of time and space, both in the geography of Tokyo and in the historical flow of institutional evolution. Tsukiji's players perform to a script shaped not only by the internal, day-to-day exigencies of the marketplace but also by historical legacies of the marketplace's location and development.

This chapter—something of a walk through the physical environment of the marketplace—may seem to freeze the place in time. But, of course, the market constantly changes; one can barely walk through the same marketplace once, let alone twice. Immediate daily fluctuations jostle with the effects of longer-term trends and gradual transformations, each obscuring the other from clear view. On almost any visit evidence of change catches the eye: bits of the past lurk behind stacks of crates as glimpses of possible futures reel off fax machines. Here I point out a few changes in passing, leaving detailed discussion of their causes and effects to later chapters.

TABLE 4. *Who's Who at Tsukiji*

Participants	Function	Licensing
Regulators		
Ministry of Agriculture, Forestry and Fisheries (MAFF)	Supervises central wholesale markets *(chūō oroshiuri shijō)* throughout the country, licenses fishing and some distribution activities, and authorizes municipal authorities to operate central wholesale markets.	Issues licenses
Tokyo Metropolitan Government (TMG)	Owns and maintains the marketplace's facilities, licenses some businesses within the marketplace, and provides overall regulatory supervision of the marketplace.	Issues licenses
Players		
Producers *(seisansha)*, consignors *(ninushi)*, and consolidators *(shūkasha)*	Supply Tsukiji with seafood for sale on consignment by Tsukiji's auction houses. They include domestic and foreign producers, fishing cooperatives, fishing companies, trading companies, provincial seafood buyers, seafood processing firms, brokers, and wholesalers from other markets.	No market licenses required; fishing licenses regulated by MAFF
Truckers and shippers	Deliver seafood to the market.	No market license required
Stevedore companies *(koage kaisha)*	Receive consignments from truckers and unload, deliver, sort, and arrange consignments within the marketplace as subcontractors for auction houses.	Licensed by TMG
Auction houses *(oroshiuri gyōsha,* "wholesale traders," also known as *niuke gaisha,* "consignment companies")	Receive seafood from producers and brokers on consignment, or purchase products on their own accounts, for sale at daily auctions.	Licensed by MAFF
Auctioneers *(serinin)*	Conduct daily sales as employees of the auction houses.	Licensed by TMG
Licensed buyers/ intermediate wholesalers *(nakaoroshi gyōsha)*	Purchase seafood at daily auctions and resell it at their stalls within the marketplace.	Licensed by TMG

TABLE 4. *(continued)*

Participants	Function	Licensing
Players (cont.)		
Licensed buyers/ authorized traders (*baibaisankasha*)	Purchase seafood at daily auctions for use or resale outside the marketplace. Authorized traders primarily represent large-scale users, such as supermarket chains, hospitals, commissaries, and food processors.	Licensed by TMG
Trade buyers (*kaidashinin*)	Purchase seafood from intermediate wholesalers within the marketplace. They include retail fishmongers, restaurateurs, sushi chefs, buyers for supermarkets and department stores, outer market dealers, fish processors, specialty wholesalers, caterers, and peddlers.	No market license required
Loading dock agents (*kainihokansho,* "merchandise custodians")	Receive trade buyers' purchases from intermediate wholesalers and hold them at loading docks (colloquially called *chaya,* "teahouses") for pickup by trade buyers or by delivery services.	Licensed by TMG
Delivery services	Pick up purchases from loading dock agents and deliver them to trade buyers' businesses throughout Tokyo.	No market license required
Outer market dealers	Have shops located in the outer marketplace (*jōgai shijō*) that supply retailers and restaurateurs but also welcome retail shoppers. Some outer market dealers have licenses as authorized traders and may participate in Tsukiji's auctions. Outer market dealers may also purchase from stalls inside the market or directly from producers.	No market license required
Retail customers	Are discouraged from buying within the Tsukiji marketplace proper, but may shop freely in the outer marketplace.	No market license required

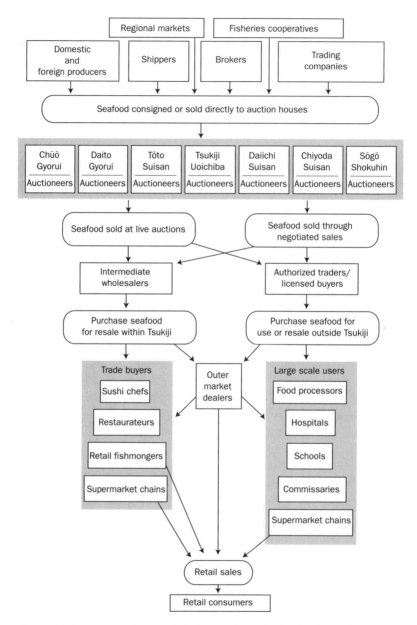

Figure 10. Levels of trade at Tsukiji. Companies and individuals are shown in rectangular boxes; modes of transaction are shown in rounded boxes.

This chapter introduces Tsukiji as a *place,* both internally structured by and externally situated in particular spaces and times—a theme I continue in chapter 3, where I sketch the historical development of the marketplace both as place and as a set of institutions. Time and space—both now and then, micro- and macroscopic—significantly construct the social structure of the marketplace, just as they do any complex organization. My discussion of tempo and place focuses on the central players in Tsukiji's cast and on the stage (especially the backstage) that frames the market's trade.[4] Later chapters (especially 5, 6, and 7) focus on several of the most important sets of leading players—particularly the intermediate wholesalers and the auctioneers—and analyze how patterns of economic transaction and institutional structure take form within the social fabric of the marketplace.

SURROUNDINGS

Only a few seagulls float above the mouth of the Sumida River where it enters Tokyo Bay below the Tsukiji marketplace. Long experience, perhaps, has taught them that the market's thrifty wholesalers throw few scraps away; the gulls instead hover further south, over the huge landfills that year by year push the bay farther away from what was once its shoreline. In the seventeenth century Tsukiji, too, was shoreline and landfill—the name means "built (reclaimed) land"—a pleasant expanse of gardens and estates for feudal lords. Today, one still stands, located just across a turbid canal from the marketplace: the Hama Detached Palace (Hama Rikyū), now an imperial garden open to the public, once a seaside preserve for the shōgun.

Although the fish market did not move to Tsukiji until the 1920s, for centuries the Sumida River has been a busy thoroughfare, where barge traffic supplying the city's wharves mingled with pleasure craft and fishing vessels that harvested the waters of Edo Bay within hailing distance of where the marketplace stands today. The cultural symbolism of the Sumida River for the city during the Edo period included its literal associations with the aesthetic concept of the "floating world" *(ukiyo)* of pleasure and sensuality, and important parts of Edo's culture centered on the "city of water" (Jinnai 1995; H. D. Smith II 1986: 27–30).

When the Tokyo municipal government built the present market here in the 1920s and 1930s, planners put priority on convenience for Tokyo's fishing fleet, but land reclamation and pollution (especially since World War II) have destroyed the bay's nearby fishing grounds. The development of Tokyo during the 1950s and 1960s increasingly cut the city off from its waterways.[5] Even for the marketplace, the waterfront gradually became its backdrop rather than its gateway. There is no Tokyo fishing fleet today; fish arrive by truck.

Nowadays the grubby Tsukiji marketplace incongruously sits astride some of the world's most expensive real estate, amid the high-tech glitter of a self-consciously postindustrial society. Just a few blocks outside the market gates, Tokyo's slick shopping districts and financial centers seem worlds away from Tsukiji's low-tech, high-touch trade. Market regulars relish Tsukiji's down-to-earth homeyness, emphasizing it in the catchphrase "Tōkyō no daidokoro"—"Tokyo's pantry." At the same time, they feel pride of place, viewing the marketplace as a perhaps ungainly but nonetheless historically venerable institution at the heart of the city (maps 1 and 2).

Directly to the west, across Shin-Ōhashi Avenue, the high-rise headquarters of the *Asahi Shimbun*, one of Japan's leading newspapers, and the research complex of the National Cancer Center tower over the marketplace. Slightly farther to the west lies the Ginza, by day a cornucopia of expensive department stores and extravagant boutiques bearing elegant European names, by night a fairyland of exclusive sushi restaurants that trade on their proximity to Tsukiji and of expense-account bars where no sane reveler would go without the solid assurance that someone else will pick up the tab. A few blocks still farther west stand the staid headquarters of Japan's leading corporations; just beyond them, the august isolation of the Imperial Palace.

Harumi Avenue, a wide, straight street that cuts roughly east-west through central Tokyo from the harbor to the Imperial Palace, runs just to the north of the marketplace, linking Tsukiji to the Ginza. Midway between the two districts stands an imposing ferroconcrete example of old-fashioned theatrical architecture, the Kabuki-za, one of Tokyo's major theaters for kabuki (another important kabuki house, the Shinbashi Enbujō, is also nearby). Although the Kabuki-za stands just outside the boundaries of the Tsukiji neighborhood—measured by purists as the parish boundaries for the Namiyoke Shrine, home for Tsukiji's tutelary Shintō deity—Tsukiji traders feel, or claim to feel, a certain affection for kabuki. In this they carry on the tradition of an earlier generation of Tokyo merchants, for whom a hobby of classical dance, haiku poetry, or friendship with a noted figure from the kabuki stage marked their success and cultivation.[6] Younger Tsukiji traders may regard possession of a classic Harley-Davidson or a Mercedes convertible as surer signs of urbane sophistication, but they too appreciate the aesthetic unity of the floating world that links theater and cuisine and thus reflects glory on Tsukiji. Through these contemporary affinities, however distant, and historical connections, however contrived,

Figure 11. Tsukiji from the air, ca. 1996. The marketplace is seen from the Sumida River (lower right) looking north toward central Tokyo. The headquarters of the *Asahi* newspaper and the National Cancer Center are in the upper left. Reproduced with permission of the TMG Bureau of Markets.

Tsukiji traders view both themselves and the denizens of the kabuki world as heirs and guardians of the culture of mercantile Edo.

To the south of the marketplace, the Hama Detached Palace is now a public park, hemmed in by elevated expressways and by huge concrete seawalls. Beyond the park lies the former location of the Shiodome rail freight terminal, once the portal for much of Tsukiji's fish supply. After the railway closed and demolished the terminal in 1986, the site stood largely vacant; part was used to display model homes built by major Japanese housing construction firms. During what is now, in hindsight, called the "Bubble Economy" *(baburu keizai)* of the late 1980s—a decade of real estate and stock speculation and poorly collateralized bank loans, before the Japanese economy took a nosedive in the early 1990s—the government hesitated to release the parcel (then said to be the world's most valuable piece of unused land) into Tokyo's overheated real estate market for fear of launching an explosive spiral of land speculation on a scale that could have rocked financial markets around the world. After the Bubble Economy imploded, the land became available for redevelopment, but there were no takers. In the late 1990s, as an unprecedented surge of skyscraper construction gathered momentum throughout Tokyo, redevelopment of the Shiodome site finally

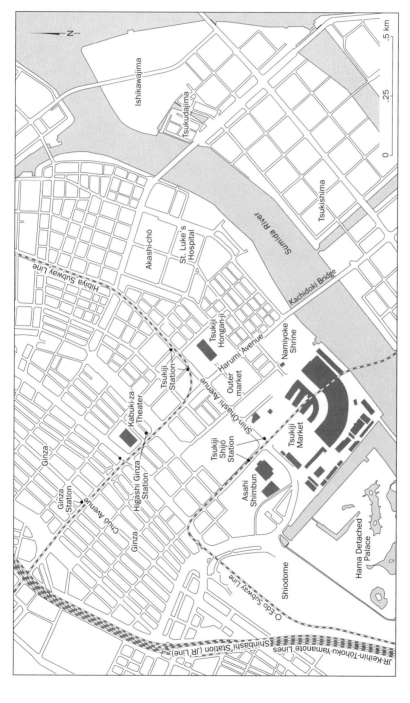

Map 1. The market and its surroundings.

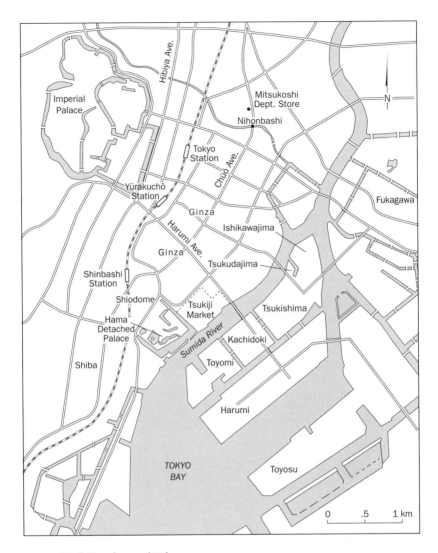

Map 2. Tsukiji and central Tokyo.

began. In 2003, more than a dozen towering office buildings and condominiums were completed. This dense vertical cluster reshapes the skyline
and further sets the marketplace apart from the new central city.

Across the Sumida River to the east, a chain of small islands—some natural and some not, all reshaped by landfill and seawalls into neat rectan-
gles—defines the far bank of the river channel. The southern portion of the
archipelago consists of three largely industrial islets created from landfill:

Figure 12. New mercantile Tokyo, viewed upriver from the Tsukiji wharf. The skyscraper on the left, closest to the marketplace, houses IBM Japan; in the distance on the right is a condominium tower built on Ishikawajima, next to Tsukudajima, the site of the late-sixteenth-century fishing settlement.

Kachidoki, the Toyomi Suisan Futō (the Toyomi Fisheries Wharf), and beyond them Harumi. They are covered by motley gray concrete cold-storage warehouses, fisheries research centers, bases for harbor patrol boats, office buildings for fisheries companies, and apartment blocks for their employees. The Kachidoki Bridge rumbles with the flow of trucks arriving at the market from the east. The bridge, which crosses the Sumida just north of the market, was built in the 1930s to link the mainland of central Tokyo to Harumi; both bridge and island were finished in time for the 1940 Tokyo Olympics, canceled as war loomed.

The northern islands of the archipelago, Ishikawajima, Tsukudajima, and Tsukishima,[7] contain remnants of tightly knit communities that can trace their origins to fishing villages established there in the late sixteenth and early seventeenth centuries. When the shōgunate commissioned Tsukudajima's fishers as the official purveyors of seafood to the castle, they became the first proprietors of the fish markets that were Tsukiji's forerunners. Protected by the Sumida River, these islands survived the fires that ravaged central Tokyo twice in the twentieth century, first in the aftermath of the 1923 Kantō earthquake and again during the American firebombing of World War II. Since isolation from the mainland sheltered the islands from development until the 1980s, they still contained quiet residential commu-

Figure 13. Old mercantile Tsukiji. An early-twentieth-century shop and home just north of the marketplace.

nities of tightly packed wooden houses lining narrow alleyways. In the 1980s the area suddenly became popular: the Japanese mass media rediscovered the old-fashioned *shitamachi* way of life just as Tokyo's real estate boom began to nibble away at the last of the islands' old neighborhoods. New subway lines—including the Ō-Edo line, which opened in 2000 with stations at Tsukiji Shijō (Tsukiji Market), Kachidoki, Tsukishima, and, in 2001, Shiodome—now make the archipelago almost instantly accessible to Tokyo's business centers, and from north to south old fishing villages, residential neighborhoods, and freezer warehouses are quickly being replaced by high-rise condominiums and office buildings.

To the north of the marketplace, towering office buildings for Dentsū, IBM, and other leading companies dwarf a few blocks of two-story wooden houses, the last remnants of old shitamachi neighborhoods still occupied by the homes, offices, and workshops of some Tsukiji traders. In the nineteenth century, this area was Tokyo's window to Western civilization, the Tsukiji Foreign Settlement (Tsukiji Kyoryūchi). Little marks the passage of the diplomats, the adventurers, and the missionaries who moved on to now more prestigious regions in the western parts of the city after the foreign settlement disbanded. Among its prominent institutions, only St. Luke's Hospital stayed in Tsukiji. In the early 1990s, the hospital tore down its art deco buildings built after the 1923 earthquake—leaving only the delicate facade of the chapel for St. Luke's school of nursing—and put up a towering skyscraper to house its clinics on the banks of the Sumida River where the original American Legation had stood.

In contrast, the ornate architecture of South Asian Buddhism unexpectedly graces the huge Tsukiji Hongan-ji temple complex at the northern edge of the marketplace. Hongan-ji is the Tokyo headquarters for Jōdo Shinshū, one of the major popular sects of Japanese Buddhism. After the 1923 earthquake, a new temple was built in reinforced concrete in an intentionally pan-Asianist style that symbolized Japanese imperial ambitions of the day. The present temple complex opened for worship in 1934. A major landmark of central Tokyo, it is often the site of massive funerals for leading public figures: politicians, business executives, and movie stars.

A handful of back alleys tucked away behind Hongan-ji preserve something of the visual texture of prewar Tokyo. Amid modern three- and four-story apartment buildings, low houses and storefronts still stand clad in the hammered copper sheets used early in the twentieth century for fireproof facades. Potted greenery grows in tiny clumps by doorways, along curbs (where curbs exist), underneath latticed windows, perched on tiny verandas outside second-floor windows, and crowding rooftop platforms used for airing futon and drying clothes. Carefully tended bonsai stand alongside shrubs plunked into large white polystyrene (Styrofoam) boxes salvaged from the marketplace and deep blue ceramic pots of morning glories, strung up in cones of twine and bamboo. In the early part of summer, when intense humidity alternates with torrential downpours, the dusty light blue of hydrangea seems to cool the weatherworn grays and browns of the old wooden houses, a few of them still occupied by Tsukiji families as home (or dormitory) and office, warehouse, or processing workshop.

THE OUTER MARKETPLACE

To the south of this quiet backwater, wedged between the growling, gaseous wall of traffic along Harumi Avenue and the marketplace proper, is the so-called outer market—a dense maze of alleys lined with tiny food shops; restaurant suppliers who deal in chopsticks, ceramics, or cutlery; wholesale fishmongers who cater to the public; and hole-in-the-wall sushi bars. Professional Tsukiji traders sharply distinguish the "outer market" (*jōgai shijō*) from the "inner market" (*jōnai shijō*). The distinction is not merely spatial but refers as well to significant differences in the character of the trade—the outer market has a large retail sector, the inner market is almost

Figures 14–16.
(Top left) Retail shoppers in the outer market.
(Above) A trade customer buying supplies for the day.
(Left) Squid drying on a *neko* (cart).

entirely wholesale—and in the institutional structures of the marketplaces themselves. The TMG owns and administers the inner marketplace, and its traders require wholesale licenses; the outer marketplace is simply a collection of independent businesses. For most Tokyo residents outside the food trade, however, this outer market *is* Tsukiji.

Until the 1920s this outer area contained the halls of worship and the graveyards of several dozen sub-temples of the main Hongan-ji temple just to the north. In the aftermath of the Kantō earthquake of 1923, most sub-temples relocated to other parts of the metropolitan region, and shops and businesses attracted by the newly established wholesale market moved in. After World War II, many of the merchants who moved into the area were squatters. (Reportedly, the tenacious defense of squatters' rights persists

Figures 17–20.
(Top left) Sun-drying *katsuo* (bonito).
(Top right) A shop banner in the outer
market with *yagō* symbol. The symbol,
a pair of inverted overlapping V's that
indicate a notch or gap *(aki)* in the
mountains *(yama)*, is read *Akiyama*.
(Above) Dishes for sale on the curb in
the outer market.
(Right) Hawking tuna retail in
Ameyoko-chō.

and bedevils urban-planning officials who have tried to redevelop the outer
market area.) Like other open-air marketplaces in Tokyo (e.g., Ameyoko-
chō, or "Candy Alley," near Ueno Station), the Tsukiji outer marketplace
was the site of a thriving black market *(yami-ichi)* in the years immediately
after World War II, and something of that aura lingers, although just barely.

In the late 1980s, merchants in one section of Tsukiji's outer market collectively built a gleaming high-rise office and shopping building and relocated their businesses onto the first several floors to create a modern shopping arcade. Sales plummeted and some shops went out of business. Other
local merchants debate the reasons for this decline, and one common opinion is that the kind of shoppers who come to the Tsukiji outer market are
not looking for something slick; products that seemed appealing and inviting to shoppers in the old setting appear merely cheap in the new. Other
outer market merchants and municipal planners ponder this lesson as they
contemplate ways to rebuild the physical infrastructure yet preserve the
atmosphere of the tumbledown outer market.

Today there is nothing black about the market, but the warrens of alleys
and dilapidated storefronts exude a seediness—at every turn, signs warn of
pickpockets—that lures shoppers with the unspoken suggestion that the
goods on sale are, at the very least, great bargains.[8] The outer marketplace
has a certain raffish appeal, especially for young shoppers who regard it as
quaintly old-fashioned yet cutting edge, an authentic slice of old shitamachi
mixed with the gourmet delights of haute cuisine. The three merchant associations that constitute the outer marketplace try to capitalize on this allure
with glossy posters and brochures for shoppers. They also sponsor a bi-
monthly magazine, *Tsukiji monogatari (Tales of Tsukiji)*, that features short
articles on market lore, local culinary specialties such as dried bonito flakes
(katsuobushi, an indispensable ingredient for making stocks and soups), and
the history of Japanese cutlery. The magazine also records nostalgic recol-
lections of life in the old neighborhood by longtime residents, and the casual
observations of a foreign visitor to the outer market (T. Bestor 1990–91).
And, of course, lots of advertisements for local shops.

From time to time, popular women's magazines run pieces on Tsukiji.
Then the outer market is flooded with groups of young women timidly pok-
ing around this hot new place. For example, *Hanako,* a trend-setting magazine for young women (which takes its title from a common woman's name
and which in the 1980s became the bible for unmarried, twenty-something
women with lots of disposable income and an eye for fashion), "discovered"
the outer marketplace around 1990. After each issue came out, hundreds of

Figure 21. "Feel a Little Like a Pro" is the slogan used on this pamphlet and shopping map distributed by the shopkeepers' association of the outer market. Reproduced with permission of the Tsukiji 4-chōme Seinenkai.

shoppers descended on stores unaccustomed to trendy fame. According to one story that went around the market at the time, an elderly proprietor was heard to complain, "Komatta na! Ore mo shiran. Uchi e okyakusan o annai shite kureta Hanako-san tte in no wa dare da?"—"It's frustrating! Who is this Hanako who steered all these customers to my shop?"

The outer marketplace contains roughly 500 businesses, grouped into three geographically defined merchant associations. Offices and storerooms for traders from the inner marketplace stand next to sushi bars and noodle stalls. A handful of sub-temples and their graveyards still remain, with space along their outer walls now rented out for shallow booths and stalls, some only a meter deep. These shops range from exclusively wholesale to entirely retail, with many somewhere in between. Ceramics dealers, knife shops, dealers in dried fish flakes, pickle dealers, butchers, fishmongers, and dealers in chopsticks collectively provide everything a restaurateur might need and more than enough to stock any home kitchen. Other outer market merchants are wholesaler-retailers who are both customers and competitors of the inner marketplace's intermediate wholesalers, buying products in the inner market for resale in the outer. Many of these merchants cater to a largely retail clientele, and on weekends the outer market is crowded with homemakers on shopping excursions.

When the inner market is closed, the outer market closes as well. The neighborhood then seems a ghost town, inhabited only by grandmothers and cats. Like much of Chūō-ku, the ward in which Tsukiji is located, the number of residents of the area has fallen dramatically over the past generation, and the difference between nighttime and daytime populations is enormous. The outer market neighborhoods, once home to many who worked in the marketplace, now barely survive as residential areas. The three administrative subdivisions *(chōme)* that encompass the inner and outer markets together (Tsukiji 4-, 5-, and 6-chōme) have fewer than 2,500 residents (unpublished population figures from the Chūō Ward Office, September 1997).

To the west, in the direction of the Ginza, the outer market merges almost imperceptibly into a restaurant district. One section is informally known as "Edogin Village" (Edogin-mura), so called for a famous sushi bar, Edogin, that has prospered and expanded into several separate shops and banquet halls spread across several blocks. Other well-known though much more intimate sushi shops abound in the area, drawing on their Tsukiji addresses for cachet. Less visibly, the area also houses a handful of highly exclusive restaurants, known as *ryōtei*. These are elegant and exceedingly discreet establishments, more like private clubs than public watering spots, built in the style of traditional mansions behind high walls. Tsukiji ryōtei are favored by high-ranking politicians, business leaders, and literary and artistic figures who savor an atmosphere of impeccable seclusion. Most ryōtei open their gates only to those previously introduced by a regular customer. Some ryōtei are legendary: one just across the street from the outer market is famous as the place where former Prime Minister Satō Eisaku died in 1975 and where the jury meets annually to select the winner of the prestigious Akutagawa literary prize.[9]

The Tsukiji ryōtei often engage geisha from the few *chaya* ("teahouses" or, in this instance, geisha agencies) left in the area, the last survivors of what was once the thriving Shinbashi geisha quarter. The ryōtei and the geisha lend an aura of dignified, restrained old money (and new power) to the Tsukiji area; their chefs are, of course, discerning customers of the best merchants in both the inner and outer markets; and the geisha associated with the ryōtei occasionally brighten Tsukiji festivities. Ryōtei and geisha, evocative of the floating world of Edo culture, enrich Tsukiji's claims to the same cultural ancestry.

At one corner of the outer market stands a small Shintō shrine, the Namiyoke Jinja, built alongside an old canal (the Tsukiji-gawa), now filled in, that divides the outer from the inner marketplace. The Namiyoke Shrine long predates the Tsukiji marketplace, although its maritime name—the shrine to protect one from waves (*nami* means "wave," *yoke* means "protection")—is apropos to Tsukiji's trade. It is an Inari shrine—Inari, symbolized by a fox, is, among many other things, a guardian deity of shopkeepers—and the Inari enshrined here is the tutelary god for the outer marketplace and several adjacent neighborhoods. Every other year the gigantic lion's head *mikoshi* (a palanquin for carrying a god) that otherwise rests behind glass just inside the shrine's gate is paraded through the parish streets. By virtue of proximity, the Namiyoke Shrine is also favored by traders from the inner marketplace. The shrine buildings are dotted with votive signs, banners, and lanterns emblazoned with the trade names and shop symbols of Tsukiji businesses. In the early morning hours one often can spot traders—wearing their characteristic tall rubber boots—pausing to enter the shrine to offer a quick prayer at the foot of the shrine's staircase. Some, even more hurried, simply bow deeply at the shrine gate, then stride off to the inner marketplace across the small bridge in front of the shrine.

THE INNER MARKETPLACE

This short bridge—Kaikōbashi—crosses the filled-in canal that separates the outer from the inner marketplace. The inner marketplace is clearly visible, although it is effectively terra incognita for the ordinary shopper. The inner market is set apart by an intimidating air of purposeful bedlam that conveys to the visitor the sense that one should enter with caution, if at all. Large signs at the gates advise that the market is "for wholesale transactions only," and this admonition alone is sufficient to ward off most Tokyoites during the market's busiest morning hours.[10]

Seen from across the bridge or through the main gate opposite the headquarters of the *Asahi* newspaper, the marketplace is a dilapidated jumble of office buildings, sheds, shops, stalls, freezer warehouses, processing workshops, ice plants, loading docks, parking garages, incinerators, and wharves sprawling across 22.5 hectares fronting the Sumida River. Rusting metal adorns dingy, mottled gray concrete. Many of the market's major buildings date to the opening of the market in 1935, and those added since have received so little care in the intervening years that they too can pass for prewar construction. The market complex includes two almost entirely separate worlds of trade, housed in adjacent sets of buildings. The older buildings, closer to the water, date from the 1930s and are occupied by Tsukiji's seafood *(suisanbutsu)* division, for which the entire market is famous. A newer, smaller set of buildings built in the 1950s and 1960s on the inland side of the market complex contains the trading floors for fresh produce *(seika-mono)*; Tokyo has eleven markets for fresh produce, and Tsukiji's produce division—colloquially known as the *yatchaba,* an old-fashioned term meaning something like "the veggie place"—is by no means the largest. The seafood division far overshadows the produce division in volume of trade, in market share, and in public consciousness. Here and throughout this book, my analysis focuses on Tsukiji's seafood division.

In 1990, in what was to prove the last flush times of the Bubble Economy, the TMG launched an ambitious plan to reconstruct the entire marketplace. Piece by piece, existing prewar structures were to be replaced with modern market buildings to form a high-tech complex integrating all the functions of the market with state-of-the-art communications technology and efficient access to new subway lines and underground highways. Preliminary construction started in 1990 as minor buildings were cleared away and some temporary structures were put up. Construction of several of the new permanent buildings began in 1992. In the original plan, reconstruction would take place while the market continued in full operation; thus the construction would involve a complicated checkerboard plan of building, relocation, and demolition. This was to continue in phases over twelve years until 2003, when the project would be completed. However, in 1995, Aoshima Yukio was elected governor of Tokyo on a reformist platform to curb government spending; one of his administration's first acts was to suspend the reconstruction of the marketplace. The TMG halted construction at Tsukiji in fiscal year 1996–97, by which time only one new permanent building had been finished—a new multistory parking garage at the northern end of the marketplace—and so the market continued to operate in the remnants of its original buildings dating back to the early 1930s.

The TMG promised to unveil a revised plan for rebuilding the market in 1998–99, but the question of whether to rebuild on-site or to relocate the marketplace elsewhere in Tokyo dragged on and on. Finally (perhaps), in late 2001, the TMG announced its newest plan: to move the market to a site in Toyosu, east of the Sumida River, on a huge tract of industrial land owned by Tokyo Gas that has long been vacant. The new plan—more a policy announcement than a detailed blueprint—promises a state-of-the-art modern market complex with adjacent retail shopping and other amenities, possibly to be completed sometime around 2012, possibly later. As I will discuss in more detail in chapters 7 and 8, the plan to relocate the market to Toyosu is still being worked out in 2003 and complete blueprints are still at least several years off. Some at Tsukiji fiercely oppose this—bright green posters and decals dot the inner marketplace proclaiming defiant opposition to the move—while others regard opponents as sentimentalists and embrace the idea of the move (even if they are still wary about as yet unresolved details).

In the meantime, the market continues to operate in its old quarters. Generations of use and the accretions of rebuilding, expansion, and repair have altered the original layout only slightly. When the Tsukiji marketplace was designed and built in the late 1920s and early 1930s, it was an almost perfect architectural mandala of a market's idealized physical functions: "bulking and breaking"—that is, concentrating commodities in large quantities; grading, sorting, and pricing products as they flow from hand to hand through the marketplace in ever smaller streams; and finally distributing goods in minute retail quantities.

This sequence is plainly visible in the original buildings' arrangement (map 3). Most of the original buildings of Tsukiji's seafood division still stand, and a short straight walk from the Sumida River toward the market's main gate cuts through many layers in a stratigraphic cross section of a distribution system. The marketplace facilities built in the early 1930s have wide external receiving docks to accept bulk shipments; narrowing concentric arcs of auction pits and stalls through which products pass as they are unloaded, sorted, graded, and sold and sold again; and narrow shipping docks on the inner side of the arc where retail-scale shipments are dispatched on their way to Tokyo's tables. The original marketplace, influenced by the Bauhaus school and the International Style, pleasantly blended highly functional industrial design with the geometrically curvilinear style favored by the architects of prewar Japanese government buildings.[11] A collection of photographs publicizing the market's opening (Tōkyō-shiyakusho 1935) shows clean, functional lines, sparkling white facades, long sunny corridors of gracefully curved pillars forming geometrical patterns as far as the eye can see, pylons and decorative friezes and circular windows punctuating rounded stairwells. Now, beneath almost seventy years of grime, rust, and helter-skelter additions, little flashes of the architects' original ornamentation incongruously catch the eye: a circular window shedding light across a gracefully rounded banister, or the geometrical perfection of a line of arches receding along the outer wall of a curving corridor.

Curves define the seafood division's main buildings. Form followed function, and the fan-shaped sheds had a more pragmatic purpose than simply modeling the architectural aesthetic of the time. The buildings neatly fitted into the curve of a railway siding that ran between the wharves and the auction pits, and connected Tsukiji to the rail yards of the Shiodome freight terminal next to Shinbashi Station. When the market opened, seafood came to Tsukiji by boat or by rail: several express freight trains devoted exclusively to seafood arrived daily from different regions of the country. But from the 1960s on, as the nation's highway system developed, deliveries by high-speed refrigerated trucks became common. The last train delivered fish to the Tsukiji siding in 1986, and shortly thereafter the tracks were pulled up. The former rail right-of-way still defines the outer edge of the fan-shaped

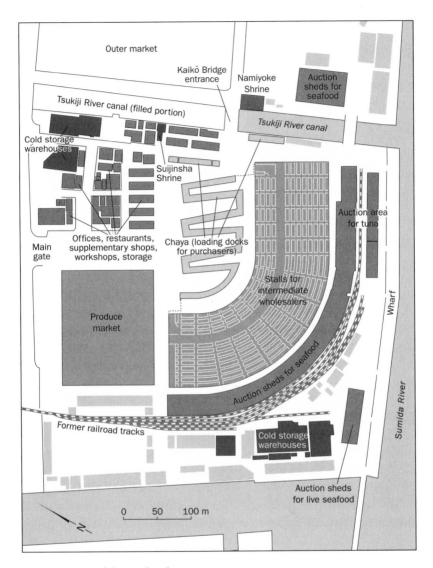

Map 3. Layout of the marketplace, ca. 1990.

buildings, running between them and the quay to the east, and separating auction pits from a row of large freezer warehouses to the south.

The curving complex of one-, two-, and three-story buildings extends from north to south along the river's edge, bending inland and westward at the southern end of the marketplace. At ground level, the curved complex contains loading docks, processing workshops, a dozen auction pits, and,

Figures 22–23.
(Above) Bauhaus on the Sumida. An aerial view of the new functionalist marketplace in 1935, with the Sumida River in the foreground. The wooded area in the upper left is the garden of the Hama Detached Palace (Tōkyō-shiyakusho 1935). Reproduced with permission of the TMG Bureau of Markets.
(Right) Form follows function. Skylights above the trading halls in the new marketplace (Tōkyō-shiyakusho 1935). Reproduced with permission of the TMG Bureau of Markets.

most important, the vast sheds containing arc after arc of stalls—1,677 in all—where the intermediate wholesalers set up shop. Over the decades, the upper floors have been rebuilt and extended piecemeal; they are mazes of meandering corridors, unexpected stairwells, and exposed catwalks. The upper floors contain the business offices of the seven auction houses *(oroshi gyōsha)* that supply Tsukiji's seafood, half a dozen auction pits, clearinghouses that settle auction accounts, and offices of the TMG marketplace administration. Scattered in the upper floors of the main complex and elsewhere are a bank, two post offices, a barber shop, a pharmacy, a library, many shops for snacks and sundries, a book store, medical and dental clinics, several coffee shops and cafeterias, the offices of several dozen trade groups, a hotel, and the Tsukiji bureaus of major Japanese wire services and trade newspapers. As Tsukiji's boosters point out, their marketplace is a little city, lacking, as they say, only a mayor and an elementary school.

The inner curve of the primary complex is filled by freight-dispatching docks, where retailers collect their day's purchases. Between these freight docks and the market's main gates to the west and north, several clusters of buildings house offices, small processing workshops, and ancillary shops and restaurants. These cater to the marketplace's workers, to intrepid tourists and bargain hunters, and to office workers from nearby skyscrapers looking for cheap lunches.

On the Waterfront

Tsukiji fronts the Sumida River across a long concrete quay. No more than one or two ships dock on any given day: most are distant-water ships offloading catches of frozen tuna and swordfish, or smaller vessels delivering tank loads of live fish from the coastal waters of southern Japan. Given the efficient network of high-speed refrigerated trucking now available throughout the country, it makes little sense for a fishing vessel to sail for Tokyo simply to unload its catch when the vessel and crew could more profitably spend their time on the fishing grounds.[12]

Little used by ships, the quay is quiet for most of the day, good for market workers who want to take a quick nap atop a stack of crates or to drop a fishing line into the river for a busman's holiday. From late evening onward, however, the quay comes alive as a delivery area. The northern end is crowded with trucks waiting until just before the morning auctions—compressors humming to maintain their refrigeration—to unload frozen tuna trucked in from the major tuna ports of Yaizu and Misaki a few hours' drive away. At the southern end, tanker trucks full of live fish pump their cargoes into flat tubs before the morning's sales.

These trucks are only the first of the thousands that will visit the marketplace during the course of a day's business.[13] Around 9:30 or 10 P.M. the bridges across the Sumida and the wide avenues that cut through central Tokyo begin to rumble with long-distance refrigerated rigs that come from almost every fishing port and regional marketing center in the country, driven hard to arrive by the auctions' cutoff time. The trucks' markings proclaim their home bases: Hachinohe Fish Express Company, Kaga Frozen Food Shipment, Hokkaidō Fisheries Cooperative Shipping, Shimonoseki

Fishport Ltd. Some trucks bear the fish trade's distinctive shop names or trade symbols *(yagō)*. Others display the red, black, and white calligraphic swirl for *uogashi* (the fish quay). The most spectacular trucks have wild murals of regional festivals, gods, or fish; many trumpet the bravado of long-distance truckers, emblazoned with pink and purple running lights, meter upon meter of burnished chrome scroll work, fanciful superstructures built over the cabs, and iridescent slogans like "Riding the morning wind, seeking the love of a fair maiden."

Plain or fancy, the trucks roll into Tsukiji, filling quay, parking lots, and loading docks. Throughout the night, compressors drone alongside cab stereos, quiet conversations, and drivers snoring in their cab berths. By 10 or 11 P.M., several of the marketplace's restaurants and bars open to cater to drivers and others whose work starts after midnight.

As the truckers relax and await the hard work of unloading that begins for most of them around two or three in the morning, forklifts start to chip away at pallets of goods intended for transshipment to other marketplaces in the Tokyo region. Although it is the largest marketplace in Japan, even Tsukiji cannot supply the entire metropolitan region. Regional shippers consigning goods to Tsukiji also send shipments intended for other nearby markets. A trucker making a run from Hachinohe at the northern tip of the main island of Honshū, for example, may drop off deliveries to other wholesale marketplaces—for example, those in Sendai or Fukushima or Utsunomiya—on his way south to Tsukiji. But if Tsukiji is his destination, cargo for the major marketplaces in the nearby cities of Yokohama or Kawasaki, or for Tokyo's other two smaller wholesale seafood markets at Ōta and Adachi, will be unloaded at Tsukiji. Throughout the night at Tsukiji, transshippers arrange deliveries to the several dozen major and minor outlying markets in the metropolitan region so that those shipments, too, will arrive in time for morning sales.

From roughly midnight onward, auctioneers *(serinin)* supervise the job of arranging fish for Tsukiji's morning auctions. Each of Tsukiji's auction houses has a subsidiary that handles much of this work, called *koage* (literally, "small lifting" or unloading). This stevedoring is considerably more difficult and more critical than its name suggests. Although the daily volume is enormous, highly perishable and fragile seafood requires gentle handling, and nothing about the final arrangement can be haphazard. The cramped, aging physical infrastructure of the marketplace impedes workers' movements, even as the highly fragmented auction system creates a large number of destinations to which the arriving seafood must be directed.

Each night a huge volume of seafood (roughly 2,300 metric tons) arrives

Figure 24. A tanker arrives at the Tsukiji wharf with live fish from Shikoku.

at Tsukiji, coming in tens of thousands of individual consignments ranging in size from entire truckloads of frozen tuna (each fish weighing a hundred kilograms or more) to three or four small crates of fish eggs, light enough to be hefted with one hand. Every shipment consigned to Tsukiji represents a separate chain of commercial transactions between one or another of the thousands of producers and consignors who regularly supply the marketplace and one or another of the seven Tsukiji auction houses that handle seafood.[14] The job of matching shipment to recipient and properly conveying invoices from trucker to receiving auction house is a mammoth one.

Having to sort and reshuffle each night's deliveries in the cramped quarters of a marketplace built before forklifts were common makes koage difficult enough. In addition, the marketplace was built to receive shipments coming in from the wharf and rail spurs along the river, whereas the trucks now approach from the opposite direction—in through the exit, as it were. The koage workers run an obstacle course each night in merely getting thousands of shipments into the auction areas adjacent to the old rail siding and the quay.

Moreover, the patchwork of Tsukiji's auctions further complicates the task. Each of the seven seafood auction houses runs its own auctions, with its own team of auctioneers. Each auction house has its own separate display areas adjacent to the common auction pits for each major commodity category. Broadly speaking, Tsukiji handles about twenty major, culturally distinct commodity categories. Only four auction houses trade in the full spectrum of goods, yet even the smallest of the houses actively deals in at least half a dozen categories. Shipments to Tsukiji therefore end up in one of more than a hundred distinct destinations, each the display area for a particular auction house's sales of a distinct commodity.

The challenge of koage, then, is first to get shipments to their proper places adjacent to the appropriate auction pits. Once at the correct display area, shipments must be sorted, graded, and arranged in time for the buyers' inspection (shitami) that starts a couple of hours before the auctions begin between 5 and 6 A.M. In preparing seafood for inspection, koage workers labor under the watchful eyes of the auctioneers for whom the precise placement and sequencing of lots of seafood is an important part of their sales strategy.

Auction Pits

Tsukiji's twenty or so major auction pits are visually distinctive, institutionally diverse, and physically dispersed. They are defined first and foremost by the different commodities they handle. Fresh tuna, frozen tuna, fresh fish—distinguishing those from the nearby waters of the Kantō, from the Sanriku coast of northern Honshū, and from the waters off Shikoku—live eels, salted salmon, live shrimp, dried sardines, shark, and fresh sea urchin roe are simply a few examples. Each pit is staffed by specialist auctioneers, their commodity category indicated by the color of their caps, their employer indicated by the neat work uniforms distinctive to one or another of the seven auction houses. Each pit attracts equally specialized traders—intermediate wholesalers and authorized traders—distinguished by the oblong plastic licenses clipped to baseball caps (seribō) they are supposed to wear during auctions. From day to day the cast of characters at any given pit is roughly the same, and each pit is a tight island of familiar faces and established trading customs, which I will discuss in much greater detail in chapter 5.

Specialization reflects the market niches that traders carve for themselves as a normal part of their business strategies. But the physical layout of the marketplace reinforces the need to specialize. Auction pits stretch from one end of the marketplace to the other, and during the morning auction hours it is impossible to move quickly through the narrow crowded corridors and alleys from one pit to any but adjacent ones. Under the awnings along the quay and on the ground floors of the outer arc of buildings are half a dozen sites for tuna auctions: smaller frozen tuna from the Indian Ocean or the South Pacific, none weighing more than 100 kilograms, are sold along the river's edge; fresh tuna, some of them giant bluefin weighing 300 or 400 kilograms apiece, from northern Japan or shipped by air from Boston, the Azores, or Tunisia, are sold inside. Next to the auctions for fresh giant bluefin tuna, large frozen tuna and swordfish are put up for sale. In long halls above the tuna auctions, buyers of fresh fish from coastal waters gather to bid on lots that are displayed in crates next to the tuna area.

At the southern end of the Sumida quay, several concrete sheds enclose the live fish auctions. An open metal building and a large refrigerated warehouse near the north gate of the marketplace are the sites of auctions for *aimono,* semiprocessed but perishable fish. Halfway down the arc, a couple of rough wooden bleachers house the morning shrimp auctions.

The morning auctions are also diverse in presentation and style. Some are held in the display areas; traders crouch over individual tuna, bidding on one while inspecting the next. Other auctions take place within viewing distance of the seafood yet separate from it. Still other seafood is on sale in auction rooms several minutes and several flights of stairs away from the display areas. Most seafood auctions at Tsukiji rely on open bidding, signaled by hand gestures; bidders study their notes and use clipboards and pocket diaries to shield their hand signals from the eyes of their competitors. Other auctions use written bids; the buyers are studies in indifference as they jot down prices on small slips of paper. In some auction pits, four or five or seven auction houses sell simultaneously at separate but adjacent sites; in others, the auction houses offer their goods in prearranged sequential rotations.

At the live fish auctions, two auctioneers' stands face a bank of wooden bleachers packed with traders wearing the signature of their specialty: neoprene diving suits that insulate them from the chilly water that surrounds their working days. Here side-by-side auctioneers from two houses conduct sales simultaneously, somehow sorting out the bids intended for them from those directed at their competitors; traders shift their attention from one to the other, and only occasionally does an auctioneer need to stop to clarify which house's products were the object of a bid. Behind the auctioneers' backs, half-submerged sea bream thrash around in wooden trays, and octopi—each in a separate mesh bag so it won't cannibalize its neighbors— bump one another in deep plastic tubs. Raspy wheezing fills the air, from a flimsy web of plastic tubing that aerates the hundreds of flat wooden trays and blue plastic tubs in which live fish are kept. Every few minutes a buzzer sounds and another pair of auctioneers from the other two houses that handle live fish mounts the stands. Traders come and go as they please, leaving to supervise a worker taking a tank of fish back to their stall, then returning for a couple of lots on which they especially want to bid.

From time to time, bidders break a tie by a quick round of the child's game of *jan-ken* (rock-paper-scissors). Two or more people—on the count of *jan, ken, po!*—simultaneously thrust out a hand: a fist to represent a rock, an open palm for paper, or two fingers extended for scissors. Each of the three objects can be defeated by one of the others and can in turn defeat the third: rock smashes scissors (and rock wins); paper covers rock; scissors cut paper. It is a simple mechanism for deciding among ties as long as the group is not too large; this and related hand games are commonplace legacies of Edo's popular culture (Linhart 1998).

In a long curving room on the third floor of the main building, crates of dried squid and tiny dried sardines (niboshi), elegantly packed tubs of salmon roe, and whole salmon cured in miso (fermented bean paste) line low tables. All seven auction houses have tables here, and when the bells ring, first one and then another house begins to sell at preset five-minute intervals. Traders crowd around, thrusting tiny slips of paper with written bids into the hands of the assistant auctioneer. Each lot goes to the highest bidder; if two or more buyers submit identical high bids, the earliest bid wins. About half an hour after the sales have begun, a bell rings to signal that the auctioneers are now free to sell the remaining products—if any—at negotiated rather than auction-determined prices.

Along the quay, tuna are auctioned fish by fish. The long rows of frozen and fresh tuna stretch meter after meter; they are sold at "moving auction." The auctioneer—flanked by his assistants, who record prices and fill out invoice slips at lightning speed—strides across the display floor just above the rows of tuna, moving quickly from one footstool to the next without missing a beat, or a bid. Knots of traders affect nonchalance, their keen interest in the proceedings visible only when—with swift flurries of sparse finger gestures—they signal a price to the roaring auctioneer. The auctioneer's guttural cadence sets the pace for the economical brush stokes of underlings who mark the buyer's name on each sold fish with a daub of red ink. Here, in contrast to other Tsukiji auctions, traders can advance the bid, but at most the price goes up only a tick before the auctioneer bellows the completion of *that* sale and is well into calling the next lot.

Above the tuna auctions, in a second-story chilled room accessible only across a narrow catwalk, the day's supply of sea urchin roe (uni) is put on display. Uni is an expensive delicacy, sold in minute lots and in highly standardized grades (the best kinds are from Hokkaidō; other varieties, judged lower in quality, come from Maine, California, Korea, China, and elsewhere); the soft, salty, golden roe is already removed from its spiny cases and painstakingly arranged in small wooden trays. Uni auctions, like most at Tsukiji, are conducted with open bidding, using hand signals. But because roe is fragile and can easily absorb noxious smells from the air, the auction takes place outside the display room, after buyers have had a chance to inspect the delicate goods inside. At the doorway to the chilled display room, plastic curtains keep away warmer outside air and inquisitive visitors. It is a no-smoking area, extraordinary in a marketplace otherwise often wreathed in smoke.[15]

The starting times for auction sales vary from commodity to commodity, and from season to season. Beginning at roughly 5 A.M., bells and buzzers punctuate the background din of the marketplace every ten or fifteen minutes to signal that yet another sale is starting. Depending on the volume of supply and on traders' interest, a given trading session may take five minutes or half an hour. By 6:30 or 7:00 A.M., the last auctions end.

But even before the first ones have ended, the focus of activity begins to shift. Traders rarely linger at an auction pit after they have made their purchases. As soon as their bids are completed they scurry off to supervise delivery of the day's purchases to their stalls. As the auctions continue, employees of the auction houses mark each lot with a trader's name and stick a copy of the invoice onto the slick wet surface of the fish or crate. Workers from the stalls heave frozen tuna or precariously balanced stacks of polystyrene crates and cardboard boxes onto narrow two-wheeled wooden barrows (called "cats" or *neko*) and onto tiny motorized flatbed carts known as "turrets" *(tāretto).*[16] Barrows and carts clog the aisles amid the impatient shouts of drivers trying to insinuate themselves into the clotted streams of delivery traffic that flow this way and that from the (relatively) open spaces of the auction pits into the narrower alleys and aisles that thread through the intermediate wholesalers' stalls.

Since *their* customers start arriving around 7 A.M., the traders quickly head back to their stalls through the turmoil of delivery, processing, and cleanup. High-pitched whines split the air, as workers in nearby sheds slice frozen tuna carcasses with electric table saws. Crews of sweepers start to clean up the soggy debris of broken polystyrene crates, plastic bags, cardboard sheets, and packing tape littering the display areas. By midmorning, snowy hillocks of Styrofoam totter at either end of the marketplace, heaped up by the forklift load, slowly depleted as passing wholesalers rummage for a sturdy box. From behind the mountains of crates unearthly groans, bloodcurdling shrieks—the eerie sounds of plastic chafing against plastic—and a molten stench escape from small plastic-recycling plants where the polystyrene is ground up and melted into huge cakes of resin for export to Southeast Asian plastics factories.[17]

Stalls

From 7 or 7:30 A.M., the swirling activity shifts to the cavernous sheds housing the 1,677 stalls where the intermediate wholesalers do business. Retailers and restaurateurs begin to arrive shortly after 7 A.M. Until then workers in the stalls busily sort the morning's purchases and prepare seafood for sale; until about 10 or 11 A.M., they are occupied in filling buyers' orders.

The stalls are awash with seafood of almost every conceivable species, shape, color, and size. Black tubs of live eels *(unagi)* stand by a cutting board in one stall; next door, crates of crabs packed in moist sawdust spill out into the aisle. Colorful rows of fresh snapper *(hamadai)*, perfectly matched in size, are set off by the blinding whiteness of a Styrofoam carton. Clams spread by the square meter across shallow tanks. Amorphous mounds of grayish pink monkfish *(ankō)* liver spill over the edge of trays. Each stall differs from the next, none dealing in more than a tiny fraction of the several hundred species of seafood available at Tsukiji in any given season. One stall displays mountains of red and white boiled octopus; in the stall beyond that, trays of golden fried fish cakes; over there, squid still oozing black ink; across the way, fish pâté in neat pink-and-white blocks. Around the corner, an apprentice wields a meter-long knife to carve an enormous tuna carcass; in the next stall, a woman carefully arranges clams on dozens of trays; further down the aisle, an old man watchfully stands over open crates full of sawdust and wriggling shrimp.

Although freshness is everything, few stalls enclose their products in refrigerators or under glass. Most of their seafood is in the open, to catch the critical eyes of buyers who want to see—and perhaps smell, touch, or taste—the products for sale. So even on the hottest summer days, dealers display most seafood in open cases, on beds of crushed ice or underneath blocks of dry ice suspended in mesh bags a few inches above the counters. Drifting tendrils of vapor lazily coat the displays and swirl off into the aisles.

The stalls stand in twelve rows (with about 140 in each row), lining six major aisles in the fan-shaped complex between the auction pits and the market gate. From the auction pits outward toward the gate, the rows are numbered from 1000 to 8000 and then labeled *i, ro, ha,* and *ni* (a Japanese equivalent of A, B, C, and D); the older, numbered eight rows date from the 1930s and the "alphabetical" final four were added in the late 1950s. Two enormous sheds cover the older stalls, with two aisles and four rows of stalls per shed. Hazy skylights illuminate the sheds' high corrugated metal roofs and aging skeletons of girders. It is a murky workaday setting, but light, airy, and roomy when compared with the four rows of newer stalls. These are underneath an elevated parking lot and hence have low ceilings, thick concrete pillars, and no natural light. And since the four newer rows are on the inner curve of the fan, the stalls themselves are generally narrower than those in the numbered rows. Stalls average about seven square meters, depending on location; those packed in the sections where the curve is tightest are barely wide enough for two people to stand shoulder to shoulder.

One stall is much the same as the next, simple and unadorned, differing primarily in the kinds of fish a wholesaler specializes in and the sorts of equipment that specialty requires. The four stalls of Chiyomaru, a tuna dealer, contain little more than a few large cutting boards, a collection of swordlike knives and axlike cleavers, a couple of open-topped ice chests large enough to display meter-long slabs of tuna, and a table saw in the back for splitting frozen carcasses. Next door, the stalls occupied by Konami, a wholesaler who specializes in "sushi ingredients" *(sushidane)*, have a bank of tanks for live fish, surrounded by display tables for fresh catches of the day. Across the way at Maruju, the proprietor skewers, skins, and fillets live eels on a blood-stained cutting board standing next to stacks of black plastic buckets filled with the day's wriggling stock. Beyond him, Tsukumoto, a wholesaler who deals in fish pâté, has nothing but a few cartons opened for display and a busy fax line.

Merchandise spills out from the tiny stalls into the aisles, usually well past the small metal markers sunk into the cobblestones that indicate the outer limits of the stallholders' space. Passage is difficult, and a leisurely stroll is impossible. Buyers lugging square wicker baskets may temporarily block an aisle while they make a purchase, but they are politely yet impatiently pushed aside by other buyers hurrying to get to *their* suppliers, by stall workers rushing to deliver purchases to a retailer's waiting van, or by uniformed auctioneers delivering documents to the wholesalers. In the wider passages that intersect the rows of stalls, hundreds of motorized carts relentlessly push through the crowds. Traffic signs ban the use of these carts and hand trucks along shopping aisles during the morning's prime shopping hours after 7 A.M., but the carts continually dart along the perimeters and down transverse passageways, transporting fish from auction to stall and from the stalls to the loading docks where retail buyers collect their purchases. Large signs hang over each aisle, listing nearby shop names, intersecting aisles and passageways, and traffic regulations for that section of the marketplace, but market regulars plunge through, rarely checking their location.

Each morning an estimated 14,000 customers flock to Tsukiji's stalls. A plump middle-aged man dressed in expensive golf clothes swaggers along carrying a leather handbag holding the cash to pay for live fish for his upscale Ginza restaurant. An old woman with a rectangular bamboo basket slung across her bent back selects minuscule amounts of shrimp, octopus, mackerel, and tuna for her tiny retail shop on a back street in a downtown residential neighborhood. A wiry elderly man in a drab gray work uniform cracks rapid-fire jokes with stall workers as he inspects salted salmon and fish cakes he ordered yesterday by fax for delivery this morning to his clients, a chain of box-lunch take-out shops. A gaunt man dressed in khaki work pants and a fisherman's vest, with a perm of tight ringlets and tinted aviator sunglasses, a folded sports newspaper tucked inside his high rubber boots, saunters like a hoodlum up to a high-grade tuna dealer to select two kilos of fresh jumbo tuna for his sushi bar near a major Tokyo railway station. A serious young man, a tie and white shirt peeking out from underneath his windbreaker, pores over a clipboard and a hand calculator as he directs first one wholesaler and then another to send five crates of salmon and 14 kilos of crab to this supermarket branch, 10 kilos of octopus to that branch, and 7 kilos of tuna to yet another. Toward morning's end, a small group of intrepid homemakers—bravely disregarding the stall signs that boldly state "No retail sales"—giggle at the adventure of buying a kilo of tuna at wholesale from a stall owner who is only too happy at that late hour not to own the fish for another day.

Stalls are open, set apart from one another by refrigerated cases, display tables, fish tanks, or stacks of crates. A few stalls (particularly those that deal in processed seafoods) have built-in display shelves and roll-down shutters or gates that can be closed after hours, but most are simply open, their goods protected only by a few padlocks on freezer cases. Wholesalers do not worry much about secure storage because many of them have little stock beyond their day-to-day supply. What they purchase at auction in the morning, they sell by the close of business a few hours later. Dealers who handle frozen or processed products may, for longer-term storage, rent a locker in a freezer warehouse operated by the wholesalers' federation or by one of the large auction houses. Stock on the stall floor must be sold, not moved from freezer to display and back again. Traders pack the lofts over stalls in the older sheds (where ceilings are higher) with boxes, knives, and other odds and ends; larger equipment, such as carts and table saws, clogs the narrow passageways that run behind each row of stalls.

Plain painted signboards distinguish one stall from the next. These boards simply post the shop name, its telephone and fax numbers, and the kinds of seafood it handles. Lighting and signs are regulated. Market rules prohibit colored lighting that might obscure or disguise the quality of the seafood, so naked, untinted light bulbs dangle everywhere and bathe the stalls in even, direct light. A few of the larger wholesalers who control several adjacent stalls have invested in modest decoration: a colored awning stretching across their several stalls, perhaps a blue-and-white nautical color scheme for refrigerators and cashiers' booths, perhaps even track lighting to highlight display cases. Amulets and votive icons from popular mercantile lore decorate some stalls: a large papier-mâché Daruma doll, a bamboo rake *(kumade)* festooned with good luck symbols, or a figurine of Ebisu or Daitoku, gods of good fortune and patron saints of shopkeepers.

Women's Work

All stalls have a small booth *(chōba)* for their cashiers, a tiny counting-house, usually not much larger than a telephone booth, where one or two people preside over telephones, fax machines, abacuses, calculators, and lap-top computers as they handle the steady flow of cash and invoices. Most chōba cashiers are women; not surprisingly, many of them are wives, mothers, daughters, or daughters-in-law of the men out front.

In the construction of Japanese machismo, cooking is women's work, but culinary connoisseurship and the business of the marketplace are repre-sented (inaccurately) as male domains. In Tsukiji's stalls, however, lowly male shop apprentices pour tea for visitors; the women in the chōba con-centrate on much more important things. With hands on the cash and inti-mate knowledge of the personal networks of trade, women occupy central ground in the business of the marketplace, even when they may appear to be tucked away in the back.

In the early morning hours, especially, the marketplace *does* appear to be a man's world. Men are everywhere: unloading, sorting, checking, arrang-ing, tasting, or considering the dawn's purchases. No women work around the marketplace's auction pits, and there are no women among Tsukiji's roughly 700 active licensed auctioneers. According to TMG officials, several women have taken and passed the auctioneer's exam each year since the late 1980s, but the companies that employ them have not assigned them to the auction floor.

Along the sales aisles of the marketplace, a few women play front-line roles as sellers of seafood. They are particularly evident in shellfish busi-nesses, perhaps a reflection of the fact that many of these dealers are small-scale family enterprises only one or two generations removed from shellfish harvesting in Tokyo Bay's tide flats, labor in which women played a large part. Other seafood dealers sometimes echo the view voiced by sushi chefs—that the temperature of women's hands fluctuates too much to han-dle raw fish—to account for why they don't have more women working the fish counters.

In the late 1980s, a tuna dealer—Chiyomaru—hired Tsukiji's first knife-wielding female *eigyō-man* (salesman). It was by accident. The young woman had wished to become a sushi chef and had apprenticed herself to a sushi shop, but the shop went bankrupt. A family friend in the fish business offered to introduce her to Chiyomaru, the midsized Tsukiji tuna dealer with whom he did a large volume of business. The friend mentioned to Mr. Andō, the tuna dealer, the plight of the hardworking, dedicated sushi apprentice whose master had failed. Mr. Andō said to send the kid around. She showed up ready to work. He didn't know what to say, he told me. He hadn't ever asked whether the apprentice was male.[18] "I almost told her to go home, but then I thought, 'What difference will it make?' I didn't say anything and just put her to work." She held her own for about three years and then left to get married. Mr. Andō says she did well, and he would hire another woman for the same job—he is always looking for workers—but no other woman has ever applied.

Many of the firms at Tsukiji are family-run businesses and kinship is an important substratum of the marketplace's social order (an important topic that I will return to in chapter 6). Women embody and maintain crucial links among firms across the trading hierarchy of the marketplace, as elsewhere (Hamabata 1990). Many family firms count women among their corporate officers and registered principals, and women play central roles in the strategic decisions, personnel policies, and financial management of family firms.

In the course of a normal trading day, women appear mostly in seemingly supporting roles, as clerical workers in traders' back offices and as cashiers sequestered in tiny booths. As they handle the cash, they also keep track of the personal relationships that make most businesses run. These relationships come into play through the fact that at Tsukiji many prices are not posted and sellers determine what to charge based at least in part by calculations of personal connection. Prices therefore are communicated among shop staff in code, and the cashiers' tasks are made more complicated—and all the more vital—by this practice. A good cashier knows the customers and their relationships to the stall; she can pick up coded prices amid the banter of the trade.

Wordplay

The stalls buzz with a low hum of quick greetings and quiet negotiations. In this wholesale rather than retail trade, the kind of overt hawking that reverberates through the outer marketplace is rare. Apprentices do not assail each person who pauses with a loud chorus of "Irasshaimase!" ("Welcome!"), nor do they indiscriminately tout their wares to passersby. Tsukiji stall keepers reserve their greetings for known customers; in this marketplace, the buyer usually initiates the transaction, not the seller, and buyers and sellers often know each other well.

Mercantile phrases of indebtedness and personal relationship, so character-istic of Japanese business life in general, punctuate market talk. A stall owner called to the phone greets the caller with "Itsumo osewa-sama desu"— "Always thanks to your support." "Okage-sama de"—"Thanks to *you!*" springs forth in response to any pleasantry about the state of business. A mer-chant hands over a customer's purchases with "Maido, dōmo arigatō . . ."— "Thanks, every time . . ." Returning a friendly wave from a passerby, a stall owner calls out, "Senjitsu wa dōmo . . ."—"The other day, very . . ." The spe-cific meaning is ambiguous: "the other day I was very rude" or "you were very kind." But whether offered as apology or thanks, this phrase—like the others—notes a recent interaction that cannot pass unacknowledged.

Billingsgate, the venerable London fish market, has become synonymous with foul-mouthed abuse; Tsukiji's denizens are far more polite, but they too have their own distinctive idioms of etiquette, invective, and transac-tion.[19] Tsukiji conversations draw heavily on the slang and the imagery of *Edokko* (natives of shitamachi; literally, "children of Edo") (see Kōjiro 1986). In a transformation common in Tokyo's demimonde, syllables are reversed (Go 1963): sushi toppings, known conventionally as *sushidane* or simply *tane* ("seed" or "source"), in the slang of the marketplace and sushi chefs are *neta*, for example. Market conversations are often enlivened with brief flurries of *beranmē*, the extravagant shitamachi dialect in which even the most polite request can be issued (and received) as a bold challenge. At Tsukiji beranmē is usually deployed in jest, used in the oral sparring or *sharé*—wordplay rich in puns and double meanings—so central to the ver-bal presentation of self in shitamachi mercantile life.

This wordplay carries over into the complicated interplay between pric-ing systems and personal relationships. Many stalls do not post prices; and even if they do, they will knock down the price for good customers. The unknown walk-in buyer gets a higher price, if encouraged to purchase at all. Tsukiji traders do not publicly dicker or haggle over prices; if prices are posted openly, they are take-it-or-leave-it for a stranger. To preserve secrecy over prices offered to different customers, many stalls at Tsukiji use dis-tinctive codes known as *fuchō* when employees discuss prices among them-selves (table 5). Regular customers probably can piece together the stall's code, but occasional or first-time buyers are in the dark. Fuchō are usually nine-syllable phrases, each syllable representing a number between one and nine. Since the codes must be easy to remember, many stalls rely on stock

TABLE 5. *Coded Poetry* (Fuchō)

Code Syllables	Underlying Phrase	Translation
Nine-syllable codes		
sa-ri-to-ha-o-mo-shi-ro-i	*Sari to wa omoshiroi*	"If so, it's remarkable"
a-ki-na-i-no-shi-ya-wa-se	*Akinai no shiawase*	"The happiness of trade"
shi-ro-ha-ma-no-a-sa-ki-ri	*Shirohama no asakiri*	"Morning mist on a white beach"
Ten-syllable code		
u-me-ya-sa-ku-ra-ma-tsu-ta-ke	*Ume ya sakura matsu take*	"Plum and cherry, pine, bamboo"

SOURCES: Iijima 1972: 100–102; Takarai 1991: 83–85; *Uogashi hyakunen* 1968: 552–53.
NOTE: The actual syllables used to code numbers may differ from the spoken phrase, following standard Japanese orthographic conventions (as in the substitution of *ha* for *wa* in the first example). In other cases, simple substitutions are made to avoid duplication (*ya* for the second *a* in the second example). The last example can be converted from a ten- to a nine-syllable code simply by eliminating *ya* ("and").

colloquial expressions or semipoetic phrases, such as "shirohama no asakiri" ("morning mist on a white beach"), drawn from a customary repertoire (see Iijima 1972: 100–102; Takarai 1991: 83–85; *Uogashi hyakunen* 1968: 552–53).

As in the finger-bidding system *(teyari)* used in Tsukiji's auctions, zero rarely appears, nor is it needed since the general magnitude of the price for a specific item is obvious and all parties can be expected to know from context the appropriate level: a price quoted at 1-5 means 1,500 per kilogram when tuna is under discussion, though the same 1-5 would clearly indicate 150 yen per piece when packaged *kamaboko* (fish pâté) is up for sale. The *chōba* cashier must keep her ears open and be able to calculate rapidly the coded and abbreviated price quotations shouted by her co-workers: "three kilos at *ha-sa*" (37 or 3.7 or 3,700) or "one case for *ri-ro*" (92 or 920 or 92,000), while at the same time keeping track of other transactions that may be conducted in one or another versions of counting slang colloquially used in the fish business and widely known to habitués of sushi bars.

These slang forms, like the counting codes, reflect shitamachi fondness for *sharé*, wordplay. In counting slang *gake* is nine; in standard Japanese *gake* means cliff, and the written character for nine looks something like a cliff. *Geta* means three; *geta* are wooden sandals; and sandals have three

TABLE 6. *Counting Slang*

Number	Standard Japanese Forms	Slang Form(s)
One	*ichi; hitotsu*	*pin*
Two	*ni; futatsu*	*buri, ryan, nokku*
Three	*san; mitsu*	*geta*
Four	*yon* or *shi; yotsu*	*yotsuya, dari*
Five	*go; itsutsu*	*me*
Six	*roku; mutsu*	*ronji*
Seven	*shichi* or *nana; nanatsu*	*ya, seinan*
Eight	*hachi; yatsu*	*tetsu, bando*
Nine	*kyū; kokonotsu*	*gake, kiwa*

holes where thongs are inserted. *Bando* is eight; *bando* is a term for a belt; and by a stretch of imagination, the character for eight might resemble a belt buckle (table 6).

EBB TIDE

The traffic streaming out from the stalls crosses the loading docks where buyers take delivery of their day's purchases. There are roughly 250 loading slots, each supervised by a separate agent. Administratively, the loading docks are known (and licensed) as *kainihokansho* (merchandise custodial places), but no one uses that term. They (and the men and women who run each loading slot) are known colloquially as *chaya* (teahouses), an evocatively quaint name for so shabby and barren a collection of spaces, each really nothing more than a few square meters of bare concrete, piles of crates, and a couple of chairs. Chaya, short for *shiomachijaya* or "teahouses for awaiting the tides," is a term from the old Nihonbashi fish market, built alongside a major Edo canal, where both buyers and sellers awaited the proper tides in teahouses along the embankment before setting out by fishing vessel, barge, or peddler's skiff into the canals and tidal estuaries. By the later years of the Nihonbashi market (which was destroyed in 1923 during the Kantō earthquake), chaya had developed into full-fledged freight handling services. As they move through the marketplace, buyers simply direct purchases to their designated chaya; for their own regular customers, wholesalers know the proper chaya without asking. The chaya receive purchases from both the seafood and produce divisions as well as from shops in the outer market—a buyer may make purchases at a dozen or more stalls and shops in a day—and both wholesalers and buyers know the chaya will check, organize, safely store, transmit the paperwork, and load the entire day's purchases onto a delivery truck at a prearranged time. At Tsukiji today, nothing remains of *tea*houses—beyond the name—except the battered aluminum kettles perched on gas stoves at almost every loading slot.

Scattered among the loading docks are half a dozen canteens where a busy trader can buy a sandwich, a sports newspaper, or a pack of cigarettes. Next door to several canteens are the marketplace's icehouses. As porters position hand trucks under roaring grinders that spew chipped ice into crates, muscular icehouse workers heft 200-kilogram blocks of ice and, with a few deft cuts and a sharp blow from the saw blade, split them into neat chunks. Melting ice drips across the cracked pavement of the loading docks, tracked everywhere by workers' rubber boots.

As the last shifts of delivery vans pull out from the chaya in the early afternoon, the loading docks become workshops where itinerant fish peddlers clean and fillet fish and arrange them in refrigerated display cases mounted on the backs of their tiny trucks. In the afternoon and early evening, these peddlers make the rounds of residential areas throughout Tokyo, although fewer and fewer such itinerant fishmongers operate in Tokyo with each passing year. Many of them are workers in wholesale stalls who take advantage of their contacts in the marketplace and their employers' early closing hours to run side businesses as fishmongers. In old residential neighborhoods of central Tokyo where traditional retail shops have given way to office buildings, and in enormous suburban apartment complexes where close-at-hand shopping is scarce, truck-borne fishmongers are often the only suppliers of fresh seafood. By midafternoon, most of the peddlers, too, have packed up and driven off.

The area between the chaya and the market gates quiets down by noon, except for the ancillary shops and restaurants. A dozen hole-in-the-wall restaurants stay open through noon to cap off a morning rush of traders with a lunchtime crowd of office workers from the surrounding neighborhoods of skyscrapers. Advertising executives, journalists, and doctors are elbow to elbow with grizzled market veterans, Italian loafers next to rubber knee boots. The book shop, the knife stores, the scale dealer, the sellers of twine and plastic bags and invoice books, the vegetable shops, the seaweed stalls, and the soy sauce wholesaler stay open long enough to catch straggling restaurateurs and retailers who need supplies for their own businesses, but by the end of lunch, they too close for the day.

Tucked in among rows of shops, restaurants, and office buildings along the northeastern edge of the inner market stands a small Shintō shrine dedicated to Suijin-sama, the god of water, who is the patron deity of the marketplace and also is enshrined in many domestic kitchens as an essential household god. Unlike the Namiyoke Shrine in the outer marketplace, the Suijin Shrine (Suijinsha) usually stands locked and shuttered, its gate blocked by handcarts and bicycles, the chain-link fence that surrounds it covered with signs and posters. Market traders pass it without a visible thought or a bow; it is open for prayers only on special holidays. But as I noticed one day when poring over a market map, the Suijin Shrine is providentially positioned almost directly in a NE-SW line opposite the curve of the sheds housing the wholesalers' stalls and the auction spaces beyond them, in almost perfect alignment with the traditional idea that a deity should protect a place against ill fortune entering from the northeast.

Less mystical concerns, however, are the daily business of the market. In front of the gatehouse at the market's main entrance, a forlorn blackboard testifies to the frailty of human memory and to the honesty of at least some of Tsukiji's denizens. Each day it lists lost items turned over to the marketplace guards: a crate of frozen squid, a carton of Chinese cabbage, three packages of fish pâté, a folder of shipping invoices, a wallet containing a driver's license, and "naked money" (i.e., cold cash). From time to time the market's public address system broadcasts similar announcements: "Would the person who left three kilos of tuna in the telephone booth near the shrine please claim them at the gatehouse?"

By 1 or 1:30, Tsukiji's trading day is pretty much over. Back-office operations continue until midafternoon, but the auction floors are deserted. The arcs of stalls are quiet except for the occasional apprentice cleaning cleavers or packing ice around a stack of crates. Here and there a stall owner and his wife may be puzzling over a pile of receipts, reconciling sales with the morning's auction purchases. After the lunch crowd has departed, most of the restaurants in the marketplace close for the day. The women in the booths at the entrance to the market who sell lottery tickets (takarakuji) tot up their day's sales. About 1 P.M. sweepers pulling handcarts wind among the buildings, ringing handbells to signal the last trash pickup of the day.

By midafternoon, the marketplace is quiet, almost empty. Market administrators remain at their desks until the close of the business day as it is measured outside the marketplace. Mechanics tinker over broken turret carts, trying to resurrect them for another day's service. A solitary watchman slowly walks the rows of stalls. A few cats dart in and out of the almost deserted sheds looking for a forgotten scrap.

In late afternoon and evening, as the surrounding neighborhoods explode with beckoning neon, Tsukiji is dark and shuttered. 'Round midnight, the tide begins to change.

3 From Landfill to Marketplace

As torrential rain lashed their faces and pasted their thin cotton festival robes flat against their bodies, Tsukiji's traders hove an enormous *mikoshi*—a god's palanquin, a portable shrine—through the marketplace during a typhoon in late September 1990. The festival honored the marketplace's tutelary deity, Suijin-sama (the god of water), and deluge or not, the Uogashi Suijin-sai—the Fish Market Suijin Festival—would go on as scheduled. Organizers buoyed their spirits by noting that the weather was "tottemo Suijin-sama rashii"—"so very like the Suijin-sama."

From the palanquin's temporary resting place just inside the market's northern entry, across the bridge past the Namiyoke Shrine, through the outer marketplace, across Harumi Avenue, around the walls of the Hongan-ji temple, down Shin-Ōhashi Avenue, back past the outer market, and then through the main gate of the inner marketplace across from the headquarters of the *Asahi* newspaper, the enormous mikoshi navigated the storm. In front of the portable shrine walked a solemn, sodden procession of market elders and a troupe of their daughters and granddaughters wearing antiquated costumes and elaborate stage makeup, bedraggled and stoically miserable in the face of the downpour. Teams of young men from the marketplace struggled under the shifting weight of the slick lacquered poles that supported the heavy palanquin, trying to keep their balance on the drenched pavement.

Despite the storm, the portable shrine bounced with its predictably enthusiastic rhythm, signifying that the god rather than its bearers was in control. But, in the rain, the procession did not lurch out of bounds as it had at a previous Suijin festival, a generation earlier, when the mikoshi headed off for the Ginza, only to be blocked near the Kabuki-za theater by the police. To stop its travels further toward Tokyo's main shopping street, they had confiscated the mikoshi's support poles, leaving it to sit on the pavement until a crane could be called to lift it onto a flatbed truck for a sedate trip back to the marketplace. This time, festival organizers were pleased that the frisky Suijin-sama had surprised them with only a typhoon. The god repaid their years of planning and preparation with a safe and sane Suijin-sai.

It was all very *iki*, everyone agreed, referring to the sense of style that underlies the more flamboyant aspects of *shitamachi* life: an aesthetic that relies on painstakingly artless use of color, pattern, and visual contrast to frame flashes of devil-may-care bravado, physical derring-do, and fiscal improvidence (Kōjiro 1986; Nishiyama 1997: chap. 3). What could be more iki than spending millions of yen to refurbish an elaborate mikoshi for a parade held in the teeth of a typhoon?

For the several days of the festival, Tsukiji's Suijin Shrine—inconspicuously tucked away among shops and office buildings in the inner marketplace—opened its gates for prayers and offerings. The tiny shrine structure, itself too small for anyone to enter, was cleaned and refurbished and its compound festooned with banners offered by merchants from the marketplace. Carpenters from nearby neighborhoods built a temporary resting place for the palanquin close to the shrine. The day before the festival, a pair of enormous bulls were brought from a shrine near Nikkō to pull the Suijin Shrine's *dashi:* a cart that towers almost three stories high, topped by an elaborately carved life-sized figure of a character from *Nō* drama whose ancient silk robes were fitted to it by a dresser recruited from the kabuki theater. Auspicious red-and-white bunting decorated the loading docks near the shrine. The wholesalers' meeting hall adjacent to the shrine became the reception area and command post for the festival. For three and a half days, the normal activities of the marketplace came to a halt.

This was only the third full-blown Suijin festival of the twentieth century (the others were in 1920 and 1955); it takes place once a generation.[1] For several years, the market's festival committee had discussed putting on the festival again. During the long illness of the Shōwa Emperor and the period of mourning that followed his death in January 1989, they suspended the planning, but in 1990 Tsukiji's elders decided the time was right. It was the 400th anniversary of the occupation of Edo Castle by Tokugawa Ieyasu. Under the rule of the Tokugawa dynasty, which lasted until 1868, Edo (now Tokyo) grew to be Japan's predominant metropolis. Because of the market's claims to have originated with fishers who accompanied Ieyasu on his march to occupy Edo, the 1990 celebrations marked the putative 400th anniversary of the fish market as well. It was also the 40th anniversary of the revival of the marketplace, dated from the lifting of rationing and price controls after World War II and the relicensing of intermediate wholesalers. And in the spring of 1990, the marketplace had completed one of its periodic rotations of stalls, so the intermediate wholesalers were all established in fresh locations.

The most pressing reason to hold the festival in 1990 was that reconstruction of the existing marketplace was scheduled to begin in 1991. The massive project would tear up the market for over a decade. After full-scale construction started, there would be no opportunity to hold a festival until sometime in the early twenty-first century. With a new marketplace on the drawing boards, 1990 would be the last chance to celebrate the marketplace as it had been for most of the working lives of all but the oldest Tsukiji denizens. This was the last chance to hold the festival while some of those who had participated in the previous festival in 1955 were still active, and for them to share their experience with younger people.

Tsukiji's Suijin-sama holds title to a domain that is discontinuous geographically and, to an increasing extent, socially. The tiny Suijin Shrine at Tsukiji is a branch of a slightly larger shrine to Suijin-sama located in the precincts of the Kanda Myōjin Shrine, several kilometers to the northwest.[2] Kanda Myōjin, one of the city's largest Shintō shrines and home to one of Tokyo's three major annual festivals, is the tutelary shrine for Nihonbashi, the center of mercantile life in old Edo where, until 1923, the old fish market stood (map 4). The guardian god of the marketplace therefore defends many domains. It is a god of the domestic hearth or *daidokoro*, a protector of the fish market (which, after all, regards itself as "Tokyo's daidokoro"), and a champion of the Nihonbashi mercantile district as a whole.

Suijin-sama watches over the marketplace, not the Tsukiji district per se. The neighborhood of Tsukiji has its own guardian deity, the Inari-sama resident in the Namiyoke Shrine ever since the area was first reclaimed from the bay in the seventeenth century. A third shrine—the Sumiyoshi Shrine on the islet of Tsukudajima—houses a guardian deity also significant to some market participants. This shrine, a branch of the large Sumiyoshi Shrine in Osaka, was reputedly established in the late sixteenth century by the fishers who accompanied Ieyasu on his journey to take possession of Edo. For Tsukiji traders who trace their ancestry and that of the marketplace to that momentous event, the Sumiyoshi Shrine is an important landmark.

In staging the festival for Suijin-sama, the elderly members of the Uogashi-kai—the committee responsible for the upkeep of the Suijin shrine and for organizing the infrequent festival—called on younger generations of Tsukiji traders and workers to provide financial support and energy. The invitation did not go unheeded; firms and individuals donated millions of yen.

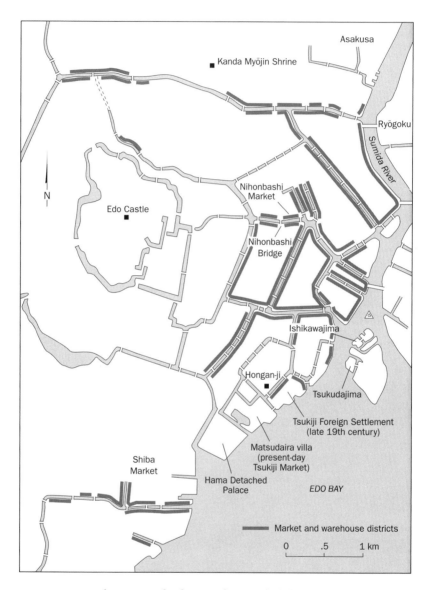

Map 4. Nineteenth-century Edo: the city of water. Shaded areas along canals were markets and warehouse districts along Edo's working waterfront. Adapted from Jinnai (1995: 73). Reproduced with permission of the University of California Press.

Wholesalers ordered thousands of cotton festival robes *(yukata)* decorated with the symbols of the fish market. Firms organized more than a hundred teams of men—eight to ten to a team—to help carry the mikoshi. Individuals spent countless hours planning the festival, renovating the mikoshi and other paraphernalia, and cleaning and decorating the marketplace.

The Tsukiji marketplace the festival celebrated in 1990 was far different from the fish market of the past, certainly different from the representations of its past that the festival memorialized. A couple of generations of change had eradicated the character of the fish market as simultaneously a workplace and a residential community, and had eroded the sense that market workers pursue an occupation situated within an all-embracing social world.

In the Nihonbashi era, workplace and home were often the same for traders, many of whom lived above or behind their shops. With the market's relocation to Tsukiji in the 1920s, the new marketplace physically separated workplace and home. Yet because the nearby neighborhoods north of the marketplace became home to many of Tsukiji's traders, family and shop remained close. Today, after a couple of decades of prosperity for the fish market and in the wake of Tokyo's astronomical real estate inflation, only a few Tsukiji traders live in the area; many commute by private car from distant suburbs.

With geographical dispersion, the daily life and social contacts of the marketplace are alien to many members of the traders' own families. Moreover, the sense of loyalty, identity, and participation in a common enterprise, a common way of life, that bound together (at least in memory) employers and employees, elders and juniors, masters and apprentices, buyers and sellers, has weakened as the business of the fish market increasingly has taken on the character of corporate Japan. Family firms now have boards of directors; workers are recruited through newspaper advertisements; some employees commute to and from company apartment complexes; apprentices can no longer hope to be set up in business by their masters (although marrying the boss's daughter remains a possibility). The marketplace is no longer a circumscribed, face-to-face community.

The older Tsukiji traders who planned the 1990 festival knew all this, of course, and would occasionally lament the passing of the spirit of the Nihonbashi uogashi, the old fish market. As the years have gone by, nostalgic recollection had blurred the sharp edges of economic and political conflict that rocked Nihonbashi throughout much of the late nineteenth and early twentieth centuries. In memory, turbulence appears as communal bustle. The festival sought to recapture some of that spirit of affinity and to mobilize—or create—a community sustained for the moment by the reflected glory of the fish market's past.

In organizing the fête to honor the Suijin-sama, the Uogashi-kai not only called on the resources of the marketplace itself but also drew in a more extensive range of people for whom such festivals have meaning. Because of Tsukiji's venerable, if at times contrived, ties to the mercantile quarters of old Edo, its festival lays claim to space in the city's nostalgic imagination. The Suijin-sama's festival is but one landmark on an almost imperceptible social topography marked off by shrine parish boundaries that both outline the territories of tutelary deities and also—for the cognoscenti—help to place self and other in a complex system of local identity and social standing. This is a dimension of Tokyo's social space in which festival aficionados identify themselves by the tutelary shrines of their neighborhoods: Minato's Teppōzu, Monzennaka-chō's Hachiman, Yushima's Tenjin. In this social world, volunteer firemen and old-fashioned construction foremen— known as *tobi* or *tobishoku*—are the cocks of the walk.[3] They carefully delineate and protect their *jiban* or *nawabari* (spheres of influence or stamping ground) and are as knowledgeable about the territorial claims of *yakuza* gangs as they are of the hierarchical layers of municipal authority. In this shadowy realm of social geography, a flash of ornate tattooing is an admission ticket, even as those so inscribed hasten to assure onlookers that they are "men of honor" *(katagi na hito)*, not outlaws (Egawa 1990; Richie and Buruma 1980).

For Tsukiji's festival to happen, the Suijin-sama was put on the shoulders of others, others with pasts constructed out of the repertoire of spatial-historical memories embodied in shitamachi identity today. Of the hundred-odd teams of men recruited to hoist the mikoshi, roughly half were from outside the marketplace: residents of nearby neighborhoods; groups of festival fans from throughout the city; volunteer firefighters from shitamachi neighborhoods; and members of the gang Kawazoe-gumi, that considers the Tsukiji district its turf. Festivals like Tsukiji's Uogashi Suijin-sai have particular force and legitimacy because they so neatly connect place, history, and contemporary social reality. For participants as much as for onlookers, the identity of locale and the sense of historically situated tradition become almost entirely intermingled: Nihonbashi, Tsukiji, and the heartland of old shitamachi.

田 田 田

This chapter depicts Tsukiji's history through a rearview mirror. The view is narrow, it bounces quite a bit, and it is seen almost entirely from the perspective of the current driver. And a rearview mirror mainly reflects land-marks of the very recent journey. Here I outline briefly a few of the central trends in Tsukiji's development that one major set of actors—the interme-diate wholesalers—sees as the most important for understanding the con-temporary marketplace. This account focuses on those aspects of Tsukiji's history that most clearly exhibit their views of their own occupation and its place in the market's development.

In the minds of Tokyo's residents, Tsukiji and its environs are now almost indelibly fused with the fish trade; yet market and place were in fact brought together quite recently, in the mid-1920s. But even though the long histories of place and market have intersected only in the past several gen-erations, the venerable institutions of the fish trade and the events that formed the Tsukiji district—the confluence of market and of place—have significantly shaped the present structure of the marketplace as well as the images of it held by market insiders and the general public alike.[4]

THE PLACE: FROM LANDFILL TO FOREIGN SETTLEMENT

Tsukiji rose during the seventeenth century out of the marshy lowlands along the mouth of the Sumida River. Throughout the Tokugawa period (1603–1868), low-lying areas in the river delta were systematically filled. Earth from the gigantic excavations undertaken by the shōgunate to build castle moats and transportation canals created space for Edo's growing mer-chant quarters and for aristocratic estates and villas along the waterfront.

After the great Meireki fire of 1657, which destroyed almost two-thirds of Edo's buildings and killed perhaps as many as 100,000 people, the Hongan-ji temple, the enormous Kantō headquarters of the popular Jōdo Shinshū sect of Buddhism based at the Nishi Hongan-ji temple in Kyoto, was relocated from Asakusa to Tsukiji. The fishers of nearby Tsukudajima—themselves transplanted from the Kansai area where the sect was based—contributed greatly to constructing the Tsukiji Betsuin (as Hongan-ji was originally known), and the temple rewarded them with hereditary sinecures as guards, attendants, and cemetery keepers.

South of the main temple, on land that is now the outer marketplace, many sub-temples were erected, numbering almost eighty in the eighteenth century. A wide swath of villas and estates of feudal lords separated the densely clustered complex of temples from the rest of the commoners' city. Still extant is the garden of the Hama Rikyū (Hama Detached Palace), a for-mer waterfront villa, now a public garden just to the west of the present-day Tsukiji marketplace. Between the Hama Rikyū and the sub-temples of

Hongan-ji were a garden and villa of the influential Matsudaira clan; the site of this estate is where the marketplace now stands.

East of Hongan-ji, isolated from the commercial center of the city, a small district of commoners' residences and workshops lay in a narrow strip along the riverbank.[5] Just across the Sumida River from this settlement was the tiny islet of Tsukudajima, poised defensively at the mouth of the river. At the beginning of the seventeenth century, Tsukudajima was home to a village of fishers, who settled there supposedly under the sponsorship of Tokugawa Ieyasu, founder of the dynasty bearing his name. Today, these fishers are popularly credited as having founded Edo's fish market and as being the occupational forebears of Tsukiji's contemporary traders.

The proximity of Tsukudajima, however, did not involve the Tsukiji area substantially in the fish trade, although in the early nineteenth century a small market briefly sprang up along the riverbank behind the Hongan-ji temple. Edo's major fish market developed in the heart of the city, at Nihonbashi (literally "Japan Bridge"). Built in 1603, it and the surrounding district just outside the main gates of Edo Castle quickly became not only the commercial center of Edo but also the symbolic center of the city and the nation. Throughout the Tokugawa period, the bridge itself was the zero point from which all distances throughout the realm were measured, and it was across Nihonbashi that all formal processions visiting or departing from the shōgun's court passed.

Edo was a city of canals. The eastern parts of the old city, the low-lying districts between Edo Castle and the Sumida River, were mostly landfill, created from the massive seventeenth-century excavations that rechanneled rivers and created defensive moats circling the shōgun's castle. In the mercantile districts, specific stretches of the canal banks became the destinations for particular cargoes—fish, vegetables, wood, rice, and so forth—and along these quays *(kashi* or *gashi)* more than fifty specialized commodity markets developed for lumber, clothing, and other products (see Suzuki 1999: 74–75; McClain 1994). The uogashi, or fish quay, was located along the northern bank of the canal to the east of Nihonbashi. The Nihonbashi uogashi, the Nihonbashi fish market, which remained there until 1923, occupied a site very near the present-day Mitsukoshi department store, and a monument to the market's long history stands at the northeastern corner of the contemporary bridge.

I will return shortly to the development of the Nihonbashi uogashi; as for Tsukiji, throughout the Tokugawa period it remained commercially a remote cul-de-sac. This isolation helps to account for the next significant

Figure 25. The fish market at Nihonbashi, in the foreground. "Clearing After Snow, Nihonbashi," by Hiroshige. From his 1856 series *One Hundred Famous Views of Edo.* Bequest of William P. Chapman, Jr., Class of 1895, in the collection and reproduced with permission of the Herbert F. Johnson Museum of Art, Cornell University.

development of Tsukiji's history: the creation in the late nineteenth century of the Tsukiji Foreign Settlement (Tsukiji Kyoryūchi).

In 1858, major Western powers negotiated treaties with Japan that opened Edo and several other cities to foreigners. The Tokugawa regime began preparations for a foreign settlement in Edo, which the new Meiji imperial government inaugurated at Tsukiji during 1869–1870.[6] The Tokugawa authorities probably had several reasons for choosing Tsukiji. It was convenient by boat to Yokohama, where the majority of foreigners had settled, and it was close to Shinbashi, the planned terminus of the railroad being built from Yokohama. Since Tsukiji had also been the site of various early efforts to cultivate "Dutch studies" (i.e., the study of the West), perhaps the area seemed already ripe for—or tainted by—internationalization.[7] But perhaps most important, the Tsukiji site was cut off from central Tokyo by canals, by a swath of secondary villas and estates of middle-ranking feudal lords *(daimyō)*, by the huge Hongan-ji temple complex, and by the general remoteness of the lower Sumida from the centers of both aristocratic and plebeian Tokyo. Foreigners therefore would be safely out of sight in Tsukiji.

Tsukiji was never popular with foreign residents; indeed, its non-Japanese population "wavered around a hundred" (Seidensticker 1983: 38). Shortly after the settlement was completed, the Ginza fire of 1872 wiped out some of the early hotels and public buildings that had given Tokyo its first glimpses of what one of the Meiji period's leading intellectuals, Fukuzawa Yukichi, heralded as "Civilization and Enlightenment." That same year, the Shinbashi terminus of the new railway that linked Tokyo with the major international port (and the much larger foreign settlement) in Yokohama was completed. Most foreign traders deserted the capital for the bustling port city, leaving the Tsukiji settlement to diplomats, missionaries, and teachers. Although many residents were undoubtedly as respectable as the missionaries portrayed in *Clara's Diary* (Whitney 1979), the journal of a young American woman who lived in Tsukiji from 1875 to 1884, others were less savory—as suggested by Tanizaki Jun'ichirō's speculations about the nocturnal occupations of the young European women who tutored him at an English language academy in Tsukiji, where he studied briefly as a young boy (Tanizaki 1988: 166–70; Seidensticker 1983: 36–42).

But the settlement's influence was disproportionate to its population. A number of institutions that have since become eminent—such as Rikkyō (St. Paul's) University, Meiji Gakuin University, Aoyama Gakuin University, and St. Luke's Hospital—can trace their origins to the efforts of Tsukiji's foreign missionaries. Nearby, the Meiji government acquired the estate of the Matsudaira clan south of the Hongan-ji temple and established on the site a naval training school, one of Japan's first Western-style military academies. It remained only until 1888, when it moved to Etajima, near Hiroshima, where it became the premier academy of the Japanese Imperial Navy.

The Tsukiji foreign settlement survived only a generation, until the Meiji government negotiated an end to the international agreements for extraterritoriality—which exempted foreigners from the laws and control of the Japanese state—in July 1899. With the abolition of extraterritoriality, foreigners and foreign institutions were free to locate elsewhere in Tokyo, and most did. The foreign legations moved to Kōjimachi and other areas closer to the Imperial Palace and the centers of national government; the churches and schools, along with most of the resident foreigners, moved to the more desirable and spacious western fringes of the city. All that remained of the foreign settlement—with the sole exception of St. Luke's Hospital—disappeared in the fires that followed the Kantō earthquake.[8]

This earthquake, which destroyed most of central Tokyo on September 1, 1923, had incalculable impact on the future development of the entire city. The earthquake and the fires that raged in its aftermath completely razed the old fish market at Nihonbashi and devastated the Tsukiji district as well.

Visiting Tsukiji a few days after the earthquake, Joseph Dahlmann, a Jesuit priest and professor of German literature at Tokyo Imperial University, wrote an eyewitness account:

> I follow the road to the spot once occupied by the great Hongwanji [Hongan-ji] temple. . . . To-day there is no trace of it left. From here on I pass through another of those terrific fire areas, which must be seen to appreciate to the full the effects of the catastrophe. The former sites of big business are now heaped with ashes from which the odor of burnt and rotting corpses urges the wayfarer to hasten. . . . Now the vista opens on the Tsukiji settlement, formerly reserved for the occupation of foreigners. . . . Heaps of ruins are the only reminder of the fact that this street was lined on both sides by neat residences in American style. The Metropole and Central Hotel in the vicinity could not be saved though they fronted on Tokyo bay, where plenty of water was available. Through the fitful shifting of the breeze the fire rushed on Tsukiji—from two, later on from three different directions, so that the inhabitants were hard pressed to escape with their bare lives. . . . Every avenue of escape was barred except one road leading into Shiba. (Dahlmann 1924: 98–100)

The earthquake and fire cleared land, at incalculable human cost, and in the rebuilding of Tokyo the marketplace moved from Nihonbashi to Tsukiji, firmly relocating the linkage between market and place in Tokyo's popular imagination.

THE MARKET: FROM TSUKUDAJIMA TO TSUKIJI

Founding the Market

Tokyo's fish market conventionally traces its origins back to 1590, the year that Tokugawa Ieyasu assumed control of Edo Castle. In the heroic history of Tsukiji, the market originated from the relationship between Ieyasu, the brilliant general who was confirmed as shōgun in 1603, and Mori Magoemon, a fisher from the village of Tsukuda in Settsu province, in what is now Osaka Prefecture.[9]

Magoemon was born in 1569 and, according to legend, encountered Ieyasu in 1582 when he became a fisher supplying Ieyasu's entourage. And when Ieyasu formally entered Edo to take possession of the city and its castle in 1590, Magoemon supposedly headed a band of thirty-odd fishers who formed a tiny part of Ieyasu's retinue.

The fishers had proved their loyalty to Ieyasu during the preceding civil wars. This fealty and the strategic location of the tiny island on which they settled gave rise to their slightly sinister reputation as water-borne spies for the Tokugawa regime and guardians of the riverine approaches to the city. Whatever their true services, Magoemon and his companions received the island at the mouth of the Sumida River—now named Tsukudajima, after their ancestral village—and fishing rights to the waters of upper Edo Bay. In return for this monopoly, they supplied Ieyasu's court with fish. In particular, the fishers were required to present the castle with the first catches of the whitefish *(shirauo)* that were plentiful at the Sumida River's mouth from November to March (Tōkyō-to Kōbunshokan 1978).

In 1603 Magoemon's son Kyūzaemon requested and received permission to sell surplus catches to Edo's commoners. In 1613 he and others opened a shop called Tsukudaya Kyūzaemon in Hon-Odawara-chō, a section of Nihonbashi. At roughly the same time, Ōwada Sukegoro, also from the Osaka region, opened a business in nearby Hon-Funa-chō serving Edo's warrior elite with live sea bream imported from the coastal waters near present-day Shizuoka. By 1641 at least fourteen fishmongers were operating around Nihonbashi, half of them affiliated with Magoemon's group from Tsukuda. Magoemon, his son Kyūzaemon, and their followers thus became credited as the marketplace's legendary founding fathers.[10]

Tsukudajima also holds its time-honored place in the history of Japanese cuisine for the delicacy known as *tsukudani* (boiled in the Tsukuda fashion): seafood and vegetables steeped in thick soy sauce. A handful of present-day Tsukiji intermediate wholesalers claim genealogical descent from the original fishers of Tsukudajima, and the first character of the name is used in several dozen Tsukiji shop names, implying to customers (though by no means proving) the shops' venerability.

Fishing and markets had existed in Edo long before the arrival of Ieyasu and Magoemon, of course. Edo had been a fishing village for centuries. In 1457 a local warlord, Ōta Dōkan, erected a castle there to control the fertile Kantō Plain. A fish market regularly operated at Shiba, along the bay to the southeast of the castle. Just outside the castle gates, a mixed market called Yokkaichi ("Fourth-Day Market")[11] sold fish—primarily dried and salted fish brought from the Kamakura area—and other necessities to both the castle and the townspeople. Both these markets, which predated the establishment of the Nihonbashi market, continued throughout the Tokugawa period; indeed, the Nihonbashi marketplace grew up next to the Yokkaichi market, which survived as a distinct entity until 1923.

The "establishment" of Edo's fish market by Magoemon's kin and followers is a historical myth that respectfully credits the dynastic founder of the Tokugawa regime, Ieyasu, with the creation of all things. But in several

Figure 26. The daily bustle of the Nihonbashi market during the Tokugawa period. Sketch by Mori Kazan.

important respects, the Nihonbashi market that developed *was* new and not simply a continuation of its predecessors.

Nihonbashi Uogashi

Against the backdrop of Edo's population growth and the increasing prosperity of its merchant classes during the seventeenth and early eighteenth centuries, the Nihonbashi marketplace developed rapidly. Its organization reflected the intricate and shifting relationships among fishers, merchants, and consumers, all dependent on feudal patronage in different ways. Shōgunal officials were always ambivalent about merchants; on the one hand, they constantly inspected the market for tax evasion, and on the other hand, they regarded merchants as a ready source of cash. The castle demanded the best seafood at nominal prices, while its elaborate sumptuary regulations prevented wealthy townspeople from (openly) enjoying the best the marketplace could offer.

Edo strategically dominated the entire Kantō Plain, and for this simple reason Ieyasu chose it as his headquarters after securing his dominion over the entire region. After the arrival of Ieyasu and especially after the establishment of the Tokugawa shōgunate, Edo grew explosively. Although population figures for the premodern city are unsystematic, around 1600 Edo

probably had no more than a few thousand residents. By the 1650s its population had reached nearly half a million, making Edo Japan's largest city.
By the beginning of the eighteenth century, the population had grown to
about 1 million, and by the 1720s, 1.3 million, making Edo the world's
largest city of the time (eighteenth-century London had a population of
about 600,000; Beijing, about 1 million). After the 1730s, Edo's population
remained relatively constant until the mid–nineteenth century (Cybriwsky
1998: 58).

As the Nihonbashi market began to supply the populace of a rapidly
expanding city, its scale quickly surpassed that of Edo's earlier markets.
Urban growth, the expansion of long-distance transportation, and the peace
imposed during the long Tokugawa rule all helped to foster prosperity and
the growth of a cash economy, despite official efforts to suppress it. Ideologically, the feudal regime espoused an economic ideal of physiocratic agrari-
anism (the idea that wealth is land and the products that can be extracted
from that land) and despised the urban artisan and merchant classes in
whose hands a market economy flourished. Even though the shōgunate
exercised tight controls over economic activity in general, merchants of the
period developed highly sophisticated commercial practices, perhaps in part
because the feudal authorities had no conception of a market economy and
could hardly recognize it as such, let alone formulate rules to contain it
effectively. The powerful Osaka merchants, for example, who controlled
much of the nation's long-distance trade during the Tokugawa period, developed what was perhaps the world's first organized futures trading. In the
early eighteenth century, the Osaka rice futures market "developed without
any guidance from financial authorities . . . a market that materialized
solely in response to the needs of market participants," without either a pri-
ori economic theorizing or the institutionalized regulatory authority that
characterizes contemporary futures markets (Schaede 1991: 340; see also
McClain 1999).

During the seventeenth and eighteenth centuries, urban commoners
(chōnin—merchants and artisans) grew wealthy as a class even as samurai
and the regime as a whole fell further and further into debt. The merchants
prospered despite rigid sumptuary regulations designed to curb commoners'
consumption, to increase revenues for the state, and to enforce the stylistic
boundaries sharply separating society's various classes from one another.
The authorities' disapproval notwithstanding, in Edo and elsewhere chōnin
developed a lively, flamboyant, hedonistic, and materialistic culture that celebrated—among other things—consumption. The fish merchants of Nihon-

bashi both catered to and reveled in this consumption, and as they prospered they too became leading patrons of Edo's urbane culture.

A satiric verse *(senryū)* alludes to the Nihonbashi market:

Yoru to hiru, asa to ni chiru nichi sen ryō

Evening, noon, and dawn, a thousand ryō are scattered each day

(Tōkyō-to Chūō Oroshiuri Shijō 1985: 4)

The lines refer to three places in Edo where a thousand gold *ryō*[12] changed hands every day: the pleasure quarters of Yoshiwara at night, the theaters in midday, and the fish market in the morning. An earthier verse with a similar message was recited to me by a Tsukiji official: "Three things that consume a thousand *ryō* a day—above the nose, below the nose, below the navel" (i.e., eyes—theater; mouth—food; loins—sex). Tsukiji legend makes the connection in other ways as well: the calligraphy for the uogashi symbol that dots the marketplace today reputedly was first used on an elaborate curtain presented to a kabuki troupe in the middle Tokugawa period by its wealthy fishmonger patrons, as an advertisement—certainly of their wealth, perhaps of their wares (*Uogashi hyakunen* 1968: 79).

The Tokugawa regime was perpetually suspicious of commerce and mercantile life in general, and the Nihonbashi fish market was highly regulated. Officially, the market was authorized, indeed required, to supply the court— it was a *goyō ichiba*, a marketplace "by appointment to his majesty"—and the feudal privileges and obligations that this status imposed closely linked the marketplace to the shōgunate. The shōgunate exacted tribute in specified amounts or kinds of seafood from fishing villages (as did local feudal lords); the rights of these villages to exploit certain waters and monopolies over particular species were themselves under the control of the regime, which could grant them, reconfirm them, or take them away almost at will.[13] The tribute exacted for control over a fishing ground was sometimes purely nominal, a symbolic token acknowledging fealty to the lord; in most cases, however, the tribute was substantial and provisioned the regime through taxation in kind.

As Edo's fish trade grew, its character changed. Traders in the older markets (like the early fishmongers from Tsukudajima) included many fishers selling their own catches; as the Nihonbashi marketplace developed, many of its traders became true wholesalers *(ton'ya)* who bought rather than caught the seafood they sold. Control over particular fishing grounds became entangled with the rights to sell the catches in Edo. In some cases fishing villages like Tsukudajima requested permission to sell surplus catches in Edo and thereby acquired a monopoly. In other instances (for example, the case of Ōwada Sukegoro and the Shizuoka sea bream mentioned earlier) fish merchants gained control over the sale of a particular locality's catch. But the end result was similar: fishers and wholesalers were quickly and irrevocably locked together under the feudal system. The business of Edo's ton'ya revolved around so-called proprietary coasts (mochiura), that is, fishing villages and grounds with which they had exclusive trading rights. Typically an Edo ton'ya would advance cash to local fishing bosses—"net masters," or amimoto—for the costs of equipment and would enter into a long-term trade relationship with net masters or with a local ton'ya in the vicinity of the fishing port. Fishers could sell their catches only through a licensed ton'ya; a ton'ya could control a catch only at the sufferance of the authorities, who granted permission at a price.

The wholesalers of Nihonbashi were also caught up in—and created by—a system of feudal tribute known as jōnō: a complicated combination of rights to engage in trade, tax exemptions, and the serious matter of provisioning the shōgun's court, his direct retainers, his garrisons, and his hangers-on. In 1644 fish merchants in the Nihonbashi area organized themselves, and the shōgunate officially recognized the "Four Guilds of Fish Wholesalers" (Uodon'ya Yongumi), each located in a distinct neighborhood within the larger Nihonbashi district: Hon-Funa-chō, Hon-Funa-chō Yokomise, Hon-Odawara-chō, and Anjin-chō.[14] The raison d'être for official recognition was the jōnō system, under which merchants supplied fish to the shōgunate in return for licenses entitling them to conduct long-distance trade and to sell seafood to the general public. The shōgunate established three uokaijo (fish offices) at Nihonbashi, to supervise the guilds and to ensure that the castle was well supplied.

In 1674 fishers from thirteen villages in the Kantō region around Edo protested the monopolies of the Four Guilds and their "proprietary villages." In response, the shōgunate established an additional marketplace in Moto Zaimoku-chō, just south of the Nihonbashi Bridge, near the Yokkaichi marketplace for dried and salted fish. This market was called Shinsakanaba (literally, the "New Fish Place"), or simply Shinba, the "New Place," and it, too, became part of the jōnō system. The merchants of the Shinsakanaba were responsible for supplying the shōgunate during the first shun—the first ten-day segment—of each month, and the original Four Guilds for the latter two shun.[15]

Although the feudal privilege of trade was, in a sense, a boon, in the long run merchants considered it "the cancer of the fish trade." The jōnō system created a class of fish merchants under perpetual obligation to provide low-cost fish to the shōgun and his massive retinue. During the system's first century, the shōgunate paid only about 10 percent of the market value of the fish it received, and its agents naturally expected to receive the finest fish available. Although wholesalers were individually obligated to provide fish according to the shōgunate's daily specifications, the members of each guild were collectively responsible for filling the appropriate quotas, and individual wholesalers frequently cooperated to cover each other in the face of shortfalls.

Official patronage had its benefits, of course, and at least in the first century or so of Nihonbashi's existence, wholesalers enjoyed both the material advantages of privileged trade and a sense of pride at being in the service of the shōgunate. The merchant guilds were constantly on the lookout for ways to exploit their connections to the shōgunate to advance their material interests. For example, in 1720 the shōgunal authorities established a port office in Uraga, just south of Edo, to control shipping and to increase tax revenues. Permits and inspections were mandatory for all ships entering Edo Bay. Seven guilds of Edo wholesalers—from Nihonbashi and the older Shiba market—who dealt in fresh fish, however, requested exemptions for their fishing vessels, carefully noting that delays would impair the quality of the fish they provided the castle. The officials evidently saw their point, and sixty-four wholesalers were designated as "certified wholesalers" *(inkan ton'ya)*, that is, wholesalers authorized to issue letters of transit to fishing and cargo vessels in their service, exempting them from inspection. Together these sixty-four wholesalers controlled roughly 1,200 vessels, both fishing and cargo craft (*Uogashi hyakunen* 1968: 70–71).

These wholesalers, however, were only a fraction of the fish trade. For example, as of 1743, the six guilds of wholesalers in the Nihonbashi district (the Four Guilds, the Shinsakanaba, and the merchants of Yokkaichi) numbered 512 members. Although the guilds had their origins in specific neighborhoods, over time their membership dispersed somewhat; thus members of, for example, the Hon-Funa-chō guild could be found throughout the Nihonbashi area as well as in other regions of the city—even as far away as Shinagawa, near the city's southern gates (*Uogashi hyakunen* 1968: 160–75). But the guilds remained tightly defined by the rights and obligations that continued to bind them to the specific fish offices the shōgunate had established in Nihonbashi to administer the jōnō system.

Wholesalers—ton'ya—whether specifically bound by the rules of the jōnō system or not (as was the case for the wholesalers of Shiba and Yokkaichi) were all beholden to the shōgunal authorities through their licenses to engage in long-distance and local trade, as well as through the monopolies that entitled them to control particular fishing grounds and catches. A secondary group of fish merchants, lacking either any entitlements to engage in long-distance trade or any specified obligation to the regime, developed at Nihonbashi and elsewhere as quasi-wholesale/quasi-retail traders, commonly known as "middle traders" *(nakagai)* or as "lower receivers" *(ukeshita)*. The essence of the trade was twofold: buying and selling fish that ton'ya had "imported," and then selling directly to the public. Many of the smaller ton'ya developed side businesses along these lines, and became known as *ton'ya-ken-nakagai* (wholesaler-middlemen). Middlemen without established places of business set up shop on the streets of Nihonbashi (which was a commercial center for many other trades as well),[16] bringing protests from established merchants that fish peddlers were disrupting the flow of other business. Eventually the shōgunal authorities imposed a compromise: middlemen were granted the rights to rent the areas in front of other merchants' shops—what one might think of as sidewalk space, except that Edo had no sidewalks. These rights, called "board rights" *(itafuneken)*, entitled middlemen to put out one or two large cutting boards apiece in front of shops, but only during the early morning hours.

Most of the major institutions and practices of the Nihonbashi market were well established and set in place by the early eighteenth century. Over time, however, the cost of jōnō grew oppressive; inflation on the one hand and the increasingly autocratic bureaucracy of the shōgunate on the other undercut those benefits of feudal protection and patronage that the system had originally provided. Repeatedly, wholesalers and fishing villages alike sought relief from the shōgunate, which sometimes assisted with land grants, the revenue from which would supposedly subsidize costs incurred in providing the fish required by the jōnō system.

Cheating was rampant. Fish merchants designed baskets with false bottoms to conceal high-quality fish; others hid fish at the bottoms of cesspools and latrines, hoping that official inspectors would not search carefully. In 1792 a new and more powerful fish office was established to regulate the trade, and its officials relentlessly extracted their due from the daily traffic in fish. Throughout the remainder of the Tokugawa period, conflicts between the fish offices and the ton'ya were frequent. Although many reforms and countermeasures were tried, none addressed the basic structural problems at the heart of the jōnō system.

Protests over the shōgunal authorities' onerous regulations, their attempts to crack down on cheating wholesalers, and reforms to correct the institutional problems all continued apace, but for nearly a century from the 1720s onward relatively little changed. By the 1830s and 1840s, however,

Figure 27. Hiding fish to avoid the tax collector. Sketch by Mori Kazan.

the political and economic power of the Tokugawa regime was in serious
danger of collapse. In the face of rising debts to the merchant classes, the
Tokugawa regime systematically debased the currency nineteen times
between 1819 and 1837. Samurai stipends (paid as fixed amounts of rice)
had long since fallen behind inflation. The regime's dependence on the
despised merchant classes clashed with its attempts to reexert feudal control
over what had become a highly sophisticated domestic economy (see
Schaede 1991; Hanley 1997). During the Tempō era (1830–44), reformers
within the shōgunal government tried to purify the economic system of
endemic corruption and to revitalize the political regime. Among many
other measures, in 1841 the shōgunate revoked the system of feudal
monopolies and ton'ya licensing. This reform was expected to lower prices;
instead, the result was wild speculation in commodities, massive inflation,
and general economic chaos. In 1851 the authorities reinstated the monopolies and guilds. Throughout this economic turmoil, the shōgunate retained
the jōnō system, and Nihonbashi's dealers remained obligated to supply the
castle with the finest catches. But the larger political and economic problems
of the Tokugawa regime continued to worsen and in the 1850s and 1860s,
rebellious clans began to rally against the Tokugawa regime in a movement
to depose the shōgun and restore imperial rule.

In the last days of the shōgunate in 1868, as armies supporting the Meiji Restoration neared the city, the Tokugawa regime appealed to the Nihonbashi wholesalers to raise troops to defend Edo. The ton'ya hesitated, loyal to the ancien régime but befuddled by this request from warriors that *they*, merchants, should take up arms. At a meeting to discuss the request, support for the shōgun—or, more likely, support for Edo—finally won the day. Fish dealers recalled that when Commodore Perry had anchored his black ships off Uraga in 1853 (coincidentally in the vicinity of the port office that regulated ton'ya shipping) and the residents of Edo had been on the verge of panic, the Nihonbashi ton'ya had bravely sent their boats out to inspect the fearsome foreign fleet. If we men of Nihonbashi could face down foreign invaders, the argument ran, how can we do less when the warriors marching on our city are simply Japanese bumpkins? (The invading armies were from the distant southern provinces of Satsuma and Chōshū.) Emboldened, the uogashi raised a body of 1,000 men, armed them with staves and pikes and huge fish cleavers, dressed them with headbands clearly marked with the symbol of the fish market (prudently assuming that if the fighting went against them, their attackers would recognize them—perhaps spare them—as mere fishmongers, not warriors), and laid plans for the defense of central Edo around Nihonbashi and Edobashi.

Their valor was never tested. The battle never came. Their pride as defenders of the city went unchallenged. The shōgunate fell.[17]

From the Meiji Restoration to the Kantō Earthquake

With the success of the Meiji Restoration in 1868, which replaced the shōgunate with nominally direct imperial rule, Japan's leaders began to establish the strongly centralized Meiji government, which was intent on unifying and strengthening the nation to resist and ultimately to equal the Western powers. To that end, the Meiji state launched policies to direct and channel massive changes in almost every realm of political, social, economic, and cultural life.

From the parochial perspective of Nihonbashi fish merchants, the most stunning immediate transformation was the Meiji government's decision in 1872 to close the shōgunate's fish offices and abolish the jōnō system. The merchants gained newfound economic freedom, but this was scant comfort as Tokyo tottered near economic collapse. When the shōgunate was disbanded, the Meiji government ordered samurai in the service of the shōgun and the regional lords to "return" to their home provinces. Although many samurai families had lived in Edo for generations as part of their lords' permanent retinues in the capital, they officially had residences elsewhere;

many went "home" as if to exile (McClellan 1985). With their departure, the city's population plummeted, by as much as 600,000, to a little more than half of its previous size (H. D. Smith II 1979: 51). A good number of samurai and former shōgunal officials remained, of course, but many of them were impoverished, as the Meiji government first reduced their hereditary stipends and then eliminated the stipends altogether. Poverty trickled down and Tokyo's tradespeople suffered.

But people must eat, and the fish market, of course, stayed in business, freed from feudal regulation and deprived of officially licensed monopolies, yet still operating through established trade channels already well developed and easily adapted to capitalism. The control and exploitation of fisheries by Nihonbashi merchants continued in familiar ways. The old system of "proprietary coasts" *(mochi-ura)*, also known as "subcontracted coasts" *(ura-ukeoi)*—that is, fishing grounds controlled exclusively by wholesalers—remained intact as merchants in Tokyo or in local fishing ports consolidated their power over entire fishing villages through loans and capital advances to local fishing bosses *(amimoto)*.[18] Although such relationships had been cemented in the past by varieties of capitalist exploitation masked by feudal privilege, during the Meiji period overt, unfettered capitalism was the rule. Wholesalers obtained exclusive rights to purchase catches at predetermined prices from fishers in exchange for long-term loans of capital and advances on operating expenses. Ties between wholesalers and fishers were those of creditor and debtor. Little or no competition existed among buyers; producers and suppliers could trade only with those to whom they were already in debt. And the chance to escape from debt was slight.

Changing patterns of economic control simply extended wholesalers' domination over fishers in new ways. Nonetheless, conditions for wholesalers shifted substantially. Without monopoly rights backed by feudal authority, wholesalers themselves had to compete with one another to control supplies and markets. With the loss of feudal protection and privilege, Tokyo's fish market became a far more fluid place. The old distinctions between ton'ya and nakagai—wholesalers who controlled the fish coming into Tokyo, and quasi-wholesaler/quasi-retailer merchants whose businesses lay entirely in the city—remained, but the lines became blurred. Many old family firms went out of business, unable to adjust to new conditions and competition from new entrepreneurs. The number of ton'ya increased and many more ton'ya operated as combined ton'ya-nakagai. During 1881 and 1882, for example, in the city as a whole, the number of wholesalers fluctuated between 318 and 503, and the number of middlemen ranged between 297 and 481.[19]

In 1889 the fish market's location became an urban planning issue. Tokyo officials sought to remove the market from the commercial heart of the modernizing city. The unseemliness of a messy, smelly marketplace in the center of the city's financial district—outside the windows of the new Bank of Japan—offended Meiji bureaucratic sensibilities, and officials argued for relocation on the grounds of sanitation, public health, and the logistical difficulties of transportation around Nihonbashi. Many Nihonbashi fish merchants stoutly resisted pressure from the Tokyo municipal government to move, and proposals to relocate the marketplace were delayed, derailed, or debated to a standstill again and again. Over the next generation, two factions—one pro-relocation, the other adamantly opposed—developed within the marketplace, with the anti-relocation camp skillfully exploiting its political clout to resist the move. A major point was compensation for rights of access to space in the marketplace, especially the ephemeral but by no means inexpensive land-use rights implied by the long-established "board rights" *(itafuneken)* exercised by fish merchants who set up for business in the early morning hours in front of shops and offices in Nihonbashi. Supporters of a relocation were generally newer ton'ya and nakagai without extensive property or usage rights in the Nihonbashi area. Resistance by Nihonbashi's established merchants and their political allies blocked any action by the municipal government.

The issue was settled—as if by a deus ex machina—on September 1, 1923, when the Kantō earthquake struck the city just before noon, when cooking fires were alight everywhere. The quake—with a magnitude estimated at approximately 7.8 on the Richter scale—and the fires it sparked destroyed more than 700,000 buildings, killed close to 100,000 people, and left 60 percent of the survivors homeless. On both land and water the destruction was nearly total. Boats and barges burned to their waterlines, choking the canals of Tokyo and paralyzing supply lines to the Nihonbashi market. Tokyo's fishing fleet was pulled out of service and put to the gruesome task of pulling corpses from the waters of the bay. At least 20,000 people drowned, particularly in shitamachi areas such as Honjo and Fukagawa, where people had sought refuge in canals to escape the raging fires (Dahlmann 1924: 93–98).

Nihonbashi's devastation was no greater and no less than that of the city as a whole. Within a day or two, facing the reality of the destruction, most of the surviving Nihonbashi merchants met and agreed to organize a temporary fish market at Shibaura (south of the central city, near the present-day Hamamatsu-chō Station), which opened for business under tents on September 17. It remained there only until December, when again the market moved—this time to Tsukiji, to the site of the old naval training acad-

Figure 28. "Before the Earthquake—West from Nihonbashi (Bridge), Tokyo, Japan." American stereopticon slide (Keystone View Company, no. V14945). Reproduced with permission of the Morita Photo Laboratory.

emy. Eventually the municipal government and a majority of the Nihon-bashi traders concurred that here a new, permanent marketplace would be erected. Meanwhile, immediately after the earthquake, a die-hard anti-relo-cation faction of Nihonbashi dealers attempted to reopen for business at Nihonbashi, with permission granted by a local police official. For several days they operated amid the rubble until the municipal government forcibly closed the marketplace for good. The police official who granted permission to the merchants to reopen at Nihonbashi was summarily transferred to Hokkaidō, the shops were closed, and some disgruntled Nihonbashi dealers left the fish business forever (Takarai 1991: 97–98).

The physical relocation of the marketplace to Tsukiji after the destruction of the old Nihonbashi market coincided with major political and economic reforms initiated by the national government to stabilize urban food sup-plies and reduce or eliminate speculation in and oligopolistic control over basic foodstuffs. These reforms were a direct response to the so-called Rice Riots (Kome Sōdō) that convulsed the country in 1918. The riots began as a protest against spiraling rice prices in a small fishing village on the Toyama coast. There the control of local fishing grounds by amimoto was near absolute, and most Toyama fishers had had to turn to migratory work, ship-ping out as crew members bound for the fishing grounds off Hokkaidō and the Siberian coast (Lewis 1990: 37–40). The underlying discontent was widespread, and economic conditions for working people in rural and urban

areas alike had been dire for many years. Within eight weeks of the first violence in Toyama, riots had broken out in 141 towns and cities across the
country. The protests' immediate targets were rice dealers accused of profi-
teering from the inflation of rice prices, but, more generally, speculative
control of the food supply was at issue; rioters attacked any "middleman
group unfairly taking advantage of scarcity" (Lewis 1990: 107).

In the aftermath of the riots, reformers proposed major legal reforms in
the distribution of foodstuffs (Lewis 1990: xix). One was to create a system
of nationally regulated central wholesale markets *(chūō oroshiuri shijō)* for
the sale and distribution of perishable foodstuffs. In 1923 national legislation, the Central Wholesale Market Law (Chūō Oroshiuri Shijō-Hō), established these markets in six major cities. The first central wholesale market
opened in Kyoto in December 1927, formed by a merger of twelve privately
operated marketplaces.

The law established several important principles: it defined the range of
perishable commodities in which such markets could deal; it mandated
municipal ownership and administration of the markets; it clearly separated
the spheres of activities of ton'ya and nakagai; it regulated the commissions
that could be charged by traders; it allowed for other private markets to
coexist with central wholesale markets; and it established an auction system
to ensure fair and open pricing. The new central wholesale market system
promised to curtail the activities of ton'ya whose operations spanned financ-
ing of fishing enterprises, monopolistic control over entire catches of particular villages or fisheries, price-fixing and attempts to corner markets, and
distribution of products at both the wholesale and retail levels through
exclusive marketing agreements with secondary wholesalers *(nakagai)*. By
instituting publicly supervised auctions as the major price-setting and
allocative mechanism within central wholesale markets and by setting new
licensing requirements for participants in the new wholesale markets, the
new system split the various functions embodied by the old ton'ya among
firms located on discrete levels within the marketing hierarchy (e.g., the
contemporary consignment auction houses, or *oroshi gyōsha;* intermediate
wholesalers, known at the time as *nakagainin;* and so forth).

None of these reforms was uncontroversial, and even as the temporary
market opened at Tsukiji and the Tokyo government began to plan construction of a permanent marketplace, heated negotiations continued
between fish dealers and the municipal (and national) governments over
financial issues. The problem of "board rights" *(itafuneken)*—the rights to
lease and use space in front of shops in Nihonbashi—proved particularly

intractable. The shops that benefited from these rights demanded compensation of ¥7,000,000 for the losses they suffered in the relocation. Over the years, the issue took on a life of its own. In 1928 it engulfed the Tokyo Municipal Assembly; open bribery by advocates of compensation became so flagrant that the Home Minister intervened to cancel a proposed settlement of the claims and to dissolve the assembly itself (Seidensticker 1990: 90–91). The board rights issue lingered unresolved until 1942, when, because the marketplace was tightly controlled as part of the wartime mobilization, the merchants were forced to settle for only ¥500,000 (Tōto Suisan 1987: 1.92).

THE TSUKIJI MARKETPLACE, 1923–50

Although the marketplace was physically relocated to Tsukiji in 1923, the new institutional framework of the market was not inaugurated until new facilities were completed in 1935. Many of Nihonbashi's ton'ya joined together to establish a major auction house (oroshi gyōsha)—Tōkyō Uoichiba K.K.—to supply the marketplace under the new auction-based rules. The company was created only after much wrangling and political maneuvering among the surviving firms from Nihonbashi. The major debate—known as the *tanpuku mondai* (the "one-or-several problem")—centered on the question of whether there should be one or several such supply houses. As was frequently the case, the debate was settled by political intrigue, bribery, and intimidation. A competing supply house sprang up, only to be quickly put out of business.

Some ton'ya took the path that linked them with the market's upstream suppliers by joining Tōkyō Uoichiba K.K.; other ton'ya, ton'ya-cum-naka-gai, and nakagai entered the new market regime as intermediate wholesalers (called, in the new system, *nakagainin*) trading within the marketplace and supplying retailers further downstream. Although the earlier marketplace regimes had usually separated these aspects of the trade, these distinctions were now made institutionally clear and in principle absolute: relations upstream with producers would be in the hands of auction houses; nakagainin would take charge of relations downstream; and relations between upstream and downstream would sort themselves out through competitive auctions.

In February 1935 the new Tsukiji marketplace opened as an official central wholesale market with divisions for produce, poultry, and freshwater fish. Later in the year, in June, sales of salted and dried fish began, followed in December by the start of trade in fresh fish.[20] During the market's first full year of operation, it handled 183,000 metric tons of seafood valued at ¥45 million, more than $20 million in 1936 dollars (Tōkyō-to Chūō Oroshiuri Shijō 1985: 9).

By the late 1930s, however, with Japan's domestic economy increasingly under quasi-military control, the hard-won institutional arrangements of the new marketplace were modified while still in their infancy. Japan's aggression in China grew year by year, and the national government increasingly put the domestic Japanese economy on a war footing. In July 1937—the month that the Marco Polo Bridge incident ignited undeclared war with China—the national government imposed price controls, and the following month it sought to regulate excess profits. In March 1940 the cabinet issued emergency policies for rationing foodstuffs. Price levels were fixed in August and September for both produce and fresh seafood, and actual rationing of seafood began in April 1941. In October 1941, less than seven years after the marketplace had begun operations, the system of nakagainin was abolished. In July 1944 all activities of the seafood division of Tsukiji were amalgamated into a single corporation, the Tokyo Marine Products Control Corporation (Tōkyō Suisanbutsu Tōsei K.K.). The ton'ya and nakagai of Nihonbashi reunited institutionally, this time as employees of a corporation whose goals were simply to distribute what little seafood could reach Tokyo's civilian population.

Allied naval operations during World War II, which Japanese often refer to as the "Pacific War," destroyed the Japanese fishing industry, particularly the distant-water fishing fleets, as well as shipping capacity for foodstuffs— whether agricultural products or seafood—reaching Japan's home islands from its colonial empire: Taiwan, Korea, Manchuria, parts of Southeast Asia, and the Pacific islands (Tsutsui 2002; Bourgois 1950). On the home front, military requisitions of foodstuffs took precedence over civilian consumption. And American air raids destroyed much of the nation's rail network, so civilian distribution of foodstuffs of any sort was extremely limited. Seafood was available only to the extent that local coastal fishing—not relying on gasoline-powered vessels—could supply nearby consumers. Civilian evacuations from Tokyo and other major cities in the last years of World War II—first of schoolchildren, later of adults—were at least implicitly intended to move the urban population to areas where food might be available.

During the war, American air raids destroyed most of central Tokyo through relentless bombing, most horrifically in the incendiary raids of March 9–10, 1945, over the shitamachi districts of Tokyo. That night at least 80,000 residents died (Daniels 1975). The Tsukiji area escaped major damage. Some residents say the Americans were careful not to bomb Tsukiji because St. Luke's Hospital still remained on the site of the old foreign settlement; others simply thank St. Luke directly.

The market facilities were largely intact when the Allied Occupation began in September 1945, but food supplies were extremely scarce. That fall, in the first flush of reformist zeal to eliminate all vestiges of the wartime regime, the Occupation authorities initially eliminated food rationing and price controls. Almost immediately, realizing that the Japanese population faced a very real threat of mass starvation, the authorities reversed themselves and restored stringent controls over food distribution. Food controls continued until 1950, and the wartime institutions of the marketplace remained largely unchanged until then. The marketplace continued to operate simply as a distribution hub. American forces took over large sections of the Tsukiji marketplace, in which they housed a motor pool and a laundry for nearby Occupation offices and billets in the Ginza and Marunouchi districts. The Occupation left Tsukiji's seafood division largely untouched, but commandeered much of what is now the vegetable division. Civilian control over all Tsukiji facilities resumed in the summer of 1955.

The postwar recovery of Japanese fishing was a priority for Occupation policy makers, for several reasons. One goal was that Japan should become self-sufficient in food production as rapidly as possible. Another was to dismantle Japan's prewar colonial empire and ensure that Japan could not reestablish control over East Asia. Japan's possessions (e.g., Korea, Taiwan, Manchuria, and various territories in the South Pacific)[21] had helped to supply the home islands with foodstuffs—including seafood, grains, and processed foods—before the war. These colonial sources of food supply were disrupted, and then, of course, entirely severed by the end of the war. Reviving Japan's production and distribution of foodstuffs—and putting markets like Tsukiji back into operation—therefore required efforts not merely to restore food supply channels that had existed previously, but to restructure Japan's food supply in light of the country's new position in the world. Protein and calories would have to come to Japan through its own efforts.

An unexpected environmental benefit of naval warfare among humans is a breathing spell for fish (Tsutsui 2002). When Japanese fishing resumed, it found unusually abundant fisheries resources in the Western Pacific. Traditional, small-scale coastal fisheries had been the least affected by the war and were able to resume relatively easily. Larger fishing vessels capable of deep-water and distant-water fishing had been largely destroyed, and although the Occupation encouraged construction of modern trawlers, it established strict limits on the extent of the Western Pacific in which

Japanese vessels could fish. After 1952, the end of the Occupation, Japanese firms began to expand much more, in terms of both the size of the vessels and the areas in which they fished. However, conflicts with Korea, China, and the Soviet Union over claims to various fishing grounds pushed Japanese vessels further and further into the North and Central Pacific (Borgstrom 1964: 22–33).

On another front, the Occupation authorities encouraged the early resumption of whaling. Small-scale coastal whaling resumed immediately. Japan's fleet of whaling factory ships had been lost during the war, but in 1946 new factory ships started whaling around the Bonin Islands and in Antarctic waters. In 1952, factory ship whaling resumed in the North Pacific.[22] Well into the 1950s, in school lunches and factory cafeterias, whale meat was a major source of Japanese protein—today remembered by some with nostalgia for their youth, by others as an unpalatable reminder of hard times.

Companies in the whaling industry were also deeply involved in the slightly later expansion of the deep-water fishing industry. As these firms developed into full-range fisheries companies, they profoundly shaped Japan's food supply—a phenomenon that I will look at more closely in chapter 5—and of course affected markets like Tsukiji.

In the late 1940s, however, as economic conditions began to improve and the food supply became more stable, traders began to anticipate the eventual decontrol of the marketplace, and private businesses that had operated in the marketplace before the wartime mobilization reincorporated themselves. Tsukiji's traders organized politically to press for the restoration of a "free" market; eventually, in the summer of 1950, the system of competitive auctions among clearly defined and separable levels of actors, licensed accordingly by the Ministry of Agriculture, Forestry and Fisheries or by the TMG, was reinstituted. The restored market regime followed the lines laid down in the 1923 Central Wholesale Market Law, which remained in force. But when wartime mobilization began to erode—and then demolish—the system, Tsukiji had operated under this regime for only a couple of years; thus the postwar restoration in fact did not return the market to its old ways but set it on an almost unfamiliar course.

TSUKIJI FROM POSTWAR TO POST-BUBBLE

Tsukiji dates its renewal from the relicensing of the intermediate wholesalers. Between June 1950 and October 1951, the TMG issued 1,647 licenses for intermediate wholesalers to operate in Tsukiji's seafood division. Under the principle of "democratizing the marketplace," all intermediate whole-salers who had had licenses when the nakagainin system was abolished in 1941 regained them almost automatically. Of the 1,647 intermediate whole-salers licensed in 1951, 1,238 (or 75 percent) had held licenses in 1941; viewed another way, 89 percent of license holders in 1941 got their licenses back when the system resumed a decade later.[23] The times were tough and unstable, however, and by 1954 the number of license holders had dropped to 1,579. These included 1,194 traders who specialized in fresh fish and 385 in dried and processed seafood (Tōkyō-to Chūō Oroshiuri Shijō 1958–63: 2.695–97). In the late 1950s an extension to the market's stalls was built and a few additional licenses were granted, bringing the total up to 1,678.[24] Today there are 1,677 valid licenses for the Tsukiji seafood division.

Across the auction blocks, more than thirty firms acquired licenses in the immediate postwar years to operate as auction houses supplying the mar-ket. Many of these new oroshi gyōsha arose from the splintering of the Tokyo Marine Products Control Corporation, the wartime company created to administer the seafood rationing system. The dominant prewar corpora-tion, Tōkyō Uoichiba K.K., reincorporated as Tōto Suisan K.K. The new company's supremacy was challenged by the economic purges initiated by the Occupation authorities against individuals who had played significant roles in the militarization of the economy, as well as the antitrust policies of the early Occupation years that encouraged competition. Some Tsukiji auc-tion houses were established at least in part with capital provided by major Japanese fisheries corporations, the most notable example being Daito Gyorui K.K., one of Tsukiji's four major full-line seafood auction houses, which was capitalized entirely by what was then the Taiyō group—now the Maruha group—of fisheries companies. Most of the newly formed auction houses—almost two dozen—were small, highly specialized, and short-lived. By the early 1960s, through bankruptcies, mergers, and acquisitions, Tsukiji's seafood auctions were conducted by the currently existing seven firms, five of them full-range, two of them specialized.

This consolidation of auction houses took place alongside the growing industrialization of the Japanese fishing industry, as large-scale, well-capi-talized corporations began to develop deep-water fishing fleets and factory ships (see Borgstrom 1964). The British fishing vessel the *Fairtry*, launched in 1954 to exploit the Grand Banks, was the world's first large-scale trawler and processing vessel—a factory ship of 2600 gross tons. The basic design was quickly copied and adapted by the fishing industries of, notably, Japan, the Soviet Union, and Poland (Woodard 2000: 74–76). Japanese firms like Taiyō Gyogyō, which had pioneered pelagic whaling in the 1920s and 1930s, quickly embraced the new technology. By the 1970s Japanese firms operated about 125 such large-scale trawler factories. These vessels and the development of new technologies for freezing or chilling fish on board propelled the Japanese fishing industry to a position as a global fishing power, operating fleets in most major fishing regions of the world's oceans. As production changed, so did the profile of supply to Tsukiji and other Japanese markets. An increasing proportion of seafood came from large fisheries corporations like Taiyō Gyogyō, Nippon Suisan, and Kyokuyō, and increasingly it was seafood from very distant waters (often in frozen form). Traditional coastal fisheries—often quite local and small-scale—declined steadily from the 1950s, and their products became less and less central to Tsukiji's business.

During the 1950s and 1960s, the fishing industry in Tokyo Bay almost completely disappeared. Industrial pollution wiped out many fishing grounds, and many areas of shallow water were filled in as large-scale land reclamation projects created tracts for still further industrial development. One such reclamation zone included the waters and mud flats off Urayasu, an old fishing village on the border between Tokyo and Chiba prefectures at the northern end of Tokyo Bay, long important for shellfish harvesting.

As both the national government and Chiba's prefectural administration pushed forward with land reclamation schemes for the Urayasu tidal flats, negotiations began over payment to the fishers for the loss of their ancestral fishing grounds and their contemporary livelihoods. In customary law and (since the nineteenth century) administrative law as well, Japanese fishing communities have held collective rights of sea tenure *(gyogyōken)* over specified fishing grounds (Ruddle and Akimichi 1984, 1989; Marra 1986; Kalland 1995). Nowadays the rights belong to and are administered by local fisheries cooperatives *(gyogyō kyōdō kumiai)*. The Urayasu cooperative negotiated skillfully for compensation for the community's loss of ancestral fishing grounds, and they finally reached agreements with developers and the prefectural government for substantial cash settlements as well as rights to some of the land that would be reclaimed.[25]

For generations, Urayasu fishers—as harvesters of clams and other shellfish—maintained extensive connections to the wholesale and retail seafood trade in Tokyo. Peddlers from Urayasu sold shellfish door-to-door in Tokyo, retail fishmongers in Tokyo bought some shellfish directly from Urayasu traders, and some Urayasu shellfish went to Tsukiji's auctions. Land reclamation ended the shellfish business, but left the Urayasu fishers with strong ties to Tsukiji and with the newfound capital to pursue these connections further. Many of the fishers ended up at Tsukiji, first as employees of intermediate wholesalers and then, after they acquired experience in the wholesale trade, as the purchasers of wholesale licenses. Today, roughly 10 or 15 percent of the intermediate wholesaling firms at Tsukiji are regarded as "Urayasu firms." These firms form an influential network marked by informal cooperation and common interest (which I discuss in more detail in chapter 6). Typically, they are in the shellfish business or in related specialties (such as supplying sushi chefs), but firms owned by Urayasu traders also include some of Tsukiji's largest and most prosperous, high-profile tuna wholesalers.

In the late 1960s, at about the same time that the Urayasu *renchū*—the "Urayasu crowd"—was beginning to become prominent in the market, the issue of market relocation surfaced once again. The arguments were familiar. Tsukiji traders, officials of the marketplace, and bureaucrats from the national government agreed that the marketplace wedged into the center of Tokyo was inconveniently situated and too cramped to handle the needs of the enormous metropolis. The market's wastes added to the pollution of the Sumida River. And transportation was growing ever more difficult, as trucks replaced boats and rail in supplying the market. But resistance to relocation arose in familiar ways, echoing the opposition voiced in earlier generations. Who would compensate Tsukiji traders for losses they might suffer if the micro-advantages bestowed by the present system and their present location were upset? What would happen to all the businesses in the outer marketplace whose trade depended on proximity to the Tsukiji marketplace?

The administration of the TMG was at the time in the hands of Governor Minobe Ryōkichi (who held office for three terms from 1967 to 1979), elected by a center-left coalition. With strong progressive, populist, and consumerist leanings, his administration was considered—by people at Tsukiji, at least—to be antagonistic to business, and particularly to businesses such as theirs, businesses perceived to profit from adding margins between producer and consumer. Minobe's administration, his Tsukiji critics argue, simply never understood the marketplace and the real work performed by auction houses and intermediate wholesalers, and hence was unsympathetic to traders' protests over the proposed relocation. The TMG went ahead with its planning, putting all efforts into creating a new marketplace rather than into renovating or reconstructing the existing one. The site for the new market was on landfill being extended at Ōta just to the north of Haneda Airport, in the southern fringe of the city. As the landfill gradually took shape, the TMG administration changed; moreover, the fiscal climate of public works projects shifted when, in the late 1970s and early 1980s, "deficit-ridden" and "public finance" became practically a single term. The project languished; with the landfill complete and plans drawn up, no funds for construction were appropriated. Tsukiji traders continued their resistance to an uncertain future.

As the financial climate for public works projects revived during the Bubble years, Tsukiji's traders found support—another serendipity—in unsuspected quarters. Over the years that the landfill had stood unused, wild birds had taken up the marshy ground as a refuge, and during the same years the incipient Japanese conservation and environmental movements had gained strength, opposing the despoliation of the environment that had characterized the high-growth years of industrial expansion in the 1950s and 1960s. As construction plans were dusted off, environmentalists demanded the creation of a wild bird sanctuary. Faced with this outcry, with the opposition of the Tsukiji merchants, with the unavailability of any other large parcel of land, and with the fiscal consequences of delay in an era of ever-increasing construction costs, the Tokyo government compromised. The birds got their sanctuary on part of the land; the plans were scaled down to create a market primarily for produce (with less environmental impact in terms of water use and sanitation); and Tsukiji traders were given the option of voluntarily relocating into the much smaller than originally intended seafood division of the Ōta Market, an option that few accepted. When the seafood division of the Ōta Market opened for business in the fall of 1990, only about three dozen Tsukiji traders had moved there—some only after exacting major financial concessions from the TMG—and about one-third of the stalls stood vacant.

The Tsukiji marketplace remained intact and in place. But the problems the marketplace faced—location, crowding, ancient facilities—also remained, exacerbated perhaps by the TMG's inattention while it pursued the Ōta project. During the long period while the Ōta Market was being planned, debated, and delayed, the physical infrastructure of the Tsukiji marketplace was frozen in bureaucratic limbo. At the same time, the context of Tsukiji's business was changing dramatically (as I will discuss in greater detail in the next chapter). In the 1970s, the Japanese fishing industry began to withdraw from distant-water fisheries, excluded by new 200-mile fishing limits in many parts of the world; at roughly the same time Japanese economic power began to enable direct imports of seafood from ever-widening regions of the globe, and the international seafood supply began to move away from fisheries companies and into the hands of general trading companies (sōgō shōsha). As global supply channels shifted, domestic distribution began to change as well. Supermarkets became increasingly commonplace, and Tsukiji faced a new customer mix with fewer small-scale retailers and more large chain stores. Frozen seafood came to occupy an increasingly large share of the market's sales, but sales of the finest fresh fish also flourished as Japan's prosperity fostered gourmet consumption. Coastal fishing declined; seafood arrived at Tsukiji more and more often by truck (and air freight) and less and less by rail or fishing vessel. None of these trends originated in the marketplace, as they reflected wider social and economic factors of Japanese growth, but their impacts were all felt in Tsukiji's trade and in the ability to carry on with the existing infrastructure of the aging marketplace.

At long last, plans were drawn up to reconstruct the Tsukiji marketplace, a particularly complex and delicate process since the market would remain in operation throughout the construction. Preliminary reconstruction started in 1990, with the clearing away of some minor buildings and the construction of some temporary ones. When the project began, TMG planners projected that the new complex would be finished by 2003. Construction of new permanent buildings began in 1992; by 1995 work on many of the ancillary buildings such as parking garages was well under way. In the 1995 gubernatorial election, a political outsider, Aoshima Yukio, a television personality running on a platform of fiscal austerity, unexpectedly beat the incumbent Suzuki Shin'ichi (who had been in office for four terms from 1979 to 1995). Among Aoshima's first moves was to cancel an ambitious waterfront reconstruction and world's fair. Less publicly dramatic measures included shelving plans to rebuild Tsukiji, with construction actually suspended in 1996. Most of the auction arenas and the wholesalers' stalls had not yet been touched when construction was halted. Nothing further happened during the remainder of Governor Aoshima's single term, and when Ishihara Shintarō, a well-known conservative politician and bestselling author, became governor in 1999, the issue was still on hold, with the expectation that plans for either a move or reconstruction would be announced sometime in 2000. As it turned out, not until late 2001 did the TMG announce its decision to begin planning an entirely new market complex for construction in Toyosu, on the eastern side of the Sumida delta, with a completion date first projected for 2012 or 2013.

Left suspended in 1996, with the existing marketplace torn up and no clear idea of whether, when, or even where new buildings might be started, Tsukiji traders worried—and continue to worry even after a new planning process was announced in 2001—about how trade would be affected by construction or relocation. Now they worry whether a new marketplace will function differently from the present one, whether their own businesses will survive to see that new market, and, if or when the new market actually opens, how some of them might (or might not) be compensated for any loss of rights and privileges they suffer in the transition. Some groups of traders strongly supported the idea of moving to Toyosu well before it became official; others were equally adamant in opposing *any* move. Everyone wants new, state-of-the-art facilities, but beyond that, the economic interests at stake vary enormously; auction houses and supermarket chains want the best possible transportation access, and see a new location as preferable to remaining in Tsukiji's awkward surroundings. Larger, more prosperous stallholders who see their businesses as dependent on solid market infrastructure also favor the construction of state-of-the-art facilities at a new location. Smaller stallholders, who are often dependent on walk-in trade, and many of their customers—chefs and independent retailers—prefer Tsukiji for its convenient accessibility from central Tokyo, and simply worry that given the economic troubles that began in the 1990s, they will not be able to afford the costs of a move in any event.

PAST PRESENT

In this chapter I have outlined Tsukiji's past, less to technically reconstruct the market's social or economic history than to illustrate the present-day understandings, the cultural accounts of the past known by, shared among, and elaborated by contemporary participants who situate themselves, their jobs, and their identities against this backdrop. In chapter 2, I sketched the physical and temporal structure of activities in the contemporary marketplace. These two perspectives are intertwined in complex ways. Time and space significantly shape social relationships and institutions. The time and space of present-day activity as well as the sense of place-and-identity are constructed out of accounts of the past. Such accounts fit the present into a trajectory of culturally coherent causality; they cloak the spatial and temporal patterns of here and now with a particular historical identity and a sense of direction.

The distinctiveness of place is not simply a product of Tsukiji's cultural boundaries in the time and space of the here and now. The past is fertile ground, and Tsukiji's legacy and the vast accumulation of market lore also serve to firmly establish the marketplace's distinctive identity as a distant and impenetrable place. As I have argued elsewhere, "traditionalism" is a device of cultural ideology that wraps the present in a mantle of venerable antiquity, thereby legitimating the social present by calling attention to its presumed antecedents and origins in the culturally sacrosanct past (T. Bestor 1989, 1992b).

These are critical tasks at Tsukiji in part because sharp institutional breaks mark the history of the marketplace. Time and time again, the entire fabric of market relationships and their institutional framework has been torn apart and rewoven. Culture reassembles the pieces, reshaping the past to maintain the present's insistence on venerable continuity. The present clumsily unfolds itself from the past in particular and idiosyncratic ways. Traditionalism reconfigures this unfolding into a sequence of inevitability. It constructs time and space to establish the significance of place—of being *here* by virtue of having been *there*. If the past is a foreign country, traditionalism is the agency that issues tourist visas to some, even as it grants permanent citizenship to others.

4   The Raw and the Cooked

Food culture is neither foreordained by nature nor an immutable aspect of a society's life. Indeed, if nations are "imagined communities" (Anderson 1983), then food culture equally imagines national cuisines as organized around essential traits: and—other than rice—what is more essential and essentialized in Japanese cuisine than seafood? Fish and the arts associated with its preparation and consumption are central to Japan's culinary heritage, itself near the emotional core of national identity. In English, "food culture" is an expression used perhaps only by anthropologists and restaurant reviewers. But equivalent Japanese phrases—*shoku bunka* and *shoku seikatsu* ("food culture" and "culinary life," respectively)—commonly appear in the Japanese press, on television, and, of course, around the marketplace. The origins of particular dishes; the harvesting and preparation of ingredients; and the proper techniques, preferred seasonal combinations, ideal implements, and appropriate accouterments for their preparation and consumption all attract wide attention.

Seafood is a pillar of Japanese cuisine, and odd bits and pieces of food lore adhere like barnacles to its consumption and preparation: Why are sea bream *(tai)* so highly prized? Because they are served at weddings and other auspicious events, for their congratulatory *(omedetai)* red-and-white coloring. Why are whole lobsters not served at weddings? Because their claws resemble scissors, which cannot be given as wedding gifts. Why is poisonous *fugu* (blowfish or pufferfish) a great delicacy? Because the numbness it induces exquisitely tickles one's senses when (or if) they return. Why do so few women sell fish in the market and why are there no female sushi chefs? Because—some men say—women's hands are warmer than men's and hence adversely affect the flavor of raw seafood.[1] Or so goes Tsukiji's folklore. Although homespun "explanations" such as these provide sushi chefs with material for endless hours of chatter with inquisitive foreigners, the features of culinary classification that fundamentally move the market are far more subtle and far more complex.

The seas provide a seemingly infinite variety of fish, and as fish become food, they become even more intricately variegated. The marketplace plays a central role in this transformation, not simply through the distributive processes of buying and selling fish. Rather, the Tsukiji marketplace and its counterparts throughout Japan are institutions in which the more subtle cultural processes that differentiate fish are accomplished according to the dictates—often changing, sometimes fickle—of culinary preference. The marketplace and its daily transactions are set into motion by and delicately synchronized along channels that assign meanings and uses, and hence economically calculable values, to particular species and grades of fish.

Marketplace practices follow from the logic of seafood within Japanese cuisine. Such cultural frameworks form the basis for what Pierre Bourdieu (1984) refers to as discrimination and taste, the raisons d'être for the professional roles of Tsukiji traders: the abilities to differentiate and validate shades of quality from which chefs and their clients can draw the satisfaction of knowing that *they* are connoisseurs. Such distinctions not only involve expert knowledge of the intrinsic qualities of seafood—a not inconsiderable attention to freshness, visual appeal, seasonality, and purity (in terms both of food safety and of ritual meaning)—but also a host of other factors such as the salience of secular seasons and ritual holidays, the aesthetics of food preparation and presentation, the regional identities embodied in specific cuisines or types of seafood, and the delicate balancing of culinary authenticity and national identity with desires for cosmopolitan consumption. These considerations, and many more, constitute the culinary logic of commodification, whereby fish become food to which economic values are attached. And finally, the translation of these principles and preferences into practice through Tsukiji's daily transactions produces and reproduces the social structure of the marketplace. Tsukiji's daily workings are organized around culinary categories and in turn create and reflect the wider patterns of food distribution and consumption that surround the marketplace.

Japanese cuisine molds the market's broad contours. But food culture is not just the abstract culinary principles of cuisine and the practices, both culinary and social, of cooking and eating. It is formed as well by myriad practical circumstances of the production and distribution of foodstuffs in social, political, historical, environmental, and at times global contexts. At Tsukiji, food culture in this broad sense is shaped by the social institutions and values of capitalism as a cultural system; traditional patterns of Japanese mercantile life; the political economy of the Japanese fishing industry; Japan's ever-changing dependence on global sources of food supply; new technologies for food processing, storage, and distribution; the structure of retailing and of the restaurant industry; trends of change in Japanese domestic living; and the complicated intersections of class and consumption.

As purveyors of fine seafoods, Tsukiji's traders—both small- and large-scale—regard themselves as stewards of Japan's culinary heritage, a not insignificant role to assign themselves, given the centrality of cuisine in defining Japanese identity and tradition. But day-to-day, they are traders who live by their economic wits. In the most straightforward terms, their daily job is to correctly evaluate supply and demand. These are common-sense terms in the vocabulary of capitalism, but in reality they are mundane shorthand for subtle calculations of extremely complex cultural and social trends well beyond the inherent daily fluctuations of the marketplace. What matters for professional traders in the longer term—and what they try to divine in the daily movements of prices—are trends of supply and demand that encompass the whole gamut of cultural, social, political, technological, and environmental contexts that make up food culture in the broad sense.

Although much of the economic life of a Tsukiji trader may seem at least superficially similar to that of a trader in steel or foreign exchange or wid-gets, it is distinctively shaped by the simple fact that *this* marketplace revolves around highly perishable commodities with vastly elaborate cul-tural connotations and equally complex patterns of production, distribu-tion, and consumption, all of which change rapidly. As a practical matter, food culture—cuisine in the abstract, as well as the social realities of pro-ducing, selling, shopping, cooking, and eating—cannot be reduced to one thing or another; the market's trading mechanisms and the culinary prefer-ences of professional traders and ordinary consumers are steered simulta-neously by both ideal and material concerns.

CUISINE AND PRACTICAL REASON

Much anthropological writing on food focuses on structural principles of classification and cognition, and on food's significance as an element in social exchange and the definition of the self. But food circulates not only in moral but also in monetized economies. Economies require institutions of trade, and trade involves commodities. Anthropologists such as Jack Goody (1982) and Sidney Mintz (1985, 1996b) have analyzed the elaborate social contexts of trade and commodity flows that surround the production, dis-tribution, and consumption of foodstuffs, particularly in industrial (or industrializing) societies. Other scholars, particularly Arjun Appadurai (1986a, 1986b, 1990) and Igor Kopytoff (1986), provide important insights on how exchange rates may be set between moral and monetized values as commodities take cultural form. The practices of seafood markets like Tsukiji in producing, reproducing, and attaching meanings that organize and are organized by Japanese cuisine provide a lens through which we can examine the ongoing cultural construction of commodities firmly grounded amid the social institutions of modern trade.

As fish change hands at Tsukiji and are carted out the market's gates, the finishing touches are put on the transformation of fish into food, a process that begins when they are pulled from the water (or even before, as commercial fishers ply their craft with the market's needs and preferences in mind). Fish are differentiated into culturally relevant categories of commodities as they pass along channels of distribution leading to and through the complex social institutions of the marketplace. Fish become commodities in the hands of traders whose calculations of value and utility are shaped by principles of Japanese culinary logic. The cultural valuation of commodities as they become distinctive items of cuisine is, of course, the basis for the economic valuation of these products as items of trade.

Writing about the process of commodification as a central feature of any economy, moral or monetized, Kopytoff has argued that commodities, commonsensically defined as objects with a value both for use and for exchange, are intrinsically cultural constructions: "For the economist, commodities simply *are*. . . . From a cultural perspective, the production of commodities is also a cultural and cognitive process: commodities must be not only produced materially as things, but also culturally marked as being a certain kind of thing" (1986: 64; emphasis added). Kopytoff proposes that the cultural nature of commodities—and of the processes, inherent to any system of exchange, that mark and classify goods—manifests itself in "cultural biographies of things": that is, the "careers" or "life trajectories" of goods within the social contexts of their production, exchange, and consumption. Along such trajectories, objects acquire or shed meanings, identities, and implied qualities that render them worthy of use and exchange. Without this culturally constructed valuation, goods can have no value as a commodity in the sense of objects of *either* social or economic exchange.

Tuna or shrimp or octopus are too unfamiliar to most Americans even to possess cultural biographies (with the possible exception of Charlie the Tuna, the spokesfish for Starkist brand canned tuna), but one can see the connections among cultural meaning, the categorization of commodities, and the institutions of exchange by comparing rabbits and cats. For Americans, these

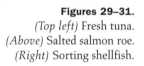

Figures 29–31.
(Top left) Fresh tuna.
(Above) Salted salmon roe.
(Right) Sorting shellfish.

animals occupy overlapping but quite different cultural spaces. Both may be pets and both are edible; although some rabbits live out their cultural biographies as adored pets, very few cats end theirs as meals (see Sahlins 1976: 170–79). The cultural structuring of commodification accounts for these divergent fates, as it leads to rabbits being sold out of galvanized tubs at farm stores (with bursts of sales just before Easter), whereas cats year-round are available either free from a shelter or at great cost from a breeder. Wild rabbits are quite literally fair game. Stray cats are not, and the distinction between wild and feral cats further complicates the categories. Feral is neither stray nor exactly wild, implying (at least for cats) a permanent escape from domestication but not necessarily from the tender attentions of humans: animal protection activists may feed and neuter feral cats, but similar efforts on behalf of wild (not feral) rabbits are hard to imagine.[2]

A colleague once jokingly objected to the relevance of this example because, he said, "No one keeps tuna as pets: you can't compare small furry mammals to larger fish that so 'obviously' deserve to be eaten." True, Americans take little cultural note of fish. Perhaps another more fishy example will make the point more clearly. Americans raised on images of clever cetaceans like Flipper are aghast that some Japanese consider dolphins a delicacy, and are befuddled to learn that although carp is also a delicacy in Japanese cuisine, some carp live for decades or longer as family treasures, traded at high price for their ornamental value. Japanese, on the other hand, regard American attitudes toward whales and dolphins as bizarre anthropomorphism and are surprised to learn of widespread American boycotts of albacore tuna to protest the by-catches of dolphins that result from *some* fishing techniques. In other words, the American and Japanese matrices within which creatures are pigeonholed as edible, ornamental, wild, or anthropomorphic are quite at odds.

In neither case—cats and rabbits, carp and dolphins—are the distinctions between the pairs of cultural biographies much related to intrinsic characteristics of these creatures: any could be eaten, any could be sold, any could be pets (or at least ornaments). Their different fates are partly the result of the various ways in which we conceive of and categorize these animals. But more important, our classification schemes motivate people to define themselves in various ways (as cat fanciers, gourmets, animal breeders, environmentalists, or commercial fishers) who create or engage themselves in different kinds of institutions (for example, humane societies, cat shows, or fishing crews), technologies (for neutering, creating hybrids, or fishing in an environmentally friendly manner), and exchange relationships (adopting pets, breeding animals commercially, or selling seafood wholesale), among other things. A cultural biography, therefore, may start from ideal categories but is inevitably shaped by the ways in which animals, goods, or services become social objects around which people organize themselves, sometimes to quite varied and different ends.

This is not the place to rehearse full biographies of tuna, or carp, or sea urchin roe.[3] Partial biographies nonetheless become obvious as one considers fish passing from hand to hand along the chains of trade that lead to and from Tsukiji. Diverse and culturally salient attributes such as nationality, domesticity, purity and pollution (both ritual and environmental), maturity, locality, form, and temporality adhere or are attached to varieties of seafood. And these cultural markings of commodities necessarily shape the social details of trade—the mosaic of prices paid, the timing and organization of sales, patterns of supply and demand, and the professional identities of sellers and buyers—that together create the social life of seafood. Tsukiji is obviously a central chapter in this biographical narrative, where seafood's varied character is constructed and embellished as fish complete their transformation into salable commodities and are then consumed.

Figure 32. Plastic sushi. Window display at a chain-store take-out sushi shop near Tsukiji.

Anthropologists endlessly theorize food classifications and the resulting food preferences and taboos. Some, notably Claude Lévi-Strauss (1966, 1970), argue that classificatory schemes for foodstuffs manifest binary or tri-angulated structural oppositions—the raw and the cooked; smoked, roasted, or boiled; free-range or genetically engineered—and that these oppositions represent (or simply *are*) the deep structures of human mentality. Materialists, on the other hand, such as Marvin Harris (1985), reject the primacy of cognitive or symbolic structures (Sahlins 1976: 166–221) and insist instead that culinary preferences are culturally explicit encodings of implicit ecological rationality. Others look at food more pragmatically. For scholars such as Goody (1982), Mintz (1985, 1997), William Roseberry (1996), and James L. Watson (1997), cultural classifications and meanings of cuisine arise from the circumstances—technological, environmental, political, and economic—of specific societies as they produce or trade or consume foodstuffs.

Goody succinctly dismisses Lévi-Strauss and others when he notes, "the presence of a concept of 'baking' [is] related to the adoption of the oven" (1982: 38). But material innovations do not by themselves alter the salience of food classifications; foodstuffs and the material circumstances that bring them forth are embedded in the highly fluid social, political, and economic contexts that structure both production and consumption. Food classifications do not exist apart from cuisine.[4] Cuisine is inextricably bound up in the complicated cultural and social contexts of consumption. And neither cuisine nor cooking and eating can exist apart from the production and distribution of foodstuffs, including what Goody refers to as "the industrialization of cuisine," a phenomenon I will return to later in this chapter.

Cuisine, in all these senses, shapes Tsukiji, and cuisine is Tsukiji's product. The complex mixtures of symbolism and material substance that circulate through and around the marketplace suggest that the food industry might better be thought of as the food culture industry. Studies of other culture industries, notably the mass media, often contrast content analyses of products with structural analyses of production and dissemination. Further, they distinguish the social relations of production (and the social worlds of producers) from those of audiences. In Tsukiji's food culture industry, too, imagery, symbolism, and social meanings of culinary content bump up against material realities of harvesting, shipping, and processing. The social contexts of production, distribution, and consumption—reflected in both symbolic and material matters onstage, offstage, and in the house—intersect and collide along complicated trajectories.

The following sections of this chapter examine various facets of the food culture industry, starting with the mass media and popular entertainment. I go on to look at cuisine and identity, and at calendars of consumption, before turning to the changing material circumstances of food supply—including the industrialization of cuisine, changes in diet and domestic living arrangements, retailing and restaurants, and foreign trade. The chapter weaves between images and trends that are experienced by consumers and those that are visible or relevant primarily to those in the business. Finally, I return to the traders in the middle, Tsukiji's *nakaoroshi gyōsha*.

A FEAST FOR THE EYES

Trends in Japanese consumption are constantly replenished—dare I say fed?—by the mass media, which keep cuisine constantly in the public eye. Television, newspapers, magazines, books, and films all draw on food for inspiration and content. Sometimes the point is news, sometimes it is practical information. Food is also entertainment, however, sometimes providing a backdrop for dramas or comedies loosely connected to cuisine, but also with culinary matters as the main dish in contemplations of travel, regional identity, and culinary nationalism.

At the most mundane level, television networks broadcast hours of practical cooking shows instructing homemakers in both basic and sophisticated techniques, and many general daytime television shows devote a segment to a "kitchen corner." Dozens of magazines provide basic recipes as well as special menus for seasonal dishes, ideas for children's school lunch boxes, and tips on preparing foreign dishes and appreciating imported foodstuffs. Increasingly, articles at the gourmet end of this spectrum appear in magazines—even *cooking* magazines—aimed at men.

Food documentaries are also common fare on television. Such programs often emphasize the folkways and lifestyles of food producers (including, of course, regional culinary specialties or oddities), but they also provide detailed overviews of the food production and processing chains that bring rice or fish or tofu or soy sauce to the local store. NHK's educational channel broadcasts many shows for children with themes such as "let's see where our eggs come from." Even during prime time, well-produced documentaries full of food-related information are common. Japanese tend to regard the ocean and the seashore as places of work and harvest as well as of natural beauty—in contrast to Americans, who think first of surf, sand, and relaxation—and certainly the Japanese media's focus on the realities of food production reinforces this viewpoint. Major national daily newspapers treat agriculture and fisheries as important topics for general readers and regularly cover economic, technological, and political stories on food production and supply, both domestically and in terms of foreign trade.

Every year, new books on sushi, seafood, and Tsukiji—aimed at popular audiences—roll off the presses. A few recent titles give a sense of the range and depth of popular interest: a brief guide to Tsukiji's seafood and its seasons (Hirano Fumi 1999); an account of how sushi chefs learn the profession (Shimoda 2001); a book on the economics of *kaiten-zushi* (Watanabe Yonehide 2002); a popular historical account of the origins and cultural background of sushi (Utsukushii Nihon no Jōshiki o Saihakken suru Kai 2003); an overview of the economics of the tuna market (Ueda 2003); a guide on how to eat at kaiten-zushi restaurants (Yagyū 2003); and an extensive collection of photo essays on Tsukiji by eighty photographers (Beretta P-03 2003).

Beyond the practical culinary, nutritional, economic, and ecological information that the media broadly disseminate to the Japanese public, food has enormously high entertainment value.[5] Long before Americans knew of *The Iron Chef*, which has attracted a cult following for competitive cooking as spectacle, Japanese audiences were hooked on food entertainment shows. The Food Network began regular broadcasts of *The Iron Chef* in North America in 1999; the original Japanese series, *Ryōri no tetsujin (The Iron Men of Cuisine)*, began to air on Fuji Television in 1993. This wildly successful series is simply one in a long line of television shows and other media productions that make food a centerpiece of popular entertainment in Japan. They appear almost at random across the television dial. (Many of the following examples date from the late 1980s and early 1990s, and although specific series come and go, the genre remains a staple of Japanese television.)

The cartoon *Anpan-man*, a hit with preschool children, stars animated foods: Anpan-man (Mr. Beanpaste Bun); his buddies Jamu Ojisan (Uncle Jam), Batako-san (Ms. Butter), and their dog Chiizu (Cheese); his allies Shokupan-man (Mr. White Bread), Kareepan-man (Mr. Curry Bun), and

Tendon-man (Mr. Shrimp-and-Rice Bowl); and of course Hamigaki-man (Mr. Toothbrush). They are locked in never-ending struggles against the schemes of Baikin-man and Dokin-chan (Mr. Germ and Little Miss Bacteria). The dominant motifs of the *Anpan-man* series are the struggle of good against evil, the value of teamwork, and the need to brush your teeth, although the program also raises fascinating themes of purity and pollution, self-sacrifice, redemption and rebirth, and auto-cannibalism. In naming characters after foodstuffs, *Anpan-man* follows a common convention, perhaps best illustrated by a long-popular animated television show, *Sazae-san*, a gentle comedy about urban middle-class family life, peopled entirely with ordinary (if cartoonish) human characters, all of whom—starting with the title character, Sazae-san (which can be translated "Ms. Winkle")—are named after varieties of seafood, fishing techniques, or other maritime phenomena.

Food can be entertaining and also instructive. One popular situation comedy of the late 1980s, *Kukingu kazoku (Cooking Family)*, featured a "typical" middle-class urban family; each episode loosely revolved around the unexpected difficulties or comic misunderstandings that popped up in readying the dish of the week (the proper preparation of which was always shown during a brief epilogue). And yet another series, *Oishinbo*, based on a popular *manga* (comic book) of the same title, featured a cynical young reporter who time and time again stumbles into a bar or restaurant and— affronted by what he is served, or by the attitude of the chef—proceeds to expose inept chefs or unmask culinary poseurs, relying on dazzlingly virtuoso demonstrations and lectures on proper technique and ingredients, often laced with strong doses of culinary nationalism.[6]

Oishinbo and other television shows present deadpan the themes that are also the raw ingredients of the satiric hit movie *Tampopo* (1985), Itami Jūzō's extended journey through the byways of Japanese food culture. The title character is a young woman who struggles to master the mundane art of making *rāmen*, noodle soup. *Tampopo* is, as well, a symbolic journey into gender, sexuality, and identity (Ohnuki-Tierney 1990; Prindle 1996), but its central plot device—the quest for noodle perfection—neatly satirizes the conventions of culinary manga, in which characters enact exemplary scripts for success, persevering against all odds toward the goal of becoming the world's greatest chef, or saving the family restaurant, or perfecting a new style of sashimi. (Of course, the specific themes of hard work, loyalty, perseverance, and success are central in many genres—stories about sports teams, business, and samurai—not just culinary manga.)

One long-running manga with a culinary setting is *Shōta no sushi*

Figure 33. "Living Fish." Title page for the story "Ikita Sakana" ("Living Fish") from *Oishinbo: Maboroshi no sakana (Oishinbo: The Phantom Fish),* by Kariya Tetsu and Hanasaki Akira (1985). Reproduced with permission of the author, the illustrator, and Shōgakkan.

(Shōta's Sushi), which first appeared as a book in 1992 (Terasawa 1992), featuring the adventures of a young apprentice sushi chef. Another series, *Tsukiji uogashi sandaime (Third-Generation Tsukiji Uogashi),* chronicles the on-the-job education of a young man following in his family's business footsteps. The eighth volume (Hashimoto and Nabeshima 2003) is subtitled *Amadai no ude,* which can be translated "the arm for *amadai* (tilefish)," but in this case arm *(ude)* is a metonym for the mastery of skills, learning to do something by training the body in the proper movements. (I discuss this cultivation of skills further in chapter 6.) At the bookshop in Tsukiji's inner marketplace where chefs pick up cookbooks and everyone gets sports newspapers, *Tsukiji uogashi sandaime* sells well; the proprietress told me that market workers buy each volume quickly and say that it is accurate in its details ("People here wouldn't buy it if it had mistakes"). And, she reported, the author himself comes to Tsukiji often, sometimes stopping in her shop to buy books on cooking and the seafood industry.

In addition to simply promoting culinary knowledge and appreciation in general terms, the mass media, particularly television, disseminate local culinary lore and imbue it with great significance, often linking it with travel.[7] Week after week, the middle-aged male hosts of television travel

Figure 34. Title page of *Shōta no sushi (Shōta's Sushi)*, by Terasawa Daisuke (1992). Reproduced with permission of the author and Kōdansha.

Figure 35. Shōta takes a visitor to Tsukiji. From *Shōta no sushi,* by Terasawa Daisuke. Reproduced with permission of the author and Kōdansha.

[1] WA-A-A-A-A-N!

[2] Woman: What a voice! What noise! It's just like a festival . . .
Shōta: Absolutely! Hey, watch out, carts come through here!

[3] Ga——————— [sound of cart rattling by]

[4] Woman: W . . . wow! It's huge!

[5] Shōta: Hey! They're cutting apart a tuna . . .

shows nibble a morsel of some local delicacy and smack their lips, exclaiming "Kore ga umai, ne!" ("This is really good, isn't it!") as they nod knowingly to the starlet who is their unlikely traveling companion for the episode's journey to the back roads of Shinshū or the lakes of Tsugaru.

Some travel shows focus directly on cuisine. Several specials broadcast during June 1991 provided contrasting views: devotional, comic, and scandalized. The first—in celebration of nouveau riche lifestyles—was devoted to Japan's most ultra-expensive *ryokan* (traditional inns), ranging in price from a lofty ¥300,000 ($2,600) to a mere ¥120,000 ($1,040) per night per couple. The show reverently showed elegant celebrity couples visiting half a dozen exclusive inns in turn. Each segment devoted about half its time to the scenery, local attractions, and the inn's appointments; the remaining half lavished attention on the inn's cuisine. As the inn's chef looked on with deferential pride, the celebrity hosts examined and made comments on every exquisite tidbit, noting each dish's use of local ingredients and its associations with local history.

A second special, devoted to regional variations of sushi, sent celebrity interviewers—younger, less elegant, and quick with irreverent comments— to explore foodways in remote villages. Sushi made from uniquely local fish were of course savored, but much of the program focused on unique forms of preparation. The clear favorite was a type of *chirashi-zushi* (a mixture of fish, rice, and vegetables) whose defining characteristic was the massive quantities of local saké in which it was marinated overnight. By way of contrast, a delicacy that only a local could love—and not even all the locals would taste it on camera—was a sushi made by preserving fish for several years in a paste of fermented soybeans.[8]

A third program took a more critical view of local cuisine and the gullibility of travelers. Using a documentary exposé format, it focused on the travel boom that followed the opening of the new bridge linking Shikoku to the main island of Honshū. The cameras, to the accompaniment of the off-camera staccato voice of an investigative announcer, plunged into the kitchens of Shikoku restaurants—with names like Amimoto ("The Net Boss") or Ryōshigoya ("The Fisherman's Hut")—that featured seafood banquets for busloads of tourists. Naturally, the cameras "revealed" the fact that their "local" specialties were created out of fish gathered from the length and breadth of Japan, and the announcer pointedly noted that the Seto Inland Sea between Shikoku and Honshū is so polluted that a local fishing industry barely exists.

But whether reverential, flippant, or outraged, the programs all underscore the importance of the "culinary experience" as an element of travel through which one can savor the local culture of one's destination. As domestic tourism emphasizes the past-in-the-present of a Japan rendered exotic even to its own citizens, television shows and guidebooks invariably lavish great attention on regional cuisine, focusing on the "famous local products" *(meisan* or *meibutsu)* that almost every town and village touts as its special contribution to Japan's culinary heritage. The vendors of box lunches *(bentō)* on station platforms throughout Japan offer "unique" local lunches that in some cases are nationally known tourist attractions in their own rights (Noguchi 1994); one national guide to box lunches lists over 500 local variations, and another covering only western Japan lists 39 local sushi specialties (Ishii Izuo 1975: 146–53; Akiyoshi 1975). During high travel seasons, department stores in Tokyo hold special sales of famous box lunches from around the country.

Visits to local markets—particularly to "morning markets" *(asaichi)* in fishing or farming areas where local vendors sell fresh fish, produce, local processed food specialties (e.g., regionally distinctive pickles or "mountain vegetables," *sansai*), and regional handicrafts—are almost de rigueur for the recreational traveler. One guidebook devoted exclusively to markets (Kodama and Otome 1990) lists thirty marketplaces, most of them retail markets or "peddlers' markets" rather than larger urban wholesale marketplaces (although Tsukiji itself is the first entry in the book).

Local pride and identity are clearly at stake in culinary matters. At least in conversations with foreigners, some Tokyoites tell of hometown specialties that allegedly people from no other part of the country can eat. They appear to take quiet satisfaction in the belief that others do not like—or cannot stomach—their own local favorites. Food preferences are part of the well-established folk wisdom of *kenminsei,* stereotyped personalities that characterize people from different prefectures (e.g., people from Kyoto are snobs, people from Tokyo spend money hand over fist, and people from Osaka like to eat larger servings and prefer sweeter flavors).

With food preferences so closely linked to identity, culinary diversity points toward separateness and division, however slight. Viewed against global gastronomy, rice and fish and soybean soup are comfortably "Japanese"; but when natives of Tokyo and Osaka—or Kyūshū and Tōhoku—are head-to-head, pan-Japanese culinary solidarity dissolves into fierce local partisanship. Chefs treasure their knives and pride themselves on wielding regional styles: a long, tapered *yanagiba* (willow leaf) for slicing sashimi in Tokyo in contrast to the equally slender but squared-off blade, known as a *takohiki,* used for the same purpose in Osaka. Soy sauce, thick or thin; the palatability of *nattō* (fermented soybean paste); or the subtle distinctions of sweetness in various regional cuisines can easily become the fault lines—usually dormant but occasionally jolting—in the culinary geography of identity.

Even seemingly trivial differences in regional food habits can spark an extended cultural exegesis. One sweltering summer afternoon, on the "Day of the Ox" *(Doyō no ushi no hi)*—the day at the peak of the summer's heat on which traditionally one should fortify oneself by eating grilled eel *(kabayaki)*—a friend from Tsukiji took me to an eel restaurant. As we ate, he mentioned that in Tokyo eels were prepared by slitting them down the back; in Osaka however, the filet is prepared by slitting the eel down the belly. He laughed and told me that since Edo was full of samurai, and Osaka wasn't, the custom in Edo was to avoid the belly slitting because it might suggest *seppuku*, the ritualized suicide of the samurai in which they cut open their stomachs.

My friend clearly was telling me this not as a point of historical fact, but only as an amusing story. Yet his and similar tales in the folklore of food illustrate two significant points. First, they underline the extent to which food and culinary differences are the subject of extensive cultural commentary. Second, they make clear that food symbolism is popularly linked—however casually—to deep currents in the cultural history of Japan. And for this reason, I believe, this penchant for focusing on minute details becomes so satisfying and so important as Japanese define themselves by what they eat.

IMAGINED CUISINE

Culinary Authenticity

Japanese and foreigners alike often regard raw seafood as one of the pillars of "authentic" Japanese cuisine. Inverting Lévi-Strauss's famous dichotomy, Emiko Ohnuki-Tierney observes: "For the Japanese raw or uncooked food is *food*, while in other cultures food usually means *cooked* food. The raw in Japanese culture thus represents culturalized nature; like a rock garden in which traces of [the] human hands that transformed nature into culturalized nature have been carefully erased, the raw food of the Japanese represents a highly crafted cultural artifact presented as natural food" (1990: 206; emphasis added).

Appadurai ascribes concern over "culinary authenticity" to outsiders rather than to "native participants in a culinary tradition," and goes on to say that "the concern with authenticity indicates some sort of doubt, and this sort of doubt is rarely part of the discourse of an undisturbed cuisine"

(1986a: 25). Yet doubt need not be an outsider's prerogative. Unease over cultural authenticity and its attempted resolution are pervasive features of Japanese encounters with themselves-as-others throughout the postwar period (T. Bestor 1989, 1992b; Kelly 1990; Gluck and Graubard 1992; Ivy 1995). And cuisine offers ample and authentic grounds for cultural concern.

Despite the enormous culinary changes of the past several generations— or perhaps precisely because of them—many Japanese maintain a strong conceptual sense of "Japanese cuisine" as a distinct category: *wa-shoku* (Japanese food) as opposed to *yō-shoku* (Western food).[9] The identification of a distinctive Japanese cuisine, of course, implicitly alleges historical continuity and stability. Yet like all other aspects of "tradition," food culture constantly evolves. Many dishes and delicacies now widely regarded as hallmarks of Japanese cuisine—by foreigners and by Japanese as well—are actually of relatively recent introduction or invention. For example, even the basic form of nigiri-zushi, a thin slice of fish atop a compact oblong block of vinegared rice—the style characteristic of Tokyo's cuisine and now the world's de facto sushi standard—was an innovation of the mid–nineteenth century.

Japanese culinary historians date the origins of sushi to perhaps as early as the seventh century, when rice was used to preserve fish through the natural fermentation that occurs when the two come into contact; the rice itself, however, was simply discarded before the fish was eaten. (This form of sushi still exists as a regional specialty, notably as *funa-zushi* from Shiga Prefecture, near Kyoto.) Fresh fish was not served over vinegared rice until the Tokugawa period. The particular style that is the hallmark of Edo-Tokyo sushi, called *nigiri-zushi* ("squeezed" or "hand-molded" sushi) or *Edomae-zushi* (sushi from "in front of Edo"), became the rage of Edo in the 1820s or 1830s (Nishiyama et al. 1984: 259–62; Nishiyama 1997: 170–73; Omae and Tachibana 1981: 105; Yoshino 1986: 16).

One common story of nigiri-zushi's origins puts it in the hands of a famed sushi chef, Hanaya Yohei (1799–1858), who invented or perfected the technique in 1824 at his shop in Ryōgoku (then one of Edo's major entertainment districts), a shop that survived until the 1930s. A nineteenth-century verse celebrated the popular innovation:

> Crowded together, weary with waiting
> Customers squeeze their hands
> As Yohei squeezes sushi

Shops named Yohei Zushi remain common, the implication—usually without foundation—being that they were originally established by apprentices of the first Yohei, who permitted them to use their master's name.

Many of the present varieties of sushi made with extremely fresh seafood were not even possible until the advent of mechanical refrigeration in the mid—twentieth century. And tastes in toppings have changed dramatically as well: until about a generation ago, *toro*—the fatty flesh from tuna bellies that is now the quintessential high-priced sushi topping—was held in such poor regard that it was given away as cat food. To fully appreciate this lowly status, one must know that the Japanese "cultural biography" of cats casts them not as adorable house pets but as necessary domestic nuisances, useful for catching rats yet otherwise pests themselves or ghostly avatars (Omae and Tachibana 1981: 12, 104–5; R. J. Smith 1992b: 23–24). Worse yet for toro's reputation, until the 1950s at Tsukiji it was referred to as *neko-matagi*: fish that even a cat would disdain (Watanabe Fumio 1991: 26).

Toro found new popularity for two reasons: the postwar diet accustomed Japanese tastes to fattier foods, and increasingly widespread refrigeration technology kept fatty foods fresher longer. The rich flavors of toro fit the new palate, and traders could handle, preserve, and ship the fatty toro more easily; in this way, a new market niche was born.

As Japanese cuisine (in the marked sense of "Japanese") has evolved, dependence on imported foodstuffs has increased. Developments in transportation as well as Japan's dominant position in international trade have created systems of trade capable of supplying Japan with large amounts of imported fresh and frozen fish, but they are received with ambivalence. The nation has long since ceased to be self-sufficient in any category of foodstuff except rice. Recently, even rice production has dwindled. A poor harvest in 1993 forced the Japanese national government to allow the first rice imports in decades; and in the face of widespread revulsion over eating foreign rice, the government required rice dealers to blend domestic and foreign rice so that consumers could not pick and choose which varieties to purchase.

Imported fish supply basic protein and calories to a food-poor country, but also provide one of the centerpieces of Japanese cuisine. Although Japan's food dependency is unavoidable and makes policy sense in terms of comparative and absolute trade advantages, it is a trade imbalance fraught with cultural tension. The mass media make food dependency (also called food security) widely known. Newspaper articles around New Year's bring home to the public their reliance on the rest of the world by cataloging the extent to which preparation of even that most resolutely traditional of Japanese feasts, the New Year's *o-sechi*, now relies largely on imported basic foodstuffs. The question of food dependency, of course, has practical political and economic dimensions involving the reliability of Japanese allies and the international flow of trade.[10] Thus protectionist responses—expressed through vigorous defense of Japanese agriculture and fisheries—often take the potent form of defending Japanese economic interests by linking them with Japanese cultural identity and its culinary components.

Many foodstuffs now or recently at the center of recurring trade disputes, such as rice, beef, citrus fruits, and seafood, are the subjects of intense cultural commentary in contemporary Japan. Some—oranges and beef are notable examples—have become famous largely as a result of controversies over trade; that is, they have become rallying symbols for Japanese economic and cultural nationalism largely because they are focal points for current disputes in international trade, not because of any particularly significant cultural overtones related to traditional aspects of their production and consumption.

Seafood, however, is another matter. Of course, seafood occupies a special symbolic niche because it is so frequently marked—by both foreigners and Japanese alike—as a distinctive element of Japanese cuisine. And so, when seafood or fishing turn up on the global stage, they do not raise *incidental* issues of trade balances and market access or Japan's status as an economic superpower; for both foreigners and Japanese, Japan's demand for seafood and the methods of catching it are *the* central issue. Cuisine—in the broad sense—itself becomes the crux of the matter; in this context, marine resource management is not a neutral technical concept. Environmental disputes rage for decades over whales, tuna, dolphins, squid, and tangled issues of high seas drift-net fishing. (Japanese whaling, of course, has become an international cause célèbre, the focus of intense, often hostile, foreign criticism for Japan's continued defiance of attempts to ban all commercial whaling, as well as of deeply impassioned defense by those who argue that whale consumption is a cornerstone of traditional Japanese culture.)[11] Seen from a commonplace Japanese perspective, environmental criticism of their nation's fishing policies and of their society's eating habits is a stinging assault on Japan itself. Many ordinary Japanese wonder whether these attacks are motivated solely or even primarily by ecological concerns, and question scientific claims marshaled by Japan's critics. They see themselves and their cuisine vilified as barbaric and regard the unending sets of foreign demands—stop whaling, classify bluefin tuna as an endangered species, protect dolphins—not as well meaning but, at best, as capriciously ethnocentric carping by Europeans and North Americans.

Purity and Danger

Cuisine is central to cultural identity, and Japan finds itself simultaneously criticized for its international fishing activities and increasingly dependent on food imports. Food from abroad—however vital to the national diet—seems somehow less culturally filling; even more worryingly, it may seem dangerous, and not just because of political controversy. Concerns about freshness and purity are a normal part of any food culture. In Japan, however, purity and pollution both have multiple meanings, and unease over dietary matters is widespread. The Japanese public in the past several generations has repeatedly come up against environmental, social, and political issues involving the fundamental integrity and viability of their country's food supply.

Domestically, the mass media frequently report on the possibility of links between various features of the traditional Japanese diet and gastrointestinal cancer. On a positive note, folk wisdom holds that heavy consumption of hot green tea or of seaweed reduces the threat of cancer. Other aspects of diet are allegedly risk factors: the talc used to coat processed Japanese rice, the charring of grilled fish *(yakizakana),* and the prevalence of pickled foods, especially in the regional cuisine of Tōhoku, the formerly remote mountains of northern Honshū.[12] Other established food habits and their links to health also fall under intense scrutiny from time to time. An outbreak of *E. coli* O157:H7 (known in Japan as O-157) contamination near Osaka in the summer of 1996, for example, caused widespread panic as more than 10,000 residents fell ill and 12 people died. The source was never conclusively identified, but the incident collided with another cherished culinary custom; uncooked foods of all kinds became suspect. Even in midsummer, consumers scrambled to eat *cooked* food, and in restaurants dishes that one could cook oneself on the table—before one's *own* eyes—such as *okonomiyaki* (an egg-and-vegetable frittata) or Korean-style grilled meat soared in popularity. Sushi and sashimi sales across the nation plummeted, fishmongers and sushi shops closed their doors, traders at Tsukiji and elsewhere were rattled, and tuna prices across the globe plummeted. (The same strain of *E. coli* has recurred in Japan—for example, in the summer of 1998, when an outbreak was traced to salmon roe.)

Beyond the risks of favorite dishes and "normal" ingredients, Japanese consumers have faced a long history of contamination and threats to the integrity of foodstuffs. Perhaps the most dramatic case, shortly after the end of the American Occupation, touched the rawest nerves. On March 1, 1954, the ill-fated *No. 5 Lucky Dragon (Daigo Fukuryū-maru),* a small tuna longliner out of the Japanese port of Yaizu, was roughly 150 kilometers northeast of Bikini Atoll just as the United States detonated a hydrogen bomb at its test site there. Twenty-three crew members suffered severe radiation sickness and one—Kuboyama Aichi, the radio operator—died six months later (Lapp 1957). After the *Yomiuri Shinbun* broke the story on March 15, the incident

Figure 36. Hot tuna, 1954. Health officials check tuna at Tsukiji with a Geiger counter, after the American hydrogen bomb test at Bikini Atoll. Reproduced with permission of the TMG Bureau of Public Health.

and subsequent American attempts to minimize it unleashed a storm of anti-U.S. sentiment and fueled the nuclear disarmament movement in Japan. The public reaction spawned Gojira—Godzilla—the prehistoric creature awakened from the primordial ocean depths by American nuclear tests, who began to ravage Japanese cities in the first Godzilla film produced later that year by the Tōhō studios (Kalat 1997: 33–34). And the tragedy of the *Lucky Dragon* destroyed the market for tuna for months; haunting newspaper photos show market officials checking tuna with Geiger counters.

Other, shattering threats became apparent as a series of notorious domestic pollution cases, which came to light in the late 1960s and early 1970s, rocked confidence in the safety of foodstuffs produced in Japan. In place after place, local residents gradually and painfully discovered major pollution incidents in which food chains—particularly aquatic food chains—and foodstuffs were contaminated, sometimes lethally, by industries' flagrant disregard for human and environmental welfare. As cases were revealed—Minamata, Yokkaichi, Kanemi—almost invariably after official denials and orchestrated cover-ups, food contamination entered the political arena and it has remained a volatile issue (W. E. Smith and Smith 1981; Huddle, Reich, and Stiskin 1975; Reich 1991).

During the late 1980s, concern over food preservatives and additives used in processed foods became an issue around which Japanese agricultural protectionists were able to rally widespread opposition to liberalizing food imports from the United States. Even the Japan Socialist Party, long dependent on urban voters who might be expected to favor greater reliance on imports as a means to lower food costs, managed to straddle the issue by opposing liberalization on the nominal grounds of protecting Japanese consumers from food adulterated with excessive preservatives and other contaminants.

Other recent cases keep Japanese consumers nervous about foodstuffs and make the entire food industry edgy, as markets are affected even when their own products are not in question. The scandals surrounding Snow Brand milk products in 2001, when 13,000 people were sickened by milk processed in equipment that had not been properly cleaned (the now-defunct company compounded the problem by attempting to recycle unsold milk into still *other* products), put the entire food distribution system on the defensive. Equally, concerns over such things as mad cow disease (bovine spongiform encephalopathy, or BSE), discovered in Japanese herds in 2001 (after repeated assurances from MAFF officials that BSE would never reach Japanese shores); the unknown risks of genetically modified organisms (GMOs); and the potential for contamination in seafood raised by aquaculture all rattle consumer confidence and cause market traders to be constantly vigilant for flawed products (a point I will return to shortly).

On entirely different grounds, foreign foods are often regarded as simply inferior; other things being equal, Tsukiji traders prefer domestically harvested or produced food items (known and labeled as *kokusan*—literally, "national product") over imports. Thus, although sea urchin roe from Hokkaidō and from Maine are almost indistinguishable, Hokkaidō roe command a premium at Tsukiji. And, of course, the indistinguishability and the premium give rise to grumbling by American producers that some Japanese importers process and repackage Maine roe in Hokkaidō before sending it to the marketplace. Japanese importers counter that the quality of the product is better if it is shipped in the shell to Japan and processed there, and that in any case Japanese workers are much more highly skilled in packing the roe in neat, uniform, attractive ways.

Preferences for domestically produced foodstuffs may in part stem from fundamental Japanese parochialism, but they also reflect issues of *kata*, or idealized form, and the inability of foreign producers to live up to Japanese standards. The ideal of perfect external form adds an extra dimension to assessing foodstuffs. The slightest blemish, the smallest imperfection, or the most trivial deviation from a foodstuff's idealized form can make a product—or entire shipment—languish unsold. That is, the outward appearance must be perfect, since imperfection outside may signal imperfection within, just as the etiquette of wrapping symbolically ensures both ritual and hygienic purity (Hendry 1990).

Even where concern over the integrity of the inner product is not directly at issue, the question of kata bedevils the international fish trade. An American lobster producer from California once told me that he had given up trying to ship lobsters to Japan; apparently his Japanese broker rejected sample shipment after sample shipment, complaining that the individual lobsters in each lot were too varied in size. "I gave up. I don't sort that carefully for anybody," the American producer told me disdainfully. Instead, he concentrates on the American restaurant market, where the normal lobster dinner is served individually and often priced according to the weight of the lobster. People dining together may indeed all order lobster, but they are unlikely to compare their individual lobsters closely; and if they do, the differences in price by size will usually account for any obvious disparities.

Across the Pacific, a Tsukiji lobster trader tells another side to the story: "Hotel banquet halls buy almost all the lobsters at Tsukiji. The auspicious red-and-white color of a lobster tail makes it very popular at wedding banquets. Everybody's plate has to look exactly like the one next to it. If a guest sees that his lobster tail is smaller than that of the person sitting next to him, everyone gets uncomfortable."

Almost every Tsukiji dealer in imported fish has his favorite horror story about the improper handling of fish by foreign producers and brokers; in retelling these tales traders return again and again to issues of Japanese food preferences as they are made manifest through "Tsukiji specs," the demanding specifications with which the Tsukiji auction houses expect suppliers to comply (and which foreign exporters often seem to ignore or dismiss, according to Tsukiji traders). One salmon dealer, for example, recounted with dismay his visit to an Alaskan fishing port where salmon were being unloaded by crew members wielding pitchforks, rendering the lacerated fish worthless in Japan. He went on to show me how even the size and placement of an external scar could make a difference. A scar running lengthwise along a salmon (parallel to the spine) would make the fish unsalable as a fillet; on the other hand, a fish scarred at right angles to the spine could be salvaged because it could be cut into slices or salmon steaks, and the portion with the damaged skin simply discarded.

Finally, although the Japanese appetite for fish is enormous and enormously varied, Japanese consumers are conservative in adopting new species of seafood. As an official of one of the auction houses with long experience in managing imports told me, "I always tell foreign producers who want to sell at Tsukiji to look carefully at what is on sale here, then go home and find the fish closest to what you saw. Send us that one, don't send us anything unfamiliar." Far from breeding contempt, familiarity promotes peace of mind. Reassurances of safety and predictability are encoded in preferences for domestic products and in the reliance on ideal form as an index of both purity and culinary authenticity.

The Wild and the Caged

The crucial distinction between "wild" or "natural" fish (those harvested by fishermen operating in open waters) and cultivated fish is another important conceptual dimension in the seafood trade. Cultivated fish raised through aquaculture are referred to as *yōshoku* ("cultivated" or "cultured," as in cultured pearls); fish that are captured in the wild and raised to maturity in pens (such as bluefin tuna raised in "farms" in Spain, Australia, or Croatia for export to Japan) are known as *chikuyō*. When it is necessary to distinguish "wild" fish from their farm-raised cousins, fish caught in open waters are called *tennen* (literally, "natural" or "spontaneous").[13]

Japanese aquaculture is centuries old, and in recent decades Japanese researchers have advanced aquacultural technology enormously, both by increasing the domestic production of species (such as eels and shrimp) that have long been cultivated and by developing techniques for cultivating species that have been generally free-range. Vast amounts of salmon, snapper, and yellowtail, for example, are raised through aquaculture. And tuna, a highly migratory fish that can cover thousands of miles in a season, is also the object of intense aquacultural research. Since the early 1970s, the Fisheries Laboratory of Kinki University, in Wakayama, has been carrying out extensive and increasingly successful research on breeding bluefin tuna in captivity. In 2002 the laboratory successfully hatched bluefin fingerlings that were themselves the offspring of bluefin tuna bred in captivity—yōshoku fish to the second generation, the grandchildren of wild fish (*Japan Times,* July 6, 2002).

As industrial food, cultivated fish have become particularly popular in the supermarket and mass-market restaurant industries, where there is great demand for highly standardized seafood available year-round in large and predictable quantities.[14] Cultivation is popular among producers and shippers as well, for it regularizes capital expenditures and product flows and minimizes some of the risks associated with other forms of fishing.

To Tsukiji traders, such developments are mixed blessings. For easy-to-cultivate species, the volatility of supply and hence fluctuations in prices are generally dampened. Stability and standardization of supply, however, make it easier for—and more likely that—supermarkets will develop their own direct connections with producers, bypassing markets like Tsukiji altogether. Indeed, many aquaculture ventures, both in Japan and abroad, are financed at the outset by trading companies or supermarket chains with precisely that in mind. But Tsukiji is not insulated, and markets for cultivated seafood can also suddenly collapse—for example, when speculative investment leads to sudden spikes or crashes in supply, as in the boom-and-bust cycles of cultivated silver salmon—leaving trading companies, auction houses, and even midlevel wholesalers to scramble for cover.

Furthermore, Tsukiji traders and their professional customers, like sushi chefs, usually regard cultivated fish as inferior. All other things being equal, a wild fish will command a premium over its cultivated cousin, and the wild one is more likely to be sold through an auction, while the cultivated counterpart is more likely to be sold at a negotiated price.[15] The conceptual distinctions between wild and cultivated mirror those between pure and impure, and domestic and foreign, products.

Generally, cultivated fish suffer by comparison in flavor, fat content, and the firmness and tone of their flesh, because—in the Tsukiji view—fish raised in captivity eat an unvarying diet of prepared feed, get little exercise, and cannot range freely through different waters. Their image in the marketplace is also tainted by fears of hazards potentially posed by contaminated feed, by pollution of the Japanese coastal waters in which much aquaculture takes place, or by close captivity, which may enable illness to spread throughout an entire fish farm.[16] These very real environmental dangers, along with the risk of speculative overcapacity, make aquaculture a highly chancy venture. Adding insult to market risk is the fact that even if a producer gets cultivated fish safely to market, they are generally disdained by traders and culinary professionals.

Although the average consumer may well share environmental fears over the purity of cultivated fish—and perhaps hold them more strongly than do professionals—the typical shopper or restaurant guest is unlikely to know much about aquaculture or be able to actually distinguish a cultivated from a wild fish. Under such conditions, connoisseurship's snob appeal flourishes. Elite sushi bars and Japanese-style restaurants, *ryōtei*, make a point of *not* serving cultivated seafood; some avoid serving even "wild" versions of seafood widely available in cultivated form simply to underscore their discretion. Cultivated seafood ends up in supermarkets, midlevel restaurants, and processing plants.

INDUSTRIALIZING CUISINE

Since the 1940s, Japanese foodways and foodstuffs have changed enormously, following several generations of sweeping alterations in Japan's culinary life since the mid–nineteenth century (Cwiertka 1999; Ishige 1995, 1999, 2001, n.d.; Nakagawa 1995; Ashkenazi and Jacob 2000), when Japan resumed and expanded its contacts with other societies. The evolution of

Japanese cuisine—both before and after World War II—reflects many interrelated factors, of course, including exposure to foreign cuisines, the expansion of scientific knowledge about nutrition, and the development of new technologies of production, transportation, and processing (some of which have already been mentioned in chapter 3, particular those occurring after World War II). These have all changed the availability, production, and trade of foodstuffs, as well as the social contexts of consumption, cultural attitudes toward particular foodstuffs, and the relationship between cuisine and personal, regional, or national identity.

The Japanese fishing industry's ability to exploit formerly inaccessible distant-water fisheries made octopus from the West African coast, tuna from the Atlantic, and squid from throughout the Pacific staples of the Japanese diet. New technologies have revolutionized storage, refrigeration, and processing—flash-freezing freshly caught tuna to minus 60 degrees Celsius, turning Alaskan pollack into simulated crab meat *(surimi)*, and using anaerobic technology to ship live fish by air in a state of suspended animation. The development of interregional (and later international) trade and transportation made crabs from Hokkaidō easily available in Kago-shima, and Norwegian salmon common in Tokyo. Aquaculture supplies Tsukiji with eels from Hamamatsu and Guangzhou, shrimp from Thailand, sea bream from Wakayama, yellowtail from Baja California, and catfish from Louisiana.

Leaving aside the impact of such developments on raising nutritional standards and ensuring stable food supplies, a homogenized national fare has gradually replaced regionally varied ones, which were based on traditional foodstuffs and locally idiosyncratic techniques of preparation. These transformations of the Japanese diet, both over the past couple of generations and throughout the past century and a half, are often presented—by Japanese, to Japanese—as instances of "Westernization" (Cwiertka 1999).

To be sure, the introduction of foreign foodstuffs and dishes—by no means exclusively Western—has had tremendous impact on the diet of the average Japanese. More fundamentally, however, the evolution of Japanese cuisine reflects the "industrialization" of the food supply, a phenomenon that Goody (1982: 154–74) points to in nineteenth-century western Europe and North America as well as in colonial Africa. By Goody's definition, this is the process in which the entire character of a society's sustenance—selections of food resources; methods of production and processing; the reengineering of familiar foods for mass distribution, and the creation of entirely new foodstuffs as well; techniques of distribution, sales, and advertising;

daily rhythms of eating; and the nutritional content of the daily diet—is adapted to and shaped by industrial, capital-intensive production. Typically, such industrialization of food changes the repertory of goods available to consumers, increasingly substituting highly standardized, processed and manufactured foodstuffs for widely varied, locally produced, raw and semi-processed ones.

The industrialization of food affects consumers, of course, but is fundamentally propelled by changes in the economic, political, and social institutions that produce, process, and distribute foodstuffs. On one side of the equation, Goody points out that the nineteenth-century industrialization of food centered on new large-scale techniques for canning, baking, preserving, and flavoring. On the other hand, new techniques of food processing developed hand in hand with new forms of retailing and advertising. Proprietary brand names were attached both to newly developed products and to products that previously had been simply generic items from the culinary public domain. Advertising promoted brand-name goods. Wide-spectrum grocers replaced specialized provisioners.

On the production side, there are striking Japanese examples of traditional foodstuffs developing into industrialized products widely marketed under proprietary brand names. Kikkoman soy sauce is a case in point: Kikkoman has become the world's leading producer of soy sauce by creating a nationally standardized manufactured product out of what was traditionally an item of local craft production (Fruin 1983).[17]

A more recent and more highly technological example is the transformation of traditional fish pastes, such as *kamaboko,* a kind of fish pâté, into a new industrial foodstuff with a global appeal. *Surimi* is known to those in the trade as extruded pollack and is widely sold to American consumers as imitation crab meat (sometimes marketed under brand names such as "Sea Legs").

At the retail level, industrialization heralds a shift away from products sold generically (e.g., soy sauce, soy paste [*miso*], or rice), as commodities in the economist's sense of the term, possibly distinguished by the merchant's house brand name or that of a local producer, and toward brand-name goods (e.g., Kikkoman soy sauce) distributed regionally, nationally, or internationally in standardized form, interchangeably available from one retailer or another.

But the industrialization of Japanese *seafood* has been most clearly visible in the technologies of catching, transporting, and storing fish rather than in the creation of entirely new products. The results, therefore, are almost invisible to consumers, who find familiar seafood available for consumption in seemingly unchanging ways—although perhaps more cheaply, in greater quantity, and of more standardized and perhaps higher quality than before. Of course, even if developments in production (such as fish-farming) or in transportation (such as airfreighting fresh fish from international sources to markets in Japan) are not immediately obvious to the consumer, they are linked to major transformations in the structure of the fishing industry, of distribution channels converging on the Tsukiji marketplace, and of the retail sectors of the food business.

As the repertoire of products available to consumers changes, so too do the sellers. Closest to the experience of consumers, supermarkets grow at the expense of small-scale retailers (T. Bestor 1990, 2002a). As standardized packaged goods become increasingly *the* staple products, wide-spectrum grocery stores displace narrowly specialized purveyors in all but those fields where freshness is paramount and brand names are almost irrelevant. Clearly greengrocers, fishmongers, and butchers are among the culinary specialists best able to resist the encroachments of supermarkets.

Processed products can fill entirely different culinary niches than their unprocessed counterparts. Goody's analysis pays particular attention to the development of new nineteenth-century industrial processing techniques such as canning. To be sure, Japanese culinary tradition includes many examples of processing techniques, such as pickling, salting, or fermenting, that are adaptable to industrial production. But canned and fresh fish are not interchangeable in most Japanese dishes. None of the standard dishes of "traditional" Japanese cuisine (i.e., *wa-shoku*) ordinarily are made using canned goods, whereas many Western dishes can easily be prepared with either canned or fresh products.

Because fresh foods undergo relatively little industrial processing, it is difficult to establish brand names for otherwise undifferentiated generic products (e.g., fresh Atlantic flounder versus Mrs. Paul's Golden Fish Fillets). And because fresh products usually remain generic commodities, the skills and reputation of the individual purveyor as judge of quality remain central. A merchant's ability to discriminate and validate these culinary distinctions is an important source of his or her cultural capital, within the trade and among consumers at large. For all these reasons, although wide-spectrum grocery stores and supermarkets can try to duplicate the specialties of the greengrocer, the fishmonger, and the butcher, even a deluxe superstore cannot redefine every culinary specialty so completely that the skills—and the cultural capital—of the independent merchant are rendered obsolete.

The Gourmet Boom

Since the early 1980s, what I call the gentrification of taste (what people in the trade call the *gurume būmu*—the "gourmet boom") has also created enormous demand for what were formerly "luxury" foods, which are now within the grasp of many if not most Japanese. Of course, fine fresh food-stuffs are central to this gourmet boom. And as standards of taste have risen, local culinary styles—with their emphasis on fresh, locally produced or harvested foodstuffs—have paradoxically been reinvigorated, with corresponding premiums now attached to regional cuisines as well as to the ingredients on which they depend, an example of what Bourdieu (1984) refers to as "distinction"—the elaboration and refinement of class and personal identities based on consumption.

In analyzing cuisine, Goody also discusses the relationship between class structure, the existence or elaboration of "high" and "low" cuisines, and the forms of food production common within a society (1982: 97–153). Not surprisingly, "industrial food" is deeply embedded in class structures. Although Goody does not address the gentrification of taste or the rediscovery and elevation of regional cuisine, it is not difficult to extrapolate this postindustrial development from the earlier industrialization of food. It is another facet of the postindustrial responses discussed earlier that contribute to what Appadurai (1986a) identifies as concern with culinary authenticity.

On the one hand, culinary industrialization has shifted the balance away from locally available, rather generic or anonymous foodstuffs to nationally distributed, brand-name commodities; on the other hand, in the postindustrial economy, formerly anonymous local foodstuffs now have cachet as brand-name merchandise. One Japanese example is the recent boom in *jizake* (local saké), which has—as a genre of brand-name goods—limited distribution but national (if esoteric) prestige among connoisseurs; the efflorescence of microbreweries in the United States is roughly parallel, although in jizake's case local makers often loudly (although sometimes spuriously) trumpet their preservation of long-standing regional traditions. Such culinary connoisseurship appears to emerge in response or reaction to the earlier process of culinary industrialization. And, although fresh seafood has not undergone industrial transformation, the reinvigorated popularity of particular local specialties is a roughly parallel response.

The current popularity of *Edomae* (literally, "in front of Edo") cuisine is a good example. The media and canny restaurateurs accord tremendous prestige (at elevated prices) to sushi and other specialties supposedly made from seafood caught in the waters of Tokyo Bay, on the principle that this is the freshest possible fish and shellfish. Although such seafood has become increasingly scarce—because landfill claimed most of Tokyo Bay's fishing grounds long ago and those that remain are severely polluted—sushi chefs and food writers have revived the term "Edomae" not only to indicate the style of sushi developed in Edo and still eaten in Tokyo (also known as *nigiri-zushi*) but also as a "concept" used to tout newly popular styles of fresh seafood cuisine featured in expensive Tokyo restaurants.

This appeal to authenticity, like so many others, relies on an allusion to Edo's proximity to the sea. But Edo culture had at best a "vague and even hostile conception of Edo Bay," except perhaps for "its productive harvest of fresh fish, an [appreciation] that remains today in the phrase *Edo-mae* . . . as a synonym for sushi eaten raw (rather than pickled, as in Western Japan)" (H. D. Smith II 1986: 28). Although the original, seventeenth-century term referred to a particular fishing ground of the bay, it came more generally to mean high-quality fish or shellfish, not sushi ingredients per se. Eel shops during the Tokugawa period, for example, used the term (Yoshino 1986: 16, 95). The "Edomae" catchphrase came into common use by sushi shops only after World War II—long after the bay had ceased to be a major source for fresh seafood—and has now become simply a general term for Tokyo-style sushi as well as an implied assurance of freshness.[18]

The industrialization of the food supply (or, in this case, reactions against it) not only shapes products but also affects its purveyors. As the gourmet boom and the gentrification of taste have reshaped Japanese preferences, they also have refocused attention on the independent merchants whose implicit stock-in-trade is precisely their specialized knowledge and discernment. Some trends help sustain traditional, small-scale merchants and restaurateurs in the face of supermarkets and franchised family restaurants, even as they make the Tsukiji trade still more global and complex. The boomlets of recent years—whether for gourmet foodstuffs or for eating out—create parallel demand for high-priced and often esoteric foodstuffs. As what were formerly considered luxury foods become increasingly ordinary items in the daily diet of many Tokyoites, the frontiers of conspicuous consumption are pushed further. In the gentrification of taste, urban restaurateurs and retailers have rediscovered and widely promoted regional culinary styles. The hallmarks of such cuisines—emphasis on fresh, locally produced foodstuffs, often prepared in locally idiosyncratic combinations or manners—meet the demand for "natural" food that is culturally and regionally authentic, yet esoteric enough to have cachet. And ever-higher standards of freshness, as well as the demand for exotica and the sheer volume of Tsukiji's appetite, have led to an enormous increase in the use of cargo jets to transport fish from distant ports (domestic and foreign) and spurred Japan Airlines to develop anaerobic technology to transport jetloads of live fish in suspended animation, carried in almost no water.

Old-fashioned retail fishmongers and their supermarket competitors strive to position themselves to meet consumers' varied and often contradictory demands. Retail fishmongers struggle to improve the quality of the fish they sell and to stock increasingly exotic species, as well as to instruct consumers both in basic culinary techniques and in the familiar uses of unfamiliar varieties. Supermarkets put increasing emphasis on selling seafood already cleaned, sliced, and even arranged on platters, accompanied with the necessary condiments to simplify home cooking.[19] Traders at Tsukiji try to adjust their product mix and their client base accordingly, wondering whether the future holds a system of brands for fresh seafood and, if so, whether they, like retail merchants, will find the market value of their reputations as judges of seafood deflated.

Domesticity and Cuisine

Against the changing supply side of the Japanese seafood business, shaped by industrialization and international trade, the consumption patterns of ordinary Japanese have changed enormously. But culinary homogenization, rising standards of food preference, the renewed celebration of fresh ingredients and regional cuisine, and other changes in Japanese diet have not occurred simply because of technological advances in production, supply, or distribution. They result specifically from wider changes in the lives of ordinary Japanese over the past two generations, many of which—at first glance—bear little direct relationship to food culture and culinary habits.

Rising prosperity has led to greater disposable income and has fueled the gourmet boom along with greater consumption of luxury foods, both domestic and imported. In the seafood realm, for example, live fish *(katsugyo)* have become popular, and trendy restaurants and retail fish markets flaunt their expensive fare with large, well-stocked tanks from which a patron may select a specific fish to be prepared for the coming meal or packaged to take home.

Since the 1950s, the palate of Japanese tastes has broadened to offer an ever-widening choice of foreign specialties. This has coincided with the expansion of Japan's role as a global economic superpower and the rise in opportunities for ordinary Japanese to travel internationally for both business and recreation. Entirely foreign culinary traditions have become popular in urban Japan, including Thai restaurants, tandoori grills, and Parisian bistros. Kentucky Fried Chicken has sold the idea that traditional American

[1] Hostess: Welcome! I can give you advice.

[2] Hostess: This one could be served *ikezukuri* [live, as sashimi], or if it's that fish . . .
Woman: Ahh! So lively! They look delicious!

[3] Man: OK, this one and this one, please.
Man with net: That comes to ¥2,800.
Hostess: I'll take your fish to the kitchen.

[4] Woman: It's really the fish I picked out! *Itadakimasu*.

[5] Woman: It was delicious. You'll bring me again . . . ?
Man: OK! (. . . and this doesn't hurt my wallet, either!)

Figure 37. The gourmet boom, ca. 1990. A menu from a seafood restaurant, Tōkyō Kaisen Ichiba. Reproduced with permission of the illustrator, Okeguchi Mako.

Christmas meals center on fried chicken, to the tune of "Our Old Kentucky Home" (Nathan 1981). Other foreign restaurant chains (such as Denny's or Red Lobster) also have entered the Japanese domestic market aggressively, and Japanese food producers have themselves eagerly promoted new food-stuffs and dishes from abroad. Many nominally "foreign" dishes have become so much a part of prevailing Japanese mass-market tastes as to be now virtually indigenous; obvious illustrations include curried rice and McDonald's hamburgers (Ohnuki-Tierney 1997). And, with the notable exceptions of Korean cuisine and, very recently, Southeast Asian and Latin American dishes, immigration and the creation of ethnic communities within Japan have had only minor impact on culinary innovation for the ordinary Japanese consumer (unlike many other societies, in which immigrant populations are the primary stimulus for culinary diversification). In some cases, dishes regarded as parts of "foreign" culinary traditions are thoroughly adapted to Japanese tastes: sea urchin roe pizza, for example, or hearty fish sausages.

But international culinary cross-fertilization is not one-sided; "Japanese" cuisine has simultaneously diffused abroad and sometimes rediffused itself back "home." Even as sushi has become an icon of North American yuppie tastes, and as nouvelle cuisine has become a major influence at the highest echelons of international cuisine, the "Franco-Japonaise" culinary styles currently popular in New York and Los Angeles have swept haute Tokyo as well. Attribution of "national" identity to stylistic developments in a transnational expressive context is familiar in culinary circles (see Jeffrey Tobin 1992 on "Franco-Japonaise" cuisine; Appadurai 1986a), as well as in many others, such as the international high fashion industry (Kondo 1992).

Japanese living arrangements have also altered the social context of cuisine. Since the mid-1950s, revolutionary appliances have saturated Japanese homes: everything from refrigerators, gas ranges, and electric rice cookers to microwave ovens, automatic bread makers, and devices that make rice cakes—glutinous *mochi*—from scratch. Hirano Minase (1997) chronicles the introduction of about ninety electrical and gas household appliances between 1948 and 1992. The high-tech inventory of an ordinary Tokyo domestic kitchen today stands in stark contrast to the meager lists of household goods compiled by Ronald Dore in the early 1950s, when only 12.6 percent of households owned iceboxes (not yet refrigerators) (Dore 1958: 51–52); between 1960 and 1970, Japanese kitchens with electric refrigerators shot from 10 percent to 89 percent (Hirano Minase 1997: 63).[20]

Households—and hence the domestic hearth—have themselves changed considerably (see White 2002). Throughout urban and rural Japan, nuclear and quasi-nuclear families have replaced extended ones. Not only are family units smaller on the average but they are less likely to include members of several generations. Even when extended families live together, it is not uncommon for the generations to maintain somewhat separate cooking facilities and eating schedules (Kelly 1986). The increasingly individualistic schedules of young and old alike have eroded patterns of family dining. Children returning late from cram schools may eat separately from their parents and siblings, and numerous surveys show that the average urban male white-collar employee eats dinner at home less often than he eats out.[21] Particularly in urban areas, single-person households—of the very old and of those just coming of age—have become common. In many urban areas, so-called one-room mansions (condominium studio apartments) have almost entirely replaced family dwellings.

Taken together, the culinary impact of these trends is profound. More and more foodstuffs consumed at home are commercially prepared fast foods for the microwave, packaged in single-serving portions. And fewer and fewer home cooks learn or feel comfortable with traditional culinary skills. Tsukiji traders joke about possibly apocryphal young brides who do not own a *hōchō* (an ordinary Japanese-style kitchen cleaver) and who misconstrue *sanmai oroshi* (filleting a whole fish) and *daikon oroshi* (grating a radish) as related culinary techniques.

As the culinary connotations of home and hearth have diminished, domestic responsibilities—or at least expectations—have changed. Traditionally, Japanese women were obligated to take charge of all aspects of household food preparation, and good wives and wise mothers were assumed to be highly concerned with diet, nutrition, and health (Lock 1980: 73–74, 104–6). Women today may be expected to be familiar with a wide and varied range of culinary styles (e.g., domesticated versions of Chinese, Indian, Italian, and French cuisine), and to have a repertoire of fancy dishes for special occasions, but many neither know, nor need to know, as much about basic foodstuffs or start-from-scratch culinary techniques as did their mothers or grandmothers.[22]

Many of my Japanese friends admit freely they do not know how to make many of the dishes they ate as children (although they can easily put together much fancier meals with prepared and semiprepared ingredients from grocery stores). Almost everyone acknowledges that this generation knows far less about food preparation than their mothers' generation. Tsukiji traders, both men and women, agree, and make disparaging comments about contemporary women's culinary knowledge and cooking abilities.

Bridal training classes *(hanayome shugyō* or *o-keikogoto)* generally include education in culinary arts to prepare young women for their careers as "professional housewives" (S. Vogel 1978). But rather than focusing on everyday skills of domestic cooking, the training often revolves around preparation of special dishes for formal events—such as the elaborate, highly stylized cuisine for the New Year, *o-sechi ryōri*. Of course, since the hallmark of o-sechi dishes is that they are prepared ahead of time, in order for all members of the family, including the cook, to relax during the holiday itself, commercially prepared food for takeout lends itself to the New Year's banquet. Traditional mom-and-pop purveyors and, increasingly, department stores, supermarkets, and even convenience stores (known as *konbini*) offer everything from single dishes to entire packaged banquets. The 7-Eleven chain does a booming business catering family New Year's parties. Some Tokyo department stores even offer total packages for the holidays, including not only the banquet but also housecleaning beforehand!

Although commercial alternatives to home cooking are ever-increasing, the popularity of cooking classes at private academies and municipal adult education centers suggests that many Japanese women enroll in formal culinary training at one point or another in their domestic careers as brides-to-be, wives, and mothers. Cooking has become, at least in some cases, intensely competitive. For example, Anne Allison's analysis (1991) of mothers preparing box lunches *(o-bentō)* for their nursery school children argues that the task is framed on the one hand by enormous social pressures to prove one's mothering skills and on the other hand by cultural constraints on "appropriate ingredients" that reflect culinary nationalism. And from nursery school onward, children's eating habits and table manners are regarded as evidence of their socialization and character development, and hence of their mother's dedication to motherhood (Hendry 1986: 76–78; Ben-Ari 1997).

As the industrialization of food alters women's traditionally defined roles as "good wives and wise mothers" *(ryōsai kenbo,* in the ideologically charged phrase from the period before World War II), the distance of women from the world of professional culinary accomplishment widens. Most women do not possess the specialized knowledge in which the largely male population of Tsukiji traders takes considerable professional pride. This alienation of culinary expertise affects some of the criteria by which Tsukiji traders themselves judge food. Tsukiji workers, both male and female, often commented to me that today's urban Japanese homemakers, despite their apparently wide knowledge of culinary provenance and technique, are not necessarily comfortable with mundane foodstuffs. The ordinary consumer, in approaching grocery shopping or cooking, lacks easy familiarity with raw ingredients and a willingness to substitute or make do with what the marketplace can provide.

Rather than judge foodstuffs by their quality and suitability for particular uses, many consumers rely instead on highly detailed but (in the eyes of food professionals) highly superficial notions of what constitutes perfection for any given item of fresh food. As one supermarket executive put it to me, many of his customers are "uneasy" about fresh foods. To the "nervous" eyes of a shopper, he grumbled, even the slightest blemish, the smallest imperfection, or the most trivial deviation from the ideal—defects with no possible link to either the food value or the usability of the product—may damn it: cucumbers must be straight, the cherries' stems must be uniform in length, the fish's tail must be unscarred. His suppliers must take pains, therefore, to ensure that the outward form—the *kata*—of the product is perfect, since imperfection outside might signal imperfection within. Consumers' concerns about ideal outward form, this attribute of kata, force Tsukiji traders to focus their own attention on appearance (sometimes over quality); not surprisingly, this focus reinforces an ever-upward spiral of emphasis on the aesthetic appeal of seafood among both consumers and professionals.

Kata can refer to an ideal shape, as in a mold for candies, or to an ideal form, as in the motions of a trained calligrapher, the routine of a kabuki actor, or the maneuvers of a martial artist. When seafood is under discussion, kata can imply the static physical form an object takes: the appearance of a flawless specimen of silver salmon, or a shipment of lobster perfectly matched in color, weight, and claw size. Or kata can refer to the dynamic process that results in a specific ideal outcome: the fluid but precise moves of a master sushi chef as he fillets a block of tuna, or the careful attention to detail that results in an exquisitely arranged tray of sea urchin roe. Ideal shape is a matter of both product and process, and attention to both is crucial for buyers at Tsukiji because kata is a fundamental element in Japanese food culture and in consumers' notions of quality. For many retail shoppers—and here is the problem faced by the supermarket executive—kata implies a standard against which a product can be judged; it is often the sole criterion by which a shopper can assess the quality, freshness, purity, or taste of a product wrapped in plastic. So the professional buyers at Tsukiji must make sure that what they purchase will meet the idealized expectations of shoppers who buy seafood by sight and image (T. Bestor 1995).

The Impersonal Touch

Standards of consumer judgment redefine the ways in which food is prepared within the home, and the relationship between home itself and food consumption is also changing dramatically. Car culture—what David Plath (1992a) calls "my car-isma"—increasingly drives domestic groups to meals at "family restaurants." The American chain Denny's and its many Japanese clones now have thousands of such restaurants in urban areas and along major highways. They promise an enjoyable meal as part of a simple outing in the family car. And whether their menus focus on a "Japanese" culinary realm or are more "international" in their appeal, such chain restaurants offer a range of dishes far more eclectic than do traditional Japanese restaurants, which typically specialize in a particular culinary genre, such as *tonkatsu* (pork cutlets), sushi, tempura, or *rāmen* noodles. The new family restaurants not only offer much broader ranges of cuisine than do traditional Japanese restaurants but also encourage or appeal to individuality in ordering; at traditional restaurants, in contrast, it is common for a party of diners to order the same dishes with at most minor variations in accompanying drinks or side dishes.

Some major chains, however, offer fare from a single culinary spectrum with menus almost entirely devoted to seafood—mostly served as "traditional" Japanese dishes—extending from sushi to *nabemono* (seafood stew or bouillabaisse). The Kyōtaru sushi chain illustrates both the popularity and the volatility of these new restaurants. In 1989, during the year of its greatest success, this chain ran 752 shops nationwide, 346 of them in Tokyo alone (figures from Kyōtaru's official report to the Ministry of Finance, December 1989). The shops operated under several related names with similar culinary themes, although focused on different market niches: some were located along suburban highways, some in urban shopping districts in front of major railway stations; some were sit-down restaurants, others specialized in take-out orders. The chain filed for bankruptcy in early 1997, brought down largely by poor real estate investments (although it was also badly hurt by the public panic and precipitous decline in sushi sales during the summer of 1996 following the outbreak of *E. coli* contamination near Osaka).

The increased popularity of family restaurants is only one facet of what trend-mongers call the *gaishoku būmu*—the "eating-out boom." Trade publications regularly report data on rapid increases in the percentage of meals eaten outside the home and of total household food expenditures on meals in restaurants (e.g., Shokuhin Ryūtsū Jōhō Sentaa). Retailers naturally view the growth in eating out with alarm; restaurateurs fiercely compete for market share among these diners.

Although this expansion of the restaurant industry looms large at Tsukiji, putting on pressure for more precisely standardized seafood, it is really little more than a blip within much broader changes now reshaping the retail world, the restaurant industry, the food-processing industry, and Japanese culinary habits generally.

Even as the gourmet boom, a renewed interest in regional cuisines, and an incipient "Slow Food" movement have continued to create demand for the finest that Tsukiji can provide, another trend—reflecting the economic hard times of the 1990s—has diminished sushi consumption, at least in the eyes of Tsukiji traders. *Kaiten-zushi*, sometimes translated as "rotary sushi," gained wide popularity among consumers during the late 1990s.

Kaiten-zushi is served on a conveyor belt; chefs make up small batches of different kinds of sushi and place them on a moving track, and customers take one plate of this or one plate of that (usually two pieces of sushi, as in a traditional serving). Each plate is priced (and the total is later calculated) according to the color or shape of the plate itself, and at the end of a meal, an employee simply sorts and then counts the different kinds of plates the customer has stacked up to arrive at a total. Kaiten-zushi restaurants make a point of their low prices—100 yen per serving, or 150, or 200—for basic offerings, with higher prices for servings that make the rounds on fancier plates.

Kaiten-zushi was invented in the 1950s and gained a reputation (deservedly so, in many cases) as quick, cheap, and often tasteless. Such restaurants were places to catch a bite before getting on a train. Ambiance did not come around the belt.

In the recession of the 1990s, however, kaiten-zushi became popular (even trendy) and its image (and quality) improved. Its newfound popularity (and the idea—oxymoronic to some—of gourmet kaiten-zushi) reflects the impact of the recession on consumer spending habits and the wider availability of inexpensive imported seafood (thanks to the revolution in distribution channels discussed in chapter 5). In addition, the technology of the fast-food industry has been applied to sushi: careful portion control, scanners that can read barcodes or microchips embedded in each plate, and low-paid staff who simply assemble sushi rather than master it. Some critics add that a growing preference among young Japanese to avoid interaction with others makes the anonymity of a conveyor belt preferable to the sociability of an interactive chef. (For a sense of the popularity of kaiten-zushi, see Akamoto 2002 and Yagyū 2003;[23] for its economics, see Watanabe 2002.)

Whatever the reasons, kaiten-zushi became one of the booms of the 1990s. Tsukiji people of course welcome the interest in seafood, but most of the seafood served as kaiten-zushi doesn't come from their shops. Kaiten-zushi restaurants more often get their fish from channels that run outside the market (see chapter 5) than from those within it; generally Tsukiji traders regard kaiten-zushi restaurants as bottom feeders, but for many consumers kaiten-zushi has become the standard.

The good and better kaiten-zushi shops have chefs who actually prepare the sushi in front of the customers (and respond to special requests). Other restaurants rely on "sushi robots," the array of mechanical devices that can cook rice, squeeze it into blocks, and plop precut pieces of fish on top, all in the back room where the conveyor belt slips out of sight. Still others depend on premade sushi, often frozen, sometimes prepared overseas and shipped to Japan.[24]

Top-of-the-line kaiten-zushi restaurants now have comfortable family atmospheres, nice lighting, and friendly chefs behind the counter to fill any order that a customer hasn't seen on the conveyor belt; but, most important, they have reasonable prices and good-quality, if not great, sushi. The concept also allows for immense variety, and so dotted among the plates of sushi passing by, one can pick out a green salad, some yakitori, or a piece of cheesecake. The Automat has been reborn.

In the retail world as well, convenience stores and supermarkets take full advantage of technological innovations to expand, and in many areas they have all but replaced old-fashioned, small-scale local retailers. Ready-to-eat meals and box lunches, many of them using newly developed industrial foods—such as surimi imitation crab or flash-frozen premade sushi—crowd the shelves of modern stores, in some cases almost eliminating the traditional raw or semiprocessed ingredients on which earlier generations of consumers relied.

The burden (and the profit) of provisioning the urban Japanese household has shifted from neighborhood mom-and-pop stores to convenience stores and supermarkets. Old-fashioned local shops are often quite specialized, dealing in a single category of foodstuffs: saké, or fish, or rice, or vegetables, or pickles. Such shops, of course, handle at least some nationally known brand-name goods, but their stock-in-trade is frequently those almost generic commodities for which the merchant's reputation (as processor of homemade pickles, as knowing buyer of fresh fish or produce, etc.) is important to the shop's clientele. That is, you may shop at Mr. Saitō's fish store with the knowledge—or at least the hope—that Mr. Saitō personally selected only good-quality fish when he visited the Tsukiji marketplace, and perhaps because Mrs. Saitō's homemade pickles are your family's favorite; the fact that they are neighbors and know your children adds to the relationship.

On the other hand, supermarkets deal largely in brand-name merchandise, and thus the reputations on the line are more the manufacturers' than the merchants'; the supermarket's stock-in-trade is the promise of convenience and greater variety for the daily diet and, sometimes, a lower price. As a shopper, you may bypass the Saitōs' shop for the Daiei or Jusco supermarket at the nearby station. You hope to shave a few yen off your bill, knowing that the freezer case is full of Nichirei's ready-to-heat fish cakes and that at the fresh fish counter something of everything—not Mr. Saitō's fresher but more limited and idiosyncratic selection—will be available, even if the fish were cleaned and wrapped several hours earlier. (And maybe you will return home along a back street to avoid flaunting your purchases in the face of your neighbors, the Saitōs.)

The landscape of shopping continues to shift dramatically. In addition to the struggle between retail fishmongers and large supermarket chains, a third factor is the spread of the now-ubiquitous *konbini* ("convenience stores"; Bestor 2002c). Some are outlets or franchises of major Japanese chains such as Lawson's and 7-Eleven;[25] others are local stores revamped through their affiliation with a regional or national marketing group. Small supermarkets and convenience stores exist in part because Japanese retail laws sharply distinguish between "large-scale" retail stores (such as supermarkets and department stores) and small-scale, independent shops. The former are strictly regulated in their sites, hours, product lines, and local competitive strategies, while the latter can operate with much greater freedom. Small supermarkets and convenience stores have expanded rapidly in the market terrain between conventional local shops and the large supermarket chains, through their ability to bring sophisticated distribution systems to tiny local shops. At their most stripped-down, convenience stores may sell nothing more than snacks, soft drinks, magazines, and prepackaged foods (often in single-serving portions) suitable for microwaves. More elaborate convenience stores may carry a few perishable foods, but only the most rudimentary assortment and no more than a handful of ingredients. Nonetheless, for many young and single consumers (and some who are neither), a convenience store *is* the local food store.

Shopping trends illustrate this shift. The TMG regularly conducts surveys of consumers' shopping patterns for perishable fish and vegetables. During the first half of the 1990s, shoppers who depended on retail fishmongers declined by more than 20 percent (49 percent in 1991, 39 in 1994, and 27 in 1996), while those who shopped in small supermarkets, including convenience stores, increased by 8 percent (12, 8, and 20 percent, respectively), the same increase reported for large supermarkets (21, 32, and 29 percent). Consumers who purchased seafood in department stores or specialty chain stores (often found in department stores) increased slightly (4, 7, and 8 percent), as did shoppers who relied on consumer cooperatives (*seikyō*) (12, 11, and 13 percent). One category of shopping disappeared between 1991 and 1996: in 1991 almost 3 percent of consumers reported they purchased fresh seafood from peddlers, but that was the last year the category was large enough to be reported separately. Not surprisingly, shoppers in their twenties were most likely to patronize small supermarkets and convenience stores (30.4 percent in 1996); those in their thirties were most partial to large supermarkets (36.0 percent); and shoppers over the age of sixty favored retail fishmongers (37.1 percent) (*Shijō memo* 1992: 108; 1995, 119; Tōkyō-to Chūō Oroshiuri Shijō 1996: 8–13).

TIME TO EAT

Temporal patterns of Japanese life embedded in cultural beliefs and social behaviors—some contemporary and others with venerable pasts—also define foodstuffs and shape their consumption. In today's commercial culture of consumption time defines buyers' tastes and preferences, and therefore shapes conditions of supply and demand. Some patterns are self-evident. Weekends stimulate demand across the board; bars and restaurants stock up for their increased trade, and retailers buy heavily on Fridays and Saturdays. Weekends are popular days for eating out and for shopping, and the marketplace is closed on Sundays.[26] The major monthly paydays for salaried employees also stimulate demand for somewhat fancier grades of seafood than what might sell on an ordinary Monday or Tuesday.

The political calendar plays a role, too. When Tokyo is the site of a major international summit meeting or when a major world leader pays a visit, the demand for expensive seafood drops. Why? Because the tight security imposed on central Tokyo forces ordinary citizens to stay at home and avoid the entertainment districts. And the exclusive Japanese-style restaurants *(ryōtei)* and sushi bars of the major hotels suffer a loss in business as high-rolling Japanese patrons are replaced by foreign visitors with little appetite for the more exotic and expensive seafood delicacies that are these restaurants' normal stock-in-trade. Other exceptional events make themselves felt as well. When the pall of the Shōwa Emperor's impending death lingered over Tokyo from September 1988 until early January 1989, many normal recreational activities were curtailed in the name of "self-restraint." The restaurant trade was among the industries that suffered, and Tsukiji's orders from hotels, ryōtei, and sushi restaurants dropped dramatically for several months.

On more subtle levels, too, the symbolism of foodstuffs is complex and often linked to times of transition and rites of passage. A couple of illustrations may demonstrate some general contours; a full analysis of seafood symbolism alone would call for an entire book of its own. Sea bream *(tai)*, as mentioned earlier, is almost required for wedding banquets, because of a play on words and visual imagery. *Omedetai* means "congratulations," and the combination of the fish's reddish skin and its white flesh mirrors the red-and-white combination almost universally used on celebratory occasions in Japan. This same color symbolism works for other seafood as well, so lobster tails are also standard fare in wedding halls. (Lobster claws, however, must be avoided because they imply cutting, perhaps severing the marital bond even before the knot is fully tied.) Another example, also involving weddings, is abalone *(awabi)*, a delicacy prized so much that in recent years abalone grounds on the West Coast of the United States have been closed because catches for the Japanese market threatened to wipe out the species. Traditionally, abalone was a key component of auspicious offerings and gifts, implying by its presence that the gift came with sacred blessings. However, abalone also has had a long history in poetry, dating back to the earliest anthology of Japanese verse, the *Man'yōshū* (compiled in 759 C.E.), signifying unrequited love by drawing a symbolic parallel between one-sided love and the abalone's single shell. For this reason, in the folklore of cuisine, abalone cannot be served at wedding banquets, although other bivalve shellfish are often eaten.[27]

The annual cycle of holidays and festivals also underscores links among time, food culture, and consumption. O-Shōgatsu, the New Year, is the most prominent example. The typical New Year's banquet of o-sechi, an elaborate buffet of traditional delicacies, makes great use of seafood; some varieties, such as herring roe *(kazunoko)*, are virtually synonymous with the New Year's holidays. But throughout the year, dozens of other holidays, both national and local, tend to have a culinary component, skillfully magnified both in the restaurant trade, where chefs seek to emphasize seasonality, and in the women's magazines that stimulate their own sales by extending the definitions of what every homemaker ought to know about cuisine.[28] Even if there is no particular seafood delicacy associated with a holiday, families tend to eat somewhat fancier meals on days when people are off work, and Tsukiji traders can count on the little bursts of demand for sashimi- and sushi-grade seafood that normally precede any holiday.

The simple passing of the seasons and their impact on the dining table is obvious in any food culture. Seasonal tastes echo harvest times, months in which particular kinds of seafood are freshest and most plentiful, the depths of winter when hearty soups and stews are preferred, or periods of scarcity when pickled dishes take the place of fresh ones. Japanese culture marks the passing of time closely; each day of the year has its unique constellation of cultural undertones that shape its culinary character. Several sets of calendrical considerations—seasonal and ritual—interact to define the foodstuffs that ideally, or at least appropriately, may or should be consumed. Certainly no one in his or her own daily life thinks about, let alone chooses, a diet based on all the possible permutations. But the calendar's arcane complexities steer food preferences nonetheless and form a background against which consumption and demand ebb and flow.

Calendrical precision begins with the system of *rokuyō*, a six-day cycle of ritually lucky and unlucky days, listed in almanacs and on many calendars to designate appropriate days for funerals, weddings, and other events. The day known as "Great Peace" (Taian), for example, is favored for weddings; Tsukiji wholesalers who supply hotels and catering firms in the wedding business anticipate that the demand for sea bream, lobster, and other seafoods popular for wedding banquets will fluctuate more or less predictably according to the complicated intersections of this with other secular cycles (such as weekends, national holidays, or school vacations).[29]

The customary Japanese calendar traditionally divides the year into twenty-four segments of roughly two weeks apiece.[30] Each such micro-season *(sekki)* has its own distinctive name, evocative of weather or agricultural conditions. And each micro-season is marked in a wide range of ways, including appropriate greetings, artistic motifs, poetic allusions, recreations, festivities, rituals, styles of traditional clothing, and of course cuisine. Particular kinds of seafood or specific dishes are often regarded as hallmarks of a micro-season.

The popularity of *iwashi* (sardines) on Setsubun, a holiday in early February, is one example. Setsubun (usually February 2, 3, or 4) marks the beginning of the micro-season conventionally regarded as the beginning of spring. Shrines hold popular public ceremonies to drive away goblins *(oni)* and bring on good fortune for the coming year, and supermarkets and sushi shops advertise foods that are supposed to augment one's luck. Oni do not like the smell of sardines, according to goblin lore, so they are one delicacy of the holiday; sushi rolls *(maki-zushi)*—signifiers of clubs with which to thrash goblins—are another, to be eaten while facing in an auspicious direction.

A more dramatic example of the identification of seafood with a particular holiday occurs on the midsummer "Day of the Ox" (Doyō no ushi no hi), mentioned earlier, traditionally considered to mark the hottest period of the year, when one is supposed to eat eel to maintain one's stamina against the withering heat. The particular specialty, at least in Tokyo, is grilled eel, called *kabayaki*. On that day, eel restaurants have lines of customers stretching around the block, supermarkets schedule special sales of eel, and the eel trade is in full frenzy. In 1979, on the eve of this peak eel season, a massive traffic accident involving a tanker truck destroyed a vital tunnel on the Tōmei Expressway, which links Tokyo to the major domestic eel-producing regions around Hamamatsu in central Japan. For several days, while the tunnel was closed, the Tokyo news media focused on the disruption of the Day of the Ox almost as much as on the accident itself.

A common explanation for eel's popularity at this time of year is that its high oil and protein content fortify the stomach *(hara)* against the mid-summer heat; customary Japanese views of health and illness pay careful attention to the temperature of the stomach (Lock 1980: 86–88). The calendrical symbolism behind the Day of the Ox, which reinforces this set of beliefs, stands at the intersection of several overlapping methods of marking time;[31] it also draws on other complicated aspects of cultural tradition.[32]

But Tsukiji traders, wily in the ways of commerce, explain the custom's origins and continuing popularity much more simply: advertising. One story reports that an eighteenth-century Edo *unagi* (eel) restaurateur had the bright idea of commissioning a famous calligrapher to make a simple sign proclaiming, "Today is the Day of the Ox." The fame of the calligrapher ensured that passersby would notice the sign and the eel shop, and make the desired assumption that there was something special about the day and its relationship to unagi. Once made, the connection stuck, illustrating the principle later enshrined in twentieth-century American advertising lore as "Don't sell the steak, sell the sizzle."

Whatever the arcane origins of the culinary practice, the Day of the Ox is obviously no trivial matter for eel dealers, restaurateurs, or supermarket managers planning July and August sales campaigns. Roughly one-third of Tsukiji's annual eel sales occurs during the doyō micro-season. During 1995 and 1996, July alone accounted for about 24 percent of Tsukiji's annual sales of live eels (129 and 126 metric tons out of respective annual totals of 538 and 531); an additional 64 (12 percent) and 60 (11 percent) metric tons were sold in August of those two years (Asakawa 1997).[33]

Culinary calendars are constructed in other ways as well. Seasonality (known as *shun*—written with the same character that indicates the traditional ten-day divisions of the month)[34] fixes the limits of sushi; better sushi chefs do not serve seafood that is not in its peak season. Seasonality defines varieties of seafood not just by availability and quality but by their essential characteristics. That is, fish of the same species may be known by different names depending on the time of year they are caught, their size, their maturity, or the location in which they are caught (all of which, naturally, may be closely interrelated). Yet as one sushi chef carefully explained to me, to his refined palate these are distinct varieties of seafood,

Figure 38. Selling the sizzle. A balloon above Tsukiji advertising the Day of the Ox in 1937. Reproduced with permission of the Mainichi PhotoBank.

each with its own characteristic flavors and textures, each with its own best methods for preparation and consumption, and each to be judged by its own standards of quality. Since they are not necessarily interchangeable, to substitute, say, *meji* (an immature tuna) for *maguro* (a mature tuna) would be to miss the point of the cuisine. The shun for meji is not the shun for maguro; meji is neither more nor less delicious than maguro; each size or season offers its own unique flavors and qualities to be savored on its own merits. Yellowtail, for example, is known variously as *hamachi, mojako, wakashi, inada, warasa,* or *buri* according to size and maturity, and different culinary uses await each form; these are the distinctions in the Tokyo region, and in other areas of the country different names and different dishes are common (Yoshino 1986: 40). One guide (Rakugo 1990) discusses in detail some seventy sushi toppings *(tane* or *sushidane)* and their seasons of perfection.

The concept of *hatsumono* ("first things," or more specifically "the first products of the year, or of the season") underscores the seasonality of fish as seafood. Hatsumono have special importance in determining the values (both economic and cultural) assigned to commodities in the marketplace, and the social worlds of producers and dealers celebrate their arrival (a point I return to in chapter 8). The first catch of a new season—*hatsuryō*—in many fishing communities occasions great celebration. Beforehand, priests bless vessels and crews; bamboo fronds, banners, and amulets bedeck the vessels; and captains and vessel owners receive auspiciously decorated casks of saké. Afterward, when the first catch is landed, captain and crew distribute portions of the catch to those who gave saké or other gifts to the vessel, and the captain or owner may host a round of banquets featuring the first catch. The reciprocal gift-giving of saké-for-fish and the distribution of large portions of the catch to relatives, neighbors, and friends can constitute a major element in the carefully balanced social life of a fishing community (see Akimichi et al. 1988: 41–51).

For Tokyo's consumers and the markets that supply them, hatsumono do not, of course, carry the full range of meanings that the hatsuryō implies for communities that make their living by fishing. Nevertheless, hatsumono are significant. The first catches arriving in the marketplace (known as *hatsuni*, "first freight") are heralded with high prices and intense competition among wholesalers to obtain scarce supplies. The first shipments may arrive bedecked with ceremonial banners and accompanied by delegations of fisheries representatives. Retail shops and restaurants celebrate hatsumono with sales and special menus, and the availability of a particular seafood marks the coming of the seasons in the public eye as well as in the market's calendar. For the citizens of old Edo, *hatsugatsuo* (the season's first *katsuo* [bonito]) was almost emblematic of their civic identity: one famous verse exults, "To be a man, born in Edo and eat the first katsuo of the season." Another is by the famous poet Yamaguchi Sodō (1642–1716): "Fresh green leaves to see; the cuckoo's song to hear; and the first katsuo to taste" (Sunada 1980).

FISH FIGHT BACK

Fish, of course, are products of the natural world, and there is at least symbolic uneasiness over the relationship between human domination of nature and nature's capacity to sustain or to chasten its exploiters. Many ritual beliefs and practices surround the harvest of marine creatures in Japanese fishing culture. Fishing communities throughout the country engage in similar rites to ensure the safety of crews, to pray and give thanks for bountiful catches, to propitiate the deities that control the seas and the destinies of those who live by them, and to calm the souls of the marine creatures fishers capture.

The traditions of Japanese popular religion provide for ritual memorials for lives—even of marine creatures—taken for food. Whaling communities, for example, commonly held Buddhist memorial services for the dead, known as *kuyō*, to honor the souls of whales (see Akimichi et al. 1988: 52–61). Whales are perhaps more likely than other marine species to be the objects of such ritual concern, if only because they can be anthropomorphized. Whales are mammals whose behavior can be glossed as "human": for example, mothers nurse their young, adults engage in long-term monogamous mating relationships, and parents and offspring live together in stable family groups. These traits, quite apart from recent considerations of cetacean brain size or possible linguistic capabilities, may contribute both to the ambivalence of whalers toward their hunting activities and to the avidity with which such memorial services were performed. The very real dangers of whaling—and the well-documented cases of whales turning on their hunters—may also account for the ritual care taken to placate their souls.

At Tsukiji, dealers do not confront the dangers of fishing and navigation, and they do not anthropomorphize their products; they do not regard taking the life of fish as a moral issue. A Tsukiji dealer or fishmonger or chef with qualms about gutting a fish would not last long. And yet the term "cruel cuisine" *(zankoku ryōri)*, sometimes used to describe still-living fish served for sashimi, suggests ambivalence. Indeed, some Tsukiji traders *do* take elaborate ritual note of the killing of fish. In general, such observances are collective rituals joined in by members of occupational specialties who deal in—that is, kill—fish that arrive in the market alive.

The association for unagi dealers holds occasional observances at Mount Takao, a holy mountain on the western fringes of the Tokyo metropolitan region. The eel dealers hold their rituals at a temple with a reputation for warding off eye problems and brain disorders. Unagi dealers believe they are prone to suffer blindness or strokes in retribution for their trade. Watching Morioka-san, a middle-aged proprietor of a Tsukiji eel stall, as he rapidly skins and fillets whole live eels, pinning each wriggling unagi to his cutting board with a pick stuck through its eye socket, the cause-and-effect fears of this occupational superstition are obvious.

Much more immediate dangers lurk in the trade in fugu—the poisonous blowfish or globefish that can be sold or prepared only by dealers and chefs with special licenses issued by the prefectural authorities. Many Japanese regard the fish *(Fugu rubripes)* as a great delicacy. But some of its organs, especially the liver *(kimo)*, concentrate toxins. If toxic fugu is eaten, the first symptoms are a tingling sensation on the tongue and a numbness of the fingertips; in severe cases, paralysis or death may occur within hours. Toxicity varies from fish to fish and can be judged only by eating the fish in question or by later, perhaps posthumous, laboratory analysis. If a trained chef properly removes the organs, the remaining flesh is entirely harmless. However, the flesh can be easily contaminated by a punctured organ or an improperly cleaned knife. From time to time, such mishaps cause death; but the most celebrated cases result not from accidents but from a seemingly perverse culinary aesthetic. The tingling sensation one reportedly feels on one's tongue when eating fugu liver is judged by fatalistic gourmets to be an exquisitely sensual delight. In January 1975 the famed kabuki actor Bandō Mitsugoro, a "Living National Treasure" *(ningen kokuhō)*, died after eating four servings of fugu liver at a Kyoto restaurant. Faced with the dilemma of refusing the dangerous request of a celebrated artist or of breaking the law and serving the dish, the chef catered to his patron's whim. Police questioned the chef and ultimately his license was revoked for violations of Kyoto Prefecture's fugu regulations (*Asahi Shimbun,* January 16, 1975, evening ed.).

Each year, the fugu association at Tsukiji holds an annual *hōryū,* a service to release animals to the wilds. After prayers at a temporary altar on the river bank, several hundred live fugu are released into the Sumida's waters. (Tsukiji's rites became the model for a similar ceremony now held at Shimonoseki, the major marketplace at the western tip of Honshū and the fugu trade's center; see Omura Baijin 1990: 18–19.) One Tsukiji dealer, Suzuki-san—a deceptively boyish dealer in top-of-the-line fish for elite restaurants who himself handles fugu, among many other products— jokingly complained to me that releasing fugu into the Sumida River (long known for its pollution) was itself an inhumane act, another injustice begging for further retribution. And, since the ritual takes place at the peak of the fugu season, when the fish are at both their highest quality and their highest price, the whole exercise struck Suzuki as doubly wasteful.

Ambiguity is inherent in kuyō, since the services are intended as much to ward off retributive dangers—the poison of the blowfish, which could in a sense exact revenge even as one eats it, and the sympathetic magic believed to be exercised by eels seeking vengeance for the particularly brutal manner of their death—as simply to express respect for the souls of animate beings. The concept of *tatari*—retribution, especially supernatural retribution—is the cultural rationale behind these rituals (R. J. Smith 1992b).

Kuyō have become increasing commonplace in Japanese life during the past generation, for a wide variety of commodities. The underlying motivations vary, according to William LaFleur (1992: 146), who posits a continuum from apology (mixed perhaps with concerns over retribution) to appreciation. At the most somber end of the spectrum, memorials for unborn fetuses *(mizuko kuyō)* embody the most profound forms of spiritual apology (see also Hardacre 1997); somewhat less intense memorials, for creatures consumed as foodstuffs or sacrificed in service to humans, mix apology with gratitude; other objects used in daily life are memorialized simply with thanks. Examples of these latter include such diverse and mundane items as needles, tea whisks, brassieres, and computer chips (LaFleur 1992: 143–46; Hoshino and Takeda 1993: 175–78; Sanger 1990). The Bentendō temple in the middle of Shinobazu Pond in Ueno Park— long patronized by Tokyo merchants seeking good fortune—is dotted with memorial tablets for both the animate and inanimate, ranging from chickens, turtles, blowfish, and seafood in general to kitchen knives, calendars, eyeglasses, and Japanese musical instruments including the *biwa* and *koto.*

Just to the north of the Tsukiji marketplace, the courtyard of the Namiyoke Shrine contains a small row of stone monuments memorializing fish. The monuments honor three broad species of seafood by name—shrimp *(ebi),* clams *(hamaguri),* and monkfish *(ankō)*—and two general culinary categories, *sushidane* (sushi toppings, i.e., the assorted and often exotic varieties of seafood that are a sushi shop's stock-in-trade) and *katsugyo* (living fish, i.e., fish that arrive at Tsukiji alive and then are killed either at the market or in restaurant kitchens). Dealers in omelets for sushi bars have also erected a meter-high, egg-shaped monument.

In an article on Tsukiji (T. Bestor 1991), I included a photograph of the memorial tablet for sushidane with a caption about "honoring the memory of fish that had given their lives for sushi." An incensed reader wrote me that the fish had not "given" their lives; fishers *took* their lives through wanton, barbarous slaughter. The reader's advocacy of strict vegetarianism and animals' rights would win no converts at Tsukiji, but nonetheless her view that fish suffer at the hands of humans resonates with the impetus behind memorialization. People in the seafood trade know full well that fish die so that humans may eat, and Japanese Buddhism and folk belief not only posit a consequence of this (that the innocent dead may harm the living) but also provide a means to atone and avoid retribution.

The half-dozen monuments—erected by various trade groups repre-

Figures 39–40.
(Left) Memorial for sushi, Namiyoke Shrine.
(Right) Memorial for live fish, Namiyoke Shrine.

senting Tsukiji traders as well as chefs and fishmongers from outside the marketplace—also stand as reminders of the social worlds of the marketplace in which both trade and commodities are culturally constructed.

WEBS OF CUISINE

The codes of Japanese culinary logic permeate the marketplace, as cultural tradition and elaborately variegated social structure resonate with one another. Tsukiji traders navigate the complex currents of Japanese food culture as a matter of course. They must be as attuned to the significance of holidays as to the complex interactions of international food dependency. They must be as aware of the purported links between diet and cancer as of the growing demand for convenience food. They must respond as acutely to seasonality as to the qualities of seafood raised through aquaculture.

As individuals, Tsukiji traders are as much the products of and participants in Japanese culture as are their customers; all share and are influenced by broadly similar sets of fundamental beliefs about food. At the same time, the traders have vested interests in promoting the complex of culinary attitudes, including those celebrating freshness, abundance, purity, and national identity. They are therefore both passive and active agents of the culinary mystique, only *sometimes* the self-serving instigators of the refinement, elaboration, or transformation of cuisine.

But regardless of how far they collaborate in sustaining the general norms of food culture and in synthesizing and disseminating particular attitudes about fish as food, Tsukiji traders are first and foremost operating in a marketplace that feeds and responds to consumer demands. In that sense, Tsukiji traders think that it matters little what they themselves think about the fish they handle; they believe that what matters to them is what their clients think about the fish they handle.

To be sure, Tsukiji's traders have technical information and professional skills related to seafood far beyond those of the general public. From their perspective—with cultural capital in the bank, so to speak—the public's naive assumptions about the foodstuffs they purvey seem at times worthy of quiet scorn, and they are cynical about the cultural attitudes and processes that govern demand if not supply. Yet even as they joke about the rigmarole, shaking their heads over the seemingly iron grip that social events and cultural beliefs have over their trade—marveling over the enormous demand for whale meat after the International Whaling Commission banned whale hunting, grumbling over the business lost during international summit meetings, or bemoaning the release of hundreds of expensive fugu in propitiatory rituals—they still know, in their merchants' hearts, that the customer is always right.

And they, too, enjoy the romance of food culture that not only shapes the profiles of demands for their products but gives them a role in the great chain of Japanese tradition. Hearing a tuna dealer lasciviously describe the products of his trade, with sometimes explicit references to the curve and feel of a woman's body, or listening to a dealer in pickled fish talk animatedly of the intrepid band of sixteenth-century fishers who founded Edo's fish trade and perfected the techniques of *tsukudani,* or watching a trader explain "sakana no kaiwa"—conversation with the fish—to an apprentice as the art he must master in order to appreciate the technique of filleting, one is left with the unmistakable impression that many at Tsukiji view their jobs as a way of life, almost as a calling, enriched by deep associations with cultural identities embedded in tropes of Japanese machismo, Edo's demimonde, and the heritage of food culture.

Clifford Geertz proposes that "man is an animal suspended in webs of significance he himself has spun" (1973: 5). Tsukiji's traders have hardly spun all the webs of food culture themselves; in fact, many view their occupation as suspended on strings pulled by the fickle tastes of consumers, by the social forces that drive the eating-out boom and other such trends, and by the political and economic policy makers whose actions enable supermarkets to spread. Nevertheless, it is the imperatives of food culture and the patterns of production, retailing, and consumption of foodstuffs that culturally and socially construct the Tsukiji traders' frame of reference. These competing demands and constraints influence the buying and selling of fish and their transformation into culturally relevant commodities to which values of both use and exchange can be attached. Although the professional knowledge and skills of a Tsukiji trader may incline him to be skeptical of many of these culturally relevant attributes, nonetheless he and his colleagues are the agents of the process; they can resist its imperatives only at their peril.

The cultural logic of Japanese cuisine and its effects on the seafood trade are written through the social structure and institutions of the Tsukiji market. Culinary principles and practices stand as a root explanation for many elements of Tsukiji's trading system, but currents in the political economy of Japanese production and consumption exert influences that, focused through marketplaces like Tsukiji, reshape and redirect the flow of Japanese food culture. The interaction between culinary meaning and the social practices of trade permeates the marketplace. Commodity specializations define the professional lives and reputations of individual intermediate wholesalers, and classifications of foodstuffs provide the central organizing principles around which trading communities form within the marketplace. These definitions are embodied and enacted in the sets of institutions that sustain Tsukiji's auction system, and in the formation of formal guilds or associations, called *moyori gyōkai*, through which intermediate wholesalers organize for collective action. Chapter 5, "Visible Hands," examines more closely Tsukiji's auctions and their place in the vertical integration of distribution channels. The two following chapters—"Family Firm" and "Trading Places"—focus on intermediate wholesalers, both as independent businesspeople and as members of guilds that coordinate their collective activities and attempt to address issues of competition, cooperation, and equity among traders.

The seemingly detached movements of the market, which Tsukiji traders attribute to others—to the vagaries of consumer preference as it operationalizes culinary logic, and to the impersonal forces of a market economy—traders themselves delicately calibrate every day by their own hands, through institutions of their own making.

5   Visible Hands

Around 6 A.M. bells and buzzers clatter loudly across the marketplace. The workday started several hours ago. Since midnight, employees and subcontractors of the auction houses have been arranging, grading, labeling, and rearranging the seafood for the morning sales. Since 4 or 5 A.M., hundreds of other market participants—traders and their employees—have been inspecting lots: spearing out tiny fragments of flesh from frozen tuna and rubbing the slivers between thumb and forefinger to judge the fat content, opening Styrofoam cases of salmon to check the consistency of multicrate shipments, tasting tiny dried sardines or eyeing the color of sea urchin roe neatly lined up in small wooden trays, or watching live flounders as they flop around in flat plastic tubs. The bells and buzzers do not end this hubbub; they signal the opening of the auctions. At roughly fifteen- or twenty-minute intervals the several dozen auction pits scattered across the marketplace burst into life. Any given auction may last only a few minutes, but for more than an hour and a half, someone is bidding on something somewhere in the market.

Tsukiji's auctions proceed at a lightning speed, in cryptic exchanges between the auctioneers' throaty growls and the silent hand gestures of impassive buyers. Auctioneers cultivate showmanship and style that rivet attention on them; with voices like chainsaws and staccato hand gestures they command center stage as they pull out the bids during their brief minutes on the block. They can roar through a dozen lots in only a minute or two, and an outsider can barely tell who got each lot and for what price. A burst of abbreviated jargon; a blur of waving hands; quick, almost imperceptible gestures: all signify prices asked and offered, then a sale is over.

Traders flash finger signals to register their bids and shout at the auctioneer to get his attention. Some traders are wary, lost in a silent, secret, calculating reverie; others furtively check coded notes shielded under their jackets; still others toss off bids with nonchalant poker faces. Mostly they register little reaction to winning or losing a bid, though sometimes they tip their hands with grins or grimaces after the bidding is over. Occasionally laughter sweeps the auction pit if an auctioneer fumbles or if a trader offers an outlandishly low or high bid; anger flashes once in a while if someone feels that the auctioneer ignored his bid. But by and large, the traders quietly chat with friends, glance over faxed orders from clients, scrutinize their bidding notes, watch the crowd, and feign indifference when the lots they want come up for bid. As a sale concludes, the traders quickly scatter, rushing off to another auction or back to their stalls to await their own customers, perhaps pausing only to whisper instructions to a waiting apprentice, to supervise a stevedore as he loads the day's purchases onto a wooden dolly or tiny motorized cart, to pick up a scribbled invoice from an assistant auctioneer, or to whip out a cellular phone to report a prize purchase or a disappointing price to someone waiting somewhere for vital news.

When the auctions end for the day, by 7 or 7:30 A.M., roughly 2.3 million kilograms of seafood, worth about ¥2.1 billion, will have changed hands through competitive bidding (1999 figures; *Tsukiji Shijō gaiyō* 2000: 3). In many respects, Tsukiji's auctions are classic examples of spot markets, where cash-and-carry purchases are made of goods available for immediate delivery, where buyer and seller need not know or care about one another, where each transaction is an end in itself, and where the prices at which the market clears—at which supply and demand cancel each other out—constitute irrefutable indicators of market conditions. Auctions are the central mechanism of the Tsukiji marketplace, and, to an outside observer, they convey an odd sense of mysteriously frenzied process combined with utterly familiar competitive purpose. The puzzlement is in the details—why *that* fish? why *that* gesture?—but auctions are so fundamental to notions of how capitalist markets operate that the procedure itself seems a natural outcome of supply meeting demand as sellers and buyers hammer out a price.[1]

The auction's underlying principles appear obvious and straightforward—sell high, buy low, act now!—but its actual performance is considerably more complex. Its staging is inherently the product of social institutions and cultural understandings that together shape such features as the informal norms and formal regulations that frame participation in the sales, the patterns of access to information, and the potential for competition and collusion among bidders.[2] The outcome of a given auction—who gets what, how much of it, and at what cost?—may seem mechanically calculable, but the participants can make such calculations only after the market's underlying codes of

Figures 41–44.
(Top left) Frozen tuna on the wharf at dawn, arranged for buyers' inspection *(shitami)*.
(Above) Inspecting fresh tuna before the auction.
(Center left) Bidding for fresh tuna. Intermediate wholesalers bid with hand signals from the auction bleachers. Their caps have auction licenses attached: the sign behind them warns that caps with licenses *(seribō)* must be worn at all times and cannot be lent to other buyers.
(Left) After the auctioneer has moved on, a worker marks frozen tuna with buyers' names.

Figure 45. After the auction, whole tuna are lined up next to a wholesaler's stall, where they will be cut and trimmed. The numbers and paper stickers are auction markings.

competition, obligation, fair play, exchange, and transaction have been created or routinized as seemingly automatic or natural.

To say that auctions are culturally framed and socially instituted, however, is *not* to argue that they are a "traditional" part of a society's cultural ethos, in Japan or elsewhere. Nor is it to claim that auctions are common or a prevailing symbolic motif in a society's life. Indeed, auctions are not widespread in Japan. In the United States, significant numbers of nonprofessional buyers participate in what are sometimes called estate sales or country auctions or in charity auctions. Few Japanese have such experiences (although since the late 1990s eBay has become popular in Japan, at least among young people).[3]

Auctions—or other transactions involving open competitive bidding—in Japan exist largely within well-defined markets where both buyers and sellers belong to the same occupational community: stock exchanges, cattle markets (Longworth 1983: 142–51), art and antique markets (Kerr 1996: 87–95), and the construction industry (McMillan 1991).[4] Rice exchanges based on auctions opened on a trial basis in Tokyo and Osaka in 1990, and started regular sales in 1997.

Although auctions are not commonplace, they are culturally familiar both to ordinary Japanese who may never see one and to professionals who matter-of-factly participate in them every day. The cultural logic of market behavior—"economism," in Michèle de la Pradelle's term (1995)—is a compelling and pervasive part of Japanese life, just as for most residents of advanced capitalist or capitalizing economies in the world today.[5] Auctions reflect this logic and are created out of social and cultural processes that are themselves rooted in broader institutional structures of everyday economic life (Bell 1976; Bourdieu 1984; Herzfeld 1992).

Like markets more generally, auctions are imbued with the cultural principles of economism and are inherently embedded in networks of social relations (see Granovetter 1985; Geertz 1978, 1979). These social ties and cultural processes are *not* market imperfections; rather, they make markets and their components—economic processes such as auctions—viable. Auctions in the real world are inseparable from the social institutions and cultural meanings that frame them. Auctions have many characteristics and outcomes, only one of which is to sell products competitively to the highest bidder (C. Smith 1989). This is, of course, a central and explicit purpose of the Tsukiji marketplace; but to make sense of how such sales transpire one must look to the wider cultural and institutional contexts of Tsukiji's auction system.

Tsukiji's auctions stand at a fulcrum between primary producers and consumers, and the market's auctioneers and traders are the turning point. Both literally and figuratively, they repackage a large volume of relatively similar commodities (e.g., frozen tuna, farm-raised eels, or silver salmon) into the smaller units and wider variety of foodstuffs restaurateurs or consumers can actually use. This function of a market system is "bulking and breaking." Upstream from the marketplace, brokers assemble catches from many separate producers into larger and larger flows of commodities of increasingly homogeneous character for auction at Tsukiji and similar wholesale seafood markets. Downstream from the marketplace, however, customers do not demand large quantities of single commodities; they want small amounts of a wide range of varied products. After all, only a rare retailer or restaurateur wants to sell or serve nothing but tuna or shrimp or octopus; almost no one can handle an entire 200-kilogram shipment of any single product. So the crucial task of the auctions and the traders is to match supply with demand, by transforming one bulky product stream into another that is much more diverse. In the language of economists, seafood products are "lumpy" commodities—items of trade that have their own individual characteristics, according to the judgments of traders and the uses to which their clients will put the seafood—and Tsukiji is in business for the lumps.

This is all in the market's daily work, its calculations closely attuned to the principles and practices of Japanese food culture. As I showed in the previous chapter, the market reconciles supply and demand through inherently cultural processes of classification and commodification that reflect both the categories relevant to producers and shippers and the somewhat different cultural criteria that define foodstuffs in the eyes of consumers. This generation and elaboration of cultural meaning is also inherently a social process. It animates and defines the microsocial worlds of Tsukiji's auction pits and their specialized communities of traders; these in turn are constructed by the broader institutional framework of the auction system and the market.

Networks of both vertical and horizontal relationships unfold outward from the auctions. Vertically, relatively stable alignments among suppliers, auctioneers, and intermediate wholesalers revolve around the exchange of products and the information flows that such transactions require. Horizontally, trading communities coalesce around specific commodities. These groups become significant institutional actors themselves that create, constrain, and channel particular forms of cooperation and competition among traders operating at equivalent levels within the market system. Thus, in a sense, Tsukiji's auctions are concurrently suspended in vertical columns of transactions—of products, information, and money—that lead to coordination, if not integration, between producers and buyers and also in a horizontal web of relationships that define the terms of competition, cooperation, coercion, complicity, and sometimes collusion among buyers. This chapter focuses primarily on vertical aspects of the market's organization; the next chapter will concentrate on the horizontal relationships.

Up, down, and sideways, market relations are constrained by explicit government regulations intended to secure the fairness and transparency of the marketplace, as well as by a variety of customary practices and institutions that aim to ensure the market's smooth functioning. Poised between these not always compatible goals, Tsukiji's auctions are drawn toward more systematic vertical integration even as they seek to rely on more diffuse, personalistic ties of long-term connection and obligation. Neither set of impulses characterizes what might otherwise be regarded as a spot market. Rather, Tsukiji embodies many relationships best called "relational contracting" or "obligational contracting," terms used in transaction cost economics (see Macneil 2001; Williamson 1985; Williamson and Masten 1999) to describe the durable but only quasi-formal economic ties that occupy the middle ground between the hierarchical structure of a firm and the free play of a spot market.

Three sets of transactional relationships structure Tsukiji's auctions: on one level, those between auction houses and their suppliers, whose products furnish Tsukiji; on another, those between auction houses and the intermediate wholesalers, who purchase their stock at Tsukiji's auctions; and on the third, those between these traders and their own clients: retailers and restaurateurs. At each level, these relationships exist against the backdrop of a national system of markets, in which Tsukiji plays a major but not exclusive role. In broad terms, this national system structures the vertical relationship between supply and demand, defines the contexts and limits of horizontal competition, and mandates specific types of trade—particularly auctions—in order to routinize market forces. To understand Tsukiji's auctions, we must first understand these national systems.

UPSTREAM, DOWNSTREAM

The Tsukiji marketplace does not stand alone; it is the flagship of the Tokyo central wholesale market, a system of eleven main markets (including Tsukiji) and four smaller branch markets, which variously sell seafood, fresh produce, meat, and flowers, both cut and potted (map 5). In addition to Tsukiji in the center of the city, two other markets in the system handle seafood: Ōta and Adachi, in the far south and the northeast of the city, respectively. Tsukiji is by far the largest. In 1995 Tokyo's three seafood markets together handled 738,236 metric tons of products with a value of 680.2 billion yen; Tsukiji accounted for 86.7 percent and 87.7 percent, respectively, of these totals *(Tsukiji Shijō gaiyō* 1996: 16–17).

By virtue of its size, the massive Tsukiji marketplace is unique. No other market in Japan—no other market in the world—handles the volume of seafood that passes through its auctions daily: some 2,345 metric tons. In 1994 Tsukiji alone handled 20 percent of the national trade in seafood products.[6] But though its scale sets it apart, Tsukiji is nonetheless part of an extensive and complex national system of wholesale markets for perishable foodstuffs; altogether almost two thousand wholesale markets throughout Japan trade in seafood, fresh fruits and vegetables, fresh meat, and flowers. Some markets deal in all four types of commodities; others specialize in only one or two.

The classification of these markets and the details of regulations surrounding their activities are admittedly arcane topics, but a brief overview of the several categories of markets, layers of licenses, and transactional

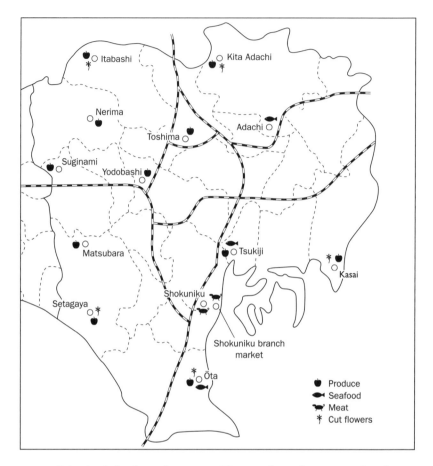

Map 5. Tokyo's wholesale market system. The map shows fourteen markets for seafood, meat, produce, and cut flowers operated by the TMG. Also shown are the boundaries of the twenty-three wards of central Tokyo and the central city's major commuter rail lines. Reproduced with permission of the TMG from the website of the Tokyo Metropolitan Government Central Wholesale Market, www.shijou .metro.tokyo.jp.

domains that make up Japan's market system helps to show where Tsukiji stands and how it is organized internally.

Categories of Markets

Japanese law classifies wholesale markets as either "central" *(chūō)* or "regional" *(chihō);* regional markets are further divided between those that serve "production regions" *(sanchi)* and those for "consumption regions" *(shōhichi).* Nationwide, seafood is sold in 54 central wholesale markets

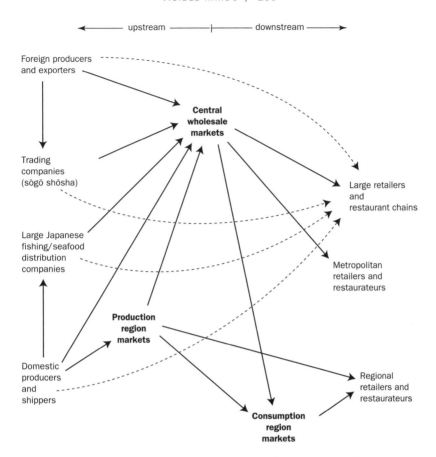

Figure 46. Distribution channels surrounding central wholesale markets. Solid lines represent established channels of the market system *(jōnai)*; dotted lines represent new channels taking on increasing importance outside the market system *(jōgai)*.

(chūō oroshiuri shijō) and in more than 700 regional wholesale markets *(chihō oroshiuri shijō)*, including 335 "production region markets" and 370 "consumption region markets."

Their positions at opposite ends of the distribution pipeline determine each market type's characteristics. At upstream markets—that is, production region markets—some of the catch may go for local consumption, but fishers primarily sell to brokers, processors, and agents of urban markets. These traders, in turn, bulk or consolidate catches into larger shipments for sale or consignment in markets closer to urban consumers. In their turn, downstream markets disassemble commodity flows into lots small enough to be of use to a retailer or restaurateur.

Central wholesale markets and smaller consumption region markets occupy functionally comparable positions at the downstream, breaking end of distribution channels. But beyond this utilitarian similarity, these two types of markets differ greatly. Central wholesale markets are governmentally operated, urban, much larger in scale, and more directly connected to producers as well as to lower-level markets. Consumption region markets are generally privately owned, in suburban or rural areas, small-scale, and dependent on higher-level markets for their supplies.

While the vast majority of production region markets are operated by local fisheries cooperatives *(gyogyō kyōdō kumiai)*, consumption region markets are mostly owned and operated by private corporations.[7] The overwhelming corporate ownership of consumption region markets stands in marked contrast to the cooperative-operated markets in fishing ports or the government-operated markets that serve larger urban populations. The interests of producers are well represented in the market structure; those of consumers are not.

Large or small, urban or rural, publicly or privately run, for producers or for consumers, Japan's wholesale markets form an integrated system. Daily trade flows link tiny production markets in remote fishing ports to provincial central wholesale markets, to metropolitan markets like Tsukiji, and finally to suburban consumption markets.[8] And the national system of laws, licenses, regulations, and bureaucratic institutions weaves them inextricably together as well.

Layers of Licenses

The national market system embodies two interlocking strands of vertical organization. One of these—just outlined—defines and organizes connections among markets at different levels: regional versus central, production versus consumption. The other thread is the hierarchy of traders whose roles take shape around these markets and the chains of transactions that link fisher to fishmonger. Both dimensions of vertical alignment are reinforced through a complex system of licensing for markets and traders at different levels in the system.

Under the Central Wholesale Market Law (Chūō Oroshiuri Shijō Hō) originally passed in 1923 and revised in 1971, the Ministry of Agriculture, Forestry and Fisheries (MAFF) charters central wholesale markets, run by local governments, in cities with populations greater than 200,000. MAFF sets national standards, enforces policies to ensure fair trading practice, and grants licenses to the auction houses or primary wholesalers that supply these markets. Local authorities, for their part, oversee the day-to-day operations of these markets, issue licenses for local wholesalers, and enforce local regulations governing market operations, such as hours of operations, allocation of space, and categories of goods to be traded.[9]

Primary wholesalers or auction houses, known officially as *oroshiuri gyōsha* (wholesale dealers) or *niuke gaisha* (freight receivers; i.e., consignees), are licensed to operate in each market; their licenses give them exclusive rights to make markets for seafood in a specific location and also require them to attract a steady supply for that market's demand. In central wholesale markets, MAFF licenses these businesses directly. Across Japan there are ninety-eight such auction houses, each licensed to operate only in a specific marketplace; Tsukiji has seven auction houses, most central wholesale markets have two, and many have only one. Tsukiji's major auction houses are many times larger than most others.

These auction houses in turn sell to intermediate wholesalers *(nakaoroshi gyōsha* or *nakagainin)*, who are licensed by the municipal authorities who operate each market. Nationally, there are about 3,800 intermediate wholesalers (Suisansha 1987: 201–5), each licensed—just like the auction houses—to operate only in a single marketplace. Roughly 900 intermediate wholesalers—just less than a quarter of the national total—operate in Tsukiji, but most markets have no more than a dozen or two nakagainin.

This system of licensing centers on access to auctions, which are the core of Tsukiji and all other central wholesale markets. Auction sales are specified by national legislation; in the official view, auctions ensure that transactions are "impartial and equitable" *(kōhei to kōsei)*. The rules and regulations under which auctions must take place are spelled out in general terms by national regulations and in minute detail by local ordinances as well as in the customary understandings that surround trade in a particular marketplace. Just as auction houses and intermediate wholesalers require licenses, so too auctioneers *(serinin)* are licensed by municipal authorities. At Tsukiji, approximately 700 auctioneers hold TMG licenses. Employees of auction houses can take the necessary examination after several years of on-the-job training.

To become a licensed serinin, a prospective auctioneer must pass a detailed examination on seafood, mathematics, and market regulations. To take the exam, one must have three years' experience working for an auction house; to receive a license, one must be employed by an auction house that supports the license application. Not all serinin are active auctioneers, however. A serinin license is a prerequisite for advancement within the auction houses, and so the license symbolizes becoming an *ichininmae:* a "full plate" or a "full serving," someone who has passed from apprentice to full adulthood in his trade. Therefore, almost every senior manager holds a serinin license, even though he may not have sold a fish in years.[10]

Transactional Domains

At the center of the auctions are the interactions among buyers and sellers—producers, auction houses, auctioneers, and intermediate wholesalers—who make the market. Overall, the system of licensed auctions and the carefully defined roles of the different licensed actors who can participate in them create several distinct strata or domains of trade, each with its own characteristics. At Tsukiji, as elsewhere throughout the national market system, there are three primary domains of transactions: supplier-to-auctioneer, auctioneer-to-wholesaler, and wholesaler-to-retailer (or wholesaler-to-restaurateur); the first two are directly concerned with the auctions.

The first transactional domain links Tsukiji's seven auction houses to tens of thousands of producers *(seisansha),* brokers, shippers, and other seafood traders throughout Japan (and indeed throughout the world). There are two generic roles in this domain, those of *niuke* (receivers of freight or consignees; i.e., the auction houses) and *ninushi* (shippers or consignors). Ninushi are a wildly disparate category, including the individual owners of fishing vessels who ship their catches directly to Tsukiji; brokers in provincial ports or markets who consolidate local catches for shipment to a few major markets; subsidiaries of major multinational fishing companies, for whom Tsukiji is merely one of many outlets; tiny, Tokyo-based firms acting as local agents for distant producers; and the import divisions of major Japanese general trading companies *(sōgō shōsha)* that may handle everything from rolled steel to fresh monkfish liver. Licensed auctioneers, who are employees of the auction houses, are immediately responsible for maintaining contacts and managing transactions with ninushi on the one hand, and with Tsukiji's traders on the other. The auctioneers therefore simultaneously play pivotal roles in both this and the next transactional domain.

The second domain comprises the transactions between Tsukiji's auction houses and traders who purchase seafood at the market, generally through competitive auctions. These traders fall into two groups. In the larger category are approximately 900 intermediate wholesalers *(nakaoroshi gyōsha)* who are licensed by the TMG to participate in auctions and to resell seafood from stalls that they individually operate within the marketplace itself. The second category consists of roughly 375 "authorized buyers" *(baibaisan-kasha)*—generally agents for supermarkets, restaurant chains, hotels, schools, hospitals, and other large-volume purchasers of seafood—who are also licensed by the TMG to participate in Tsukiji's auctions and who can resell what they buy only outside the marketplace. The intermediate wholesalers account for the overwhelming majority of the market's trading activity in this transactional domain; except where specified otherwise, my discussion focuses on them.

The final major domain of transactions at Tsukiji involves the trade between intermediate wholesalers and their customers: retail fishmongers, sushi chefs, restaurateurs, secondary wholesalers, peddlers, caterers, and box-lunch makers.[11] Market administrators calculate that roughly 36,000 such buyers come to Tsukiji on an average day, based on a 1998 survey, a number that steadily declined during the 1990s (from more than 42,500 per day in a 1989 survey) (*Tsukiji Shijō gaiyō* 1991, 2001). Most are from Tokyo, but some bypass other major markets in nearby cities (e.g., Yokohama, Kawasaki, Chiba, or Funabashi) or smaller suburban markets in order to take advantage of the vastly larger selection Tsukiji has to offer. Buyers need no license to purchase at Tsukiji. Although in principle trade at Tsukiji is restricted to wholesale transactions, in practice anyone can purchase seafood directly from intermediate wholesalers. Ordinary consumers, however, are discouraged from doing so. Auctioneers play no direct role in this third domain and usually do not interact with these buyers, but they carefully monitor the sales of their own customers, the intermediate wholesalers, to glean information on market conditions further downstream.

Across these three domains, patterns of vertical alignment—in the flow of products, payments, and information between producers and purchasers— are most directly maintained by auction houses and their employees, the auctioneers.

Auction Houses and Upstream Integration

Tsukiji's auction houses organize the flow of products into the marketplace. Their fundamental roles are to maintain direct contacts with producers, suppliers, and importers; to ensure a steady supply of products; and to sell those products to Tsukiji's traders. Six days a week, from the late afternoon till almost dawn, thousands of refrigerated trucks arrive at Tsukiji from throughout the country to deliver fresh, frozen, and processed seafood to one or another of Tsukiji's auction houses. Oceangoing long-liners unload their cargoes of Indian Ocean tuna, flash-frozen on board to last in storage for up to two years. Coastal freighters from Shikoku pump out tankloads of live, farm-raised fish. Trucks from Narita unload cartons of salmon air-freighted from Norway. Some shipments may be no more than a few crates of fish eggs from Hokkaidō or a couple of Styrofoam cases of abalone from Los Angeles. Other shipments—of farm-raised shrimp from Southeast Asia, for example—may fill an entire freight container.

In lots large or small, by truck, trawler, or handcart, seafood arrives at Tsukiji in one of only two ways, economically speaking. Either products are consigned by a producer or supplier, for sale by a specific auction house, or an auction house purchases goods outright in order to offer them for sale on its own account. The first pattern—consignment *(itaku hanbai)*—is the more typical, especially for fresh seafood. In the case of itaku hanbai, the auction house acts as an agent for the producer or supplier (the ninushi), offers the seafood for sale at auction, and receives a commission at rates set by market regulations. Alternatively, auction houses may directly purchase products (a process called *kaitsuke*) and resell them at Tsukiji; since the auction house owns these products, it does not pay or charge commissions. The key distinction between these two modes of transaction lies in who assumes the market risk, and thus the profit (or loss). Direct purchases by auction houses ordinarily are concentrated among frozen, processed, or aquacultural products for which the supply is steady and controllable, cost factors are known, and market risks (for the auction house) are low.[12]

Once goods are in the hands of an auction house, whether by consignment or direct purchase, there are again two economic alternatives. All sales by auction houses to traders are conducted by auctioneers, the only employees legally authorized to undertake these transactions, but sales may take several different forms. Primarily, sales are conducted by competitive auctions *(seri)* that involve bidding either by hand gesture *(teyari)* or by written offer *(nyūsatsu)*. (When the two kinds of auctions need to be distinguished from one another, sales involving bidding by hand signs are called *seri-uri* and those using written bids are called *nyūsatsu-uri*.) Otherwise, under limited and carefully specified circumstances, seafood may be traded through negotiated or private contract sales *(aitai-uri)* between auction house and trader.[13] Auctions are by far the more important mode of sale; almost 100 percent of sales for fresh seafood and for high-value products such as tuna (both fresh and frozen) take place through auctions, and auctions account for roughly two-thirds of all sales at Tsukiji.

Direct purchase or consignment, auction or private contract sale: the permutations of these economic alternatives are solutions to complicated equations of competitive performance. They factor in issues of risk and market volatility, assurance or doubt over the future performance of a trading partner, the potential for opportunism versus the compelling tugs of obligational ties, judgments of the competitive advantage of one market over another, pat-

Figures 47–48.
(Left) Finger bidding *(teyari):* hand signals for one through nine. There is no sign for zero (or ten) in this system; the number's magnitude is known from the context of the bidding. A quick wag of the hand indicates two repeated digits (e.g., 1-[wag]-1), and a quickly clenched fist indicates the transition from one digit to another (e.g., 3-[clench]-5). Drawings by Kim Kachmann.
(Right) Bidding at Nihonbashi. Sketch by Mori Kazan.

terns of access to information either freely shared or closely held, and the ever-changing calculations of liquidity, trust, supply and demand, and market power that inevitably color any transaction. Amid all the potential variations that structure any individual transaction, sellers and auctioneers connect with one another in disparate ways. These ties can be highly idiosyncratic, involving as they do the fit among a supplier's circumstances, the peculiarities of the market for the kind of seafood being sold, and the attributes of the auction house. No two relationships are necessarily the same, nor do they remain unchanged over time. Each is a single strand of vertical linkage in the flow of products and transactions from producers, suppliers, and importers to auction houses. Taken together, however, these strands construct durable connections, coordinating if not integrating the work of business partners. They reveal repeated transactions rather than opportunism, deployed one exchange at a time. Yet with all their potential variations and with all the possible trading partners offered in the vast Tsukiji market, how (and why) are patterns of vertical connection maintained?

GOVERNANCE

Viewed with this question in mind, Tsukiji's auction system seems riddled with paradoxes. At first glance, Tsukiji appears to be a spot market: multiple sellers disposing of products through competitive bidding from multiple buyers in cash-and-carry transactions that do not require either repeated trade or ongoing involvement between buyer and seller after the deal is struck. But if auctions do exemplify a spot market, then there should be no particular need for stable, long-term, vertical trading relations. Yet Tsukiji's auctions, as social institutions, enhance rather than erode stable long-term trading relationships, enabling trading alliances to readily emerge and survive in the midst of a competitive market.

In the language of institutional economics, vertical integration coalesces around determinations of "transaction costs" and alternative forms of "governance structure" (Williamson 1981, 1985; Williamson and Masten 1999; see also Coase 1988); these are, of course, social institutions and systems of norms familiar to anthropologists in other guises (Acheson 1994, 2003). In this view, economic institutions emerge from the effort to minimize transaction costs: the costs of doing business, which include not only profits, losses, and overhead expenses on specific exchanges but also the costs of ensuring reliability among partners, guaranteeing stable sources of supply, enforcing compliance with agreements, monitoring the fidelity of agents and employees, discovering information about market conditions, or assessing the trustworthiness of associates (see Geertz 1978). Is it cheaper for a business to get something from the external market (e.g., markets for skilled labor, legal advice, or transportation), or is it cheaper for it to provide its own services internally (through on-the-job training, in-house counsel, or ownership of a fleet of trucks)? Different governance structures form as solutions to problems such as these. The solutions for any particular business become manifest not only in the ways businesses (or business partners) are related to one another but also in the social organization of the firms themselves. Governance structures are therefore institutions susceptible to the kinds of social and cultural analyses that anthropologists generally deploy.

Governance structures range along a theoretical continuum, from "market governance" to "governance by hierarchy." In the first, a firm relies on the "pure" competitive forces of a spot market to obtain the goods, services, and degree of reliability it requires; in the second, a firm expands into a vertically integrated organization that controls the suppliers of goods, services, and compliance through direct ownership and management. Somewhere midway between the two are various forms of governance by "relational" or "obligational" contracting (Macneil 2001), in which partners in an ongoing exchange relationship agree, formally or informally, to do business with one another over time, relying on the strength of personal ties (such as trust) to overcome problems that may arise in the relationship because not all the terms and circumstances of trade are (or can be) specified ahead of time.[14]

Studies of Japanese economic organization, whether they use the terminology of transaction cost economics or not (and most do not), generally rely on a similar tripartite typology. Economic institutions are examined for their reliance on competitive market forces (spot markets), on institutional factors (notably vertical integration through, for example, the combines known as *keiretsu*), or on social and cultural patterns of long-term obligation and reciprocity (often glossed as "traditional" Japanese cultural practices). Typically, economic analysts see institutionalized vertical integration and obligational contracting as more characteristic of Japanese economic organization than responsiveness to competitive market forces.

These theoretical and ethnographic perspectives suggest several obvious interpretations of stable, vertical ties between suppliers and auction houses. Long-term trading relationships may form as a result of competitive pricing and superior performance by auction houses as they provide their services to suppliers. Another possibility is that durable ties come about through managerial or ownership control that links producers and auction houses, such as through keiretsu affiliation. And a third possibility is that ties take shape in response not only to price or outright managerial control but also to less tangible social factors—such as feelings of trust and reliability, or the ability to exchange information quickly—that encourage interdependent forms of obligational contracting.

In the following pages, I examine Tsukiji's vertical integration from each of these perspectives in turn: market governance, keiretsu, and interdependent, informal contracts in the form of information flows. In the ideal constructions of economic and sociological analysis, the distinctions among these organizational forms can seem clear-cut, although in reality they are hard to distinguish from one another.

Governance by Market: Competitive Auction Houses

The operations of the auction houses, regulated as they are by national and municipal agencies, are essentially similar, although the seven firms vary widely in their financial scale and in the range of products they handle (table 7). The common purpose of the auction houses, in the national scheme of things, is to ensure that suppliers have competitive alternatives and that a monopsony—a single buyer arrayed against several sellers—does not dominate the wholesale market. But in their regulated uniformity, the actual scope for direct competition among Tsukiji's auction houses is

TABLE 7. *Tsukiji's Seven Seafood Auction Houses (sales in 2002)*

	Quantity (million kg)	Value (billion yen)
Full-range auction houses		
Chūō Gyorui K.K.	128.99	125.29
Daito Gyorui K.K.	134.66	111.71
Tōto Suisan K.K.	117.61	112.12
Tsukiji Uoichiba K.K.	116.26	88.28
Daiichi Suisan K.K.	55.78	42.81
Specialized auction houses (processed seafood only)		
Chiyoda Suisan K.K.	73.84	44.86
Sōgō Shokuhin K.K.	10.38	10.96

SOURCE: TMG website, data for the year 2002: "Tōkyō-to Chūō Oro-shiuri Shijō, Shijō Torihiki Jōhō" (TMG Central Wholesale Market, Market Transaction Information), www.shijou.metro.tokyo.jp/frame02 .html.

narrow. Nevertheless, they do compete in subtle and not so subtle ways, against one another and against other rivals outside the market system. This competition, as auction houses seek to attract both suppliers upstream and buyers in or downstream from the market, occurs in several different arenas: they compete against one another within Tsukiji; they compete with similar auction houses in other markets; and they compete with other distribution channels that entirely bypass the national wholesale market system.

The four largest firms—Chūō Gyorui, Daito Gyorui, Tōto Suisan, and Tsukiji Uoichiba—are full-range auction houses that handle almost all varieties of seafood in all its forms: fresh, frozen, and processed. Another smaller firm, Daiichi Suisan, deals in most varieties of fresh and processed fish, but with a slightly smaller range (it lacks its own large-scale freezer facility and so deals only minimally in frozen products). The two other houses, Chiyoda Suisan and Sōgō Shokuhin, are much smaller in size and confine their dealings to processed products, such as salted, smoked, and dried fish. Each of the seven firms runs its own auctions, with its own team of licensed auctioneers, and every house has its own display areas adjacent to the auction pits for each major commodity category. For each of the two dozen or more product categories a major firm may handle, it holds a separate auction. Only the four largest auction houses sell the full spectrum of goods, but even the smallest actively deals in at least half a dozen categories. So on any given morning there are, in effect, perhaps a hundred separate auctions, with most commodity categories being the object of four, five, or seven distinct auction sequences (depending on the number of auction houses that handle a particular commodity). From the points of view of both upstream ninushi and in-market traders, there are four, five, or seven auction houses actively competing for their attention and their patronage.

Rivalry among auction houses is almost palpable, although the niches of competition may be extremely narrow. Some otherwise obvious forms of competition—competitive pricing, for example—are impossible in an auction market. Auction house cannot guarantee prices to their suppliers, unless an auction house buys the products outright *(kaitsuke)*. Auction houses make their money primarily from commissions on sales, all charging the same commission rates, set for most fresh seafood by TMG regulations at 5.5 percent. The regulations permit different commission rates under some specified circumstances, but auction houses cannot freely adjust rates to their own immediate advantage.

Competition by undercutting or discounting commissions is illegal; rebates based on the volume of trade, however, are permitted by the TMG: if a producer or supplier surpasses specified semiannual benchmarks for the volume of consignments sent to a particular auction house, the auction house returns a fixed percentage of its commissions as a rebate. These rebates offer a producer or shipper incentives to concentrate its dealings on one or two auction houses to reap these volume-based rebates—just as travelers may cluster their flights on one or two preferred airlines to reach higher levels of frequent flier awards. The rebate system may encourage repeat business, but auction houses themselves cannot legally manipulate rebate rates to attract clients.[15]

Along other dimensions of competitive performance, auction houses try to distinguish themselves by the range and quality of services they provide to their steady suppliers: swift and accurate accounting for sales, fast payment of auction proceeds, the ability to handle foreign-language correspondence, introductions to other potential trade partners, timely and detailed information on market conditions, and the like. None of these services guarantees a competitive edge in and of itself, but an auction house that fails to offer these, or fails to handle them reasonably well, would be at a serious disadvantage. That is, their absence would be noticed, even though their presence is largely taken for granted.

The most crucial aim of the competition among auction houses is to be the market maker. An auction house becomes the market maker for a specific kind of seafood by virtue of a delicate blend of factors: the share it commands of a particular product entering the marketplace, the corporate culture of the auction house and the kinds of auctioneers it trains, the reputation it has for being innovative in developing new sources of supply, the quality of the products sent to its auctions, the number and reputation of the traders its auctions attract, and, of course, the prices it obtains at auction. Since Tsukiji is a highly segmented market, no single auction house dominates across all product categories; there are different market makers for different kinds of seafood. And being a market maker is inherently a Janus-like position; an auction house must successfully turn both upstream and down, because the ability to attract the best suppliers and the ability to attract the best buyers are interdependent. Such matches are always both relative and approximate: for the producer of a particular grade of shrimp, the best buyer may be a Ginza sushi chef, and for the producer of another type, a supermarket buyer. The two buyers may or may not rely on the same auction house, but the gradations in commodity categories are so finely calibrated that the two are unlikely ever to be bidding head-to-head on the same lots.

Tsukiji's auction houses attract both sellers and buyers with relative ease. After all, Tsukiji occupies a position of almost unassailable dominance, sustained by the enormous scale of its domestic and foreign catchment area and the immense consumer market it supplies in Japan's largest metropolitan area. No market elsewhere in the country (or in many overseas fishing ports, either) can ignore the prices and market conditions established at Tsukiji. Tsukiji's auction houses as a group possess an inherent advantage as they seek to maintain their positions as market makers for most products.

Jockeying for competitive position by Tsukiji's auction houses vis-à-vis other markets is directed primarily upstream toward suppliers, since most of the buyers who purchase at Tsukiji's auctions are themselves more or less captive to the Tsukiji market through their licenses, even though they are not tied to a specific auction house. Although intermediate wholesalers may not have the option of going outside the Tsukiji auctions, their own customers (retailers and restaurateurs) may be able to move their trade between Tsukiji and other nearby markets or to nonmarket distribution networks.

Straightforward price competition is only one factor in the positioning of Tsukiji's auction houses against the nationwide opposition. Some stakes center on regional food preferences. Shimonoseki at the western tip of Honshū, for example, is the major national marketplace for *fugu* (blowfish); the leading production regions are close at hand and fugu itself is a highly regarded delicacy in western Japan. Tsukiji dominates the global market for bluefin tuna, in part because its high fat content and the delicately marbled quality of its flesh are both highly prized by consumers in the Tokyo area. But these same features make the tuna less attractive to Osaka consumers, and in Osaka and other major Kansai markets, yellowfin tuna, much leaner than bluefin, is the reigning fish.

Technical considerations and the development of different rules of market practice account for other differences among markets. Since tuna are sold whole at Tsukiji, a buyer may have 200 kilograms or more of fish on his hands with a single purchase. The risks inherent in purchasing such a large fish may substantially depress its value, so under some market conditions a savvy supplier might send his largest fish to the Sapporo market, where terms of trade (favorable to intermediate wholesalers) allow tuna to be sold split or quartered rather than whole. In Tokyo's suburbs some markets, like Funabashi, compete with Tsukiji by offering favorable trade conditions tailored to large-volume buyers, like supermarket chains.

For an auction house, generating the best prices may be more a result than the cause of being a market maker. Nonetheless, in the competition among auction houses at Tsukiji or among different markets, prices are a critical factor; both suppliers and auctioneers straightforwardly explain that good prices determine desirable business partners. In the publicly espoused economism of the market system, any supplier, presumably, will eventually switch from one auction house to another—or avoid the first altogether—if the second house is consistently able to get better prices at its auctions, or if the performance of the first auction house is unsatisfactory.

Yet only rarely does a supplier actually break off ties to one auction house and establish new ties to another, because the costs of such a break can be considerable. At the least, a supplier will lose a good source of information about market conditions, introductions to other business contacts, and the like. Suppliers also run the risk that if, at some time in the future, they want to resume business with the spurned auction house or need to find outlets for an oversupply of seafood, the firm may refuse to do business with them. Maintaining some level of connection, therefore, is a form of insurance against future needs. There are more subtle risks as well, including the cost to one's reputation as a steady, reliable supplier. And the potential disruption of social networks—in a business world where personal introductions from family members, old school friends, customers, and local politicians are crucial social lubricants—may dissuade a supplier from cutting ties with a particular auction house.

Several more indirect possibilities for switching one's allegiances exist, and these include the potential for playing off intra- and intermarketplace competition. Most simply, suppliers often have ongoing dealings with more than one Tsukiji auction house, and so they may react to auction house performance by reducing consignments to one while increasing them to another. When difficulties arise, they can adjust their strategy without ever openly breaking ties with one auction house or the other. Better yet, a supplier may set auction houses at Tsukiji off against auction houses in other major markets (e.g., Osaka, Kyoto, or Yokohama) and send larger proportions of consignments there. Since the advent of high-speed refrigerated truck transportation in the late 1960s, producers and shippers in most parts of Japan have exercised great flexibility in choosing among competing marketplaces. Tsukiji is now within one day's trucking distance from most ports in Honshū, Shikoku, and parts of Kyūshū and Hokkaidō, and producers in these places benefit greatly. But just as Tsukiji can now receive goods from all over the country, so too can producers and suppliers easily redirect their shipments to almost any auction house in almost any major central wholesale market in the country. Such flexibility is possible both because of these advances in transportation and because price information is widely and almost instantaneously available. Telephone calls and fax messages from auction houses flood the wires, and several national daily market papers provide detailed price information. These may seem unremarkable developments, but to auction house officials—middle-aged or older—who recall the days when seafood was delivered to Tsukiji by rail and auctioneers had to book long-distance calls to suppliers ahead of time, the flexibility of delivery and the simplicity of communications in today's market are regarded as phenomenal changes. Now, many provincial suppliers maintain active transactional relationships with one or more auction houses in each of several central wholesale markets, making daily decisions about where to send their consignments. Sometimes, Tsukiji's auction houses themselves play a role in this process, steering regular suppliers to their own affiliates in other markets.

Inside and Outside the Market System

The ultimate competitive arena for Tsukiji's auction houses is between central wholesale markets, generally, and other channels of distribution that avoid or bypass the national market system. Beyond affecting the narrow interests of any given auction house, this opposition between central wholesale markets and alternative channels challenges and reshapes the fundamental character of Tsukiji and similar markets. Incrementally, it leads them to adjust their own mix of products and desired clientele in response to changes in consumer tastes and the retail environment. Traders make a generic distinction between *jōnai ryūtsū*, "within-the-market" distribution channels, and *jōgai ryūtsū*, "outside-the-market" channels: that is, between products and transactions that go through the regulated auctions and traders of the national market system, and those that rely on direct, private contract deals among producers, brokers, retailers, and others. In the shorthand of the trade, these alternatives are called simply *jōnai* and *jōgai*.

Outside-the-market transactions, large or small, sidestep the auction system, the auction houses, and the licensed intermediate wholesalers. A large supermarket chain may make a deal with the import division of a general trading company for 1,000 metric tons of frozen tuna to be delivered over the course of a year; a restaurant chain may establish direct dealings with a Maine lobster pound or a Thai producer of farm-raised shrimp; a Tokyo fishmonger may have his cousin ship several crates of crabs from the Japan Sea coast by an express service; a Hokkaidō fishing company may sell salmon directly to a wholesaler operating in the outer market of Tsukiji. (And that wholesaler may decide, depending on market conditions, to offer some of it for sale within the market, consigning it to a Tsukiji auction house and thereby putting products into within-the-market channels at almost the market's gate.) The national market system does not require that seafood be sold exclusively within formally regulated markets, although the legal framework does confine some traders to the system, exclude some other traders from it, and leave the matter open for still others.[16] The two channels, jōnai and jōgai, therefore operate concurrently as competitive arenas for seafood trade.

The growth of out-of-market channels is directly related, on the one hand, to developments in communications and transportation over the past generation (particularly the flexibility that refrigerated trucks on high-speed expressways offer to producers and buyers alike). On the other hand, during the same period there has been an enormous expansion of mass-market outlets for seafood, such as chains of supermarkets, franchised restaurants, and fast-food shops that require and can consume large quantities of highly standardized seafood products of medium quality. As a result, these days ordinary seafood—of the kinds available in large quantities, in relatively predictable supply, and at relatively moderate prices—is more likely to go through out-of-market channels than are high-priced, seasonally fluctuating, specialized, luxury seafoods. Thus, traders at Tsukiji increasingly are concentrating on high-end, luxury seafoods for chefs, independent restaurateurs, and specialty fishmongers, accepting that an ever-greater portion of the mass supermarket trade is apt to go elsewhere. Yet even so, supermarkets and other mass marketers still rely on markets like Tsukiji to a large degree, particularly for specialty products for which it would be difficult or economically counterproductive to establish their own independent supply lines. A supermarket chain simply cannot develop its own supply channels, for example, for products only available in small amounts, from scattered producers, and at highly unpredictable times, or for products such as live fish that require high levels of skill in handling. The more specialized the product (what transaction cost analysts call "asset specificity"), the more likely that supermarkets will rely on market relations rather than their own distribution channels.

The auction houses and the system of markets in which they operate are embedded in a competitive environment across many different levels. But as is suggested by the play of distribution channels within-the-market against those outside-the-market—whether privately held or internally managed transactions—alternative structures of governance shape relationships among producers and auction houses. As I pointed out earlier, *markets* as a mode of organization often stand in contrast to governance by hierarchy, that is, to forms of formal vertical coordination achieved through ownership or direct management control.

Governance by Hierarchy: Keiretsu Affiliations

The Japanese economy is noted for an institution of vertical integration known as *keiretsu:* groups of companies organized into quite formal hierarchies based on interlocking stock ownership, exchanges of managerial personnel, coordinated fiscal and marketing strategies, and preferential trading practices among group members. Marubeni, Mitsubishi, Mitsui, Saison, Sumitomo, Tokyū, and Toyota are just a few among the many famous Japanese business groups, old and new, that rely on keiretsu ties. Keiretsu affiliations affect trade channels that run through Tsukiji, and important aspects of the regulatory framework of the central wholesale market system are in place precisely to control or limit these forms of vertical integration.

The levels of licensing and classification of wholesale markets in the national system rest on the clear definition and separation of actors at Tsukiji. These levels were largely set forth in the original Central Wholesale Market Law of 1923. One of the key motivations for this reformist legislation was to address patterns of vertical control of urban wholesalers over producers and suppliers, the exclusive rights that some wholesalers exerted over the catches of fishing villages, and the speculative trading rings that had characterized the Nihonbashi marketplace during much of the preceding half century. By encouraging competition and open trading at each discrete stage in the flow of products from fishers to consumers, the institutions of the new market system aimed to create barriers to vertical integration. During the late 1930s and early 1940s, this system was almost entirely dismantled in the cause of wartime mobilization; but in 1951, when Tsukiji resumed operations as a competitive marketplace organized around auctions, the various distinct categories of licensed actors and markets were revived and, at least in principle, vertical division rather than integration was restored as a guiding purpose of the market system.

Vertical division, horizontal fragmentation, and the auction mechanism define the operating rationale for the national market system. These features were introduced to prevent the formation of either oligopolies (markets with only a very few, powerful sellers) or oligopsonies (markets with only a few, powerful buyers). In theory, oligopolies or oligopsonies can occur at any or all of three transactional levels: between suppliers and auction houses; between auction houses and traders; and between traders and trade buyers. At first glance, the effort to limit market power seems least effective at the level of the auction houses; these seven (four of them well-capitalized and full-range in their product coverage) tower above the thousands of independent producers and brokers upstream and the roughly 1,400 small-scale traders operating at Tsukiji. The institutional structure of trading relationships, however, creates more balanced market power than number and scale would initially suggest, and patterns of formal vertical integration do not predominate.

In the early years following World War II, more than thirty firms received licenses to operate as auction houses at Tsukiji, but the economic turbulence of postwar recovery and the reinauguration of open trading at Tsukiji left only a few survivors by the end of the 1950s. The seven auction houses in existence today are heirs to this generation of mergers and acquisitions. As corporate entities they all can trace some connection to each of the others: some are descended from the same *ton'ya* (wholesale merchant houses) of the Nihonbashi fish market; others are fragments of one of the

large auction houses that existed during the few years the market func-
tioned before the war; and all shared common corporate identities and fates
during the forced wartime mergers.

Several of the leading postwar auction houses developed as companies
affiliated with large vertically integrated keiretsu in the fisheries industry.
Daito Gyorui K.K. offers the clearest example: the majority of its stock is
held by Maruha, one of Japan's largest fisheries companies. Maruha and its
other affiliates control about 53 percent of Daito's stock.[17] Personnel are
rotated among Daito and other firms in the Maruha group. And products
caught, processed, or purchased by Maruha affiliates regularly pass across
Daito's auction blocks.

The relationship between Daito and Maruha represents the most comprehensive case of keiretsu affiliation among the Tsukiji auction houses,
involving a high degree both of formal vertical integration (through capital
holdings, personnel transfers, and the flow of merchandise) and of informal
coordination. The other three publicly held Tsukiji auction houses—Chūō
Gyorui, Tōto Suisan, and Tsukiji Uoichiba—are more independent. Each
has significant trading relationships with one or another of the major
Japanese fisheries companies (the so-called Big Six; tables 8 and 9), but none
is as dependent on a sole major supplier as Daito is on Maruha. Among
them, only one auction house, Chūō Gyorui, has any significant stock holding by a Big Six firm (in this instance totaling only about 5 percent). There
are no personnel transfers among these Tsukiji auction houses and major
fisheries companies. Three other, smaller auction houses at Tsukiji are privately held companies, and their connections to major fisheries companies
are even less distinct; market observers regard them as independents.

The Maruha group is a keiretsu of more than 200 companies active in
almost every aspect of fisheries production, processing, distribution, and
marketing. At the end of the 1995–96 fiscal year, the Maruha group con-
sisted of 208 companies, with combined sales of 1.02 billion yen and 22,091
employees. In 1996 the group comprised 9 fishing companies, 20 wholesale
auction houses, 29 food processors and distribution companies, 16 cold storage companies, 12 aquacultural firms, 9 marine transportation companies, 5
equipment suppliers, 4 jewelry firms, 3 real estate companies, 63 overseas
subsidiaries, and 38 other miscellaneous enterprises, including a professional
baseball team: the Yokohama BayStars, formerly known as the Taiyō
Whales (Maruha sold the team in 2002).

The group takes its name from its old-fashioned shop name *(yagō)*.
"Maruha" literally signifies a circle *(maru)* surrounding the syllabic character *ha*, which has been the graphic logo of the group's companies for

TABLE 8. *The Big Six Fisheries Companies*

Fisheries Companies (suisan gaisha)	Annual Sales (billion yen)			Percentage of Sales from Fresh and Frozen Fish[1]		
	1990	1995	2000	1990	1995	2000
Taiyō Gyogyō K.K./Maruha[2]	581	421	316	59	50	69
Nippon Suisan K.K.	438	401	309	62	59	50
Nichiro Gyogyō K.K.[3]	219	173	176	47	(40)	(34)
K.K. Kyokuyō[4]	198	161	141	73	(66)	(58)
Hōkō Suisan K.K.[5]	116	72	63	75	(43)	(29)
K.K. Hōsui[6]	26	13	15	90	(95)	(99)

SOURCE: Tōyō Keizai Shinpōsha, winter 1990: 38–44; winter 1995: 65–70; winter 2000: 70–75.

NOTE: Because sales figures are categorized differently across the years, precise comparisons cannot be drawn from these figures.

[1]Seafood sales for companies no longer directly engaged in fisheries production appear in parentheses.

[2]Taiyō Gyogyō changed its name to Maruha in 1993.

[3]Nichiro ceased direct fishing operations in the early 1990s and now concentrates on development of processed seafood products and importation of products such as canned salmon, crab, and surimi. In March 2000, 58% of sales were from processed foods.

[4]Kyokuyō ceased its trawling operations in 1992 and transferred remaining fishing activities to its subsidiaries. It now focuses on frozen and canned foods, as well as extensive importation of processed and semi-processed food products from China. Sales as of March 1995 and 2000, respectively, were 65% (58%) from trading in marine products, 25% (36%) from food processing.

[5]Hōkō withdrew from direct fishing operations, and now is a seafood trading company.

[6]Nippon Suisan owns 63% of Hōsui's shares. Hōsui withdrew from direct operation of fishing vessels in the early 1990s, in favor of trading and processing. Sales (as of March 2000) include 84% from seafood trade and 15% from retail sales of seafood.

TABLE 9. *Ties among Auction Houses and the Big Six*

Auction Houses	Fisheries Companies
Daito Gyorui	Firmly within keiretsu of Maruha
Chūō Gyorui	Independent, with close ties to Nippon Suisan and Kyokuyō, two of its major suppliers
Tōto Suisan	Independent, with ties to Nichiro
Tsukiji Uoichiba	Independent

SOURCE: Interviews with Tsukiji traders.

decades. Like many trade symbols of this sort, the Maruha logo and name can be read as a rebus. *Ha* is a homonym for the ideographic character for wave; *ha* is also the first syllable of the original name of the company, Hayashikane Shōten, which was founded in 1880. The *maru* that encircles the *ha* can connote many things: cycles, harmony, completion, totality, and fullness. Truth is *marugoto* (the whole facts); *maru* is the infinity of Zen calligraphy; the impregnable inner keep of a castle is the *maru;* the suffix -*maru* ends the names of Japanese vessels, indicating a seaworthy craft, a complete unbroken hull; and, in the marketplace, a fresh whole fish is sold *maru de,* "in the round." Many businesses at Tsukiji and elsewhere in the seafood trade draw on *maru* as a element of their business names, officially or informally: Maruuo, Tsukumaru, Marunaka, Maruzen, Maruhachi, Marubeni, or Kanemaru.

The complicated iconography of this corporate symbol is quite typical of old-fashioned firms in the seafood business, and many Tsukiji firms use similar oral renderings of graphic logos as their primary form of corporate identification. For years, people in the industry have used the Maruha name as a colloquial way of referring to the companies that make up the group, and the graphic logo has adorned everything from freezer warehouses and the smokestacks of fishing vessels to cardboard boxes and company uniforms. But Maruha did not become the legal corporate name of the parent company until 1993, when it changed its name from Taiyō Gyogyō K.K. Even as the company adopted its old trade symbol for its official name, the company changed its graphic logo (called a "symbol mark" in contemporary Japanese advertising and design circles) from the old-fashioned and highly literal representation of a circle around the phonetic character *ha* to a stylized white wave against a red disk—still a *ha* in a *maru*—stylistically evocative also of the "hi no maru" rising sun of the Japanese flag.

Twenty firms in the Maruha group are auction houses, including Daito Gyorui and seven others that operate in major central wholesale markets across Japan. In addition, in almost every port and almost every marketplace, whether large or small, there are affiliated firms that belong in some fashion to the Maruha group: *kogaisha* ("child companies" to the *oyagaisha* or "parent company" of Maruha), subsidiaries that may or may not have any capital or personnel from Maruha but are linked to it through longstanding transactional relationships. These Maruha agents vertically integrate Maruha production with its marketing subsidiaries by handling Maruha catches and cargoes wherever they are landed. They also extend Maruha's reach by directing catches from non-Maruha producers into

Figure 49. Maruha logos, old and new.
(Left) The old corporate logo of Taiyō Gyogyō K.K. is a
circle *(maru)* surrounding the syllable *ha*.
(Right) The new corporate logo of the company, renamed
Maruha Corporation, is a white wave in a red circle.
These are registered trademarks of the Maruha
Corporation and are reproduced with their permission.

Maruha's channels very early in the chain of distribution. Local brokers
and distributors are identified as being part of the Maruha group, as are
independent producers whose catches are regularly funneled into Maruha
channels. Officers of Maruha's auction house at Tsukiji, Daito Gyorui, can
knowledgeably discuss the operations of, for example, an independent producer operating a single vessel out of the port of Abashiri on the Sea of
Okhotsk, one out of some 2,500 separate producers whose catches regularly
pass over their auction blocks.

Despite the formidable size and scale of Maruha's integrated reach
throughout the fishing industry, two points are important to note. First,
even in this most overt case of keiretsu affiliation, Daito is not solely dependent on products from its "parent" or other Maruha affiliates, nor do members of the Maruha group send products only to their affiliated auction
house. According to senior executives of the firm, only about 22 percent of
Daito's products come from Maruha, and Maruha products are regularly
shipped to all of Tsukiji's auction houses—that is, to Daito's direct competitors. In short, neither Daito nor Maruha is exclusively or even predomi-
nantly reliant on its corporate partner. Even Maruha divisions sometimes
find that because another auction house is the market maker for particular
kinds or grades of products, it can offer them more profitable trading opportunities than Daito.

Second, one might expect the structural affiliations between Daito and
Maruha to create enormously close connections between the auction house
and its suppliers, or at least with suppliers from the Maruha group. Yet

according to many experienced participants in the market, Daito and its Maruha suppliers are not appreciably closer to one another than are other auction houses and their steady suppliers. Keiretsu affiliations may have an effect, therefore, but they do not appear to take precedence over the kinds of connections that other auction houses and other suppliers are able to establish with one another without a keiretsu tie.

In practice, the nature and quality of ties between suppliers and Tsukiji auction houses are substantially similar for Daito and all of its more independent, less keiretsu-embedded competitors. That is, formal aspects of vertical integration—capital, personnel, and product flows—in the Daito–Maruha case do not necessarily ensure closer ties between auction house and suppliers, nor are other auction houses hampered by a lack of keiretsu ties on which to rely.

Just as competition and market governance cannot fully account for all the ways in which companies maintain relationships, neither does governance by hierarchy—in this case, the much-noted Japanese keiretsu system—offer a complete explanation for the existence of vertical integration or coordination within the Tsukiji auction system.

Governance by Obligation: Auctioneers, Information, and Relationships

Governance structures and modes of articulation among business partners lie along a continuum between the theoretical poles of perfect markets and total hierarchical control. In this middle ground are the various messy and flexible relationships of real-life economic and institutional affairs that are neither one thing nor the other. What keeps trading partners together if, on the one hand, they might be able to get a better economic deal elsewhere—even one only momentarily better—or, on the other hand, no structural or legal reason binds them? For Tsukiji's auction houses and the producers and suppliers upstream, what indeed?

Competitive positioning partly explains why suppliers stick with Tsukiji auction houses, though it seems likely that the marketplace—its scale and economic power as a center of demand—is more the attraction than any specific firm. And keiretsu affiliations explain part of the enduring connection, although (as the Daito case suggests) even in the face of a structural relationship, suppliers maintain other ties as well. In attempting to create or maintain such bonds, auction houses all appear to stand on a relatively equal footing; neither competitive advantages nor keiretsu ties provide a complete explanation for long-lasting trade ties. So what is the glue of "obligational" or "relational" bonds?

Relational ties are facilitated by and organized around a broad array of exchanges between trade partners; chief among them is the flow of information, which is closely linked to the character of Tsukiji's auctions and the roles of auctioneers. Auctioneers have great influence over the circumstances of particular sales, based both on their intimate knowledge of their suppliers' products and on their knowledge of the buying preferences of their regular customers. An auctioneer cannot effectively satisfy the demands of one side to these transactions without reasonably satisfying the demands of the other, and in each case vast amounts of information must be transmitted back and forth among parties on both sides of the auction block.

These information flows and the close relationships that form between auctioneers and suppliers on the one hand, and between auctioneers and traders on the other, are possible and necessary because of the structure of the auctions themselves and the organization of the traders into distinct trading communities with particular specialties.

Any individual auctioneer is normally responsible for only a small, carefully defined subset of the products offered by an auction house at a particular auction. He may be on the block for only a few minutes, selling a few dozen lots, before yielding the podium to a colleague who will continue with a few dozen more lots of a related but subtly different category of products. Thus, auctioneers survey minuscule domains about which they command vastly detailed information about the relevant commodities, their producers, and the preferences and purchasing patterns of traders.

Arranging an auction is the point where everything comes together. The advantages of competitive positioning—of being a market maker—are evident through the selection of seafood a particular auction house can offer for sale. At the same time, the auction display is a carefully orchestrated deployment of information, and the auction itself garners still more. Not only is the auctioneer responsible for calling the lots and soliciting bids from the traders, he is in charge of structuring the sequence and groupings of products offered for sale at each display auction. He supervises (or at least checks) the grading of products, their arrangement on the auction floor, the sequence of lots to be offered in a given trading session, and the size of the lots to be offered. That is, the auctioneer determines whether an entire shipment, say of fresh shrimp, will be offered at auction as a single unit or broken down into smaller amounts to be offered as several lots. Such determinations are based on the auctioneer's judgments about current conditions of supply and demand, which may fluctuate according to many factors such as season, weather, holiday schedules, and price.

Decisions about the disposition of consignments may extend to redirecting shipments to entirely different auction pits within Tsukiji (or even to other, smaller outlying markets in the Tokyo metropolitan region). Some products are sold in several different auction pits to entirely separate sets of traders. For example, distinct grades of frozen tuna are apportioned among different auction locations for sale to traders whose own customers represent widely differing market niches, including up-market and low-end sushi shops, supermarket chains, and independent retail fishmongers. Some types of fresh seafood, such as fish from nearby coastal waters, may be diverted toward different auction pits according the suitability of that day's fish for sushi or for other, less demanding, uses. The auctioneers are responsible for making these allocational decisions among different auction pits based on the supply, the grade or quality of the products themselves, and their knowledge of the buying preferences of different sets of traders.

Arranging the night's shipments for sale in the morning auctions is an immensely complicated task because of fragmentation of Tsukiji's auctions, but it also plays a vital role in the discrimination among fish as they are classified into salable commodities. Of course, the process of classification and discrimination is begun much earlier, by producers, dockside brokers, and provincial shippers, but at Tsukiji during the unloading and arranging of shipments, auctioneers make a final check against so-called Tsukiji specs. The auctioneers supervise workers who specialize in *koage*, or unloading, a difficult job in the crowded and highly fragmented marketplace. And once shipments have arrived in the correct display area, then the most critical tasks of koage come into play: the seafood has to be laid out for the buyers' inspections *(shitami)* that start a couple of hours before the auctions begin. The koage workers—themselves employees of subsidiaries or subcontractors to the auction houses—set up for display the next morning's sales. Individual lots must be clustered and arranged according to category and subcategory, grade and subgrade. The auctioneers record each lot as it arrives, make decisions about how the lots should be displayed and sequenced, and study the overall array of products that will make up their morning's sale. And, of course, these auctioneers ultimately are responsible for roaring through a long, carefully sequenced list of lots a couple of hours later.

In principle, goods for auction are expected to be offered for sale in the order they arrive on the auction floor at Tsukiji. If first sales command a premium price, that price should go to the consignor *(ninushi)* whose goods first arrived at market. But within any given general category of seafood, there are many subcategories and grades determined by subspecies variation, catch zone, size, and quality. When lots are called for auction, these cannot be jumbled helter-skelter because, as auctioneers argue, doing this could perplex bidders and result in lower prices for consignors. So the individual lots must be clustered and arranged according to these subcategories, which themselves reflect auctioneers' judgments about quality, value, and price. Auctioneers prove the value of their products by their own careful discrimination, which is visibly on display in their ordering of the lots on the floor.

The auction house and the auctioneer must be able to signal their own estimates of the relative value of lots up for sale (Milgrom 1987: 287), and the sequencing of lots, from most valuable to least, is a critical means of doing just that. Auctioneers explain that to do otherwise "confuses the buyers." Such sequencing highlights the collaborative, subjective quality of the auction as a price-setting mechanism. Put another way, in deciding what they should bid, buyers require and find confirmation of their own estimations in the auctioneers' implicit evaluations; buyers are then prepared to offer prices that in turn confirm (generally) the auctioneers' judgment.

Officials of the auction houses contend that they can maximize prices on average only if they can manage effectively the presentation of the goods for sale, and that effective management is possible only if they and the producers share sufficient information: not just price information, which is readily available, but the more interpretive information on market conditions that cannot always be decoded simply from prices. Prices are simply an incomplete, inadequate proxy for the fully contextualized information that supplier and auction house together need from each other. And, they argue, such information exchanges are possible only through long-term stable trading relationships. Thus, it follows, auction houses can obtain the highest average prices only for suppliers with whom they are in frequent if not constant contact. And the information transfers that such contact implies take place on a two-way street.

For their part, auction houses provide suppliers with detailed and highly customized information on the supply at Tsukiji of particular commodities, and on the precise day-by-day competitive outlook for a particular shipper's specific products, taking into account all other lots of similar products consigned to Tsukiji that same day. Both the general and the specific information are intended to assist suppliers in maintaining quality standards, applying appropriate grading criteria, and controlling the flow of shipments to sustain profits and to avoid glutting the market.

In return, auction houses want detailed information from suppliers about current conditions in local ports and about specific consignments in the pipeline, so the firms can intelligently plan their display auctions. Auction-eers can obtain high prices only if their auctions pull in traders, and close communication between an auction house and a supplier is thus part of the collaboration necessary to attract traders.

The relational or obligational aspect of transactions between suppliers and auction houses does not therefore depend on formal vertical integra-tion, nor even on the scale and resources of the auction house as a whole. It is an intensely personalized relationship between a particular auctioneer and a particular supplier—they may work with one another for years— that forms around information exchanges, and this relationship is possible precisely because of the role played by the auctioneer in making sales to traders. Moreover, the traders themselves contribute to the auctioneer's ability to transmit information. As I will show in the next chapter, the closely knit trading communities organized around particular commodities act somewhat like cartels of like-minded buyers. These groups actively shape and adjust trading rules for particular auctions, subtly shifting the balance of market power between the auctioneers and buyers, and shaping the kinds of information over pricing strategies and buying preferences that an auctioneer can accumulate. They also stabilize the boundaries of trading communities and hence contribute to the consistency of information on which linkages of vertical coordination depend.

The management of information flows by the auctioneer is a crucial aspect of vertical linkage and coordination between different levels in the dis-tribution chain. Thus, even though the auctions are seemingly a spot market, producers, auction houses, auctioneers, and intermediate wholesalers are able to maintain stable long-term ties with preferred trade partners in a fashion that resembles patterns of "obligatory" or "relational contracting."

Vertical trading patterns exist in this spot market because the central institution of the market—the auction system—requires highly specific currents of market information that travel upstream and downstream across the auction block. These streams of information simultaneously structure and are structured by the institutional framework of the auctions them-selves. Buyers and sellers equally rely on this reciprocal movement of infor-mation, and such communication is both embedded in and one of the causes of the stable long-term transactional relationships—Clifford Geertz's "grooved channels" (1978)—that habitually lead customers again and again to the same suppliers.

Patterns of vertical alignment—the sense of enduring linkage between producers and distributors—are achieved through institutional arrange-ments that structure transactions. That is, vertical ties across Tsukiji's auction blocks are produced by institutional structures that shape and are shaped by transactional behavior. Such alignments and the stability of long-term trading ties are not reflections of static cultural predispositions or abstract social principles (e.g., generic Japanese dispositions toward reciprocity, long-term planning, or social harmony). Instead, alignment and stability are continually created, re-created, and modified through economic activity on many transactional levels that both mold and are molded by institutional arrangements.

TRADE BUYERS, DOWNSTREAM

Chatting one day with Mr. Andō, a tuna wholesaler and president of Chiyomaru, I was introduced to one of his customers, Mr. Taguchi, a quiet man about the same age as Andō (mid-fifties), who runs a sushi shop in the western suburbs of Tokyo. He left a few minutes later, after purchasing a couple of kilos of the highest-quality bluefin tuna, without asking or being told the price. As he left, Andō directed one of his clerks to deliver the tuna to the sushi chef's *chaya*, where he would pick it up after making purchases at several other regular suppliers. When he was gone, Andō told me that Taguchi was the second generation of his family to come to Chiyomaru for tuna, and that Taguchi's father was Andō's first long-term customer. Andō had met the father when he apprenticed at another firm in the late 1950s, and when he returned to his own family's business, the elder Taguchi moved his patronage to Chiyomaru.

The final link in the Tsukiji hierarchy of trade relations is people like Taguchi: the approximately 14,000 trade buyers—the sushi chefs, retail fishmongers, hotel chefs, supermarket purchasing agents, restaurateurs, peddlers, and bar owners—who come to Tsukiji each day (or, now, in many cases fax in their orders the night before). Members of this highly heterogeneous and fragmented category of buyers require no special licenses to make purchases in the marketplace, and they are therefore outside the regulatory schemes of the TMG marketplace administrators.

While their patronage of particular clusters of intermediate wholesalers is conditioned by their own specializations and product preferences, their choices of specific wholesalers among the hundred or more in any given specialization is far more complex and individualistic. To attract and keep regular customers, intermediate wholesalers generally offer them generous credit terms, delivery services, implicitly discounted prices, and assurances of supply when products are scarce; irregular or occasional drop-in customers pay top prices in cash-and-carry transactions and may be turned away if products are in short supply. Although the average trade buyer visits roughly ten wholesalers on each trip to the marketplace (according to an unpublished survey by Tō-Oroshi), many chefs and fishmongers told me they usually do business regularly with only two or three intermediate wholesalers in any given specialization.

Here, too, information (and hence relationship) seems to play a far more important role than immediate price considerations; customers rely on their wholesalers to know the customers' businesses, to understand the peculiarities of their products, and to keep them up to date on changing conditions in the market. Many of the higher-grade wholesalers post few if any written prices; employees use private codes to discuss prices among themselves. Customers are thus charged varying prices, dependent in large part on their long-standing relationship to the wholesaler. Openly dickering or haggling over prices is not regarded as appropriate. At the same time, the risks of doing business with a relatively unknown wholesaler are high. So, buyers are generally willing to forgo shopping around for better prices and will stick with an established trade partner. This parallels the behavior of traders in what Geertz (1978) calls "bazaar economies," who weigh the trade-offs among flows of information, prices and transaction costs, and the risks of unstable relationships and supplies. By the same token, many intermediate wholesalers at Tsukiji do little to encourage walk-in trade, and sometimes will even turn away an unknown customer.

Trade buyers can and do switch their allegiances among competing intermediate wholesalers, hence the concern with locational advantages and stall rotations (to be dealt with in the next chapter) to ensure that every wholesaler has an equal chance over time to attract new customers. These may come from among buyers looking to switch suppliers and from among the so-called floating customers who never establish close ties to any particular stall or stalls. Nonetheless, in many cases personal relationships between stall keeper and customer are all-important, and often these ties can be measured in generations. Yet the trust implied by such venerable ties between trading partners of long standing is not always what one might assume.

In his backstreet shop a couple of blocks from one of Tokyo's busiest train stations, I interviewed Wakita-san, the second-generation master of a prosperous fish restaurant. He told me about his long ties to various Tsukiji stalls, some of them dating back to his father's generation. Earlier in the day, Wakita had taken me through the market as he did his biweekly shopping, and he had introduced me to several intermediate wholesalers, including Isomura-san, a dealer in high-quality local fish *(kinkaimono)*. Wakita and Isomura were obviously old friends, and so I later asked about their relationship. Wakita opened an album of photographs that was close at hand and explained he had known Isomura since they were boys. He flipped through it to find an aging photograph of a formal wedding party, clearly taken many years before, and pointed out Isomura's parents alongside Wakita's own mother and father, the bride and groom in the photograph. Wakita explained that Isomura's father had been the go-between for Wakita's parents' marriage half a century ago. I made some appreciative comment about their deep ties and said something about how long-standing personal relationships were the basis for the trust and confidence needed to maintain good business ties.

Wakita stopped and looked at me quizzically. He shook his head and explained with resigned patience, "No, that's not it. You stick with your established suppliers not because you trust them more, but because you mistrust them less."

6   Family Firm

Suzuki-san, a youngish forty-something with a smile and a joke for every-one, is the proprietor of Konami, a firm that specializes in *jōmono*, top-quality seasonal fish—both live and fresh—for top-of-the-line restaurants. Suzuki is always sharply dressed in stylish sports clothes, in contrast to Harada-san, his *bantō* (the old-fashioned term for a head clerk or a chief apprentice), who spends his days clad in a sleeveless wetsuit. Harada presides over a cutting board surrounded by tanks from which he plucks live fish that he expertly cleans for Konami's demanding customers. His voice worn to gravel from years of cigarettes and whiskey, he greets each cus-tomer with a throaty "Irasshaimase." In the division of labor in the Konami firm, Harada buys and sells the live fish, Suzuki buys and sells the fresh fish, and Suzuki's mother—in her seventies—sits in the cashier's booth handling the accounts on a laptop computer. Suzuki's father, the son of a fishing family from Fukagawa, close by in the Sumida delta, himself hated fishing and got a job working for a wholesaler at Tsukiji. Eventually he set up shop on his own, just before World War II. After the war, he reopened when intermediate wholesalers were again issued licenses in 1950. He died young and his son found himself proprietor of the business in his mid-twenties. The younger Mr. Suzuki carries on his business with a light, almost whimsical air that belies the fact that Konami is a very successful firm with two licenses and hence a double stall, positioned advantageously in a corner location at a major intersection in the marketplace only a few steps from the auction floors.

The next four stalls are occupied by the firm of Chiyomaru, a midsized but highly regarded wholesaler of fresh and frozen tuna. The two Andō brothers operate the firm, which they inherited from their father about twenty years earlier. Including the two of them, the firm employs about a dozen and a half people, working on the trading floor or in their office in the outer market. The older brother also owned a small sushi bar—so elegantly discreet that one could barely find it—on a side street of the Ginza. (He closed the sushi shop in the late 1990s, citing the long recession.) The Andō brothers are at least the fourth generation in their family to operate Chiyomaru. Before that, the older Andō brother says, "Granddad always claimed to be the fourteenth generation in the fish business. But who knows? He claimed lots of things." They are nonetheless justifiably proud of their shop's history. On the shop wall, right next to a photograph of Jimmy Carter, who visited their stall once, they display a copy of a plaque offered to the Narita Shrine by 108 Nihonbashi wholesalers in 1889. Chiyomaru is one of only four shops listed that is still in business at Tsukiji.

The Andō brothers hold three licenses themselves, and a few years ago began to use a fourth stall and license that they rent from a now retired dealer. With this fourth license in hand, they hired Eguro-san, their chief assistant, to handle frozen tuna, while the Andō brothers are in charge of the various grades of fresh tuna. Men of this generation, who view their enterprises as corporations, have put aside the old-fashioned term "head clerk" *(bantō);* so Eguro has a corporate title, *reitōhin buchō* (manager of the frozen products division).

Eguro, the manager at Chiyomaru, and Suzuki, the proprietor of Konami, are close friends and constant companions. Their friendship was one chance factor in determining the choice of stall location that both firms made in the late 1980s. At the time, Eguro himself had worked for Chiyomaru only a year or so. But Suzuki decided to pair himself with the Andō brothers on the strength of his friendship with Eguro and the implied assurance that any firm capable enough to engage Eguro was a worthy next-door neighbor.

Wedged into a tiny stall in the most densely packed section of the marketplace, where the curve of the buildings creates the tightest spaces, Uehara-san is the harried owner of a single stall that deals in many types of *kamaboko*—fish pâté, pastes, and dumplings—a general category of goods known as *neriseihin.* His stall is so narrow that with his arms outstretched he can touch both neighbors' merchandise at once. Although he began his adult life as a junior high school teacher of English, there was no one else in the family to carry on the business after his father's death, so Uehara resigned his position and became the third generation of his family to operate the shop.

The shop's trade name *(yagō)* is Fukuizumi, dating from his grandfather's day. His grandfather was apprenticed to a fishmonger named Matsuizumi in the old Nihonbashi market, and when the shop's master helped set

Uehara's grandfather up in his own independent shop, part of the shop's name was bestowed upon him as well. Although the original shop, Matsu-izumi, vanished decades ago, the name fragment *-izumi* (meaning "spring or fountain") survives in Uehara's shop and in seven others, also descended in some fashion (Uehara himself is unsure of the details) from the old Matsuizumi. Uehara imagines that his father, and certainly his grandfather, must have relied on the proprietors of the other *-izumi* businesses— Takaizumi, Washiizumi, and so on—for mutual aid in the form of loans or introductions to clients and the like, but by now the connections are so attenuated that he feels nothing but a vague affinity for the other *-izumi* proprietors of his own generation, none of whom are named Uehara and with none of whom does he recognize any kinship.

Because Uehara's business centers on fish pâté, a manufactured product, supply and demand are reasonably stable, prices and quality don't vary much, and most of his customers deal with him by phone or fax. The cramped space and difficult-to-find location of his stall therefore do not cause him much concern, and his business day generally ends early enough that he can take it easy for an hour or so having lunch in the ramshackle library-cum-salon of a group known as the Ginrinkai (Silver Scale Society); Uehara edits their magazine, *Ginrin*, a compilation of notes on current mar-ketplace affairs, reports on seminars and formal discussions about market administration between wholesalers and market administrators, essays on the history of Tsukiji, haiku by marketplace poets, and articles about Tsukiji reprinted from major newspapers and magazines (see *Ginrin* 1951–).

Another regular at the Ginrinkai is Muramatsu-san, a gruff, blunt, fast-spoken man in his early sixties. Together with his son, he operates a single stall that specializes in fresh tuna. He and his son collaborate with Muramatsu's cousin, who also deals exclusively in fresh tuna in the single stall next door. The two cousins occasionally go in together to purchase fish at auction, and they employ a single cashier for their side-by-side stalls. Although they share equipment and lend each other a hand, they maintain entirely distinct sets of customers, because Muramatsu specializes in top-grade tuna for sushi chefs while his cousin concentrates on less expensive tuna for retail fishmongers. Muramatsu's business is small, and often he buys only one or two fish a day. Like many wholesalers, he sent his children to expensive private schools; and although his son joined the firm after graduating from college, his daughter went on to graduate study in German literature and now works in Berlin as a translator.

Over nouvelle cuisine in a tiny *ristoranté* near the marketplace I was introduced to Nakane-san, the president of Marunami. Among the darkened tables of young couples on expensive dates, Nakane conspicuously sat dressed in a *yukata*, talking with officials of the wholesalers' federation about the success of the festival for the water god held earlier that day. The previous year his college-aged American nephew had spent a summer working as a delivery boy for the firm; I had met him one morning as I dodged his cart. By luck—the gods of ethnographers smiling on me—that evening more than a year later, I somehow recalled my encounter with the nephew and thereby pleased the uncle.

Nakane is the heir of an old Tsukiji family, an adopted son-in-law *(mukoyōshi)* who married into his wife's household from a distant branch of the lineage; his wife knows the business as well as he does and supervises the cashier's booth every morning. Grandfather Nakane had no male heir and left the day-to-day running of the business largely to his chief clerks. In family lore, Grandfather Nakane, long dead, was a man-about-town, as familiar with kabuki and geisha as with flounder, more often seen in straw sandals than in rubber boots. He cultivated the nonchalant attitudes toward money, work, and domestic responsibilities that befitted the old *shitamachi* aesthetic of *iki*, stylish bravado and devil-may-care insouciance. His descendants regard him as an exemplar of the old-style trader, who immediately funneled the daily profits of business back into the water trades. Grandfather is said to have expired in a posh geisha establishment with the words "Moo kekkō desu," the meaning of which can be shaded between "One more for the road" and "That's it." The contemporary members of the Nakane family, all very earnest themselves, agree that granddad sent himself off with a very iki flair.

Grandfather may not have left much of a business but apparently he arranged the match between his daughter and adopted son-in-law well. Together they have built the business into one of the market's leading wholesalers, a model of an innovative family firm. Marunami specializes in seasonal fish from coastal waters *(kinkaimono)* for the supermarket trade. The firm's two stalls look like a neat little warehouse of snowy-white polystyrene crates, with few customers and little of the noisy hustle that characterizes many stalls nearby. A casual passerby might think, mistakenly, that the stalls were backwaters. But most of the business is done by fax, telephone, and Internet, and Nakane and his eldest son, who holds the title of managing director, have the friendly social skills necessary for corporate buyers and boardrooms. Nakane has established a small cluster of companies to accompany the main business of Marunami; his second son runs a seafood restaurant near the Tsukiji market, and the senior Nakane operates yet another business as a broker, purchasing directly from producers and selling through Tsukiji's auctions.

When this brokerage firm was set up, Nakane consulted a specialist in *seimei handan,* the divination of naming, in order to select a name, written in syllabic katakana, that would appropriately resonate in meaning, euphony, fortune, and numerological significance with the long successful Marunami. If his back office—fashionable address, understated lighting, leather furniture, state-of-the-art computers, and streams of faxes on market conditions neatly collated by a couple of secretaries wearing trim corporate uniforms—is any indication, his business strategy of combining traditional mercantile intuition with the latest marketing trends has paid off.

SMALL BUSINESS

By their numbers, their variety, and the complexity of their interests, affiliations, feuds, and partnerships, Tsukiji's intermediate wholesalers define much of the character of the marketplace. If its auction houses face upstream, toward shippers and producers, then Tsukiji's intermediate wholesalers face downstream toward restaurants, fishmongers, and ordinary consumers. When New Year's festivities at the market are covered on television, it is the rituals of the intermediate wholesalers that are broadcast; when NHK does a serial drama, a soap opera, using Tsukiji as its setting, it focuses on the family life of an intermediate wholesaler. The auctioneers are widely visible symbols, the technicians of the market process, but in the public conception intermediate wholesalers really make the marketplace. Intermediate wholesalers themselves, of course, agree. They have pride of place and many of them care about continuities—or seeming continuities—that link their ways of doing business and their ways of life to Tsukiji's historical antecedents in the Nihonbashi fish market.

Most of Tsukiji's intermediate wholesaling firms are family-run enterprises that rely largely on the labor of family members. Although the image of family firms operating out of crowded marketplace stalls suggests marginal enterprises in the informal sector of the economy, Tsukiji's intermediate wholesalers averaged gross sales of 535 million yen per firm in 2001 (Tōkyō-to Chūō Oroshiuri Shijō 2003).

By way of contrast, the other major set of economic actors—the *oroshiuri gyōsha,* the seven auction houses—are large corporate entities that would be familiar to many white-collar Japanese, if not in the specialized details of their businesses then at least in the broad outline of their organizational forms. They belong to a world of companies listed on major stock exchanges, affiliated in various ways with integrated commercial combines, or *keiretsu*—companies that rotate corporate officers and personnel from branch to branch or one affiliated firm to another, and that recruit college graduates into large bureaucratic enterprises that (used to) promise secure lifelong employment. Although some officers and employees of the auction houses are descended from families long connected with Tokyo's fish markets and are knowledgeable about both its history and the nature of intermediate wholesaling firms, their orientation and outlook on the culture of *their* business are more typical of large-scale corporate sectors of the economy than of the world of the small family-run firm.

The intermediate wholesalers belong to this other business world of older mercantile traditions that mix family and business relationships to a much greater degree than is the case in the detached residential and business realms of white-collar Japan. In their own fusions of households and workplaces, Tsukiji's intermediate wholesalers often have more in common with the small mom-and-pop stores that dot Tokyo's streets—their own customers, in many cases—than with executives of the large trading companies and fisheries companies that dominate the auction houses.

Despite their long hours and the uncertainties of their own businesses, Tsukiji traders are sometimes almost smug in their feelings of superiority over the white-collar, salaried middle classes. They prize the flexibility and autonomy that come from running their own business. They value the kinds of freedom their work offers in forming and cultivating close interpersonal ties in a highly interdependent social world. And they take quiet pride in belonging to working families. Their idealized entrepreneurial family not only embodies young and old working (and perhaps living) together; it also rests on notions of hierarchy, authority, and continuity.[1]

At Tsukiji the business of the family is the family business. A Tsukiji family revolves around its business; indeed, it is difficult to say with precision where one ends and the other begins, nor is it entirely clear which takes precedence. To be sure, intermediate wholesalers are confronted with the same problems of corporate continuity, risk and credit, labor and capital, supply and demand that any business must face. The sales volume of their businesses may be many times larger than that of the tiny mom-and-pop stores that characterize the small-scale sector of the Japanese domestic economy (Patrick and Rohlen 1987; T. Bestor 1990), and in many cases they are incorporated as joint-stock corporations *(kabushiki gaisha)*, albeit unlisted ones, but the idiom in which they speak of credit, labor, or capital and the devices by which they arrange to solve these problems are common to

Japanese small businesses across the board: kinship, personal connections of mutual obligation, apprenticeships, and myriad ties of self-interest embedded in communal social, ritual, and religious affiliations.

The daily business of intermediate wholesalers is framed by complex sets of personal ties, obligations, feuds, political interests, family connections, and patterns of patronage that are hammered out daily, against a backdrop of years if not decades of similar calculations. Personal affiliations are the prisms through which reputation, trust, and reliability are refracted. Traders develop complex relations of interdependence and rivalry with their immediate neighbors in the marketplace, sometimes forming alliances among adjacent stallholders. The networks that spread across the marketplace bring trade partners together and are useful as well for finding workers, placing apprentices, or arranging marriages. On a day-to-day basis, informal social insurance and emergency sources of supply flow back and forth through these networks.

The sources of affiliation and the concrete relationships that develop out of them are varied. In the following sections I will introduce several distinct (but of course intertwined) dimensions of affiliation. Old school ties and common hometowns provide significant social linkages, especially for people who hail from the half dozen Tokyo neighborhoods and nearby fishing ports that have sent sizable numbers of people to work at Tsukiji over the years. Kinship ties among traders run thick and deep, overlaid by and shot through with fictive kinship relations among shops, in many cases based on histories of apprenticeship. And naturally the specializations of traders—as octopus or shrimp dealers, sushi suppliers or tuna traders—create powerful affiliations that are deeply embedded in the institutional structure of the marketplace as a whole.

OLD SCHOOL TIES

Shared connections to hometowns create ties and identities for oneself and others, and native places often are also reflected in stylized motifs adopted for shop names, *yagō* or *kigō*.[2] In some cases affiliations based on common place of origin are loosely institutionalized into *kō*, nominally religious pilgrimage groups that focus devotional (and recreational) energies on a particular shrine or temple that symbolizes a specific locale.

Hometown ties are the basis for *kai*, or clubs, for traders from a particular town or region. One such group represents the several dozen wholesalers who trace their origins back to the Fukagawa district of Tokyo, just north of

Tsukiji, where until a generation or two ago fishers could still exploit the estuary of the Sumida River. Two groups draw their members from old fishing communities sixty or seventy miles from Tokyo, one from the Jōban coast to the northeast, the other from the deep-water fishing port of Chōshi due east on the Pacific coast of Chiba. The members of yet a fourth group trace their ancestry back to Nagoya. Hometown groups like these are rarely specialized in terms of trade—they are not all tuna dealers, say, or shrimp merchants—and so create networks that crosscut many of the functional divisions of marketplace life. Such groups easily mix recreation and relaxation with all kinds of informal mutual assistance, such as providing introductions to potential customers, finding jobs for recent arrivals from the hometown, or picking reliable next-door neighbors for a relocated stall.

Native place is a very strong motif in the cultural representation of identity in contemporary Japanese society, expressed as much in the exegesis of regional food culture as in the folk ethnography of regional configurations of culture-and-personality that characterize and differentiate, say, people from Tokyo, Kyoto, and Osaka. But hometown ties among people in Tokyo generally provide a weak basis for collective organization—the networks of affiliation they represent tend to be affective rather than instrumental—in contrast to many other societies in which formal organizations based on places of common origin *(Landsmannschaft,* in sociological terminology) play socially, politically, and economically prominent roles, particularly among populations of recent migrants to urban life (see Cohen 1969; Zenner 1991).

Colleges, senior and junior high schools, and even elementary schools, however, spawn highly cohesive alumni groups and networks of old boys ("O.B.") whose interactions with one another continue for decades. Clearly, alumni ties—for example, from a particular fisheries high school or fisheries college—also may be hometown bonds, but they focus on the experience of a particular school and its institutional culture. At Tsukiji such O.B. networks frequently are deployed for the kinds of introductions used by job seekers and marriage go-betweens.

In a few instances, hometown ties per se have crystallized into control over a particular economic niche. Tsukiji's most prominent example, mentioned in chapter 3, is what some market regulars call the "Urayasu *renchū*"—the "Urayasu crowd"—from the old fishing port of Urayasu, located just across the head of Tokyo Bay from where Tsukiji stands at the mouth of the Sumida River. Like "middleman minorities" in many societies (Bonacich 1973; Cohen 1969; Zenner 1991), traders from Urayasu can exploit existing, shared affiliations (in this instance not ethnic but regional) to create dense networks of information and exchange that enable them to dominate some segments of the market.

Roughly 10 to 15 percent of the intermediate wholesaling firms at Tsukiji are regarded as "Urayasu firms." Typically, they are in the shellfish business or in related specialties (such as supplying sushi chefs); but the Urayasu firms also include high-profile tuna wholesalers who operate some of Tsukiji's largest and most prosperous companies. The emergence of Urayasu traders as a powerful—and none-too-well-loved—group at Tsukiji occurred over the past two or three decades. As shellfish harvesting ended in Urayasu in the 1960s, many Urayasu fishers gradually transformed themselves into Tsukiji traders, first working as employees of intermediate wholesalers and then, as they acquired experience in the wholesale trade, purchasing licenses to become intermediate wholesalers themselves.

The success of Urayasu firms elicits grudging admiration from other Tsukiji traders, although their comments sometimes cast even virtue as dark conspiracy. Detractors grumble that the Urayasu wholesalers succeed because—as former fishers—they are willing to work hard and long under miserable conditions; women and children from Urayasu are not accustomed to luxury and are willing to work in the stalls with the men; they are clannish and help each other out; and they have enormous amounts of capital. The unspoken implication of the last point, of course, is that their capital is both unearned and undeserved, although it originated in the payments provided by the government to compensate for the loss of their preexisting fishing rights (as described in chapter 3). Urayasu fishers have, in fact, benefited from a succession of extraordinary windfalls. With their original government payments, many acquired licenses at Tsukiji; most already owned land in Urayasu and many used their compensation to invest in still more. As real estate values grew explosively throughout the 1980s, Urayasu landowners became millionaires who, if so inclined, could borrow against their land to finance further expansion at Tsukiji during the speculative period of the 1980s, now regarded as the "Bubble Economy." They particularly profited from the extension of a Tokyo subway line that made Urayasu one of the suburban bedroom communities most convenient to central Tokyo. And to crown their good fortune, Tokyo Disneyland was built in Urayasu in the 1980s, bringing with it the development of a slew of luxury hotels. Land values rose still further. To the wondering eyes of other Tsukiji traders, Urayasu indeed became a magic kingdom.[3]

Financial compensation for the loss of fishing rights did more than provide many Urayasu fishers with large amounts of capital to invest at Tsukiji:

it also contributed to their sense of solidarity and common identity. The government's recognition of collective rights—in this case the fishing rights of Urayasu—and subsequent compensation for their loss were crucial factors in the formation and maintenance of this interest group. As Urayasu traders have became a major bloc at Tsukiji, the collective interests of the past continue to provide a basis for identifying mutual interests in the present. This fusion of collective interests and local identity institutionally locks in the solidarity of Urayasu traders. Although the Urayasu group is not a formal component in the institutional structure of marketplace administration, its members wield considerable influence within various trade guilds of intermediate wholesalers—particularly those for sushi toppings (*tokushumono*) and tuna (*ōmono*), the two specialties in which Urayasu traders are most concentrated.[4]

MARRIAGE AND ALLIANCE

The collective trajectory of Urayasu traders, with its emphasis on hometown ties, is exceptional, however. For most Tsukiji traders the significant realms of social ties are individual and personal, based on kinship and its fictive equivalents. The many examples offered earlier of interlocking connections among stalls demonstrate the pervasiveness and character of the kinship ties that run throughout the marketplace. Because most family/firms have been in business for at least a couple of generations and intermarriage among wholesaling families is common, almost every firm has at least a few other firms allied by some sort of kinship connection; some firms boast dozens of such relationships. Each generation can renew or revive such ties through marriages, adoptions, or apprenticeships. For some traders, kinship relations are irrelevant to their daily businesses, but for many dealers, the fundamental issues of kinship—marriage, inheritance, succession—are inextricably linked to property, capital, and labor.

Morimoto-san, a woman who—like her two sisters and their mother before them—has had long experience as a *chōba* cashier, estimates that roughly half of the men who run Tsukiji dealerships and their successors (*atotsugi*, i.e., sons or sons-in-law who will carry on the businesses in the next generation) are married to women who are themselves daughters of Tsukiji dealers. The proportion of such marriages probably has declined in the past generation, but nonetheless these marriages represent the norm, in her view and in the conventional wisdom of market regulars.

People at Tsukiji offer several reasons why such marriages are common. The first is simply opportunity: Tsukiji firms depend on successful marriages for their survival, and the marketplace's large and dense social network is a fertile field for matchmaking.

Second, marriages at Tsukiji are often regarded as alliances between families and firms, and are arranged as such. For example, a couple of years ago, the heir apparent of the Chiyomaru tuna firm, Andō Hideki, married the daughter of another Tsukiji dealer. The father of the bride, Yamamura-san, is the proprietor of Uorokubun, a firm that specializes in *sushidane*, sushi toppings. Yamamura has no sons, so the marriage carried with it the suggestion that Hideki may eventually become heir to the Uorokubun firm as well as to his own family's Chiyomaru. The match is advantageous for the Andō family, not only because the young couple are happy together, but also because the two Tsukiji firms are complementary and hold the promise of a future consolidation that can create a much more diversified top-of-the-line supply house. And Hideki's father-in-law comes from an old Tsukiji family. The main branch of the Yamamura family built their old Nihonbashi *ton'ya* into the core of what has now become one of the leading auction houses at Tsukiji. Because Hideki's father-in-law was a second son, he was expected to go off on his own. In the 1950s he founded Uorokubun as an intermediate wholesaler, and as a result Yamamura family members today are in business on both sides of the auctions. Through Hideki's marriage, the Andō family has further added to its extensive and influential network of kin throughout the marketplace.

And third, intermarriages among Tsukiji families are desirable because spouses from Tsukiji families can easily understand the lifestyle that goes with the business. In the Miyano family, proprietors of Marumiya, a middling-sized dealer in dried, salted, and smoked fish *(himono)*, the two sons who run the business are both married to daughters of Tsukiji wholesalers. Neither of the wives work in the marketplace now, but before their children were born, both worked as cashiers in the tiny booth at the back of the stall. One of them quipped to me that the only reason her husband had courted her was because she had been raised to think that the interlocking schedule of work and family time at Tsukiji is normal.

In many intimate details, the rhythms of the market pervade traders' lives and their own sense of social existence. Traders of a certain age joke that they all know each other's wedding anniversaries. For years the market operated seven days a week, with one day a month as a holiday, and only brief vacations at New Year's and during the O-Bon season in August. If a Tsukiji family was holding a wedding, the only way that kin, friends, and co-workers could attend was to hold it on the 22nd, the one day each month the market closed. Nowadays the market closes every Sunday and for most national holidays, as well as for a five-day stretch over the New Year's holidays and for three days during O-Bon. But except around major holidays, it is difficult to close the market for longer than two days at a time. To give workers more time off (and to make the marketplace more attractive to prospective employees), the market administration now schedules a couple of extra closings each month. To avoid creating long weekends (*renkyū*, or "consecutive holidays"), these are scheduled for midweek, usually on the second and fourth Wednesdays.

Tsukiji exacts a heavy workload. And even with the added time off, this schedule isolates Tsukiji workers and families from the common rhythms of daily life that most urban Japanese share. Whatever advantages there may be to having a Wednesday off when recreation spots aren't crowded, these are outweighed in most people's view by the fact that one's children are in school and other family members and *ippanjin* friends (that is, "ordinary people," without Tsukiji connections) are probably at work. Thus the calendar reinforces the sense that Tsukiji is a separate world. Husbands and wives alike remark that marriages within Tsukiji work best. It goes without question, among Tsukiji families at least, that the wife fits her own schedule to her husband's early hours and oddly punctuated weeks.

The significant effects of seemingly trivial details of market holidays are just one reminder that the social institutions of the marketplace produce and reproduce much of the social topography of traders' lives. The density of kinship ties within the marketplace is no random occurrence. Marriages like that between the Andō and the Yamamura families are dynastic in their implications, at least to those who plan them. As important as arranging the proper marriage is obtaining an heir to ensure that the family and its business can be passed on to following generations. When one does not follow from the other, customary Japanese kinship practices provide another means of ensuring succession: adoption, particularly of a son-in-law. The mukoyōshi marries into a family, adopts his bride's family name, and becomes heir to the family's station in life. The practice is old-fashioned but by no means moribund; indeed, it is common among urban entrepreneurial households (see Hamabata 1990: 43–45; T. Bestor 1989, 1990). Conventional wisdom is divided on the subject of adopted sons-in-law. Proverbial advice to young men contemplating such a marriage tells them, "If you have even a cup of rice bran to your name, don't become a mukoyōshi." On the benefits to a family, however, another proverb is positive: "Three generations of mukoyōshi ensure a family's fortune." Adopted sons-in-law are commonplace at Tsukiji, and successful businessmen such as Nakane, the proprietor of Marunami mentioned earlier, are often held up as exemplars. Although

the merits of adopting sons-in-law are often noted, the success is most frequently—and publicly—attributed to the son-in-law, not to the daughter
and bride who must also make the relationship and the family business
work successfully.

INCORPORATING KINSHIP

Kinship provides one means for successfully continuing a family firm.
Corporate law provides another. In either case, the legal and social frameworks of household and business are thoroughly intertwined.

When intermediate wholesalers regained their market licenses in 1950,
their businesses were legally regarded as individual proprietorships *(kojin)*,
as they had been before the war and before the wartime consolidation of all
dealerships into a single larger corporation. Under the licensing terms of the
immediate postwar period, the market assigned one stall per license and one
license per wholesaler. The legal status of proprietorships had and continues
to have many implications for taxation and insurance purposes, but here the
important point is they are individual, personal licenses, suited at least
implicitly to family enterprises in which the head of the household is the
head of the firm. In a proprietorship of this kind, there is no entity with
legal standing separate from the individual who runs the business. The proprietor, by definition, cannot have partners with controlling interests in the
firm; ownership cannot be divided; and so, of course, the possibilities for
raising capital are limited. When the proprietor dies, the firm itself does not
live on as a corporate entity, although the right to hold the individual license
can be conveyed to a member of the inheriting generation. Significantly, the
rules of the market system restrict each proprietorship to a single license.

All these factors made proprietorships extremely static, and in the 1960s
marketplace administrators began to encourage changes that over time
would result in what they hoped would be a "rationalization" of the marketplace, with fewer but larger and more economically viable intermediate
wholesalers. This was a response to a wide array of factors, including the
decline of the local fishing industry in nearby waters, the growing reliance
of the marketplace on shipments from large-scale producers operating out
of distant ports, the development of high-speed transportation networks
and efficient freezing technology, shifts in consumption away from fresh
seafood and toward processed seafood, and visions of supermarkets shim-
mering on the horizon. Such trends suggested that small-scale proprietorships would lack the capital, the management skills, and the technical
sophistication to meet future challenges. Market regulations were therefore

amended to promote market rationalization by allowing and encouraging personal proprietorships to become incorporated firms (limited liability firms or joint-stock corporations).[5] Incorporated firms (known, collectively, as *hōjin*) are able, under Japanese law and market regulations, to accept infusions of capital, to split ownership and management among several individuals, and—most important—to hold more than one license and to operate more than one stall. Market officials clearly state that the rationalization drive was and is aimed at reducing the number of intermediate wholesaling firms roughly by half, from 1,677 to about 800, while leaving the numbers of stalls and licenses intact.

It has been a gradual process: throughout the 1970s and 1980s, the total number of firms steadily decreased and more and more proprietorships transformed themselves into corporations—kojin into hōjin. These trends accelerated in the early 1990s, as the post-Bubble slump began. From the mid-1980s through the late 1990s, the number of proprietorships declined by about a dozen and a half a year, some transforming themselves into incorporated firms and others being absorbed into larger firms that had already become incorporated. In April 2003, there were a total of 901 *nakaoroshi* firms: 155 proprietorships and 746 corporations (*Tō-Oroshi*, May 2003, p. 18).

Tsukiji licenses are in some ways like New York City taxi medallions or seats on a stock exchange. The licenses themselves take on economic value in a complex and rather shadowy way. There is nothing tangible to buy or sell when a license is transferred; in many cases very little in the way of capital assets, inventory, or equipment is attached to a firm, and since the trade depends so much on day-to-day reinforcement of existing personal ties, goodwill is difficult to value (see Dore 1987). Yet licenses can be incredibly valuable, trading at astronomical prices precisely because they are an enfranchisement to participate in a market with limited entry. During the height of the Bubble years, licenses traded for ¥100 million or more, equivalent to the cost of a fancy new house in Tokyo's suburbs. But following the slump of the 1990s, licenses go begging for buyers. According to dealers, many strapped wholesalers would jump at the chance to sell their licenses, but even though the asking price these days (in 2003) is in the vicinity of ¥15 million, there are few buyers.

Technically, intermediate wholesalers' licenses are not for sale: they cannot be bought and sold at will. TMG regulations allow "transfers" under certain specific circumstances, including inheritance; conveying a license to employees, such as to chief clerk or apprentice; or, in the case of an incorporated firm, bringing in new corporate officers who themselves may assume managerial and financial control. The TMG requires that new license holders—whatever the method or the circumstances of the transfer—meet certain standards: he or she must have five or more years of experience working in the market, be of good character (e.g., not be a convicted criminal or have a history of bankruptcy), and have sufficient working capital (the minimum is absurdly low, set years ago at ¥5 million, or roughly $43,000). Absolute newcomers to Tsukiji therefore cannot obtain a license, and licenses trade hands among people who already participate in the marketplace.

This is where kinship meets corporate law. As proprietorships, both by legal definition and in practical reality, the businesses can be passed on through inheritance only without division among heirs. But the norms of single inheritance, typical of the old-fashioned stem family of mercantile life, have faded.[6] Inheritance laws now require—and contemporary social norms suggest—that property be divided in some reasonable fashion among all children and the surviving spouse. When the value of a Tsukiji license was negligible, its indivisibility caused few concerns; but as these values skyrocketed, proprietorships became too valuable to ignore. Today, despite the recent economic slump that has substantially reduced the market value of a license, a family that owns a proprietorship faces the quandary of having a valuable asset that cannot be divided among heirs. In addition, even if there is a sole heir, he or she must also pass the scrutiny of the TMG regarding fitness to operate a business in the marketplace, following the general requirements described above. A Tsukiji family contemplating inheritance and estate planning, if it is to secure this valuable asset, must either have a sole heir willing, qualified by experience, and with sufficient personal capital to take over a proprietorship—a combination that can by no means be assumed these days, when many children do not want to follow in their fathers' footsteps—or convert the business into an incorporated firm.

There are few compelling reasons to maintain a proprietorship as such. Inertia is certainly one factor, and indeed for some aging traders that may be reason enough. Why bother to change a small-scale proprietorship into a small-scale corporation that has more difficult paperwork? Others may question the benefit of forgoing the tax dodges available by blending household and personal expenses into the costs of the business. Still others may wish to enjoy the independence of a business that can provide walking-around money for *asobi* (playing)—with women, with drink, with gambling debts. Some dealers, according to their gossiping colleagues, maintain their firms as personal proprietorships for precisely these reasons.

But sooner or later, most Tsukiji families have an incentive to convert their businesses into incorporated firms, particularly if no one wants to take the firm into another generation as a proprietor. Bluntly stated, an incorporated firm can be sold and the family can realize the value of intangible assets. As an incorporated business, a firm's ownership and management can be divided among family heirs, if any are interested in continuing the business. One heir can buy out others. The firm can be put up as security for bank loans in ways that a proprietorship cannot. The business can be sold outright or can remain independent with infusions of capital and management divided among several individuals, including family members, other relatives, employees, and newcomers to the marketplace. And, of course, it can expand by buying up the licenses of other incorporated firms.

Data on the inheritance of proprietorships, drawn from records kept by the wholesalers' federation, illustrate the familial character of the marketplace. License applications record the relationship of an heir to the deceased license holder, and in the sample of records I examined for the period from January 1985 through February 1991, 56 proprietorships were transferred by inheritance, at a rate of a bit less than one a month. These 56 transfers occurred among a total of 419 proprietorships that existed at the start of the period; thus, during the six years covered, about one in eight of these firms was inherited. Heirs were overwhelmingly males (77 percent), and eldest sons *(chōnan)* were precisely 50 percent (28 out of 56) of the total heirs recorded. Other heirs included other sons (12), wives (9), adopted sons-in-law (3), daughters (3), and an adopted daughter (1).[7]

Male primogeniture in no way ensures that transitions are smooth. Tsukiji is full of stories about fathers and sons who barely speak to one another after working side by side for years. Nowadays, many children simply refuse to carry on their families' businesses, and although their rationales—a desire to study French literature, for example, or a lifelong interest in engineering—are undoubtedly compelling, the prospect of working with dad must be daunting for many merchant sons. Those sons who do carry on their father's businesses frequently are sent off for training under another wholesaler, in part because of the well-known volatility of father-son apprenticeships. Indeed, even positive relationships between fathers and heirs can have negative consequences for other family members. For example, Kawabe, an eel firm with a single stall, a proprietorship, is operated by a middle-aged man, Takemoto-san; his wife; and his son. Takemoto inherited the business from his father after his older brother—the firm's heir-apparent—died in his twenties. Takemoto still bitterly resents that his father bestowed all his attention, affection, and pocket money on the older brother, the chōnan, who, in the time-honored traditions of old-fashioned mercantile families, was the sole heir to the business as well as to the family's identity and status.

Incorporation does not remove all these potential problems; but once a firm incorporates, issues of inheritance and succession are cast in a different light, since as a legal entity an incorporated firm can outlive any of its principals and the firm can hire people to fill any necessary role. Nevertheless, even incorporated firms tend to continue as family-run businesses, and kinship relations continue to be crucial, although in its outward form the business has been transformed into a modern corporation. The firm continues to hold its market license, while shares in the enterprise and positions as officers of the corporation may shift from individual to individual, whether by inheritance or other means.

Applications to register corporate officers do not systematically record kinship information about individuals, so they are not exactly parallel to the inheritance records mentioned above. But in some cases kinship information is recorded, and within the files for the same six-year period, such data were noted in sixty applications, coincidentally almost the same number as inheritances. The kinship relationships stretch much more broadly across generations and on both consanguineal and affinal sides here than when proprietorships are inherited, since regulations surrounding inheritance restrict the eligible range of kin; and, of course, an incorporated firm can have many corporate officers whereas a personal proprietorship necessarily has only a single owner. Furthermore, these registrations of corporate officers do not necessarily coincide with inheritance or succession; in most cases the registration appears to have taken place shortly after a proprietor has reorganized his enterprise into an incorporated firm with himself as president. The relationships (implicitly recorded from the former proprietor's point of view) include eldest son (22), wife (9), other son (7), mother (4), daughter (2), daughter-in-law (2), older brother (2), son-in-law (2), father-in-law (1), mother-in-law (1), and grandchild (1), as well as bantō (4) and bantō's wife (1). In three cases the new officer was simply identified as the former proprietor or officer of another firm that had just merged with or been acquired by the surviving firm. If nothing else, these registrations suggest that the positions of corporate officers provide somewhat greater opportunities for women's participation and financial stake in the business to be legally recognized, although such data say nothing about actual day-to-day management or decision making.

Appointments of corporate officers draw on a wider range of kinship ties for two obvious reasons. First, the degrees of kinship required in the civil code constrain possibilities for the inheritance of proprietorships, but they do not prevent a family from appointing relatives as officers of a (family) corporation. Second, appointment as a corporate officer does not necessarily require active participation in the company or the marketplace. It may simply reflect a division of family property. Thus grandchildren, daughters-in-law, mothers, nephews, fathers-in-law, and other kin, distant or not, may be included as officers if they have a financial stake in the enterprise (or even if they did not have a prior stake).

WORKERS

As families/firms transform themselves into family-held corporations, they remake the institutions of labor. Within the lifetime of older traders, a system of arduous long-term apprenticeships, known as *detchibōkō*, has all but disappeared, and the possibility has vanished that a successful bantō eventually might be set up with a shop of his own. Today the market faces a perpetual labor shortage. The grandsons of bantō, in this generation now prosperous entrepreneurs with corporate titles, scramble to hire workers from a generation that idealizes itself as *furiitaa* (free-timers): young people who work at part-time jobs more or less by choice rather than by necessity, preferring no-strings employment to the entanglements of career and workplace commitment. Even in the midst of the long recession of the 1990s—the aftermath of the Bubble—when economic unease supposedly permeates society and when some large corporations have suspended all hiring for a year or more at a time, Tsukiji traders have difficulty finding workers. Even as white-collar Japan is laying off people who thought they had lifetime guarantees of employment, no one wants to start out with a blue-collar job.

During Japan's boom years and even in the long slump of the 1990s, young workers spurned low-level jobs as "three-k" *(san-kei);* this buzzword describes a variety of bad working conditions, all of them beginning with "k": *kurai* (dark), *kitanai* (dirty), *kiken* (dangerous), *kitsui* (hard), *kane ga nai* ("no money," or low pay), and *kusai* (smelly). The "k"s in question shift according to the speaker or the job, but any of them apply to Tsukiji, which abounds in three-k jobs. No question, work at Tsukiji is tough (the documentary photo essays in Motohashi 1988 and Beretta P-03 2003 powerfully illustrate that point): the hours are early and long, the work is backbreaking physical labor, and the prospects for making a career in the place are slim unless one stands to inherit a business. No amount of pay or benefits can change those facts. And so there is rapid turnover, and intermediate wholesalers are continually searching for workers.

A typical advertisement from *AN* (*Arbeit News;* June 29, 1998, p. 135)

Figure 50. "K" is for *kiken,*
a dangerous job. A worker
slices a whole frozen tuna
on a table saw.

seeks a male between twenty and thirty-five years of age, with an ordinary driver's license, to work for an intermediate wholesaler who handles dried and salted seafood. Among the roughly 100 pages of listings, this position falls under "market staff" *(shijōnai sutaffu)* and involves packing, delivery within the marketplace, and light labor *(karui sagyō).* The ad describes the shop as "an 'at-home' *(atto hōmu)* kind of place." And "applications are welcomed from people with no experience." The position offers a monthly salary starting at ¥330,000 (more with experience; raises after one year), as well as biannual bonuses, health insurance, commuting allowance, and one meal a day. The hours are from 3:30 A.M. to 12:30 P.M.; Sundays, holidays, and two market closings a month are days off. The employer writes, "Tsukiji always has a lively atmosphere, and you'll have lots of friendly co-workers *(tanoshii nakama ga takusan)!* Even inexperienced workers are OK, because we provide kind guidance *(shinsetsu shidō),* so feel at ease in applying." (The pay offered in this friendly ad is higher than for roughly comparable jobs advertised in the same issue of *AN.*)[8]

Most nonfamily workers in the intermediate wholesaling firms are nonunionized, hourly employees. Two labor unions at Tsukiji actively attempt to organize the lowest rungs of labor, especially delivery people or porters.[9] Their leaflets, posters, and large wall slogans dot the marketplace, written in the incendiary prose and revolutionary calligraphic styles of the Japanese New Left. However, since many employees at Tsukiji have a substantial stake in their employer's interests (e.g., as family members, heirs, or salaried corporate officers), the marketplace is not a welcoming place for labor organizers. Many of the other employees who potentially might be union members regard themselves as floating, part-time workers, and hence have little interest in collective efforts to improve their working conditions.

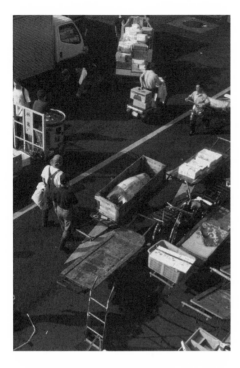

Figure 51. *Neko* (handcarts) and motorized *tāretto* move goods outside the auctions.

Tsukiji is not unique in this; the small-scale sectors of the Japanese economy and particularly the employees of family-run enterprises have markedly low rates of union participation.

Workers in the stalls are roughly divided among three categories. Men are either menial delivery people or porters (*haitatsunin,* or "staff," as the ad calls them) or more skilled *eigyō-man* (roughly translated as "sales-man," although their jobs entail much more than sales). Women are cashiers in the chōba or workers in "back offices" located outside the marketplace proper.

The workers pulling or driving the carts—officially and publicly termed "delivery men" (*haitatsunin*), privately and pejoratively called "coolies" (*karuko*)—are near the bottom of Tsukiji's labor force. Some are full-time employees of the intermediate wholesalers; most are part-time day laborers. Not surprisingly, in recent years Tsukiji firms increasingly have recruited foreign workers. A 1990 survey by the TMG found 451 foreign workers at Tsukiji—no doubt a vast underestimate—the great majority (404) from the People's Republic of China.[10]

Employers favor Chinese workers because they can read the ideographic characters used to write both Japanese and Chinese. Signs are everywhere in

Figure 52. The Tsukiji workforce. From a children's book, *Uogashi*, written and illustrated by Sawada Shigetaka (1985). Reproduced with the permission of the author and Hyōronsha.

the market's complex spatial and visual environment, and sending out an expensive tuna in the care of someone who cannot decipher even the simplest shop name would be a risky proposition.[11] Foreign workers not literate in Japanese or Chinese—such as Iranians, Brazilians of Japanese descent, Malaysians, or Bangladeshi—also work in the marketplace, but usually in even more menial jobs in the icehouses or as sweepers.

Japanese and foreign workers generally get along, and what disputes arise are usually short-lived and easily resolved, but occasionally violent fights erupt. For example, in the fall of 1990, a brawl broke out among delivery workers over some minor disagreement between a Chinese and a Japanese worker. Accounts of the incident vary, but one common version had it that a Chinese worker failed to observe the implicit rules of the road as he was navigating his cart through the loading docks; a Japanese worker began to yell at him, a crowd of Japanese workers gathered, and the Chinese worker was roughed up by the crowd and later required minor medical treatment. The incident became an instant cause célèbre throughout the marketplace, and Chinese workers put up wall posters denouncing Japanese racism. Several Tokyo newspapers picked up the story. Leaders in the marketplace—TMG officials, intermediate wholesalers, union representatives—all sought to downplay the event as an isolated one. After several weeks, overt signs of continuing antagonism disappeared, although tension remained for some time.

As seen by Japanese, foreign workers pose a problem only insofar as they do not understand the unstated rules for getting along. From the point of view of Japanese workers and employers alike, the work environment of the crowded marketplace requires a high degree of social consensus, coordination, and communication. Linguistic competence is important, but body language is crucial. These unspoken principles embrace diverse bodily behaviors ranging from etiquette to seafood handling that are "obvious" to Japanese, yet which foreign workers "fail" to learn. Japanese employers and co-workers complain that foreign workers do not bow properly and that they carry themselves impolitely, with insolent swaggers or penetrating stares. They don't seem to understand the proxemics of queue behavior as they pull a heavy cart through clogged passageways and cut in front of others. When handling seafood, they lack the proper attitude and care that traders gloss as *kata*, proper form, referring to, among other things, the precise motions of a skilled artisan. The phrase "to learn with the body" *(karada de oboeru)* describes mastery of these physical principles of work, and Japanese employers and co-workers are often mystified that foreign workers do not intuitively grasp these often unarticulated codes. If they don't, Japanese complain, foreign workers only create problems for others and hence for themselves.

The porter's job is young man's work, but not all engaged in it are young. Some of the older Japanese men working as porters hold down two jobs. Some fish peddlers, for example, work morning jobs as a market porter and spend their afternoons selling fish in residential neighborhoods. Others have entirely separate occupations. For instance, Umeda-san runs a small dry goods store on a shopping street in Miyamoto-chō in the southern part of Tokyo and works in the mornings at Tsukiji to put aside enough money to build a new house; he was introduced to the marketplace by two of his immediate neighbors, a fishmonger and a sushi chef, who shop together at Tsukiji.

The lowest rungs on Tsukiji's employment ladder—a few of these delivery jobs in the stalls, as well as jobs for sweepers who clean the market in the afternoon and the nighttime *koage* crews that unload and arrange seafood for the display auctions—are sometimes filled by workers recruited on a daily or weekly basis from the casual labor markets *(yoseba)* for construction and other semiskilled workers in slum areas such as Yokohama's Kotobuki-chō and Tokyo's San'ya. These labor markets are often controlled or contested by gangsters (Fowler 1996; Gill 2001; Stevens 1997), and Tsukiji's unions try to guard against similar influences at Tsukiji (Nakamura 1980, 1990).

At the other end of the employment scale, eigyō-man are—or become—skilled workers, who clean, cut, and arrange seafood for display, greet customers, take orders, and package seafood. Some eigyō-man have long careers in the marketplace, working for decades for the same stall; they may eventually rise to being a manager or an auction buyer for their employer. An eigyō-man with family connections in the marketplace may work as someone else's employee for a while to learn the business before taking over his own family's market stall, restaurant, or retail shop. Sons of sushi chefs and fishmongers may seek out employment at the market—or their fathers may seek it for them—to get serious seafood experience and make a few contacts for their future trade; likewise, some Tsukiji wholesalers send their sons off to work in another shop for a few years of training. Other eigyō-man work in the market for a year or two and then leave for employment with better conditions.

Introductions from clients and colleagues play a large role in recruiting workers, particularly eigyō-man and cashiers, but there is hardly ever a surplus of workers with prior connections to the marketplace. A graduate of a fisheries high school looking for a career at Tsukiji would gravitate toward one of the auction houses or a large trading and fishing company, not toward an intermediate wholesaler's stall. Wholesalers have to scramble to find workers, and must compete for them with all the other more glamorous and less demanding employers in a city where young adults have grown very finicky about the work they want to do, if any. The contemporary attitude frustrates Tsukiji's hardworking dealers, but through word of mouth and advertisements in Tokyo's many help-wanted magazines they always manage to find a few new workers.

Many of the young men they hire have no great interest in the marketplace and no particular incentive to stick out the tough working conditions. They may be looking not for a career but simply for decent pay with no long-term obligations. Tsukiji has always been a good place for a young man to find a temporary job. Generations of university students have found part-time jobs at Tsukiji, and I have met dozens of middle-aged men in all walks of life who nostalgically recall working at Tsukiji as a part of student life. Now it is being turned to by a generation of furiitaa. Tsukiji is a fine place for a muscular young windsurfer, rock musician, or student radical to find a job that pays reasonably well—¥12,000 or more a day, plus a couple of hearty meals—and leaves the afternoon and evening free. But they quickly find that the morning comes very early at Tsukiji, the eight-hour day stretches into twelve, and the free afternoon and evening are spent in sleep. And so, sooner or later, they move on.

APPRENTICESHIP

Members of the established older generation, like the Andō brothers, the proprietors of the tuna dealer Chiyomaru mentioned at the beginning of this chapter, simultaneously sympathize with young workers and decry their lack of commitment. The older Andō brother himself was trained in the late 1950s as an apprentice *(detchi)* in the old-fashioned style of apprenticeship *(detchibōkō)*, which he remembers as grim—no pay, bad food, living under his master's roof, and working all the time. They don't make detchi like that any more. The Andō brothers treat their own assistants like ordinary employees, but they run a tight ship. Their shop gleams and their employees are neatly dressed; all are unfailingly polite and well-spoken, and some are apprentices by other names. Most of the time the sons of one or two other wholesalers are working for them, and the Andō brothers turn them out as apprentices who make their parents proud.

Like many wholesalers, the older Andō groomed his own son, Hideki, to take over the business by sending him to train under the supervision of another tuna dealer. Hideki, now in his thirties, first attended a commercial college overseas, where he studied management and food services. After he returned to Japan, his father apprenticed him with another top-level wholesaler, Marukyū, where Hideki worked for two years to learn the ropes of the tuna trade before coming back to Chiyomaru to work with his father and uncle. One of the apprentices now working at Chiyomaru, under the supervision of Hideki and his father, is the son of yet another leading tuna wholesaler: Aritomo, a firm with a market genealogy stretching back to the seventeenth century.

Andō can talk passionately about the artisanal spirit of the trade—the long, repetitive, hard work that goes into learning the business and the proud self-assurance of mastery that it produces in the end, when one becomes a journeyman artisan, a full-fledged *shokunin*. The colloquial term for this achievement, as noted earlier, is to become an *ichininmae*, literally a "full plate" or a "full serving," a full-fledged practitioner of his (or her) trade. Tools are not merely means to an end in this world. They are extensions of the body and as such become personal objects. A chef's knives are his own, and no chef who would use another's knives prepares food worth eating. Knife dealers chisel a chef's name or a trader's symbol *(yagō)* into the haft of a blade. Tsukiji's knife stalls are gleaming sanctuaries to neatly aligned fetish objects. As one old market regular gravely instructed me early in my fieldwork, the key to Japanese food culture lies in the exactitude with which a chef selects the proper blade—from among dozens of shapes and

Figure 53. Tools of the trade. A knife shop in the outer marketplace.

sizes available—for the specific culinary task at hand. An apprentice spends two hours each afternoon sharpening a single tuna knife longer than a man's arm. A sushi chef should spend ten years as an apprentice, the first two just learning how to cook rice, before even beginning to wield a knife. Or so goes the folklore of artisanal apprenticeship.

Andō's assistants must learn what he calls *maguro no kaiwa*—"the conversation of the tuna"—that is, to listen to the fish as they are cutting it; to gauge the pressure of forearm and wrist on the hilt of the knife and on the back of the blade from the smooth sound of a blade sliding through a block of red meat; to be alert for the small, sharp crunch when the blade reaches the bottom, outer layer of skin; to respond to that crunch—almost before they hear it—with a short concentrated push to put the blade cleanly through to the cutting board.

There are no ragged edges on a piece of tuna cut by an Andō apprentice; Andō talks an assistant through the cutting like a coach helping an athlete visualize the perfect swing. "Stealing the secrets" is how John Singleton (1993, following Irie 1988) describes the process of an apprentice becoming a full master himself; but in Andō's shop at least, these secrets are drilled again and again, until the arm itself can converse with the tuna.[12] This too is part of the discipline of apprenticeship and mastery: to make the physical rhythms of the trade an unconscious part of the body itself. Andō uses the common Japanese expression *karada de oboeru* (to learn with the body) to speak of his training, describing what David Plath (1998) calls "getting culture under your skin."

The narrative of artisanal apprenticeship is one of mastery through discipline acquired firsthand from suffering under (sometimes) cruel tutelage. No one at Tsukiji speaks well of the experience of detchibōkō, although many who went through it express later realizations of indebtedness. No fathers say that they want their own sons to experience the same thing, although many complain that members of the younger generation have not learned what they should have. Both the complaints and the nostalgia are to be expected. Andō's accounts of sleeping under his master's eaves in the late 1950s, of eating leftovers from the master's table, of being paid only in pocket money, all echo common tropes of artisanal and mercantile apprenticeship throughout shitamachi (see Wagatsuma and DeVos 1984; Kondo 1990).

Stall owners like Andō, who went through the arduous training of detchibōkō themselves, know that Tsukiji's old apprenticeships were difficult and demoralizing. And they know, both from the number of wholesalers' children who choose not to (or flatly refuse to) take over their families' businesses and from their difficulties in recruiting workers from the outside, that young workers today consider Tsukiji to be an undesirable workplace. Andō and other wholesalers who have transformed their businesses into modern corporations have done so, in part, because they recognize that the terms of employment provided by the corporate model may be more attractive to workers. But at the same time, both traditional modes of training and apprenticeship and modern corporate terms of employment—promotions within a bureaucratic structure and profit-sharing plans, as well as health insurance and retirement contributions—are geared toward long-term employment; the benefits of either system can be realized only if employees stick around.

Andō's training methods, and indeed those of the marketplace in general, are what Jean Lave calls "situated learning" within "communities of practice" (Lave and Wenger 1991), or "learning in likely places" (Singleton 1998)—learning by doing, on the job, with an eye to mastery of skills over the long haul. Situated learning occurs when both teachers and pupils feel themselves engaged in a common, ongoing social framework or relationship. In the old days of detchibōkō, with all its hardships and exploitation, at least there was little ambiguity over the social framework; today, when labor is recruited through help-wanted ads and Tsukiji struggles against the image of three-k working conditions, neither employer nor employee holds much hope that on-the-job training will go far beyond the rudiments of what is day-to-day work. And so Tsukiji traders realize that there is little chance to pass on what is, for them, the real essence of their working selves—their craft, in both its mundane details and its elaborate embellishments of culinary and social tradition—to another generation.

For Andō and his peers, the hard-won self-image of shokunin unifies the enterprise; it is a status that all are (or should be) either striving to achieve or supporting others in that effort. For young workers, the concept of artisanal mastery is probably not a bridge but a break: a generation gap, a divide between labor and management, an ideological crevice between the ethos of live-to-work and that of work-to-live.

FICTIVE KINSHIP

The fading artisanal spirit reflects the decline of apprenticeship and the changing relationships among labor and management, and this decline also affects the social fabric of the marketplace as a whole. Sending a son out to work as an apprentice in a friend's or a cousin's shop for a few years has long been a way for firms to develop and maintain relationships with one another. Andō is still close to a couple of wholesalers who went through detchibōkō together with him; and around the corner from his stall is one owned by an old friend, a few years older than Andō himself, whose term of detchibōkō training was with Andō's father when Andō was a kid. As mentioned earlier, Andō's son was trained by another dealer, even as Andō trained the sons of several other competitors. Such ties permeate the marketplace, a network of generalized reciprocity in professional skills. Training under the tutelage of a respected rival creates currents of affiliation and trust among traders that correspond and intertwine with other layers of mutual obligation and exchange formed among firms, generation after generation. Although these ties contribute to (and draw from) reservoirs of goodwill and mutual obligation that percolate throughout the marketplace, they grow weaker as fewer and fewer heirs continue the business and the transmission of an artisanal spirit is attenuated. Relationships created today from the experience of apprenticeship pale in comparison to the ties of fictive kinship established in the past, according to traders like Andō who have seen both.

Dense networks of fictive kinship created through master–apprentice relations often mingle with those of consanguineal and affinal kinship. Older firms can trace either kinship or master–apprentice connections with dozens of other shops that have split off from the main shop over the generations. One common pattern was to establish a second son or an apprentice as a journeyman with his own business (Nakano 1964); the custom was called *norenwake*, or "dividing the *noren*," referring to the curtain emblazoned with a shop's name and logo that hung in the doorways of many businesses.[13]

Within recent memory, apprenticeship was a path to succession at Tsukiji. The corporate records mentioned above include a handful of head clerks registered as corporate officers, cases that represent perhaps the last stages of the corporate transformation of Tsukiji's venerable apprenticeship system. Bantō are everywhere at Tsukiji, although these days they usually have corporate-flavored titles such as *reitōhin buchō* (manager of the frozen products division) or *eigyō tantō* (sales supervisor). These linguistic mutations mark the corporate transformation of the marketplace; *danna* (master) has become *shachō* (president), *wakadanna* (young master) has become *senmu torishimariyaku* (managing director), and bantō has become buchō. Still, in everyday conversation they are often still called bantō, and largely function as such. A bantō has extensive experience in the trade and considerable authority over a shop's employees, its stock, its dealings with customers and suppliers, and its day-to-day operations.

In the marketplace before World War II, older Tsukiji traders reminisce, bantō often ran their master's businesses almost entirely. As one dealer told me—speaking of his father's and grandfather's generations—in those days, the bantō wore boots and the shop owner *(shujin)* and his son (the wakadanna) wore straw sandals *(zōri)*. Bosses didn't have to worry about getting their feet dirty, since the bantō and other employees did all the work. If today's stories are any guide, it was often the business acumen and hard work of the bantō that kept many fish wholesalers' businesses afloat. The golden days, when an owner and his son had little to do but sip tea, chat with customers, and watch the cash roll in, are long gone, but bantō or their now more bureaucratically titled successors are still crucial to the success of many wholesalers' businesses.

In the past, a hardworking and intelligent bantō could eventually aspire to a business of his own, set up in part with his savings and in part with aid from his former master as reward for years of faithful service. When a bantō set out on his own, he might, through norenwake, receive the favor of using part of the original shop name in his own, as a kind of commercial imprimatur and symbol of the (ideally) close relationship between former master and former employee. Thus, a bantō named Tanaka Yūkichi who had apprenticed in a shop named Matsushio (Pine Tide) might take as his own shop name Matsukichi (Pine Fortune) by combining an element from his master's yagō (Matsu, "pine") with one from his own personal name (Kichi, "fortune or luck"). This practice has largely died out—in part because employment practices have changed, in part because the costs of establishing a new shop are now exorbitant, and in part because the move away from proprietorships to incorporated businesses has created newer corporate avenues for rewarding bantō: by making them corporate officers and partners. These shop names testify to relationships established in the past. Groups of stalls that trace descent as the result of sons, cousins, nephews, or apprentices setting out on their own from ancestral main shops, some no longer extant, indicate their common origins through their variations on a common theme; for example, stalls descended from a shop called Isemoto, long vanished, may repeat part of the original name in their own shop names, such as Isetomo, Isehachi, Isemata, Isenami, Maruise.[14]

The half dozen shops whose names begin with *Tsuru* (crane) can all trace connections through kinship ties or employment ties to an ancestral shop called Tsurugen, no longer in existence. Several dozen shops that begin their names with *Tsuku* (from the place-name of Tsukudajima) trace similar lines of descent to firms supposedly founded by the fisher-traders who first established Edo's fish market at the beginning of the Tokugawa period. Similarly, shops whose names incorporate the characters *Izumi* (freshwater spring), or *Tora* (tiger), or *O* (tail), or *Fushi* (from Fushimi, a venerable mercantile district in Kyoto) can each claim ancestry derived from some ancient shop, usually long gone. Books about Tsukiji traders, especially their own memoirs, often trace elaborate genealogies back to the earliest years of the market or the fishing community on Tsukudajima. In his account of his family's business, the tuna dealer Takarai Zenjirō (1991: 39), for example, includes a genealogy spanning seventeen generations. But, many Tsukiji regulars note, such ancestries are traced—if traced at all—more often through generations of successful bantō than through a fish merchant's offspring.

Shop names and their symbolism weave together a number of semiotic threads. They may signify descent through kinship ties, provenance through employment ties, and vague affiliations with some distant ancestral place or province, while also relying on euphonious combinations of characters that evoke classical symbols of good fortune, luck, and prosperity (e.g., pine, bamboo, crane, tortoise, dragon). Characters with a nautical overtone or a suggestion of fishing *(maru* or *mizu)* are also popular. The numerological significance of particular character combinations (determined by the number of brush strokes required to write them) may also enter into construction of properly formed shop names. The semiotics of yagō are easy to simulate, and it is difficult (for an outsider) to distinguish a yagō such as

Figure 54. Uogashi logos and traders' yagō, carved on a shrine fence on Tsukudajima.

Matsukichi (Pine Fortune), based on venerable fictive kinship ties between one shop and another (as in the hypothetical example given earlier), from a name such as Matsuryū (Pine Dragon), created from scratch by a wholesaler named, say, Matsumoto Ryūta. One has to be part of the system of signification to distinguish the authentic from the simulated, the venerable from the recent, and the socially interconnected from the entrepreneurially independent, or even to regard the distinctions as themselves significant. To know the significance of the code as well as to have the ability to decode it requires insider knowledge from the outset.

But among those in the know, the fictive kinship ties embodied in master–apprentice relationships embellish existing alliances and create new ones with each passing generation. Over time, the ties thus created become almost indistinguishable from those of marriage and adoption. The proprietor of Aritomo, Wada-san, claims to be the nineteenth generation of his family in the fish business. Once or twice a year, Wada's firm hosts a banquet for, or takes a trip to a hot springs resort with, a group of "alumni"— O.B. ("old boys") is the term Wada himself uses for this group. It includes former apprentices and junior branches of the family whom the Wada family set up in their own businesses in past generations. At this point no one is terribly clear about which connections are which. About two dozen Tsukiji wholesalers regularly participate, although Wada himself is unsure how most of them are related to his firm or family, whether through apprenticeships, descent, marriage, or household fission. The patriarch of Aritomo, Wada's father, now retired from day-to-day business, could barely hazard a guess when I asked him how many other stalls are related to his own, let alone detail the specific connections:

"Thirty?"

"Umm, more."

"Forty?"

"Umm, more."

"Forty-five?"

Finally, all he could say was "Who can count them? All I know is I'm always being invited to weddings and funerals. Ask my wife."

She wasn't around.

7   Trading Places

Tsukiji's intermediate wholesalers hold center stage in high-roofed, cavernous halls like the long train sheds of an old-fashioned railway station. From the middle of the market floor there appears to be no horizon, just gently curving lines of tiny stalls, roughly two hundred to the aisle, going on forever. Row upon row of stalls little wider than a single parking place, strung together along aisles thronged with customers and clogged by pushcarts. Boundary markers for each stall are sunk into the cobblestones like surveyor's benchmarks, all but obscured by crates and tubs of seafood that spill over into the narrow passageways. The stalls begin just steps from the auction floors; the relentless flow of people, goods, money from one to the other blurs the functional boundary between these two main spheres of Tsukiji's daily economic whirl.

Amid the hubbub of delivery carts, buyers, inspectors, and auctioneers hurrying between auctions and stalls and the eddies of restaurateurs, fishmongers, chefs, and peddlers meandering through the aisles, the stalls themselves seem to be arranged helter-skelter: two shrimp stalls face each other across an aisle; to the left a tuna dealer occupies four stalls, then a shellfish wholesaler, another tuna dealer, and a salmon merchant; to the right a seller of fish pâté beside an octopus merchant, an eel dealer, and yet another shrimp wholesaler. Up and down the long rows, the stalls seem endlessly yet randomly repeated.

The unaccustomed eye of a newcomer can make little sense of the scene; in their immense variety the stalls seem almost featureless, as alike as trees in a trackless forest. It is easy to read the scene as pandemonium, as competitive chaos. But this impression is misleading. Tsukiji is a highly ordered place, and the lives, businesses, and daily activities of its intermediate wholesalers follow accustomed channels, woven together in a social fabric as dense and complex as the marketplace's physical environment. Within this social world, advantage, competition, risk, and opportunity are constructed by accepted rules of trade and ideologies of equity that are established and enforced at various levels in the market's institutional structure.

In chapter 5, "Visible Hands," I examined the vertical integration of the institutions and social ties surrounding and sustaining Tsukiji's auction system. But horizontal patterns of organization also take shape around the auctions. The social processes that construct or convey information, risk, trust, and competitive impulses are as central to the marketplace's horizontal structures as they are to the vertical links that extend upstream and downstream from the auctions. Horizontal institutions and social ties—through which intermediate wholesalers look out for themselves and sometimes for each other—are the focus of this chapter, in which I outline several major aspects of the wholesalers' institutional life against the backdrop of the auction system and the vertical aspects of marketplace integration. I examine how traders create self-regulating spheres of social ties and institutions. how auction communities create and enforce trading rules, how traders form guilds or cartels within the marketplace, how an ethos of equity among traders motivates at least some of their actions, and how traders' guilds rearrange the physical layout of the marketplace to erase locational disadvantages.

The auction system rigidly distinguishes participants, individually and collectively, by the structural niches or roles they occupy; it thereby fixes the market's major horizontal strata. The market's formal organizational structure is based on these strata, but many other informal groups exist alongside or nestled within them. On the institutional end of the continuum, intermediate wholesalers draw together through several kinds of formal groups structurally involved in administering the marketplace. These include customary trading communities, fleeting political coalitions, and enduring trade guilds organized around specific commodities, as well as the overarching federation—Tō-Oroshi—to which Tsukiji's intermediate wholesalers all belong. At the informal end of the spectrum, traders create and activate an enormous variety of networks and groups based on friendship, camaraderie, family, bonds of ritual kinship, and apprentice–master relationships, as well as connections through pilgrimage organizations and clubs for people from the same province, town, or high school.

Whether brought together by institutional structure or by personal affiliation, intermediate wholesalers organize themselves to fashion Tsukiji's social and economic environment to their collective and individual advantage. They exert cartel-like customary control over many aspects of the marketplace. They make vertical integration work; trade guilds, for example, define and enforce the trading rules for each of Tsukiji's many distinct auction pits. These rules and other practices keep the market moving smoothly, erecting some kinds of vertical integration and impeding others to preserve the competitive position of intermediate wholesalers as a group.

At the same time, ties among intermediate wholesalers dampen overt competition and level the market's playing field, at least for those already on it. Wholesalers' groups reconfigure the layout of the marketplace to redistribute economic advantage and risk. Their aim is to diminish socially disruptive competition by downplaying structural difference and amplifying a sense of egalitarianism. The intermediate wholesalers can accomplish this, in part, because the market system recognizes their collective interests and allows them a measure of autonomy and self-regulation, especially over matters that directly affect their daily economic lives.

AUCTIONS AND TRADING COMMUNITIES

Under the awnings along the Sumida quay and on the ground floors of the outer arc of market buildings nearest the river are half a dozen auction locations for tuna. Smaller frozen tuna are sold along the river's edge; fresh tuna as well as larger frozen tuna and swordfish are sold inside. In large halls above the tuna auctions, fresh fish from near and distant coastal waters are auctioned. At the southern end of the quay, several concrete sheds enclose the live fish auctions. An open metal building and a large refrigerated warehouse near the north gate of the marketplace house the auctions for salted, smoked, or dried fish *(aimono)*. Halfway down the arc of buildings, a couple of rough wooden bleachers mark the site for the shrimp auctions.

Trading communities form around specific auctions, the specializations of each group of intermediate wholesalers directly reflecting the demands created by Japanese food culture (table 10). The premium on fresh seafood and the vast array of species and grades of seafood used in the many styles and seasonal varieties of Japanese cuisine are obviously critical in defining the trade. Not only are the culinary skills, processing techniques, tools, and market knowledge necessary to deal in, say, shrimp, distinct from those necessary to trade in eels, but the demand structures differ as well. A sushi chef comes to Tsukiji looking for seafood very different from that sought by a neighborhood fishmonger, an owner of a tempura restaurant, a catering manager of a wedding hall, or a buyer for a supermarket chain.

Specializations do not simply reflect culinary trends. They are the basis for social institutions embedded in and created both by the formal structure

TABLE 10. *Major Seafood Trade Categories*

*Aimono	Semiprocessed but perishable fish
*Ebi	Shrimp
*Enkaimono	Fresh fish from Japanese coastal waters distant from Tokyo; these fish are used primarily for sushi and seasonal cuisine
*Enkangyo	Salted and dried fish, including dried squid *(surume)* and dried sardines *(niboshi)*
*Enyōmono	Pelagic fish
Himono	Dried, smoked, and salted seafood
*Hokuyōmono	Salmon, salmon roe, crab, and other North Pacific seafood, including fresh, frozen, and salted varieties from Hokkaidō
*Ise ebi	Pacific spiny lobster
Kani	Crab
Katsugyo	Live fish
*Kinkaimono	Fresh fish from coastal waters near Tokyo; these fish are used primarily for sushi and seasonal cuisine
*Kujira	Whale
*Neriseihin	Fish paste and fish pâté products, including *kamaboko*
*Ōmono	Tuna and swordfish
Reitōhin	Frozen products
*Samé	Shark and other fish for processing into fish paste such as *kamaboko*
*Tako	Octopus
*Tansuigyo	Freshwater fish, including eel; many species are sold alive
Tegurimono	Trawl catches of fish such as mackerel, sardines, or saury
*Tokushumono	Top grades of fish for the restaurant trade, especially for sushi chefs
*Tsukudani	Boiled and pickled seafood products
Uni	Sea urchin roe

*Commodity categories represented by specialized trading associations (*moyori gyōkai*; see table 11).
Some *gyokai* represent traders across two or more closely related commodity categories (for example, *katsugyo* is regarded as a subspecialty of *tokushumono*). Terms (and categories) sometimes overlap; some are informal trade jargon and others are bureaucratically institutionalized terms.

of the marketplace and by the informal social ties that link traders. Some
specializations are fraught with social significance but not much economic
power, like the small but diverse group of traders who are appointed suppliers by the Kunaichō, the Imperial Household Agency; other specializations,
like that of the tuna dealers, wield enormous clout economically, institutionally, and in the wider world of Japanese fisheries politics. Most specializations occupy a middle ground, consequential in their own niches within
the marketplace but little noted outside the market.

Many institutional factors—among them the rules and practices that govern licensing requirements, participation in auctions, and allocation of space within the marketplace—shape these specializations. Ties between intermediate wholesalers and their customers, of course, coalesce around commodity specializations, and these specializations also largely structure traders' relationships with the auction houses. Collectively, wholesalers in any given niche negotiate the terms of their trade with the auction houses, and these terms themselves both institutionalize the specialization and shape its social boundaries. Intermediate wholesalers therefore respond to the fragmented demands of Tsukiji's retail clientele, define their firms' niches in the crowded market, and end up at a particular auction surrounded by like-minded competitors. Each of Tsukiji's couple of dozen major auction pits operates more or less independently of the others. The different commodities they handle visibly distinguish them, but each also is defined socially as a separate and distinctive trading community of intermediate wholesalers and auctioneers.

Any seasoned spectator can pick out the specialist auctioneers by the color of their caps—every major commodity category has a separate color—and by their neat work uniforms, slightly different for each of the seven auction houses. The communities of regular buyers are equally specialized but not so readily spotted. The TMG licenses buyers, all of whom wear—or are supposed to wear during auctions—a plastic badge, roughly 10 × 15 centimeters, clipped to a baseball cap (known as a *seribō*, an auction hat). Some wear distinctive caps issued by their own trade groups, or a T-shirt or jacket from a supplier that flaunts their specialization—"Cape Quality Bluefin," "Royal Norwegian Salmon," or "Hokkai Crab"—but they are as likely to wear a windbreaker from Tokyo's Disneyland, a sweatshirt from Tenerife, or a jacket from the Yomiuri Giants. Nothing really sets crab dealers apart from traders in sea urchin roe or shellfish specialists. But they know who they are, and day after day, the same buyers appear in the same pits to buy the same products. Some greet their competitors warmly; others pretend they don't know a soul in sight.

The trading communities that surround each of the dozens of auction pits consist of intermediate wholesalers *(nakaoroshi gyōsha)* and authorized traders *(baibaisankasha).* In total, fewer than 1,300 firms currently hold licenses to participate in the market's auctions: about 900 intermediate wholesalers and roughly 375 authorized traders. The two categories are largely indistinguishable on the auction floor, but the terms of their licenses make them dramatically different. As noted in chapter 5, intermediate wholesalers can participate in auctions and operate stalls inside the marketplace, where they resell to chefs and retailers products they purchased from auction houses perhaps only minutes before. Authorized traders, on the other hand, participate in auctions but cannot maintain stalls or resell seafood within the marketplace; they act as purchasing agents for large-volume consumers outside the market, such as restaurant chains, commissaries, hospitals, schools, and supermarkets. Of the two, intermediate wholesalers are vastly more significant to the general operation of the market—the value of their trading is about 64 percent of the total—and they are the primary focus of this discussion.

Nothing in the licensing regulations or trading rules limits an intermediate wholesaler to handling only a particular kind of commodity or prohibits a firm from participating in *any* of the marketplace's many distinct auction pits. Specialization is an outgrowth not only of culinary distinctions and the market niches that traders carve for themselves as a normal part of their business strategies but also of the marketplace's physical layout. Auction pits are scattered from one end of the marketplace to the other, and during auction hours it is often physically impossible to move quickly across the crowded trading floors between auction areas. And the licensing system—which bundles auction participation with the right to operate a stall in an exact one-to-one correspondence between licenses and stalls—itself reinforces the specializations of intermediate wholesalers and the exclusivity of auction participation. Their licenses are concretely signified by the oblong badges without which they cannot bid at auction; and though a firm can rotate its badge(s) among its employees, any single badge obviously cannot be used in more than one auction pit at a time. Sometimes a buyer completes a bid and turns suddenly to toss his cap to a colleague waiting to hurry off to another auction site, although most firms participate in only a limited number of auctions.

A firm gets one stall for each license, and most intermediate wholesalers hold no more than a couple of licenses (the average is a little less than 1.9). A few firms control half a dozen or more, and the largest has sixteen. Firms with more licenses and stalls, of course, can have buyers at several auctions and can deal in a wider range of seafood. But because auction times overlap, a firm with one, two, or three licenses usually participates in only one or two auction pits each day and hence must specialize in a clearly if narrowly defined range of products.

Specializations—whether artifacts of the licensing system or niches carved out of the market's culinary terrain—lead wholesalers to concentrate their attention and their activity around no more than a handful of auction pits, where they interact every day with almost the same set of similarly specialized wholesalers. Not surprisingly, distinctive trading communities with their own norms and trade practices take shape around each pit.

TRADING RULES

As each auction starts, the regulars take their places on the bleachers facing the auctioneer's stand. From one day to the next the cast of characters is roughly the same: each auction pit is a tight circle of familiar faces and established trading customs. All auctions are conducted under the general regulations of the marketplace, yet each is governed by subtly different sets of rules and norms, based in part on cumulative agreements between auction houses and the wholesalers who constitute a trading community for a particular commodity. Each auction pit is a separate and somewhat autonomous social system in which economic advantage and disadvantage are differentially structured. Trading rules therefore vary from one to the next. Each trading community is defined not only by *what* it trades but *how* it trades; these rules and norms are hammered out collectively over time, reflecting the prevailing relations between buyers and sellers, among competing sellers, and among competing buyers. The seemingly straightforward and impersonal process of selling and buying goods at auction is embedded, in practice, in complex social contexts. These in turn exert their own pressures to define, modify, or maintain the particular universes of buyers and of sellers and their interrelationships that are embodied in any given auction pit. Trade rules are the outcome of social processes to manage or deflect competition, seeking to stabilize risk or assign it elsewhere; the methods of bidding used in different auction pits provide good examples of this. The varying auction regimes, negotiated and renegotiated by the auction houses and the trading communities involved in the sale of any given commodity, offer opportunities for the continual adjustment and calibration of the trading rules. Such readjustments provide checks and balances in the swings of market power among and between auction houses and traders (see Acheson 2003: 7–8).

Officially, the auction system's fundamental purpose is to promote fair and equitable trade, but the municipal authorities do not mandate uniform practices. There is great diversity in the ways in which auctions take place, in the bidding rules employed, and even in whether or not auctions are held for specific categories of commodities. These variations, themselves folded into the market's administrative regulations, are the products of disparate forces. Some result from technical particularities that shape trade in specific commodities, whether live, frozen, or processed; others arise from the social and political influences inherent in the relationships of market power, trust, competitiveness, and self-interest that exist among and between producers, auction houses, intermediate wholesalers, and their customers. Whatever their origins, trading rules are accretions of customary practice, modified in occasional flurries of political deal making, institutionalized in the market's regulatory structure, and incorporated into the informal norms that govern the trade in any particular commodity. They reflect the continual efforts by market participants to reach acceptable trade-offs as they manage risk and competition.

Differences among bidding practices are sometimes minute and may seem little more than arbitrary stylistic variations, but different auction formats and bidding practices—secret versus public, one-shot versus incremental—clearly frame patterns of competition within given trading communities (and between auctioneers and buyers) in different terms.[1] Bidding may be done by gesture visible to all (as is the case with most fresh fish), or in writing seen only by the auctioneer (as in many auctions for salted and dried seafood). These different auction styles create different opportunities for traders to shape their own bidding strategies as their competitors' bids are revealed (or not). A secret bid eliminates almost all knowledge of competitors' calculations, and increases the risk to buyers that a winning bid may be far above the prices competitors would have paid. ("Buyer's remorse" is a common reaction in this bidding system, in which a winner can never be sure whether or how much he overpaid.) Public bids provide much richer information about competitors' intentions; and if there are not opportunities for successive upward bidding, over the long haul this kind of system results in bids that are relatively close together, which obviously works to the buyers' collective advantage. If rising bids are allowed, as in fresh tuna auctions, sellers benefit on the whole and decisive buyers with deep pockets can prevail. Smaller players are shut out, because they lack the capital to risk the competition or are unnerved by the intimidating displays of power that bigger players can deploy.

For most commodities at Tsukiji, bidding is a one-shot affair; as mentioned in chapter 2, if two or more buyers offer tying bids, they decide a winner with a quick round of the child's hand game *jan-ken* (rock-paper-scissors). Such tie-breaking commonly occurs, for example, in the fresh and live fish auctions. But in other trading communities—centered, for example, around the tuna auctions—competing buyers can offer higher bids, if they act within a split second. Rising bids work to the sellers' favor, of course, while auctions that end in a stalemate, broken by rock-paper-scissors, are to the advantage of the buyers. Where tie-breaking is used, the buyers have established collectively that it is not worth their time and effort to haggle over every last yen. That is, supplies are plentiful, these are buyers' markets, and the auctions in such cases allocate supplies as much as or more than they set price levels (see C. Smith 1989).

Some commodities are sold at a kind of display auction (known as an *idōzeri*, or a moving auction) where auctioneers and buyers walk through the lots on display, making bids on each as they pass by; this is the practice, for example, in selling tuna and *niboshi* (tiny dried sardines). In other auctions, such as those for shrimp, live fish, and most fresh fish, the products themselves are inspected beforehand and are out of sight during the bidding. Bidders can more easily see who their real competitors are in a moving auction than in a stationary one. In an auction at which goods are out of view rather than on display, buyers can much more easily conceal from competitors and auctioneers their enthusiasm for particular lots.

Some large fish, including tuna and swordfish, are sold piece by piece; most other kinds of seafood are sold by weight or by fixed quantities. The choice of one sales method or the other is based on factors such as the sheer size of the fish traded, their average value, the likelihood of variation or consistency from one lot to the next, and the availability of knowledge about producers' reputations for skill and care (if these are known at all). Such determinations—made over the long run, not day by day, through the ongoing negotiations of trading communities, auction houses, and market administrators—are judgments of risk factors. For high-risk transactions (like buying a whole tuna, whose price is high and quality tricky to judge), risk is minimized by allowing sales fish by fish. Where risks are negligible, seafood is sold by the lot—shrimp by the ten-case batch, for example.

Cultural and economic calculations frequently intermingle. The culinary and stylistic preference for wild products *(tennen)* over cultivated ones *(yōshoku)* parallels the economic commonplace that wild products fluctuate in value much more than do cultivated products (whose production costs and risks, in theory, ought to be more stable). And so wild seafood generally is sold at auction, whereas aquacultural products generally are sold through negotiated sales.

The timing of sales, too, can be critical. For some commodities, rival auction houses run their competing auctions simultaneously at separate locations, while for other kinds of seafood several auction houses take to the same trading block in prearranged sequences. The consequences of such variations are real. Whether auctioneers can sell a given commodity by sequential or simultaneous auction reflects the ability of an auction house to control the transactional environment and to limit buyers' participation in multiple auction pits. At the live fish auctions, for example, auctioneers from two competing auction houses mount the podium together—standing only an arm's length from one another—and cry their lots to a single bleacher of intermediate wholesalers who can bid on the lots offered by either auctioneer. The competitive balance of power lies with the buyers, who are not constrained to deal with just one array of merchandise at a time. On the other hand, tuna auctions, held separately by different auction houses in distinct (although adjacent) locations at overlapping times, force buyers to select one auction and bypass others. The competitive balance in this instance lies with the sellers, who—at least for that moment—have a semicaptive audience.

Sales concluded by negotiation, rather than by competitive bidding, also reflect and shape different competitive environments. Under some specified conditions, auctioneers have the option of suspending the auction and concluding negotiated sales; under other conditions (and for some commodities), they do not. For example, most frozen seafood and aquacultural products may be sold by negotiation, whereas most fresh seafood must be sold at auction. Freezer warehouses enable trading companies and the larger auction houses to precisely tune the supply of frozen seafood (e.g., frozen tuna), and sellers' interests therefore tend to dominate in those auctions. Many kinds of processed seafood are also available through channels outside the market system, and so auction prices fluctuate only slightly around current contract prices. Since the subtleties of the live fish trade require accurately coordinated distribution, negotiated sales are common. Supply and price factors for aquacultural seafood products are usually stable and well known (at least in the short run), and for these products auctions are more important in allocating supplies among different buyers than in setting price levels. In many shrimp auctions, for example, an entire multicase lot is put up for bid at once and the winning bidder specifies how many cases he wants to take; the auctioneer then moves on to a second round of bidding for the remaining cases (at the same or only a slightly lower price), and so on until all the cases are sold.

Sakidori

In most sales, bidders must be present to participate; in a few others, select buyers can take purchases away before the bidding begins and let others set the price. This is known as *sakidori*, literally "taking before." The alternative forms of sales depend in part on vastly different relationships of power between smaller- and larger-scale traders in different commodity specializations. Where take-away sales are permitted, this trading rule exists as the result of complex political accommodations among shifting alliances of producers, auction houses, auctioneers, traders, retailers and restaurateurs, and the consuming public at large.

Supermarkets and small-scale retailers, for example, are constantly at odds with one another, and their rivalries carry over to the traders who serve one clientele or the other. Because supermarkets require earlier delivery times than do small-scale retailers to prepare and package seafood in large quantities and to stock counters for the day's business, supermarkets and their allies press for earlier auction times or permission to make purchases without waiting for the auctions. Auction houses want to accommodate large-scale customers like supermarkets, but small-scale retailers and their intermediate wholesalers wield substantial political power over issues of market administration. The uneasy compromise is a modification of the ordinary trading rules through sakidori.

Sakidori enables traders who supply outlying markets and supermarkets to take away carefully specified quantities and grades of products, but they must match the top price of the day for the privilege; their price is thus determined after the fact by other bidders, their competitors. For an auction, this is an odd situation, but it reflects the political balance struck among powerfully opposed forces, each with a stake in the market.

The explicit rationale for sakidori sales is to ensure adequate supplies for other outlying markets. The other central wholesale markets and many smaller regional consumption markets around the Kantō region get much of their seafood directly from producers and shippers, just as does Tsukiji. But the enormous volume of goods shipped to Tsukiji, and its consistent ability to attract the highest-quality products, means that these other markets turn to Tsukiji for some of their own supplies. However, Tsukiji's auctions are scheduled to give Tokyo's retailers time to get their products ready for sale to consumers on the same day. If outlying markets had to depend on Tsukiji's morning sales, their own customers—suburban retailers and restaurateurs—would be unable to purchase and resell in a single day. Clearly, even a one-day delay can lead to deterioration and lower value. Smaller markets are thus at a disadvantage, and without corrective measures, consumers in outlying areas would have access only to seafood of lesser variety and lower quality. To balance the availability of high-quality foodstuffs throughout the metropolitan region, the TMG permits sakidori sales; intermediate wholesalers and authorized traders at Tsukiji can select and transship fresh seafood and produce well before Tsukiji's sales begin. The sakidori system is a long-standing political compromise that equalizes food supplies throughout the metropolitan region, at the cost to suburban consumers of slightly subsidizing consumers in the central city.

But the real political contest is between supermarkets and small retailers. Sakidori sales also meet the needs of supermarket chains and other large-scale retailers, whose processing and distribution tasks are more complicated and time-consuming than are those of the small-scale retailer. As one market official put it to me, all the small retailer has to be able to do is "get his purchases home, open a box or two, and toss a couple of fish in a cooler." And indeed, the typical small-scale fishmonger in Tokyo does a great deal of cleaning, boning, and filleting of fish as a customer waits rather than ahead of time; many fishmongers do most of their business in the late afternoon, when homemakers ordinarily are shopping for that evening's meal. By contrast, supermarket chains operate, by definition, on a large scale in a highly standardized fashion. Each lot of seafood must be carefully divided among stores and then retail-sized portions have to be prepared, wrapped, weighed, and labeled so that the consumer will find them on display when the supermarket opens its doors (usually precisely at 10 A.M.). Some supermarkets do in fact directly purchase at Tsukiji's auctions and get seafood to their stores an hour or more before opening time—their own distribution centers can be models of awe-inspiring efficiency and attention to detail—but for most chains it is more convenient if they can get earlier delivery of products, an efficiency enabled by sakidori.

Risk and Arbitration

Other instances of social processes striking balances among competing economic and political interests can be seen in efforts to reduce or spread risk. Institutionalized arbitration, for instance, helps hedge some risks in high-priced tuna auctions, risks posed by the juxtaposition of bidding rules and incomplete information; tuna are sold whole, and it is impossible to know a tuna's quality with absolute certainty until it is cut apart.

Such risks arise largely from the auction rules themselves, which permit auction houses to put up for sale whole tuna—round fish—rather than fish already cut apart into halves or quarters, and which prohibit traders from making invasive inspections of the tuna on display for auction. These rules reflect many technical considerations: for example, an uncut round fish spoils less quickly than one already cut open and is in less danger of contamination. And clearly, a tuna can be destroyed by too much probing and cutting by buyers. Also at work is the market power of the auction houses: because of this rule, the consignors, not the auction houses, pay the cost of shipping a heavy round tuna, and the purchasers bear the entire cost of cutting and processing the round fish. And because of the scale of Tsukiji's demand for tuna and the number of specialized tuna buyers there, many Tsukiji buyers can easily handle an entire tuna (unlike those in central wholesale markets in smaller cities, like Sapporo, where tuna are sold split). The auction rules for tuna reflect the relative power of buyers and sellers in a given market and assign accordingly the various risks of judging each fish's quality, or of making a substantial outlay of working capital.

When fresh tuna are first landed, tuna buyers on the docks use long meat thermometers to read internal temperatures; they then extract slender samples of inner flesh, much like a geologist's core samples bored from rock, using hollow metal tubes that look like long soda straws; and finally they carve off half rounds by the tail cut to inspect for inner color, temperature, oil content, and disease. By the time a tuna arrives at Tsukiji, however, it is thoroughly chilled and Tsukiji traders have to rely on external indicators of quality. Other than carving tiny samples from the cut tail and feeling inside the slit belly, the rules for inspection at Tsukiji prohibit further piercing or cutting so that a tuna carcass won't be in shreds and tatters before it is sold.

At Tsukiji, fresh and frozen tuna are sold whole, although with heads off, bellies split, guts cleaned, and tails removed just where the bodies sharply taper down to a narrow stem. An experienced tuna buyer can tell a lot about the condition and inner quality of a tuna by a quick examination of a handful of mostly external indicators. The shape of the body is a crucial indicator of the likelihood of finding good meat inside. The condition of the skin; scrapes, marks, or wounds or other signs of struggle; the feel and texture of fat inside the tuna's belly—all these provide important clues as well. For a visual check of inner quality, buyers peer intently at the small cross section—about the width of an adult's open hand—where the tail has been cut off. Examining the tail cut is rather like reading tree rings on a stump, but for structure and texture rather than for age. It reveals the size and shape of the layers of edible meat, the patterns of fat deposits, and whether the marbling is grainy or smooth. An experienced buyer can judge the fat content of the fish by feeling the tail cut and then rubbing thumb and forefinger together to test the slipperiness. The color and translucence of the tuna's flesh are also important indicators of quality.

But however careful and discerning the external inspection may be, there remains a risk, for buyers, that damage or disease deep in the middle of a fish cannot be detected until they have purchased it, taken the fish back to a stall, and cut it open. Possibilities include internal parasites, damage caused by *yake* ("burn," resulting from the improper chilling of a fish that has built up enormous body heat during its struggle against a fisher), or the mysterious condition known as *yamai* ("illness," a whitish stain that sometimes clouds the flesh of a tuna for unknown reasons and in no discernible pattern). In some cases, a careful buyer will spot these internal conditions, but they can remain undetectable despite thorough visual inspection. All external clues notwithstanding, buyers sometimes are surprised when they cut open a tuna they just purchased. The rules governing sales inevitably create bad deals based on the limited ability of a buyer to judge internal quality.

Overall, the auction houses' hold on market power sustains the whole tuna auction rule at Tsukiji; but to limit risk to buyers, the social institutions of the marketplace create a countervailing set of rules regarding arbitration. Late each morning a small series of conferences is held to one side of the tuna trading floor. Representatives of the tuna traders and the five auction houses that deal in tuna meet there under the supervision of a TMG official to hear the complaints of midlevel wholesalers who have found that a fish they bought that morning is somehow defective. Every day half a dozen or so wholesalers trundle up a tuna carcass to bring a case before this panel. It first judges whether the buyer should have been able to detect internal defects by careful external examination, or whether defects could have been spotted only after the buyer cut open the fish; buyers are liable for their own bad judgments or careless inspections, and adjustments are made only when the fish's faults were truly invisible. If this was the case, the panel then determines how much of the fish is affected—a half, a quarter, a belly slab—and announces a binding adjusted price between buyer and auction house.

Arbitration and sakidori are both examples of how the social institutions of the marketplace shape the rules of trade. Both the resulting trade rules and social institutions that frame them are products of political accommodation and negotiation among different parties to the auctions, with different interests and slight differentials in their power shaping the processes to meet their ends. But in each instance, whatever incremental advantage may fall to the powerful parties, an at least implicit ethos of equity generates countervailing practices to temper the risks that are shifted toward the weaker parties. Thus in sakidori, powerful agents of supermarkets may be able to take away the choice merchandise, but their weaker competitors can set the prices later. In the case of risky tuna auctions, the overall terms of the sales may favor the auction houses and the producers, but the possibility of arbitrating reduced prices on substandard fish significantly reduces the dangers to small traders posed by the inability to thoroughly judge an uncut tuna.

Throughout the auction system, institutionalized devices spread risk or equalize slight differentials in power. For example, trading rules seek to overcome or minimize monopolies of locational or sequential advantage that might otherwise benefit one auction house at the expense of others by regularly rotating the sites and ordering of the various auctions. Every few months the five auction houses that sell frozen tuna exchange the stretches of quayside where they hold their daily auctions. And every day, the sequence of tuna auctions is changed, so that every auction house will have an equal opportunity to sell first, last, and in the middle. Upstairs, where fresh fish from western Japan are auctioned, the sequencing is even more strictly set, by establishing a rotation of auctioneers that changes daily and by allowing each auction house only five minutes on the podium at a stretch; if goods remain unsold at the end of a house's allotted time, their auctioneers have to wait for another turn at the end of the day's queue. In other auctions, such as for dried fish, the sequence of starting times switches from day to day, with each company starting its auctions about five minutes apart and with the order of starting times shifting from day to day.

Whether adjusting the delicate equilibrium of market power among competitors (as in these devices to ensure that the auction houses conduct their sales on a more or less equal footing over time) or between actors at different levels in the market system (as between producers, auctioneers, and buyers in the tuna auctions), such trading rules and established practices are all products of the market's institutional structure. They are significant features of the market's social landscape and reflect the strength of horizontal forces within the marketplace to identify and act on issues of collective interest. At the same time, these also reverberate through the vertical linkages that make up the auction system. The subtly distinctive trading environments that result from these trading rules, and their occasional recalibrations, add another element of market information to the mix that the auctioneers must handle in their day-to-day management of auctions and must be able to communicate to their suppliers to ensure the stability of supply for the market.

TRADE GUILDS AND CARTELS

Sixteen guilds—known as *moyori gyōkai,* "customary trade groups," or simply *gyōkai,* "trade groups"—are central organizations in the formulation of auction rules and arbitration procedures. They are, in the most straightforward and neutral sense of the term, cartels: firms of similar specialization and purpose organized together in the attempt to coordinate the terms of their trade. The marketplace's system of governance implicitly and explicitly recognizes and depends on the authority of such cartels to do just that.

Each gyōkai represents the trading community of intermediate whole-salers who handle a specific commodity. Some are organized straightfor-wardly around a single species of fish (e.g., tuna, octopus, whale, shrimp, or lobster); some center around fish caught in particular locations (e.g., in near or distant coastal waters, in the North Pacific, or freshwater species); some focus on seafood handled in particular ways (e.g., live, salted, smoked, dried, boiled in soy sauce, or prepared as paste); and some concentrate on the quality of the seafood, as in *tokushumono* ("special things"), the eclectic range of top-grade products demanded by sushi chefs and other profes-sional connoisseurs.

Gyōkai membership is not mandatory, but since these trade groups are some of the most strategically important organizations of the marketplace, only a handful of firms fail to belong to at least one (table 11). Their mem-berships range in size from hundreds of firms (the largest group, by far, is for tuna dealers, with more than 300 members) to as few as half a dozen (for uncommon specialties, such as dealing in whale meat). Only a few firms belong to more than one gyōkai (the average is about 1.2 member-ships per firm), reflecting the close focus of most nakaoroshi on a single culinary specialization.

These gyōkai make manifest the social structure of the market niches formed in the interplay between cultural categories of food preference and the forces of supply, demand, and specialization. Because they institutionally represent the trading communities that gather each morning at the various auction pits, gyōkai are the most focused forum in which otherwise com-petitive intermediate wholesalers can express and elaborate mutual inter-ests. Not only do they stand for the group against other actors, but by doing so they also define the competitive environment that exists within the group, among its own members. The guilds negotiate with the auction houses and the TMG over the operations of the marketplace in general and over the very specific trade practices and bidding techniques established for each auction pit.

As I argued in chapter 4, the institutions of the marketplace play central roles in defining commodities according to culturally meaningful categories of foodstuffs, and gyōkai are pivotal to this process. By establishing trading rules and handling arbitration disputes, guilds translate the cultural classi-fications of commodities into the economic mechanisms of the marketplace. Gyōkai coordinate the activities of dealers in a given line of trade, structur-ing their perceptions and definitions of commodities. Formed around the market's typology of commodities, trade groups stand between the seem-ingly natural categories of the world of producers and the compelling yet

TABLE 11. *Trade Groups* (Moyori Gyōkai) *in 1990*

Number of Member Firms	Moyori Gyōkai Name	Commodities
335	Ōmono Gyōkai (Large Products Trade Group)	Tuna and swordfish
217	Tokushumono Gyōkai (Special Varieties Trade Group)	Top grades of fish for the restaurant trade, especially for sushi chefs
161	Enkaimono Gyōkai (Distant Coastal Water Products Trade Group)	Fresh fish from Japanese coastal waters distant from Tokyo; primarily for sushi and seasonal cuisine
96	Kinkaimono Gyōkai (Near Coastal Water Products Trade Group)	Fresh fish from Japanese coastal waters near Tokyo; primarily for sushi and seasonal cuisine
78	Hokuyōmono Gyōkai (Northern Ocean Products Trade Group)	Salmon and other North Pacific species
75	Aimono Gyōkai (Semiprocessed Products Trade Group)	Semiprocessed but perishable fish
66	Enkangyo Gyōkai (Salted and Dried Fish Trade Group)	Salted and dried fish
63	Ebi Kyōkai (Shrimp Association)	Shrimp
56	Neriseihin Gyōkai (Fish Paste Products Trade Group)	*Kamaboko* and other fish paste products
28	Tansuigyo Kumiai (Freshwater Fish Union)	Eel and other freshwater fish
25	Enyōmono Gyōkai (Distant Ocean Products Trade Group)	Pelagic fish
22	Tako Dōgyō Kumiai (Octopus Trade Union)	Octopus
18	Tōgeikai (Eastern Whale Club)	Whale
7	Ise Ebi Kumiai (Pacific Lobster Union)	Pacific lobsters (spiny lobster)
7	Tsukuwakai (Tsuku Harmony Club)	Boiled and pickled seafood products
5	Tōkakai (Tenth-Day Club)	Shark

SOURCE: Calculated from a commercial directory of intermediate wholesalers (Nikkan Shokuryō Shinbunsha 1990).

NOTE: These sixteen trade groups of intermediate wholesalers *(nakaoroshi gyōsha)* are listed according to size of membership, in descending order, along with a brief description of each group's characteristic commodities. An individual firm may belong to more than one trade group.

arbitrary categories created by patterns of consumption. They reproduce the complex set of distinctions of seafood not only according to abstract culinary principles but also in mundane terms: sources of supply, availability at particular auction sites, types of customers who patronize particular kinds of traders, and trends in retail and restaurant patronage. Gyōkai are active agents in the transformation of seafood from items of production and trade into those of consumption.

On a direct level, the sixteen trade guilds engage in regular if incremental discussions with the auction houses and TMG administrators about what products should end up in which auction pits. The product mix in various auction pits, and hence the working definition of boundaries among trading communities and commodity classifications, are always subject to readjustment. Sources of supply change; new fishing grounds are brought into the market's sphere; unfamiliar species (tilapia, for example, or Lake Victoria perch) are introduced at Tsukiji; or advances in aquaculture make a previously seasonal type of seafood available year-round (as happened with farm-raised yellowtail). Other adjustments reflect shifts in such conditions as transportation and the timing of deliveries to market, the relative demand for particular types or grades of seafood by supermarkets and by small-scale retailers, seasonal changes in levels of production or methods of distribution, and the relative abundance of domestic or imported, fresh or frozen, wild or aquacultural products. In response to these or any other fluctuations in supply and demand that alter the balance among the Tsukiji trading communities most interested in bidding on a particular kind of seafood, the affected gyōkai attempt to readjust the boundaries of auctions. And by doing so, gyōkai—as closely knit cartels of like-minded buyers—also recalibrate the scope of trading communities and contribute to the consistency of information about pricing and buying preferences on which linkages of vertical coordination rest, as outlined in chapter 5.

Trade guilds provide many very specific services as well. Some, like the *ōmono gyōkai* for tuna dealers, provide specialized equipment for members. Larger dealers provide for themselves, but smaller dealers often depend on the several cutting sheds that the tuna gyōkai operates around the marketplace; there, for a nominal charge, a trader can have a frozen tuna split apart by a gyōkai employee using one of the gyōkai's table saws. Gyōkai buy supplies for their members in bulk, ranging from note pads and rubber gloves to cutting boards and order forms. They administer mutual insurance schemes for members, offering protection against fire or other losses, and have emergency loan funds. Beyond such formal measures, these circles of traders also provide informal assistance to one another: offering the use of equipment or freezer space when something breaks down, arranging apprenticeships for each other's sons, or laying off a bit on bidding when someone is up against the wall. And, like almost all Japanese organizations, sooner or later trade groups provide assistance at the funerals for their members.

The guilds are deeply involved in the everyday politics of the marketplace, of course, and they also mobilize informal lobbying of politicians at the metropolitan and national levels around issues of market regulations, trade practices, and fishing policies that affect their own particular specialties. They organize seminars for wholesalers with speakers from government, the fishing industry, and the retail sector to discuss changing market conditions, ranging from the impact of the United Nations Law of the Sea Conference on the Japanese fishing industry to the impact of shrink-wrap technology on supermarkets' sales of fresh fish. Gyōkai engage in public relations work, providing spokesmen, for example, when television reporters want to do a story on fishing crises or seafood prices. The tuna guild even commissioned an illustrated children's book—*Maguro ga tonda* (*The Tuna Flew;* Ishiguro Kaoru 1988)—to explain the global tuna trade to schoolchildren (see figure 9 in chapter 1).

Trade guilds train wholesalers' employees and others in the trade about the proper handling and processing of seafood. For example, the blowfish *(fugu)* subgroup of the *tokushumono gyōkai* (the guild for dealers in the highest quality and most rarefied selections of seafood) teaches chefs and fishmongers studying for the prefectural licensing exams required of anyone who prepares this poisonous specialty for public consumption. Such groups organize study tours (and recreational outings) for people from Tsukiji to visit fishing ports in Japan and abroad and to meet producers of shrimp or yellowtail, perhaps inviting along auctioneers and market officials involved with the same seafood specialty. Guilds likewise host visiting delegations of producers and traders from other markets who want to tour Tsukiji. And they sponsor rituals—both secular and religious—to mark the passing of the seafood seasons, to memorialize the commodities in which their members deal, to solidify traders' own identification with the traditions of the marketplace, and to satisfy television crews looking for colorful footage.

Tō-Oroshi

The sixteen specialized trade guilds constitute only a first level in the institutionalization of identity and mutual interest among intermediate wholesalers. They are rooted within a larger federation, a higher-level, all-inclusive "horizontal" organization to which all intermediate wholesalers belong: the Tōkyō Uoichiba Oroshi Kyōdō Kumiai (the Tokyo Fishmarket Wholesalers' Cooperative Federation), commonly known by its abbreviated name, Tō-Oroshi. Tō-Oroshi encompasses all the intermediate wholesalers as individual members and all the guilds as its subdivisions. It represents the interests of the membership as a whole as well as the more specialized concerns of the various organized trade communities. (Each of the sixteen gyōkai and two other groups, based on historical alignments dating from World War II, are represented institutionally on the board of directors of Tō-Oroshi.) The federation is both the organization that speaks for the intermediate wholesalers as a group and also the chief arena in which their own internal political wrangles occur. The federation bargains collectively with the auction houses and the TMG administration, and its several dozen employees also provide a wide array of services for individual members.

Although Tō-Oroshi plays an enormous role as a central institution in the administration of the marketplace as a whole, in their daily business lives wholesalers rely on Tō-Oroshi for the services it provides them individually. The political strength of the institution rests on these services, on the many details of business that it can take care of for its members. Tō-Oroshi runs a clearinghouse for settling accounts payable with the auction houses. The Tō-Oroshi staff assists members with advice about government licensing requirements, labor regulations, insurance, tax payments, and credit. Tō-Oroshi also operates a large freezer warehouse in which members can rent individual compartments. These Tō-Oroshi services particularly benefit smaller firms by enabling these wholesalers to keep their own costs of labor, equipment, space, and overhead to a bare minimum.

On the collective front, Tō-Oroshi works hard to foster good public relations for the wholesalers (although these efforts tend to be of little concern to most dealers, who correctly regard their trade as out of sight of and hence ignored by the consuming public). But Tō-Oroshi's staff attentively arrange visits by TV camera crews. They frequently present the case that Tsukiji's multiple layers of wholesalers do *not* unnecessarily inflate prices to consumers. They argue instead that Tsukiji's prices reflect the realities of business amid wildly fluctuating supply and demand, rapid spoilage, and inevitable product shrinkage as whole fish are transformed into consumer-sized portions of high-quality seafood. Tō-Oroshi sponsors market open houses to familiarize consumers and the media with their trade. At such events, members of the federation fillet an entire jumbo tuna from round fish into sashimi. While visitors enjoy the free snack, wholesalers explain the filleting process in terms of *budomari* (shrinkage and yield). As their long tuna knives reduce the fish into smaller and smaller pieces, and the tub of bones, skin, and other unusable portions fills up, they carefully point out the reality that roughly 50 percent of the weight of a tuna sold at auction ends up as waste before sashimi reaches the consumers' plates. The retail price per kilogram, therefore, has to be at least 100 percent above the auction price just to meet the cost of the fish, even before figuring in any margins or overhead for wholesalers and retailers.

Governance, Decision Making, and Segmentary Cartels

Tō-Oroshi's position as a keystone in the market's system of governance is far more consequential than its service and publicity roles. Tō-Oroshi represents the intermediate wholesalers' collective interests in negotiations with marketplace administrators, the auction houses that supply the market, and others throughout the market system. Decisions about market operations are discussed among officially recognized and enfranchised groups or cartels representing the various sectors of the marketplace, and Tō-Oroshi is one of the major actors. These decisions, whether addressing onetime issues or ongoing matters that recur annually (or seasonally), have covered license allocations; stall placements; classifications of products and their disposition in specified auction pits; rules for standardized settlement, clearance, and credit procedures; distribution of rights to purchase outside regular auction channels; and days and hours of operation for the marketplace each year. Under the aegis of the TMG, Tō-Oroshi bargains as a unit with the seven seafood auction houses over the general conditions of auction sales. Tō-Oroshi and its sibling organization that similarly represents the intermediate wholesalers from the produce division negotiate with the twin organizations that represent the seven seafood and the four produce auction houses, respectively. They hammer out general terms of sales and licensing, schedules for construction and repair, traffic regulations, the calendar of hours and days the marketplace will operate, and other matters that affect the entire marketplace. Tō-Oroshi and a counterpart federation of authorized traders negotiate with the auction houses over what proportion of a day's sales can be made as sakidori. Tō-Oroshi and the vegetable wholesalers' federation together confer with the federations of the loading dock operators who hold merchandise for retailers and restaurateurs to establish rules of the road for carts and turrets, liability for the occasional lost shipment, and schedules for pickup and delivery.

The administration of economic affairs at Tsukiji relies on this style of indirect governance, through negotiated agreements among trade groups that represent all the individual firms of any given category. Characteristically, the marketplace administration enfranchises groups with decision-making powers (or the right to be involved in making decisions that affect their niche). Within the bounds of the rules or regulations that are thus agreed on, these same groups are accorded a fair amount of autonomy over how those agreements are implemented and how matters within that niche are internally administered. The distinct sets of auction rules discussed earlier in this chapter are good examples of this devolution of decision making and administration into the hands of cartels, which is a hallmark of the institutional structure of Tsukiji and a key to understanding the formation, persistence, and dynamics of cartels. Structurally, Tō-Oroshi and the sixteen gyōkai form a complex segmentary organization, shaped in part by this devolution. That is, at any particular level of common interest, groups come together under a common umbrella and represent themselves as a unified organization; but around almost any enduring common interest, dispute, or point of conflict, cohesive subgroups can divide from one another. These subgroups persist, whether based on contemporary concerns or more historical affiliations, in part because some fraction of the successful conclusion of any decision rests in the hands of the lower-level groups.

Lower-level groups persist over time. Organized around a common point of interest, and enfranchised with both internal autonomy and considerable power over decisions that affect their interests, groups such as gyōkai rarely relinquish their claim over a particular trade niche, nor do they easily dissolve themselves into larger groups. Once a gyōkai, always a gyōkai. Although some of the contemporary gyōkai are themselves the products of mergers of smaller groups, those precursors generally maintain a corporate identity and a controlling voice over the issues most directly concerned with their original common interests. The consolidation of groups therefore does not erase the perception of enfranchised privilege or collective mistreatment that spawned the interest groups in the first place. Moreover, the definition of common interests and the organization of traders around some set of interests, even at some point in the past, creates an institutional lock-in that ensures that the group will continue to mark its existence by maintaining common interests (or grievances)—even if only by reference to past conditions in the marketplace. Collective past experience, however long gone and whatever the resolution, can itself become the basis for defining a contemporary common interest and providing segmentary units with their raison d'être.

Some of these segmentary divisions are relatively inconsequential. For example, the tuna guild, created by a merger of groups representing tuna and swordfish dealers, still contains a subgroup of swordfish dealers. Swordfish dealers identify themselves as *nagamonoya* (dealers in long things): in market jargon, swordfish are *nagamono,* "long things," in contrast to tuna (*ōmono,* "big things"). The swordfish subgroup represents these dealers' special interests when tuna and swordfish issues diverge, as they sometimes do in the wider arena of fisheries policy, when fishing regulations for the different species conflict, or in the microworld of Tsukiji auction rules for the separate sales of tuna and swordfish. But tuna and swordfish dealers mostly find common cause, and minute organizational divisions are submerged.

A similar example is the tokushumono gyōkai, formed by a merger of several specialized groups of dealers in high-quality seafood; some of its members supply sushi chefs, others stock the kitchens of inns and traditional restaurants *(ryōtei),* and still others deal with hotels and Western-style restaurants. The different constituencies have few disagreements, but the auction rules for the different kinds of commodities in which members trade create distinctions among them and lead to organizational autonomy within the gyōkai as a whole. Each specialty therefore has its own subgroup to negotiate the specific terms of its particular subniche.

Still other subgroups crosscut the other subdivisions, such as one for the blowfish trade. Fugu, since it is potentially poisonous, requires special handling, and traders and chefs hold special licenses from the TMG to deal with it. These licenses are distinct from the wholesalers' licenses required to trade at Tsukiji (and are issued by a separate division of the TMG, under the ultimate authority of the health ministry), thereby creating for fugu traders yet another set of institutional constraints, prerogatives, and regulations around which to mobilize common interest. Because the community of licensed fugu dealers extends beyond the boundaries of the Tsukiji marketplace, the fugu association is a rare example of a lower-order group at Tsukiji not entirely contained within a larger group. (For this reason, although the fugu association functions partially within the tokushumono gyōkai, it is not itself recognized as a gyōkai in the larger scheme of things.) Thus, as the framework of institutions creates minute distinctions among sets and subsets of traders, these distinctions become the basis for the further elaboration of segmentary complexity.

Tō-Oroshi was itself created over the past several decades by the mergers of several groups of intermediate wholesalers organized not only around commodity specializations but also around licensing statuses that existed in the marketplace before and during World War II, before the current marketplace system was instituted in the 1950s. Even as these groups were drawn into Tō-Oroshi, they retained their own distinct organizational identities, either as gyōkai operating under the Tō-Oroshi umbrella or as parallel, but now subordinate, organizations that duplicate some functions that Tō-Oroshi fulfills for all intermediate wholesalers. They still maintain a voice in contemporary market affairs, even though their claims on current collective interests are based almost entirely on positions they occupied in the prior institutional framework of the marketplace.

In the marketplace as a whole, Tō-Oroshi is one cartel among many, and the structure of these groups—each made up of diverse individual firms united by common interests as intermediate wholesalers, seafood auction houses, authorized traders, or loading dock operators—is similarly framed by institutions of marketplace administration. Within this structure, licensing requirements define membership and enfranchise the members of each group with specific rights, privileges, and obligations in the marketplace; government administrators endow each group with broad powers for self-administration of their own collective affairs; and the market's administrative structure rests on the assumption that cartels, each representing a particular sphere of economic activity, will jointly hammer out coordinated arrangements with a minimum of administrative guidance from the government. As with gyōkai, enfranchised privilege leads to a segmentary structure of cartels, in which rights and prerogatives granted members of a group at some past time may continue to be the basis for at least incipient divisions in the present.

The loading dock operators provide a good example of such continuity. They number about 250, organized into three distinct groups, and all perform the same tasks. Colloquially known as *chaya* ("teahouses," an old-fashioned way to refer to an agent), these loading docks each have a regular clientele of retailers and restaurateurs for whom they receive goods from intermediate wholesalers, holding those deliveries for pickup later in the morning. An intermediate wholesaler knows, at least for his regular customers, to which chaya a purchase should be directed. Because the ordinary restaurateur or retailer patronizes a number of intermediate wholesalers— anywhere from three or four to as many as a dozen—the chaya provide a convenient means of storing and consolidating purchases made throughout the marketplace.[2]

The three chaya groups result from three different paths of institutional evolution. One group, established after World War II, is run by a federation of Tokyo retailers on behalf of its members. The other two federations represent groups of freight agents that trace their firms' histories back to the old Nihonbashi fish market: one is descended from ships' chandlers *(funayado)*, the other from land-based delivery agents known as *shiomachijaya* (tea houses for awaiting the tides) from the days when boats tied up along the canals of Nihonbashi to make or accept deliveries. After 1923, when the Nihonbashi market was destroyed, the two trades were incorporated into the new market. From the somewhat different starting points of their separate trades, with their distinct rights and monopolies, their functions converged as the new market system evolved: today they are indistinguishable but for their separate federations and historically derived identities.

Members of all three groups are now known by the same term, *chaya*. As in the persistence of gyōkai established under wartime conditions mentioned earlier, the perception of their past distinctiveness and their different structural accommodations to the new market have locked in the divisions of the institutional structure. To an outsider, their activities are indistinguishable, but as an organizational reality they maintain separate institutional identities and a sense of rivalry with one another over their positions in the marketplace.

Many other and sometimes highly consequential issues have also involved questions of rights or prerogatives within the marketplace and the institutional mobilization of common interest around those rights. Disputes involving groups possessing—or arguing that they ought to possess— inherent rights based on previous government entitlements or recognitions flare up repeatedly in Tsukiji's history. The argument over compensating Nihonbashi traders for the loss of land-use rights known as *itafuneken*, mentioned in chapter 3, is one past example; the mobilization of Urayasu fishers around the loss of their fishing grounds is another.

The most significant contemporary instance revolves around the Tokyo's new Ōta Market, near Haneda Airport, which began operations in 1990 with several dozen seafood intermediate wholesalers relocated from Tsukiji and several dozen more relocated from a now-closed market at Ōmori. The irony is that although the new market was originally planned to consolidate a fragmented distribution system, the intermediate wholesalers who relocated to Ōta almost immediately divided into three separate organizations. One of these is a branch of Tō-Oroshi representing wholesalers who were induced to move from Tsukiji, the second is an organization of wholesalers from the old Ōmori marketplace who favored relocation to Ōta, and the third is a group of wholesalers originally from Ōmori who had opposed the relocation.

When plans to build a market at Ōta were launched in the 1970s, the idea was to create a modern comprehensive market for Tokyo as a whole that would merge the operations of several existing TMG markets, including both the seafood and produce divisions of Tsukiji, the major Kanda Market for produce at Akihabara in central Tokyo, and two smaller markets at Ebara (produce) and Ōmori (seafood), both in the southern part of Tokyo near the location of the new market. The Tsukiji marketplace was to be entirely relocated because its buildings were in bad repair, its space was cramped, and its location was inconvenient for moving millions of tons of seafood. Land in the heart of Tokyo's major business and entertainment districts could be put to much better use, the planners thought, and a spacious new market could be built on land reclaimed from Tokyo Bay. The complete relocation of Tsukiji was opposed by many Tsukiji dealers themselves, by retailers who favored the more central Tsukiji location, by the ward government of Chūō-ku where Tsukiji is located (which was concerned over the loss of local jobs and tax revenues), and by environmentalists concerned over the impact of the construction on Tokyo Bay's dwindling wetlands. As the combined opposition of these diverse allies stalled the planning process, estimated costs mounted to a point where the national and municipal governments realized that the full-scale move was prohibitively expensive. In the scaled-down plan that was drawn up, traders from the old Ōmori Market would all be moved to the new facility, to be joined by a hundred Tsukiji traders who would voluntarily relocate.

Only a very few Tsukiji traders were interested. To move from Tsukiji to the new Ōta Market was, in most traders' view, to walk away from a profitable franchise in the center of the world's largest market toward a risky peripheral position as a trader on a lower level in the distribution hierarchy in a new and unproven market, competing for customers against the largely unknown and potentially hostile Ōmori traders, and competing as well with the still-functioning Tsukiji marketplace they would leave behind. The TMG therefore went to great lengths to persuade Tsukiji traders to make the move, offering various financial incentives as well as advantageous licensing arrangements. In pursuing their campaign to find volunteers, the TMG laid the basis for immediate factionalism within the new market. Fault lines were drawn between Ōmori dealers and Tsukiji dealers over the incentives offered to each group to move into the market, and, among Ōmori dealers, between those who accepted the TMG's initial plans and those who held out for incentives like those offered Tsukiji traders. Among the sixty-odd Tsukiji traders who did decide to move, the TMG created the grounds for even more factional disputes by making three separate sets of offers to traders. Those who moved in the first wave had to relinquish their Tsukiji stalls, those who were recruited in the second wave were permitted to keep their Tsukiji stalls until the Ōta Market went into full operation, and those who held out until the third wave of TMG inducements were allowed to keep their Tsukiji licenses.

Each group at Ōta maintains its own perspective on the economic rights and prerogatives they possessed in their former locations, those they possess (or ought to possess) now, and what obligations and entitlements continue to be owed them by the municipal government following their relocation. (Likewise, the relocated vegetable dealers from the old Kanda Market split between a faction that agreed to go along with the move and those who were adamantly opposed, and these two groups are now represented at Ōta by separate federations.) These perspectives provide the basis for separate institutional structures now, and the possibility of further segmentation in the future.

Differences, therefore, in the way that the government has treated otherwise similar members of the group—the separate deals and the entitlements or enfranchisements they entail—all contribute to the identification of group interests along factional lines that may fade but never entirely disappear. Often the reason why fissures that subdivide existing groups and preserve the boundaries of their predecessors persist is the government's implicit promise, when it bestows or recognizes rights over particular economic activities, that if those rights are abrogated in the future, payment is warranted. Whether the government is willing to offer compensation or entrenched interest groups are able to block action until compensation is awarded, the net effect is the same. Government recognition of a cartel's rights over particular economic spheres carries with it the promise of future remuneration should that cartel's interests be infringed.

In pressing their interests, the different groups—whether different sets of relocatees to the Ōta Market, or Urayasu fishers seeking compensation, or dealers working out the procedures and proportions for sakidori sales—aim at preserving a collective claim to a piece of the market rather than improving the competitive position of some members at the expense of others.[3] In the discourse of egalitarian fairness that traders like to refer to as *nakama ishiki* (in-group consciousness), the group should strive to create or defend market rules that maintain each member's position vis-à-vis the others over the long term, not to alter their relative status in the short term. Their goal is not to create an entirely level playing field for all members but to ensure that the institutions of the marketplace do not themselves create greater disparities, do not dig deeper potholes for some competitors while smoothing the way for others. The process is clearly illustrated in the complicated efforts of Tō-Oroshi to manage the placement of stalls.

LOCATION, LOCATION, LOCATION

Early in my research at Tsukiji I spent several days simply walking the marketplace from one side to the other, back and forth, exploring its layout and trying to commit at least its rough bearings to memory. I expected to discover an order to the place, a locational logic of internal "neighborhoods" where tuna was traded or sushi chefs congregated or Ginza restaurateurs did their shopping. After several careful inspections, I satisfied myself that there were no special shrimp sections, no enclaves exclusively for octopus, nor any other distinctive clusters tucked away in the heart of the marketplace. Products and stalls seemed to be distributed randomly.

Along with a thousand other as yet unasked questions about details of Tsukiji's operations, I wondered about the arrangements of the stalls. For the time being, I loosely surmised that the visible jumble of specialties was probably the result of little more than historical accident, the random outcome of hundreds and hundreds of individual businesses, each evolving along its own trajectory over generations.

Then one day, a few weeks into my research, Kurosaki-san—a wholesaler in dried squid, the friend of a friend—offered me his own tour of the marketplace. After an hour's stroll and conversations about dozens of topics, I casually asked, "Why aren't there separate sections for, say, tuna or dried fish? How can anyone find what they are looking for? Why are the stalls all jumbled up like this?"

"Everyone asks that," he smiled. "We used to be divided like that, but now we're all mixed together."

"So, how long have all these stalls been where they are now?"

"For about four years," he answered.

Startled by this response, which neatly demolished my tentative hypotheses about collective continuities amid historical trajectories of individual change, I asked the obvious *next* question. "What happened four years ago?"

"Oh, that's when we held the lottery to reassign stall locations. We do it every four or five years."

He went on to outline briefly a complex system of lotteries that shift incumbents from good to bad or from bad to better places in the market, regardless of their specialties, size, or social influence. As Kurosaki explained it to me, the relocation of stalls through a lottery smoothes out inequalities among traders that arise from disparities in the shape, size, and placement of stalls in the huge fan-shaped sheds that house the wholesalers.

Kurosaki described for me the vastly complicated logistics of the reconstruction. The market closes for four or five days—strategically chosen to coincide with a holiday—and crews of workers tear the place apart in a round-the-clock marathon. A fleet of dump trucks hauls away the trash from the gutted interiors of the long sheds, which are stripped bare. Stalls themselves are fairly simple affairs; each may consist of only a counter and cutting board, some trestle tables on which to display seafood, a cashier's booth, perhaps a couple of coolers or refrigerated display cases, maybe a table saw (for a tuna dealer), and, if space above the stall permits, perhaps a small storage loft. All the salvageable equipment has to be moved out—coolers, cashier's booths, table saws, cutting tables, and boxes of knives—to make way for carpenters to build afresh the elementary wooden structure of the stall. Equipment new and old has to be moved back in, as new signboards, counters, and duckboard flooring above the cobblestones are installed, and telephone and fax lines are reconnected properly. This would not be a difficult weekend assignment for a crew of carpenters working on a single stall, but all 1,677 have to be ready for business before the opening of auctions four days hence. No one sleeps, Kurosaki told me, but the market always opens on time—pungent with the smell of fresh lumber—to crowds of customers puzzling over maps to find their regular suppliers.

As Kurosaki finished, I was staggered by the thought that 1,677 stalls could change places without a total breakdown of trade, and even more skeptical that the system could possibly work as evenhandedly as he described it. Surely, in a society where connections accomplish almost everything and where there is a public face and an inner reality—a *tatemae* and a *honne*—to every level of social interaction, highly competitive wholesalers would not voluntarily let their fortunes ride on a lottery that might assign them a stall next door to bankruptcy. Surely this was one playing field that was deeply furrowed.

Over the next several months, I pursued this topic whenever the chance presented itself to question stallholders, trying to figure out why they would participate willingly in this lottery system and whether or not it really did operate as impartially as it appeared. The physical arrangement—and rearrangement—of the marketplace is tightly bound up with complicated interrelationships among Tsukiji's institutional structure, the social networks among wholesalers, and their attitudes toward risk, relationship, and fairness. As I discussed in chapter 2, Tsukiji's layout is inseparable from the market's operation as an economic and a social institution. As Henri Lefebvre notes, "space is neither a 'subject' nor an 'object' but rather a social reality—that is to say, a set of relations and forms" (1991: 116), and this is certainly true at Tsukiji. Location is a key element in how wholesalers think about their businesses, and the institutionalized system of stall rotations links the marketplace-as-space to its social order in several significant ways.

Real Estate

The market buildings are owned by the TMG, which rents stalls to intermediate wholesalers who themselves own their equipment, a license to operate in the marketplace, and the intangible goodwill of established reputation and trading relationships.

The TMG calculates rent according to a formula based strictly on stall size and volume of sales. Stallholders pay a monthly rent of ¥1,800 per square meter for space on the sales floor. For an average-sized stall of slightly more than seven square meters, the rent would be only about ¥12,600 per month. Even though the TMG has more than doubled the rent since 1979 (from ¥820 to ¥1,800 per square meter, set in 1995), Tsukiji remains a true bargain by the standards of central Tokyo's commercial rents (*Shijō memo* 1988: 24; 1995: 41). In addition, stallholders pay fees based on their sales volume: 0.25 percent of gross sales.

These TMG rents do not take into account locational advantages or the quality of the space; the operator of an airy corner stall opening onto the intersection of two major aisles and the proprietor of a narrow stall under the low overhang of a parking garage ramp located in the middle of a block far from passing foot traffic pay the same rent per square meter. And the TMG does nothing to match supply of desirable space to demand.

Yet even to a casual observer, stalls clearly differ. Some are close to the entrances, others are deep in the middle of aisles; some are narrow, others wide; some stand on the corners of broad intersections, others are in midblock; some are light, others dark; some have lots of workspace behind them, others none. Stalls along the inner four rows (below a parking garage) lack overhead storage space, while the middle and outer eight rows covered by the high peaked sheds have overhead lofts. Stalls at the northern end of the shed have access to the market's north gate unobstructed by loading docks; those to the south, although close to the market's main gate, are hemmed in by loading bays and by the vegetable market next door. At the northern end, the aisles are straight and the stalls rectangular; at the southern end, the aisles curve and the stalls are wedge-shaped. Northern and southern, close to auctions or distant, cramped or spacious, innermost edge versus outermost, accessible periphery versus buried core: these are the basic structural determinants of locational advantage.

Within these large spatial distinctions, there are many smaller ones. Some are simply the architectural peculiarities of particular stalls, where for

Figures 55–59.
(Top left) Tuna dealer at his cutting board.
Hanging behind him is a row of tags for
regular customers, each preprinted with
a customer's name and his regular chaya
for deliveries.
(Left center) Tuna wrestling.
(Left) Carving frozen tuna.
(Top right) Stalls seen from overhead
storage loft.
(Above) Doing the books at the end of
the day.

example a manhole cover precludes the placement of a large freezer case, or pillars supporting the overhead parking garage come down through what might otherwise be unobstructed workspace. Other more complex factors also affect specific stalls. The stalls themselves are arrayed in twelve rows that front six main aisles. These rows are intersected by fifteen lateral aisles of varying width that customers and delivery men use to get from inner to outer edges of the market. A stall at the intersection of two wide aisles is preferable to one at a narrower intersection, and either trumps almost any midblock location. Stalls on corners get the advantages of easier deliveries, extra frontage, and larger numbers of passersby, particularly if they are on one of the wider lateral aisles. Conversely, a stall in the middle of a block of twelve, buried somewhere deep inside the market sheds, has the poorest chance of trade from passersby; even its steady customers may be diverted by enticing displays they spot while threading their way into the middle of the market.

What makes a location good or bad is a matter of perspective. The physical and locational peculiarities of the stalls and sheds are only part of the question. Over the decades, changes in the kinds of seafood handled; in the way products are bought, sold, and transported; in the flow of customers visiting the market; and in the character of wholesalers' businesses have altered perceptions of what factors make locations good or bad. On the one hand, there is a shifting balance in the market's product flow between high-value, low-volume fresh seafood and high-volume, lower-value frozen and processed fish. More and more wholesalers handle large shipments and use freezers or coolers to hold stock for several days. For these dealers, access to the auctions and storage space are crucial features of a good stall. On the other hand, the market's clientele has changed as well; supermarket and chain store buyers have increasingly replaced small-scale retail fishmongers and restaurateurs. As walk-in trade has declined, fewer wholesalers regard the front rows of stalls as prime locations. Over the years, wholesalers have adjusted their individual businesses to respond to the changing conditions of the market as a whole, and their spatial needs and locational preferences have shifted accordingly.

Stalls on the narrow front edge of the fan-shaped market buildings offer easy access for the walk-in trade, such as buyers of small quantities of high-quality, sushi-grade fish. These stalls are closest to the loading docks where small-scale customers accept deliveries, but they are furthest from the auction arenas. They are also generally the smallest, most oddly shaped stalls with the least amount of storage space. In contrast, wholesalers whose businesses are based on bulk sales to supermarket chains regard the back edge of the sheds (nearest the Sumida River) as a better location. These stalls are furthest from the marketplace entrance and less convenient for walk-in customers, but they are bigger and more regularly shaped with larger work areas, are just a few steps away from the auctions, and are more accessible for large delivery trucks.

Wholesalers, of course, are acutely aware of the advantages and disadvantages of their own specific locations, and of the more favorable places occupied by other traders who specialize in the same market niche. Every stall has its good and its bad points, and most wholesalers can hold forth eloquently about the bad aspects of their own stall while grumbling about the unbeatable superiority of their competitors' location. This sense of deprivation is linked to a strongly held sense that location itself should not stand as a long-term source of competitive advantage, at least in the terms through which wholesalers view the impact of market institutions on their own businesses.

Locating Equity

Although intermediate wholesalers nominally regard "goodwill"—their long-standing reputations and long-enduring personalistic ties to their clients—as their most important asset, nevertheless they view the locational advantages and disadvantages of particular stalls as structural inequalities that must be evened out over time. Wholesalers like to think that personal relationships and reputation are what keep customers coming back year after year, but they are aware as well that some customers, at least, inevitably will gravitate toward stalls that are more convenient or better situated to catch the attention of passersby.

Following from the principle that participation in the marketplace should be on an equal footing, and that the rules and regulations of the marketplace itself should not cause or accentuate disparities among businesses, wholesalers regard location as a valuable communal asset that should be equitably shared. Thus, to impose some rough form of equality on at least the physical environment of business, every few years everyone moves. There is no specific legal or administrative requirement for stall rotations as such. Yet the elaborate lottery system run by Tō-Oroshi, the federation of intermediate wholesalers, has become a central institution of the marketplace's organization, providing a further example of the devolution of administrative autonomy to marketplace cartels. The most recent lottery, held in 1995, was the fifteenth such reallocation of stalls since 1951, each carried out under different circumstances and each with at least slightly different procedures.[4] My analysis focuses primarily on the 1990 cycle of the lottery and stall rotations, relying on market records and interviews with participants in that cycle, as well as analysis of market records for 1981 and 1985 and further interviews about the 1995 lotteries and planning for possible future moves.

There are several rationales for periodically reassigning the stalls. Pragmatically, the relocation provides a brief window of opportunity for upgrading the equipment in individual stalls (installing new refrigerators, for example, as changing regulations about chlorofluorocarbon emissions force wholesalers to replace obsolete units) and improving the infrastructure of the marketplace as a whole (e.g., rewiring electrical systems and adding extra phone lines for fax machines). Because stalls are small and closely packed, occasional individual remodeling that might disrupt business is difficult without the consent of one's neighbors, and the daily flow of goods through the cramped marketplace makes scheduling large-scale repairs or renovations impossible. A concentrated burst of rebuilding, lasting only a few days and affecting everyone equally, is regarded as the best solution, despite the vastly complicated logistics of rebuilding all 1,677 stalls during a four-day market closure.

The periodic relocation of stalls also allows wholesalers to rethink their operations and their market niches to meet changing conditions. At least in theory, the lotteries give each firm a chance to place itself into a block that is particularly suited to its own specialty. In practical terms, stall rotations make it possible for firms that have acquired additional licenses to combine otherwise scattered stalls into convenient and presumably more efficient clusters. This periodic chance to consolidate stalls in turn creates a boom-and-bust cycle for license transfers. As a lottery approaches, wholesalers looking to expand are eager to acquire an extra license or two that they can quickly bring together with their existing stalls, and wholesalers looking to cash out see an opportunity to realize the maximum sale price for their licenses.

During the past couple of decades, as noted earlier, marketplace administrators have encouraged small firms to merge, hoping that a somewhat smaller number of somewhat larger firms will bring about efficiencies of scale and rationalization of distribution. Changes in market regulations enable individual proprietorships *(kojin)* to become incorporated firms *(yūgen gaisha* or *kabushiki gaisha),* which can acquire multiple licenses.[5] To realize efficiencies of scale, wholesalers with several licenses try to cluster their stalls together. In the absence of a fluid market for location—for real estate—institutionalized reassignments of stalls every four or five years enable these consolidations to take place.

Of course, the system imposes the transaction costs of relocation on all participants across the board. These costs—most directly, of moving and rebuilding a stall every few years—probably fall more heavily on smaller, perhaps marginal operations. A kojin enterprise, which by definition can operate only one stall, cannot reap economies of scale from the move; all it gets is a chance at a better location. Larger firms, which are more likely able to afford to acquire additional stalls in the first place, can cut operating costs by consolidating their stalls into clusters, although their capital costs for equipping a new set of stalls with appropriately up-scale appointments may be much higher. Precisely because of the scales of efficiency they command, larger firms should be less imperiled by business fluctuations that might result from locational advantage or disadvantage. In short, the trade-off is that smaller firms have the chance to improve their locations and their larger competitors get the opportunity to consolidate their operations and improve their efficiency.

But technical considerations of marketplace efficiency and infrastructural enhancement only partly justify the stall relocations. They are premised as well on the ethos of equity in which intermediate wholesalers stake their position. From their perspective, the system overcomes short-term inequalities created by physical location to ensure that wholesalers compete on a relatively equal footing over the long run. The interests of equity among intermediate wholesalers, a principle at the heart of group dynamics, and of fairness, a concept legally embedded in the charter of the marketplace, justify the effort. No one gets to monopolize the best locations, and no one gets saddled permanently with the disadvantages of bad locations, either. Everyone shares some of the burden—the transaction costs—of the massive relocation, and the bargain implicitly promises something to all parties.

Luck of the Draw

The lotteries that accomplish the stall reassignments are intricate undertakings, requiring months of planning. For the lotteries the marketplace is split into four major blocks, containing between 250 and 480 stalls apiece. Each includes a mixture of superior, average, and ill-favored locations, but each has a general appeal for particular sets of wholesalers.[6]

Nowadays the blocks are significant only as a device for redistributing stalls, but when stalls were first assigned in 1950 (just as wartime and postwar rationing and price controls were lifted and the TMG again licensed wholesalers to operate stalls in the marketplace), wholesalers and their licenses were divided among three basic categories: fresh fish dealers, frozen fish dealers, and dealers in processed fish products (such as *kamaboko,* or fish pâté, and *tsukudani,* or fish boiled in soy sauce). Immediately after the war, the narrow range of products available and the limited technologies for transporting and handling them meant that the specialties of wholesalers were much more sharply defined than they are today. Each specialty occupied different blocks of stalls: the outer edge near the auctions for fresh fish, the inner edge near the market gate for dried and processed fish, and the middle blocks for frozen fish. The earliest lotteries simply reallocated spaces within these particular blocks. But as more and more wholesalers have expanded to handle wider arrays of products and larger volumes, reflecting changes in the technology of the fish business, in the scale of wholesalers' businesses, and in the mix of customers who come to the market, the distinctions among specialties lost much of their meaning; and so since the late 1960s, all blocks—four major ones, not three—are open to all applicants.

The outer block comprises the two rows of stalls closest to the auctions. The inner block encompasses the least accessible wedge of the fan and the innermost row of stalls closest to the market entrance. In order to make the inner block more attractive in the lottery, Tō-Oroshi gerrymandered this oddly shaped section to include some of the best stall locations as well as the worst. The central block is in the middle of the fan, and the north block is a rectangle of regularly shaped, uniform stalls unaffected by the curvature of the buildings and offering customers the best access. Not surprisingly, the outer and north blocks are the most popular; the inner is the least (map 6).[7]

The lottery goes through several stages. First, wholesalers apply for space in one of the four major blocks. For administrative purposes, individual stalls *(tenpo)* are paired into units called *koma,* each unit consisting of two stalls; these are the basic unit of the lottery system.[8] Wholesalers who operate two, four, or some other even number of stalls can go into the lottery on their own. Those with one stall (or a larger, odd number of stalls) must find a partner to create an appropriate combination of two-stall koma. Any number of wholesalers operating any number of stalls may file a joint application in the lottery, as long as their total number of stalls is even. Microcoalitions of three, four, five or more wholesalers are common, representing various combinations of holders of single and multiple stalls. In the 1990 lotteries, the average microcoalition represented 3.6 stalls and the largest single coalition operated 28 stalls.

Because the four large blocks are not equally appealing, a series of preliminary drawings match applicants to the number of stalls available in each block. In the first round of the 1990 lottery cycle, applications for the outer and north blocks far exceeded the number of stalls available, while the inner

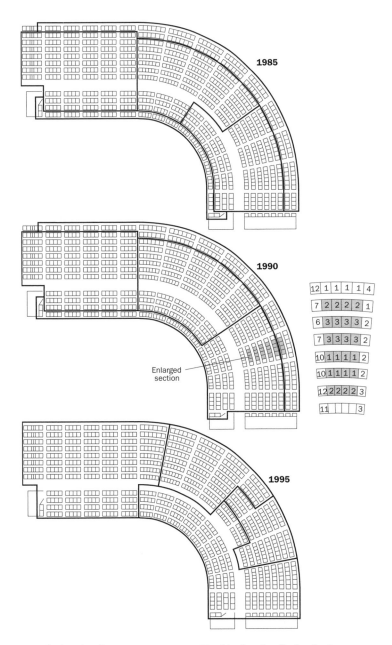

Map 6. Blocks of stalls: 1985, 1990, 1995. The blocks of stalls for the lottery are reconfigured from one lottery to the next as evaluations of competitive conditions change. The enlarged segment of the 1990 lottery map reproduced here illustrates the positive and negative ratings (the latter are indicated by shaded boxes) attached to individual stalls. Reproduced with permission of Tō-Oroshi.

and central blocks were undersubscribed. A first round of drawings eliminated excess applicants for the outer and north locations. Those who were
weeded out could then reapply for space in either the inner and central
blocks, both as-yet unfilled. But because the inner block was so unpopular,
the central block was immediately oversubscribed, and so a second lottery
assigned the surplus applicants to the inner block.

These preliminary lotteries balanced applicants and available stalls in
each block and established the order in which each applicant would draw in
the final round. In this final lottery, each group of applicants drew a number that established its place in a queue, in a fixed sequence for filling stalls.
The final lottery was *not* for specific stalls, and it did not award priority to
choose preferred locations; instead, matching stallholders to locations was
rather like putting together a train of boxcars in a freight yard. If the group
who won the right to draw first pulled number 2, the exact location of their
stalls would not be clear until eventually some other applicant drew number 1. If *that* group operated six stalls, then it would get stalls 1 through 6,
and the group that drew number 2 would get the stalls starting from number 7. If an applicant drew number 50, the exact location of that set of stalls
would become clear only after the intervening lottery numbers 1 through
49 had been matched to the exact numbers of stalls held by each coalition.

These complicated preliminaries lead to a momentous final outcome: the
lottery may dramatically affect a wholesaler's fortunes for years to come.
Although no hard figures can be calculated, many wholesalers estimate that
the locational shift can affect their sales volume by as much as 10 to 15 percent. A good location can't save a failing business and a bad location won't
ruin a strong one, but middling operations can be seriously affected; and
whether prosperous or not, no wholesaler can face a potential swing of this
magnitude with equanimity. Trading volumes and margins aside, stall rotations inevitably mean a change in a firm's surroundings and social environment: some customers simply will find another shop to be more convenient
and then disappear; a firm's new neighbors may be helpful or difficult to get
along with; a wholesaler may end up surrounded by struggling stalls that
tarnish its own image; or perhaps a small firm will find itself dwarfed by a
giant firm that occupies ten or twelve stalls directly across the aisle. A
wholesaler's best friend or fiercest competitor may end up next door.

Rebates

Stall lotteries are supposed to even out long-term locational advantages.
But what institutions give with the right hand, they can take away with the
left. Long-term equalization creates short-term inequalities as some dealers

lose and others gain business in their new locations. To counteract such fluctuations, Tō-Oroshi administers yet another complex system to *re*equalize the luck of the draw by compensating wholesalers for the shorter-term fluctuations for *individual* businesses created in each lottery cycle, based on the relative advantages or disadvantages of each stall's location.

Tō-Oroshi rates each stall individually for location as well as architectural defects (such as especially low ceilings or cramped workspace), expressed in a numerical score: the best stalls are rated +15, the worst −10. Based on these rankings, the federation assesses surcharges on favorable locations and pays subsidies to stallholders who end up in lousy ones. Holders of favored stalls pay a monthly surcharge of ¥1,000 for each positive point to the federation, which in turn reimburses the locationally disadvantaged at the rate of ¥8,400 per month per minus point.[9] After both the 1985 and 1990 lotteries, the highest assessment was ¥15,000 per stall per month and the highest compensation was ¥84,000 per stall per month. In effect, the system creates twenty-six grades of stalls with a maximum spread of ¥99,000 between the effective rents (for space) paid by stallholders in the best and worst locations. Wholesalers' fees to the market based on their sales volume (0.25 percent of gross sales) are not affected.

The ratings are assigned before each rotation and remain unchanged until the next lottery.[10] In the evaluations that preceded the 1990 lottery, the federation rated 964 stalls as "above average" in location and hence required their occupants to pay a supplementary assessment to the federation; another 280 stalls were rated "below average" and their occupants thus received rebates from the federation; 433 were "average" or neutral, and their holders neither paid nor received compensation. The advantaged locations were generally those on the extreme edges of the complex, those on the corners of major intersections inside the marketplace, and all those in the four innermost rows (nearest the main market entrance). The disadvantaged were those where the curvature of the fan-shaped rows creates the most tightly constricted spaces, those farthest from lateral aisles, and those at the southwestern end of the fan where access is generally the most difficult.

In the overall economic scheme of a multi-billion-yen marketplace, the amounts of money that are actually transferred among wholesalers through these rebates are trivial, although in some cases the rebates may be just enough to keep a small wholesaler's head above water. Cynics claim that the rebates provide a cash incentive for some wholesalers to apply for the sections in which they have the highest chances of hitting a disadvantaged stall that comes with a large rebate. No one can say how many wholesalers run their stalls for *asobi* (play)—as a source of ready cash for fooling around rather than as a serious business—but everyone seems to know a couple of them, and their willingness, even eagerness, to occupy the poorest stalls a coalition might win could make them ideal lottery coalition partners.

But the rebate system fundamentally upholds the ideal of elaborately calibrated equity among stallholders, regardless of the relatively high costs of the organization required by these transfers of modest sums of money.

Sharing Risks

Overall, the lottery system aims to dampen down the average effects of locational advantage over time. But even if the lotteries achieve *systemic* equalization, for any given stallholder they pose the risks of great fluctuation in his or her own *individual* business. The risks of such fluctuation are much greater than the cushion provided by the rebate system. Even if one set of measures begets countermeasures in an ever-narrowing oscillation, ultimately institutions cannot entirely prevent distinctions of advantage and disadvantage that their actions inevitably create. Wholesalers therefore fall back on other strategies to avoid the dangers that may lurk in institutionalized shields against risk.

When they choose a block in the early stages of the lottery they are only selecting a broad region; they can do nothing to determine *where* within that block they may ultimately land. And so, in the face of the lottery's enormous potential impact, wholesalers fall back on extra-institutional strategies to try to maximize their chances of landing in a good spot and minimize their risks of finding themselves in an awful one.

In these critical matters, some wholesalers find that the supernatural offers partial reassurance. Throughout the months leading up to the lotteries, fortune-tellers are consulted and geomancers engaged to determine the best blocks and to advise on what route a wholesaler (or his particularly charmed representative) should take on the way to the lottery drawing itself. Amulets and charms are obtained from favored shrines and temples, and unmarried daughters are carefully groomed to draw the family's fateful lottery slip. Many wholesalers belong to *kō*, quasi-religious pilgrimage groups, loosely organized around trade specialties or hometown ties; each group is centered on a shrine or temple that serves as the setting for communal rituals and a convenient destination for occasional recreational outings, like those undertaken by eel dealers to Mount Takao, a holy mountain west of Tokyo (mentioned in chapter 4).[11] During the preparations for the lotteries, wholesalers may cultivate religious affiliations more avidly as they seek intercession or oracular guidance from shrines and temples they otherwise visit for informal weekends of relaxation and camaraderie.

But most wholesalers rely on the social fabric of the marketplace—which plays so important a role in many other aspects of their personal and business lives—to solve the problem posed by the lotteries. The formation of coalitions for the lottery applications, mentioned earlier, is one crucial social strategy. Many wholesalers try to minimize the risks of a new and as yet unknown location by building coalitions with other wholesalers with whom they can jointly apply. They thereby manipulate the (future, as yet unknown) microenvironment of their business's location, by positioning it in the midst of a (currently known) social universe. Such coalitions are made possible as well as necessary by the administrative requirement that all stall assignments be in multiples of two. This offers a couple of ways to shape one's future environment: by choosing future neighbors and by arranging informal swaps of space.

By entering into a lottery coalition, a wholesaler can select his or her immediate neighbors to either side (although not across the aisle, because the stalls are assigned up and down the long rows in linear order and a space across the aisle could be as many as a hundred slots away in the lottery sequence). A firm can both avoid risk (its biggest competitor will not be right next door) and win positive benefits (a congenial and complementary neighbor beside it). With luck, a properly selected next-door neighbor will steer some of his or her established clients in your direction, even as you send some of yours to him.

Moreover, coalitions make possible some flexibility *after* the lottery. Even though a coalition cannot control where in a large block of several hundred stalls its application may land it—where on the necklace its particular bead will be—the larger the coalition, the greater the odds that the stalls it draws will include *some* better than average locations. It may not include a premier corner location, but if it is large enough it will include some corner. For example, if a coalition represents firms with a total of fourteen stalls, they will necessarily end up with at least two (and possibly four) corner stalls, since the rows of stalls are intersected by aisles every eight or twelve stalls. Members of a coalition strike private, internal deals for the specific stalls each will ultimately occupy, since they can allocate among themselves the stalls they win through the lottery. The businesses of some coalition members may be less sensitive to location than others. A dried fish dealer who deals largely with standing orders from established customers may be quite content with a "below average" midblock location. In contrast, a sushi supplier with a large walk-in trade may require the prominence and display space afforded by a corner and may enter a coalition precisely to be assured of getting that high-profile location; he will readily compensate a dried squid dealer, his coalition partner, for the privilege of moving into the corner stall. Such calculations are one key to a successful lottery coalition.

Pragmatic deal making aside, lottery coalitions are based on the same sets of social ties that operate in the everyday exchanges and transactions of market life. Coalitions are transitory, fluid structures that rise out of the ebb and flow of social relationships for a short and specific purpose before receding back into the general pool of social capital. Lottery coalitions cease to have any real organizational meaning after the preliminary negotiations, the lotteries, and the final allocations of space are complete. Of course, microcoalition members become close neighbors from one lottery until at least the next, and the ties among them may remain active even if the coalition as such does not. Some coalitions stick together cycle after cycle, and partners become closely tied to one another in many ways. Other coalition partnerships may be only onetime affiliations. As individual businesses evolve over time, their needs for—and their appeal to—particular kinds of coalition partners may change dramatically.

Dealers are guided by many considerations in selecting appropriate coalition partners; most important are the compatibility of specializations, appropriate scale, and reputation. In judging the latter, and gauging the degree of trust and reliability to be placed in a future neighbor, intermediate wholesalers call on the ordinary dimensions of personal affiliation, whether to solicit known partners or to arrange introductions to appropriate but as yet unknown ones. Cousins, drinking buddies, people who apprenticed together, brethren of religious kō, and alumni of the same elementary schools all seek each other out as coalition partners. Friends may become coalition partners, and coalition partners may become friends. In the complicated skeins of ties among dealers, it is impossible (and even pointless) to judge whether the Andō and the Yamamura families arranged the marriage of their children because they were coalition partners, or decided to place their stalls—Chiyomaru and Uorokubun—near one another because their children were engaged. It doesn't matter: the business of kinship is the family business, and as with so many things, relationships are simultaneously significant and strategic along many different dimensions.

In these coalitions—private responses to the market's formal mechanisms—institutions such as Tō-Oroshi, the gyōkai, and the lottery system all are submerged into the elaborate social fabric of the marketplace, the myriad relationships hammered out over time, and the webs of patronage and apprenticeship, of adoption and arranged marriage, of friendships and rivalries. Along these dimensions, the operations of the institutions themselves depend on the informal social ties that the same institutions are often intended to replace or codify, even as those ties become the mechanism to avoid or evade the potentially negative effects of institutionalized leveling mechanisms. The apparent contradiction stands at the heart of Tsukiji's social structure.

⊡ ⊡ ⊡

The timing of each rotation is a matter of sometimes fierce debate within Tō-Oroshi, because of its impact on the fortunes of so many stallholders and the very real costs in time and money that it imposes. A decision to hold the lottery requires negotiations with all the other parallel organizations in the marketplace as well as with the TMG administration. And since the rotation closes the marketplace for several days, it requires coordination among not only all actors at Tsukiji but also the entire seafood industry upstream and much of Tokyo's retail food industry downstream. The in-house decisions concern not just which set of days the market should be closed but in which years the rotations should be held.

Changes in the marketplace have led in recent years to a great deal of political maneuvering among factions of wholesalers with clashing stakes. In the 1950s and early 1960s, when *all* wholesalers were single-stall proprietorships, most seafood was fresh rather than frozen, and the equipment of the ordinary stall was rudimentary, the move was a relatively simple affair. Today, many firms have multiple stalls and even small stalls may have elaborate fittings and equipment; as the amount of capital sunk into a firm's space has risen, the inclination to invest in outfitting a new space has declined. As the market has diversified, a larger proportion of stalls are involved in bulk sales to supermarkets and other large-scale retailers. These stalls are less dependent on location and more dependent on fax lines. And as larger firms have captured scales of efficiency from consolidations of stalls, the potential impact of location on their bottom line has lessened. On the other end of the scale, small wholesalers remain highly sensitive to location and its impact on their sales, but as the costs of moving have risen over the years, some worry that a stall rotation might force them into the red.

The timing of the rotations has become an increasingly delicate issue, and with each passing cycle participants wonder whether it will be the last, a doubt that is delicately poised on top of the implicit question of whether growing disparities among individual wholesalers will eventually adjust the balance of self-interest away from collective risk-sharing through redistribution of space and toward an individualized notion of space as a private asset to be exploited as best one can.

Another round of lotteries and rotations was announced late in 1994, with applications and a preliminary lottery slated for February 1995, and a final lottery in March. The market would do business on Friday, June 9; stalls would move on Saturday, June 10, and Sunday, June 11; the market would reopen for business on Monday, June 12.

The stall rotations in 1995 were timed to occur just before the large-scale construction of a modern new central market hall was scheduled to begin, and the idea was that wholesalers would be more or less locked in competitive place throughout the entire subsequent construction project, which was then expected to be completed in 2003. Whether there would be stall rotations in the new market—in which all stalls were supposed to be exactly equivalent in size and amenities—was left an open question. As in previous lotteries and rotations, the specific details were altered to reflect what were presumed to be the current balances of locational advantage and disadvantage. Because the future of the market's space was so unclear, many of the complicated trappings of previous lotteries were modified in ways both big and small.

The lines of the lottery blocks were radically redrawn, in part to reflect the timing of construction plans that would over time eat away at the existing structures. And each lottery block not only designated a particular area within the existing market space, it also designated a location in a temporary market structure (to be built during the complicated reconstruction process) and a date on which occupants of a particular block would have to vacate the existing space and move into the temporary space. On the projected time line, some wholesalers would move into temporary space in 1999 and others as late as 2003, with moves into new quarters in the reconstructed market occurring in 2004 and 2005. The authorities clearly stipulated that there would be no further reallocations of space until the reconstruction was completed. Wholesalers therefore were being asked to stake their futures on a ten-year trajectory through the uncertainties of a couple of moves, within a complicated construction process, in the midst of what was (and, as of this writing, continues to be) an extended recession of the Japanese economy as a whole. Small wonder that the complicated system of premiums and rebates to further readjust locational risk could not handle unknown risks of this magnitude, and so these were set aside.

Nevertheless, in the winter and spring of 1995, the lotteries and the rotation went off as planned.

ON AGAIN, OFF AGAIN

In 1996 the TMG suspended reconstruction of the marketplace, citing enormous budget deficits. Immediately, wholesalers began to ask how long they would be expected to remain in the places assigned to them in the lottery. In the midst of the post-Bubble recession, which had depressed if not destroyed many wholesalers' revenues and had hollowed out the TMG budget, many large- and small-scale firms alike opposed another lottery on the grounds of cost, especially since the TMG moratorium on reconstruction invited speculation about all kinds of scenarios for the future marketplace. Why go through another lottery before the future of the present marketplace is decided? many wholesalers argued. Others, particularly those who considered themselves stuck in a bad spot by the previous lottery, took the other side, pointing to the lottery and its goal of equalizing individual risk as the overriding precedent. The marketplace has been organized for decades around principles of distributing and sharing risk, and what greater risks are there than those of an uncertain future for the marketplace as a whole? Should not the reassignment of spaces continue in a regular way to help spread the risks of this larger uncertainty as well?

The immediate status quo prevailed, however. The lottery was not attempted again in the late 1990s nor in the early years of the new century. Intermediate wholesalers remained where they had landed in 1995, set in place amid increasing bickering about future scenarios for the marketplace: Would the TMG resume reconstruction, rebuilding piece by piece around an ongoing market? Would a temporary structure be built nearby so that Tsukiji could be moved en masse, its site razed entirely, and a new marketplace built on the original site in an intensive, massive construction project? Would a new site be found for a permanent marketplace that would replace Tsukiji? Would the Tsukiji marketplace simply sink into second-class oblivion—overtaken perhaps by new distribution channels—before *any* plan was launched? Everyone in the marketplace had his or her own opinion of which option was likely or desirable in light of how his or her own interests might profit or be imperiled. The ethos of collective solidarity that intermediate wholesalers so often express and the institutions that pragmatically sustain or implement such solidarity were severely strained by this uncertainty.

Late in 2001, after several years of discussions aimed at forging consensus as widely as possible, the TMG formally announced its new plan. A new marketplace would be constructed and operations at Tsukiji would be moved to a large plot of land in Toyosu, east of the present Tsukiji market on the opposite side of the Sumida River's mouth beyond the rectangular islands of Tsukishima and Harumi. The site, owned but no longer used by Tokyo Gas, would be cleaned up and rebuilt as a marketplace over approximately a decade, becoming fully operational by 2012 or 2013 at the earliest.

The history of efforts to move or rebuild the marketplace is littered with abandoned plans announced with bureaucratic certainty. But whatever lingering doubts people at Tsukiji may have about whether this latest definite plan will in fact come to pass, the TMG market administration regards the matter as settled. Therefore, the plan must be taken seriously by market participants as they chart the future for themselves and their firms, whether they are pleased with the prospect of this move or prefer some other option.

At the same time, the decision reached and announced in late 2001 came when the market—and the entire Japanese economy—was in its tenth or twelfth year of a seemingly intractable recession. Tsukiji has been whipsawed by many economic factors: some of them are endemic to the wider Japanese economy, such as the effects of bank failures, plummeting real estate values, a moribund stock market, and tight credit; others are more closely tied to the specifics of Tsukiji's business, such as declining consumer demand for high-priced seafood (partly because of the slump in business entertaining), the prominent failures of several large supermarket chains, environmental issues surrounding marine species targeted by Japanese markets, and the transformation of the largest Japanese fisheries companies from seafood producers strongly focused on domestic Japanese markets into corporations that trade in processed seafood on a global stage. Against this backdrop of widespread economic change and enduring economic slump, few if any Tsukiji players could look at a future move with unbridled confidence that their firm, their segment of the market's operations, would necessarily find itself ten years hence thriving in new and untested quarters.

Many of the smaller wholesalers believe that the plan consigns them to failure. They see themselves as doomed by the costs of this future move, by the prospect that the Toyosu marketplace will be difficult to reach and will not attract their existing customers, by the fear that distribution channels will bypass their small operations well before 2013. They would gladly sell their licenses and leave the business. But times are bad, and there are few buyers for Tsukiji trading licenses. Those who want to leave the business feel trapped, struggling to keep their firms alive in the hope that they can eventually find someone to buy them out. Potential buyers, for their part, wait on the sidelines facing their own current economic difficulties. The contours of the future marketplace are still too distant to warrant heavy investments in increasing one's own ability to participate in it.

As the ambiguity of multiple possibilities that held sway during the reconstruction moratorium ended, people at Tsukiji were able to begin to calculate how a specific move would or would not be to their advantage, plotting what steps they could take for their own firms or their own segments of the market to diminish potential disruptions and to accentuate competitive advantages. Tsukiji's actors, both large and small, intensified their thinking about how to position themselves, come what may. They reexamined their affiliations and allegiances to existing institutions, organizations, and coalitions within the marketplace. As different traders glimpse different futures, existing coalitions and institutions are tested by new, or long-submerged, stresses and strains. Solidarity and an ethos of equalization are admirable ideals and solid foundations for an institutional agenda when the status quo is stable (and reasonably prosperous!), but when the only constants are bad economic news and an unknown future, the social institutions that foster cooperative market governance look shaky.

Not surprisingly, since the institutions of internal market governance present themselves as bastions of stability and solidarity—sheltering individual firms from extreme changes in their microbusiness environments and protecting collective advantages that have been built up over decades— they seem best suited for (perhaps suited *only* for) periods of overall prosperity and incremental change, such as Tsukiji experienced from the early 1950s to the early 1990s. And conversely, they seem ill suited to manage— let alone survive—radical transformations of the sort that the move to Toyosu will almost certainly bring. Yet their shakiness—evident as I complete this book in 2003—unexpectedly sheds light on the underlying dynamics of the marketplace's institutions that I have described in this and the preceding two chapters.

The social institutions that govern the marketplace and that frame the currents of internal competition generally convey a sense of continuity, perhaps stasis: implicitly these institutions suggest that their elaborate calibrations of equality, their negotiated rules of trade, and their carefully constructed balances of market power simply reflect a conservative desire to maintain some "traditional" structural status quo. The parities among competitors and the delicate balances among different market segments that Tsukiji's institutions strive to achieve, of course, may be structural manifestations of an underlying ethos or set of values, but these competitive balances are maintained or achieved—if achieved at all—only through incessant and complex institutional tinkering. They are hardly products of a social system asleep at the switch or unaware of larger pictures.

The culture of market stability masks almost constant institutional change, which itself reflects dynamic calibrations both within Tsukiji among insiders and between the internal structure of the marketplace and the wider world in which it is embedded.

First of all, the internal organization of the marketplace generates special interests, embedded privileges, and imbalances of market power, even as it simultaneously creates institutionalized reactions that seek to override or dampen the effects of those interests, privileges, and imbalances. That is, these are two sides to the same coin: the institutions of the marketplace are suspended in—created in—the dynamic space between competition and cooperation, between the accumulation of advantage and the distribution of risk, between individual reward and collective security.

And second, the internal organization of the marketplace is acutely attuned to the broad, actively shifting political, economic, social, and environmental contexts in which Tsukiji is located. Efforts to preserve advantage on a collective level or protect individual players are not simply manifestations of unchanging market values; these goals and the institutions they shape (and are shaped by) are products of the continuous reiteration and sedimentation of internal adjustments to keep abreast of changes more or less external to the daily operations of the marketplace and beyond the power of market participants to control directly. Each effort to define and sustain a status quo within Tsukiji is spawned by structural shocks and dislocations coming largely from outside the market. Changes in external conditions that affect balances of power among actors inside Tsukiji are the impetus for institutional responses to manage or contain internally the effects and impacts of those changes.

With the move to Toyosu now definite, some market participants, officials, and observers regard it as inevitable that the current structures of interest groups, collective equalizations, and careful calibrations of market power will unravel. But Tsukiji is a socially embedded economic institution (to reiterate Mark Granovetter's perspectives [1985], discussed in chapter 1) and is perhaps best thought of as *doubly* embedded (see also Acheson 1994, 2003; Plattner 1989a, 1989b). That is, the internal economic life of the market takes place through the social structures of market governance— through such features as auction rules, trading communities, stall rotations, and the institutionalized devolution of decision making—and, in addition, the marketplace is embedded in larger realms of domestic and international political economies of trade, urban planning, consumption, and natural resources. Although the social embeddedness of Tsukiji's economic life is most obvious in the internal configurations of market governance, those arrangements are often framed in reaction to structural changes in the market's position in broader contexts.

Collective decisions and actions—about distributing risk, equalizing trading positions, or setting the terms of market power within different trading communities—can directly affect only the internal organization of the marketplace. The marketplace as a whole is buffeted by and responds to a much wider world of economic, cultural, social, political, and ecological forces, which constantly devise new challenges that will spin its internal calibrations.

Tsukiji's social organization is segmentary, internally splitting into smaller and smaller interest groups over time as new issues arise externally. The rights, privileges, and advantages that groups want to collectively protect give rise to factions and schisms, and vice versa. Each aspect of the social structure and the cultural framework of marketplace organization inevitably gives rise to the other.

The institutional history of the marketplace is dotted with groups, factions, and coalitions that seek to preserve their position or some remnant of it from a prior status quo. In the complex accommodations and equilibrations among many such groups, the present status quo comes into being, only to be challenged again by events beyond the immediate influence of the market's current actors. Many examples from throughout the market's history illustrate this Hegelian logic: the complicated politics surrounding moving the market from Nihonbashi to Tsukiji; issues about compensating Nihonbashi traders for lost space, which dragged on until World War II; distinctions among traders by scale, drawn during World War II, still present in institutional structures although long since irrelevant to day-to-day trade; the introduction of lotteries for allocating stalls after the market expanded in the 1950s; the development of ties of vertical market integration that endure even after the major corporations around which such ties originated have shifted their own business operations; the turf protection among different groups of chaya (loading docks) that preserve their separateness long after the differences in their businesses have disappeared; the factional splits that developed among different groups of traders who accepted varied offers from the TMG to move their operations to the new Ōta Market; or, most recently, the jockeying among traders over whether to hold another round of lotteries during the long construction moratorium. All these are examples of the internal elaboration of the social structure of the market, of the complex social world into which economic transactions are embedded; but these adjustments, changes, or adaptations are not stimulated by internal factors so much as they are prompted by changes in the larger contexts in which the marketplace as a whole is embedded.

The move to Toyosu—as well as all the other changes projected (whether with fear or anticipation) in macroeconomic conditions, in the composition of the market's clientele, in the nature of retail distribution and sales, in the character of consumer demand—will undoubtedly set in motion massive transformations of the character of traders' businesses and of the internal organization of the marketplace. But if Tsukiji's history is any guide, the social and institutional reactions of traders will be to organize their internal interests in ways that proliferate differentiation around the preservation of what they now regard as important past configurations (however vestigial) and current distinctions in their institutionalized privileges, advantages, and sense of autonomous market governance. External changes will not sweep away the social structure of Tsukiji. The economics of the market are inseparable from the social organization of the marketplace, and no market can slip the bonds of its embeddedness. Rather, the social structure of Tsukiji— or Toyosu, the future name is not yet decided—will continue to calibrate itself with internal effect in response to external change.

8   Full Circle

Late December is the busiest time of the year at Tsukiji, as the market girds itself for *toshi no kure,* or O-kure, the end-of-the-year season: the "twilight," the "closing," the "end."

In the weeks leading up to the New Year's holidays, sales at Tsukiji reach a feverish pitch as retailers and restaurateurs lay in stock for the year-end spike in consumption. December is the month for *bōnenkai:* the "forgetting the year parties" that almost every company, office, school, and club holds to celebrate or drown the recent past. Restaurants and banquet halls are booked solid. The season is punctuated by the emperor's birthday on December 23, a national holiday since the accession of the current Heisei Emperor in 1989. The emperor's grateful subjects party on through Christmas, which has in the past couple of generations become an informal (and entirely secular) celebration, both at "home parties" and extravagant hotel dinner shows. December also includes O-Seibō, the end-of-the-year season for giving gifts—foodstuffs being leading gifts—to those with whom one has incurred significant obligations during the preceding year. The merriment climaxes with O-Shōgatsu, the New Year's holiday, which starts with Ōmisoka (December 31) and lasts until January 5. For many people, this is a week or so of quiet but often elaborate meals at home with family and friends.

January celebrates beginnings. On January 15, twenty-year-olds toast their legal majority on the national holiday Adult's Day (Seijin no Hi). And the month is dotted with *shinnenkai:* "welcoming the year parties" held in direct counterpoint to the parties for forgetting thrown by the same groups only a few weeks earlier.

Amid the gaiety of the season, people at Tsukiji work grueling hours. Because the multiple demands of the overlapping holidays pile upon one another just before the market itself closes for five days—the year's longest

Figure 60. The straw circle for New Year's prayers at Namiyoke Shrine is visited by a Tsukiji cat, December 1997.

single vacation for Tsukiji—the weeks beforehand are flat-out toil. In overall sales, December is the market's busiest month, and its year-end performance is in the public spotlight. Television news program regularly report when shipments of herring roe *(kazunoko)* for the holidays arrive in the market; newspaper articles inform consumers of the market prices for holiday specialties; and forecasters use Tsukiji as an informal barometer for economic trends and consumer confidence (rather like Wall Street's hemline indices). Tsukiji traders themselves view the O-kure season as a benchmark for their individual and collective well-being.

In the outer market, the crowds of homemakers and restaurateurs thicken in the last days of December. The merchants' association posts signs everywhere: "Beware of pickpockets." At the Namiyoke Shrine, the cycle of old year and new is marked by a gigantic straw hoop—a circular gate—through which visitors pass to offer prayers at the foot of the shrine's stairs.

The inner market is also jammed. From the point of view of harried traders, as the year closes, as prices for holiday specialties soar into risky multiples, their daily business is complicated by the influx of trade customers—both regular and occasional—looking to fill their own inventories. Because the market ends its business on December 30 and reopens on January 5, regular customers have to stock up, or risk doing without once the market closes.[1]

O-kure is also the season when the wannabes show up in force. Earnest

Figure 61. A hand towel for a
New Year's gift.

bargain-hunting amateurs try to shop for family banquets on the cheap;
showy parvenus try to impress their friends—definitely impressing themselves—through faux camaraderie with wholesalers whose culinary expertise is beyond question. The market aisles are clogged with middle-aged
housewives in expensive fur jackets and gold jewelry, well-dressed elderly
men trailing a couple of grandchildren, and small clusters of women in their
early twenties in fashionable ski parkas. Children—never seen in the inner
market at other times of the year—are everywhere. Stall keepers watch
with restrained displeasure as small children occasionally poke fingers into
the strange fish, but they tend to hold their tongues; the culprit might turn
out to be the beloved grandchild of a prized customer.

Many traders pass out token gifts to customers, most commonly cotton
hand towels *(tenugui)* printed with their shops' names and decorative
motifs of New Year's regalia or the animal of the coming year: the Year of
the Rabbit, the Ox, the Horse, and so forth. Some are quite elaborate, others quite utilitarian; but either way they are wrapped appropriately as gifts.
Regular customers accept them briskly and tuck them away quietly with a
phrase or two of holiday greeting. Wannabes collect them: grandmothers
furtively stuff shopping bags with as many towels as they can put their
hands on; young women become heavy with towel as they pack layer after
layer under their parkas.

Figure 62. New Year's at
Nihonbashi. Sketch by
Mori Kazan.

For people in the marketplace, the entire season is trying. The workload
is enormous, the spotlight of holiday publicity is on the market, and the
market is flooded with strangers. It is also the traditional time to take stock
of one's business, to settle up financial and personal obligations, and to chart
a course for the future. It is a time of exhausted reflection.

LENGTHENING SHADOWS

The scariest encounters in Japanese proverbial wisdom are with *jishin,
kaminari, kaji, oyaji* (earthquake, thunder, fire, and the old man!). Concern about fire is ritualistically heightened at the end of the year. In old-
fashioned *shitamachi* neighborhoods, community fire patrols take to the
streets, breaking the silence of cold December nights with the customary cry
"*Hi no yōjin!*" (Take care with fire!).

No one patrols the marketplace, however.

On Sunday, December 21, 1997, a fire broke out at Tsukiji around 3:00
A.M. Somewhere in the innermost rows of stalls toward the northern end of
the fan-shaped sheds, the fire started and spread. It burned unnoticed for at
least half an hour before an alarm was turned in. Most of the week, people
are at the marketplace throughout the night to prepare for the next morning's auctions. But the market is closed on Sundays, so no one was around.

By chance, I was in Tokyo that weekend, and Saturday evening I had
been barhopping with a Tsukiji friend. On Sunday morning, I got a phone
call telling me to turn on the news. With a couple of other friends, includ-

ing one who worked at Tsukiji, I rushed off to the marketplace, feeling slightly guilty at my eagerness to see the fire's aftermath. *Yajiuma* (fire horses) are the excited onlookers who rush to the scene of a disaster. When I arrived at Tsukiji, I joined throngs of other yajiuma, none looking at all abashed by their curiosity.

Fire engines were neatly parked where tractor-trailers ought to have been unloading for the Monday auctions. At the entrance to the stalls, Tō-Oroshi staff members passed out maps of the marketplace on which stalls were circled ominously in heavy black ink. Tokyo's efficient firefighters had responded quickly to the alarm, and the blaze had been extinguished within an hour or so. But it had consumed about 130 stalls, close to 10 percent of the marketplace. Inside the sheds, temporary guards indifferently manned cordons around the damaged sections. Rows of charred rubble were eerily illuminated by light unexpectedly streaming through gaping holes in the shed's roof. Several hundred people milled about, few showing much emotion except stunned shock. Husbands and wives stood quietly, staring in silent disbelief; an old man ignored the demolition crew—already tearing down the corrugated roof above him—in order to make a video of the ashen rubble that must have been his stall the day before; another man talked animatedly—to passersby, to me, to the air—about his coolers full of now-ruined tuna, not listening for any response through the motorcycle helmet he still wore.

One trader stood a few feet from his stall, unwilling to defy a fire department cordon. He talked loudly about how his stock was ruined, and because his stall had only been blackened but not destroyed his insurance would not cover his losses. Another worried that the fish in his coolers was now spoiled because the electricity had shut off, water had poured over his stock in the loft above, and the smell of smoke would cling to any fish that he might otherwise salvage the next day.

Others plunged into stalls more obviously damaged than his to clean up even if there was little or nothing to salvage. A man climbed into the loft above his stall with a broom, carefully picking up a half-melted scale to place it on top of a charred freezer, and began to sweep debris into the void. A young man dressed in work clothes hurried past carrying three shiny shovels, price tags still dangling from their handles, and pushed aside a couple of half-burned carts; he stopped short and shouted "Wow!" (in English), dumbfounded by the rubble where his stall had been. Another man arrived on a bicycle, stoically carrying a box of plastic garbage bags and a bundle of clean towels. Farther from the center of the burned-out area, a father and son stood in their undamaged stall talking into cellular phones about getting

Figure 63. Fire damage in the
marketplace. Workers clear
away rubble after the fire.

their electrical power restored, bowing abstractedly to fellow traders who
were making the rounds to inquire about the fate of their colleagues' shops.

The fire—the sixth of its kind in the past decade, in the midnight hours,
in the front ranks of stalls, on a morning when the auctions would not open
and hence the marketplace would not be fully stocked—inevitably raised
suspicions. One turn of mind asks who stands to profit. Would the possibility of insurance settlements offer a quick and anonymous alternative to
public failure for a dealer driven close to bankruptcy? Another turn of mind
looks to systemic failure. If the reconstruction or relocation of the marketplace into modern facilities had not been stymied by years of political wrangling or budgetary stalemate, perhaps modern wiring and fireproof buildings would have been in place. Doubt—fueled by suspicions of deliberate
arson or by the certainty of infrastructural failure—settled heavily on a
marketplace already deep in distress.

Only two or three days before the fire at Tsukiji, Tōshoku, a major dis-
tributor of foodstuffs including many seafood products, had declared bankruptcy. Tōshoku had been a leading firm; its stock was traded on the Tokyo
exchange and listed among the companies that make up the prestigious
Nikkei average, the index that charts the Japanese financial world. Tōshoku's

demise caused the Nikkei average to take a severe tumble, and its bankruptcy was declared at the time to be among the ten largest corporate failures in recent Japanese business history.

Of course, the failure of Tōshoku, with its ripples both through credit markets and through the food distribution industry, was not—could not have been—directly connected to the blaze at Tsukiji. But in the bleak light filtering through the burned-out roof of Tsukiji's second shed, the bankruptcy of Tōshoku, the bankruptcy earlier in 1997 of Kyōtaru (a major restaurant chain specializing in sushi), the stagnation of seafood sales in the shaky economy of post-Bubble Japan, and the near-mortal blows suffered by purveyors of fresh foods in the wake of the panic over E. coli O-157 food contamination cases near Osaka during the summer of 1996 all coalesced. The mood of traders and "fire horses" alike reflected a general conviction that times were bad; the fire could only make things worse.

Earlier that fall, a successful Tsukiji dealer had told me he thought that one hundred or more nakaoroshi would sell their licenses immediately if they could find buyers offering ¥50 million for a stall—a fraction of the price eagerly expected (and offered) only a few years before—but there were no takers. Now, surveying a blackened freezer beneath a large soot-stained kumade (the rake of good fortune) hanging next to a sheaf of plastic bags melted into a grotesque stalactite, he assured me that many of the fire's victims would never reopen.

Tsukiji's liquor store opened for business that Sunday, and—you should pardon the expression—it did fire sale business. Lines of customers waited patiently to purchase braces of saké bottles, carefully wrapped in ceremonial paper and bound together. These were taken or delivered to devastated shops, as tokens of condolence from friends, business partners, and customers of traders they had patronized and would continue to support. Here and there within the twisted skeletons of stalls, pairs of saké bottles stood as small emblems of the social ties that animate the market. Meanwhile, Tsukiji traders got on their cell phones and arranged for workmen to clear away the rubble, to restore electrical power, to build temporary scaffolds on which to hang the paraphernalia of business. They called friends to borrow the use of a refrigerator and to find space in which to do business the following morning. In concrete terms, they set about the work of making a market, much as they did every day, disaster or not.

On Monday, the sharp tang of burned wood hung in the air. Remarkably, the market was open and in almost full operation. The burned-out sections were spotty; some stalls contained only small clusters of saké bottles left by well-wishers; others were occupied by traders sitting on folding chairs at

Figure 64. Condolence gifts after the fire. Saké, cakes, and crackers from patrons and suppliers rest in an undamaged stall.

boards spread across sawhorses, talking on telephones dangling from temporary loops of wire hanging from shiny new metal rafters. Construction workers were busily stringing cables, assembling new rafters, and cutting plywood on table saws. Blackened stains remained, but everything had been scrubbed down, with almost no rubble left.

A couple of months later I had a chance to visit Tsukiji again. If I had known nothing about the fire, I might not have noticed anything unusual on this midwinter visit. In the rebuilt sections, the woodwork was fresher, some of the stalls were fashionably minimalist in their new incarnations, and the light coming through new fiberglass panels in the roof was brighter than elsewhere under the sheds. But the bustle of trade was unchanged—or, more properly, restored. The life of the market had continued. My friend's dire prediction of the collapse of dozens of firms turned out to be wrong, even if only because many stall owners can't afford to close unless and until they find buyers for their licenses.

Seen against the fire, the market's quick recovery underscored the fact that traders travel light. If the market survives disaster, an individual trader can too. Sustained by the general flow of trade and the elaborate social structure of trading relationships, even faced with complete physical destruction (on an individual level), they can be up and running the next day. Their business is in their heads and in their contacts. Social rights to space—perhaps, spatial rights to sociality—are among their most important forms of capital. The infrastructure of the trade is social and cultural; it is embedded in contexts, not in buildings, freezers, or well-honed knives. Their fundamental assets are confirmed in the exchanges—of saké, of cell phones, of freezer space—after a disaster like the fire, but more importantly, they are reaffirmed, reinvested, re-created, and recapitalized in the daily round of business.

MARKET MOVEMENT

The blaze reopened discussions of the market's place. The fire's obvious damage was repaired within weeks at most, but the larger, longer task of building a new market has barely begun. Resume the effort to rebuild on site? Move to a new location? As this manuscript goes to the publisher (in 2003), the issue of the market's location is inching toward final resolution.

Throughout the market's history, decisions to move or rebuild inevitably have raised political questions, necessarily reflecting myriad individual calculations of present and future costs and advantages. For many traders, the capital they have sunk into the market is primarily social capital, denominated in social relations and participation in the cartel-like social institutions of market governance. Therefore, their calculations of advantage or cost in any move revolve around ensuring that individual positions vis-à-vis these institutions are not compromised. A trader is loath to lose his place in a particular social context, not in a location per se.

In the early twentieth century, as noted in chapter 3, the problem of compensating the owners of *itafuneken* ("board rights," the right to occupy a space for business a few hours each day) blocked market relocation for decades; the issue was whether a move would disenfranchise those whose income depended on leasing out the space. In the 1980s, the TMG's efforts to relocate Tsukiji traders to the new Ōta Market ultimately failed because traders were asked to modify their institutional allegiances in ways that would at least potentially foreclose some future forms of participation in the market. The TMG's subsequent plan to rebuild Tsukiji in place, which foundered in the mid-1990s after construction had been under way for several years, tried to avoid these problems by preserving the status quo; if no one was forced to give up his or her social rights to space or spatial rights to sociality, then presumably no one would be institutionally disadvantaged by the reconstruction. But the financial difficulties of the TMG brought construction—and this compromise—to a halt.

Sixty-eight years after the current market facilities opened for business, the same buildings, patched and repatched over the years, are still the core of the market's physical plant. With reconstruction in place halted and with the future uncertain, the facilities continue to deteriorate. No one wants to sink funds into substantial improvements or even extensive maintenance for a marketplace that is so obviously on its last legs. Yet everyone connected with Tsukiji agrees that something must be done; clearly the facilities now are completely inadequate, and its share of the wholesale business suffers as a result (both vis-à-vis other markets and in terms of the growing percentages of the seafood trade that rely on "outside-the-market" channels of distribution).

In 2001, as noted in chapter 7, the TMG finally announced a resumption of the planning process for rebuilding the market. Ideas of constructing the market on-site, around the ongoing marketplace, were no longer on the table. Tsukiji would have to move, and the only real candidate for a new location was a tract of land in Toyosu, one of the artificial islands across the main channel of the Sumida River beyond Tsukishima and Harumi. Toyosu contains a large vacant site, surplus land owned by the Tokyo Gas Corporation. The land is close to major highways, and although other transportation links are not yet handy, the TMG promises that they can and will be added relatively easily. The TMG negotiated with Tokyo Gas, and eventually reached an agreement to purchase some of the land for a new marketplace.

The cynical but realistic view of Tsukiji regulars is that in the greater scheme of things, the TMG's efforts to relocate the marketplace to Toyosu are motivated more by the bottom-line reality of the revenue to be gained by redeveloping the Tsukiji site into something like the Shiodome project and less by deep concerns about how to improve the inner workings of the marketplace itself. Of course, TMG officials would argue that *both* are important (and legitimate) concerns. Now, in 2003, TMG officials forecast that the new market at Toyosu will open sometime between 2012 and 2016, but there are, of course, many uncertainties along the way.

As always, the politics are complicated. Some factions of the *nakaoroshi gyōsha* at Tsukiji are dead set against the move—green protest signs dot the inner and outer marketplace, declaring eternal opposition to any move—but it remains to be seen whether these are simply negotiating tactics or last stopgap measures by stall keepers who may go out of business soon. Even without the final agreement of Tō-Oroshi (as of 2003), most market regulars now regard the move as a foregone conclusion.

At the national level, the TMG and the current governor, Ishihara Shintarō, are fighting plans pushed by provincial politicians to move the national capital to some new location; three areas outside Tokyo are under study. The outcome of this is still very unclear, but if the capital (or parts of the government) were to be relocated, the impact on Tokyo's local economy—its ability to pay for a new market and indeed the amount of business a new marketplace might handle—is difficult to predict.

Closer to Tsukiji's trading floors, the political calculations focus on possible future directions of the market. Many intermediate wholesalers assume that political and economic pressures will reduce the numbers of separate firms from the present level of about 900 to half that number over the next decade or so. Those who are confident that their firms will be among the survivors look to a new marketplace as an opportunity. Those who are less confident—including most of the smallest intermediate wholesalers, the unincorporated proprietors—fear that a new marketplace will force the pace of consolidations, and they believe that their only chance to survive is to hold fast within the existing Tsukiji marketplace.

Some traders look at the auction houses and wonder whether all seven would survive in a new marketplace. Publicly, the auction houses all support a move to Toyosu. But if the number of intermediate wholesalers shrinks by about half, might a Toyosu marketplace need only three or four auction houses, especially as distribution channels outside the market system grow larger and more nimble?

The outer marketplace and the municipal government of Chūō Ward pose further questions. If Tsukiji moves, what will become of all the private businesses outside its gates? They will neither be relocated nor compensated by the TMG, presumably, yet their trade will unquestionably decline. If the TMG relocates the marketplace, the TMG is directly responsible only for the facilities that house the licensed businesses and operations of the marketplace. Businesses outside the institutional framework of the TMG market, such as the many shops in the outer marketplace—economically dependent on the TMG market though not institutionally connected to it—always raise the question of what will happen to them, as do their political representatives and the local government (the Chūō Ward Office) that collects their taxes. Simply put, the noodle vendor, the chopsticks dealer, and the bar owner across the street from the TMG marketplace, together with their political representatives, all raise issues about the destruction or uprooting of established local businesses and the impact on local community life (and municipal finances), if the marketplace moves. And what of the enormous tax revenues that now flow into Chūō Ward because of Tsukiji's trade, both from the inner and the outer markets and from other related businesses? Toyosu is located in the adjacent Kōtō Ward, so tax monies will leave Chūō Ward along with the customers of the independent businesses of the outer market.

As for the merchants of the outer market themselves, since the opening of the Ō-Edo line in 2001, many of them—the more retail-oriented shops—have flourished because of the improved access from a great number of places in Tokyo. Slick new sushi bars offering inexpensive servings now dot the outer marketplace, some of them operating twenty-four hours a day. Even *kaiten-zushi* has reached Tsukiji (and a McDonald's too)! The outer market has successfully promoted itself as a shopping, dining, and recreational destination (one poster features a famous television personality clowning as a chef under the headline "Doyōbi, Tsukiji wa omoshiroi-i-i!" ("Saturday, Tsukiji is f-u-n!"). Part of the outer market's self-promotion reflects the reality that it cannot depend forever on its proximity to the inner market, especially as planning pushes forward to move the inner market to Toyosu. The outer market needs its own identity for the general public.

But even as the outer market adjusts to the probable departure of the inner market within a decade, it faces other challenges from the redevelopment of central Tokyo. The opening of the Shiodome skyscraper complex in 2003 and 2004 threatens the outer market, now only a subway stop away. Many of the big companies that currently occupy buildings scattered around the Tsukiji, Higashi Ginza, and Akashi-chō neighborhoods adjacent to the outer market are moving into newer, larger, more modern quarters in Shiodome. The huge advertising agency Dentsū, for example, is vacating its space in half a dozen office buildings including the St. Luke's Hospital Tower (itself a glittering showcase less than a decade old). As these large companies move on, office workers will no longer flock to the outer market during lunchtime for a meal and to make small purchases. The small merchants of the outer market—coffee shops, sushi bars, noodle stalls, and even the retailers of foodstuffs—will lose much of their daily drop-in trade. This, coupled with the hard times of Japan's long-running recession, may seal the outer market's fate, even if the move of the inner market to Toyosu does not.

Whether a Tsukiji business—inner or outer—is threatened by a move to Toyosu depends largely on the kind of investment it has in the present situation. Some, like outer market businesses or small-scale, unincorporated intermediate wholesalers who depend on a walk-in trade, have their financial or social assets sunk in the status quo. Others, like the larger intermediate wholesalers, depend on highly liquid social capital, embedded not in property or equipment but in social relationships and contexts. This social capital is portable, assuming that a relocated and renewed marketplace does not alter or dilute Tsukiji's fundamental institutional order and the spatial rights to sociality that many traders depend on, now as in the past.

ROCK–PAPER–SCISSORS

Social capital may be the bedrock of trade, but surface currents of economic activity are nonetheless fluid. A trader is up one week and down the next. Markets for salmon or tuna or herring roe rise dizzyingly and collapse abruptly. Seasons come and go. Unexpected weather on the fishing grounds or long-simmering international disputes rattle the market. A trader's son marries another trader's daughter and a new strategic alliance is formed. Supermarkets expand and independent retailers retrench. Consumer tastes migrate gradually—or cartwheel willy-nilly—across a spectrum of products. Exchange rates shift, and foreign seafood suddenly becomes cheap or dear. The TMG forges ahead with plans to reconstruct the marketplace, and then freezes the project.

Change is constant, and constantly unpredictable; the marketplace is never quite the same from month to month, from year to year. In the midst of this uncertainty, Tsukiji's denizens focus on movement. Time and again, Tsukiji traders tell me how things aren't what they used to be: the marketplace teeters on the edge of a fundamental revolution! Supermarkets are sweeping independent retailers away. New specialty shops offer sophisticated seafood that supermarkets can never match. With the shambles of family life today, all anybody wants nowadays is fast food. The gourmet boom has made homemakers highly conscious of fresh foodstuffs. Rebuilding Tsukiji will destroy the place. The marketplace should have been rebuilt twenty years ago. Back in the good old days, Tsukiji traders really knew their fish. Now, with the revolution in shipping technology and the global supply network, Tsukiji traders really have to know their fish.

Most people at Tsukiji *know* they are living through great transformations. They are right, of course, probably as right as every generation has been since Nihonbashi's merchants took up arms to defend the Tokugawa shōgunate against the Meiji Restoration in the 1860s, since the Nihonbashi marketplace went up in flames in 1923 after the Kantō earthquake, since trucks replaced the railroads in the 1960s, since airfreighted Atlantic bluefin tuna became the flagfish of Tsukiji in the 1970s. Traders' convictions that, amid the unique circumstances of today, unprecedented flux is already upon them have to be seen against the background of cultural and institutional processes that shape and reshape the marketplace. The historical origins of particular market customs, or the durability or impermanence of current trends, are not really the issues on which to stake an understanding of the market. In financial circles, the predictability of technical market analysis often is hedged by the legalese that warns the buyer to beware: "past performance is no guarantee of future return." But in analyses of a marketplace in cultural and institutional terms, the past is always present and past performances count for a lot. How else could one bet the firm every morning?

Anthropologists have long argued about formalist and substantivist views of markets and exchange, counterposing interpretations that emphasize rational choice in terms of quantifiable calculations with those that focus on the socially and culturally embedded contexts of exchange. Substantivists emphasize that these contexts encourage multiple calculations of advantage, reciprocity, and other equilibrations of relationship beyond marginal utility.[2] Tsukiji's traders may be formalists in their exposition of daily economic trends, of the effects of exchange rates, interest rates, and transactions costs. But to work in a market*place,* on some level one must be a substantivist: one must intuitively engage in exchange that is embedded in social context and know that assessments of advantage and reciprocity can be simultaneously calculated in financial, cultural, and moral currencies. Even if one doesn't overtly acknowledge it, the trade—and one's success within it—depends day in and day out on social relationships and on the institutional framework that sustains them.

To be sure, buy low and sell high is always good formalist advice. But buy from whom? Sell to whom? When? Where? In a marketplace, these questions are often answered in a substantivist mode, which speaks in the patterned regularities that persist behind the face of daily fluctuation (even amid the long-term recession in which the Japanese domestic economy has been mired since the early 1990s). These regularities involve the ways in which transactions, institutional structures, and cultural meanings interact in the creation and ongoing functioning of a marketplace, a marketplace—like all marketplaces—in which economy, society, and culture mutually shape and reinforce one another. The social structure of Tsukiji's institutions and the cultural logic of transactions are the centrally defining elements of the marketplace as an economic mechanism, a social institution, and a cultural site. They make Tsukiji a marketplace, not a spot market.

Observers of Japanese economic structure and behavior fall into various interpretive camps. Some hardheaded "revisionists" emphasize fundamental economic calculation, and regard explanations that evoke cultural or social factors as the persiflage of the "apologists" of the so-called Chrysanthemum Club. Others point to the special institutional arrangements of contemporary Japanese political economy—including patterns of *keiretsu* integration, obligational contracting, or administrative guidance—to suggest that there are social differences in which economic behavior is embedded. The proponents of these varying interpretations often seem to be playing the children's game of *jan-ken:* rock crushes scissors, paper covers rock, scissors cut paper. In one or two rounds of the game, one factor can triumph. Economy can trump society, or culture can explain institutions, or political institutions can dominate cultural discourse. But over a longer run (or with more players) a different and more realistic picture emerges: culture sustains institutions, institutions shape the economy, the economy recalibrates culture, and on and on.

Market and place—economic transactions and the institutional frameworks and cultural processes that enable them—are indivisibly joined. Tsukiji's transactions cannot be isolated from their social or cultural contexts. Formalist and substantivist orientations inevitably cohabit; structure is enacted through agency, just as agency is enabled and constrained by structure. Tsukiji is highly embedded in complex social institutions that are sustained by the cultural logic of cuisine and trade, and, in turn, these logics are generated in part through the day-to-day operations of the market's institutions. The marketplace socially reproduces itself in an endless cycle.

OPENING CLOSURE

The start of trade after the New Year is the most celebrated beginning at the marketplace. The New Year's holiday—the longest vacation that Tsukiji traders get—ends on January 5, the day of *hatsuni* (first freight).[3] The arrival of the New Year's first shipments is marked by ritual, and the biggest rituals surround the auctions of the first tuna, the *hatsumaguro.*

The hatsumaguro is a harbinger of the New Year and an opportunity for spectacular displays of entrepreneurial derring-do, even during the economic doldrums after the Bubble Economy. On January 5, 2001, the first day of auctions of the new millennium, a Tsukiji trader made global news for his purchase of a 202-kilogram bluefin tuna (caught off northern Japan) for 100,000 yen per kilogram, roughly doubling the previous auction record (and vastly exceeding ordinary auction prices for fresh tuna: an exceptional tuna might bring 10,000 or 12,000 yen and an ordinary one 3,000 to 4,000 yen per kilogram). Using the exchange rate of the time, the hatsumaguro of the millennium sold for $174,138—a wholesale price of $392 per pound, skin and bones included. This auction price was widely misinterpreted in the foreign press as a benchmark, but market insiders recognized it as a publicity stunt, though perhaps one gone awry; even the buyer, interviewed by Japanese media, commented that he had gotten carried away with bidding. Nonetheless, the purchase was for some market observers a comforting, for

Figures 65–66.
(Above) First freights of the season. Crates are festooned with "Hatsuni" (first shipment) banners before the auctions on January 5.
(Right) The tuna heard 'round the world. The bluefin tuna on the left set a world record price of 2.02 million yen at the first auction of the millennium, January 5, 2001. The paper banner reads "Congratulations, First Shipment." Reproduced with permission of the Mainichi PhotoBank.

Figure 67. Ipponjime at Nihonbashi. Sketch by Mori Kazan.

others a disturbing reminder of freewheeling consumption during Japan's boom times.

Banners and New Year's decorations festoon both the auction blocks and the fish. The first trading sessions open with formal greetings from leaders of the TMG administration, the auction houses, and the traders' guilds. The greetings end with a round of *ipponjime,* a rhythmic chorus of clapping that Tsukiji traders regard as a distinctive legacy of the Nihonbashi uogashi. The president of Tō-Oroshi, himself a tuna wholesaler, leads the "fish market's time-honored cadence" *(uogashi no kōrei no ondo).* In unison, the traders join in three clusters of three evenly spaced, sharp claps, followed by a slight pause and then a single, much louder, final clap:

clap-clap-clap, clap-clap-clap, clap-clap-clap, CLAP

As the cold dawn air cracks with the sound, television cameras record the ritual and the following first auction of the year; the ipponjime of the tuna traders and similar rituals held on the floor of the Tokyo Stock Exchange are staples of holiday coverage by Tokyo's television stations, marking the New Year for professionals and the general public alike and animating the social cohesion of the bounded community of trade.

The clapping ritual is familiar throughout Tokyo's shitamachi mercantile culture, a social ceremony through which all parties to a ritual or to a transaction signal their unanimity. But elsewhere the sequence is performed three times *(sanbonjime,* literally "triple closure"); the distinctive feature of Tsukiji's version is that the sequence is performed only once *(ipponjime,* "single closure").[4] A minor distinction, to be sure, but emblematic of the marketplace as a distinctive social world. As with the wordplay common in mercantile life—the complicated interplay between written, graphic, and spoken representations of *yagō* (shop names), market slang, and counting

kyu (nine)   shime (closure)   maru (full circle)

Figure 68. Closing the circle.

codes that abound at Tsukiji—this sequence of rhythmic clapping juxta-
poses double readings of forms and meanings, of numerological and orthographic symbolism.

Three clusters of triple claps total nine *(kyū)*. The final clap represents
closure, *shime* (or *jime)*, written in commercial shorthand as a slanting tick
to indicate that a bill has been totaled or that an invoice is complete. When
shime is superimposed on the character for nine, together they form *maru,*
the ubiquitous floating signifier of the seafood trade. The common meanings of *maru* include fullness, totality, completion, circle, and cycle.

Tsukiji's *ipponjime* concludes the holiday season; the endings of O-kure
have given way to the beginnings of the New Year. Transactions are complete, a circle is closed, and another cycle commences.

And then Tsukiji's traders get back to work, their mundane work of buying and selling, of feeding the city, of making and remaking a market every
dawn.

Visiting Tsukiji

Anthropologists rarely write about the sites of their field research with the intention of guiding tourists to them. But Tsukiji has long been a destination for foreign visitors to Tokyo; it is certainly among the most spectacular sights (and sites) in a city that often strikes first-time visitors as vast, formless, and without many obvious "attractions." Tsukiji is a genuine attraction that does nothing to promote itself as such. Anthropologists and tourists alike worry about authenticity; Tsukiji is the real thing.

Although the marketplace is not set up for casual tourists, it is remarkably open. The entrances to the marketplace have large signs in Japanese that announce "for wholesale transactions only"; these deter many ordinary Tokyoites from entering, but each year thousands of foreign visitors brave the crush of traffic and thread their way through fast-moving carts, joining the daily to-and-fro of fishmongers and restaurateurs. Longtime expatriates recommend it to newcomers; visiting chefs and gourmets consider it a must; many tourist guides to Tokyo—at least the hip, adventurous ones—include Tsukiji; there are even a few commercial tours that pick people up at major hotels for early morning guided visits.

My friends at Tsukiji often ask me why so many foreign tourists visit the place. I point out that Tsukiji is famous throughout the world and that many foreigners are interested in sushi and Japanese cuisine, and therefore find the fish market fascinating. No place other than Tsukiji has so many varieties of seafood regularly on display. My punch line is jet lag: where else will they go when they wake up at 3 A.M.?

My Tsukiji friends are amused at the pragmatism of tourists who fill even the early morning with sightseeing, but they appreciate even more that Tsukiji is a unique destination.

PRONUNCIATION

Many foreigners stumble over the name "Tsukiji." It roughly rhymes with "squeegee, " but without emphasis on any syllable.

EATING, OF COURSE

This simple guide does *not* list my favorite sushi bars, not to protect my secret spots but because I do not want to repay many kind hosts with invidious comparisons. Tsukiji is a great place to eat and you can hardly go wrong in any local establishment—after all, many of their customers are food professionals, so they have to be good! The range of restaurants within the marketplace includes sushi bars, tempura restaurants, grills (featuring fish and meat), noodle stalls, curry restaurants, and at least one Italian café. The outer market includes many more restaurants across a similar culinary spectrum. (Many Tsukiji restaurants these days have menus or pamphlets in various European and Asian languages.) The outer marketplace also has quite a few coffee shops *(kissaten)*, good places to rest and get your bearings before heading on to other destinations.

Restaurants in the inner market specialize in the morning trade (some open at 2 A.M. and most close by 1 or 2 in the afternoon). Those in the outer market follow more ordinary cycles and are open for lunch and dinner, including evening snacks and drinks. Real night owls should look for a few places—most of them not sushi restaurants—around the market that cater to the timetables of long-distance truckers; they are easily recognized by the illuminated rigs parked outside.

If in doubt, make your choice according to the welcome you get when you poke your head into a restaurant's doorway. In fifteen years of visiting Tsukiji regularly, I have had only one truly bad meal, and it was in a place that failed the friendliness test.

WHEN IS THE MARKET OPEN?

The marketplace operates approximately 280 days a year and generally is open six days a week, Monday through Saturday. It is closed on Sundays, on Japanese national holidays, for a five-day period around New Year's, and for several days in mid-August for the Japanese holiday of O-Bon. The market is also generally closed on the second and fourth Wednesday of each month to give market workers an extra day off, but these midweek holidays may vary in months when there are several national holidays. The entire annual schedule of market closings is announced the previous year. If you are planning a visit (and speak Japanese), you can check if the market will be open by calling the market administration offices ahead of time (03–3542–1111); the year's calendar is also posted as the fourth item within the second category (*gyōsei jōhō*, administrative information) on the market's Japanese-language homepage (www.shijou.metro.tokyo.jp).

Auctions in Tsukiji's seafood division generally start around 5:30 A.M. and are over by 6:30 A.M. Starting times vary from season to season (later in winter, earlier in summer—Japan does not observe daylight savings time in summer), and from commodity to commodity. Auctions in the fruit and vegetable division start later, around 7:00 A.M. Goods for sale are put on display throughout the night, and wholesalers begin to inspect the day's offerings from about 4:30 A.M. Stalls inside the marketplace wind down the day's business between 10 and 11 A.M.

The outer marketplace is active until early afternoon, but is liveliest in midmorning. Saturdays are the most crowded, when many ordinary Tokyoites shop there. When the marketplace is closed, most of the businesses in the outer marketplace are closed as well and the area is like a ghost town.

WHAT TO SEE?

A satisfying visit to Tsukiji will require at least a couple of hours, and if you want at least a glimpse of the auctions, you should plan to be at the marketplace by 5:30 or 6:00 A.M. at the latest; you can break for a sushi or tempura breakfast before strolling through the outer market's stalls. (If you are interested mainly in the outer market and its mixture of seafood and other culinary shops, then you can arrive in midmorning and stay through lunch.)

At the guard boxes at the marketplace's three major gates—the Seimon (the main gate) on the western side of the marketplace just across from the headquarters building of the *Asahi* newspaper, the entrance to the market closest to the Tsukiji Shijō Station on the Ō-Edo subway line; the Kaikōbashi (the Kaikō Bridge) entrance, on the northern side of the marketplace across the bridge from the Namiyoke Shrine; and the Kachidoki entrance, at the northernmost edge of the marketplace where Harumi-dōri (Harumi Avenue) crosses the Sumida River over the Kachidoki Bridge—visitors can usually get an English-language pamphlet about the marketplace published by the TMG market administrators and a map of the marketplace that shows the locations and times for auctions at that season.

If the pamphlet and map are not available, simply head toward the Sumida River, to the east, where the auctions for tuna are held, and work your way back through the market's stalls.

My recommended itinerary begins at the river's edge where the frozen tuna are sold and turns slightly inland to the open sheds where the fresh tuna are auctioned. Then, walk through the curving sheds where the intermediate wholesalers have their stalls: walk down several different aisles to get the full impact of the variety and scale of the marketplace. From the stalls, head to the row of numbered buildings beyond the loading docks; most of the restaurants inside the marketplace are located on the ground floors of these office buildings. Afterward, leave the inner marketplace via the Kaikōbashi exit (crossing a bridge over a now filled-in canal) and visit the Namiyoke Shrine on the right. From the shrine, walk down the street perpendicular to its gate for two or three blocks and turn right into one of the main passages into the outer marketplace.

A few general tips for a safe and successful visit:

·   Watch out for carts! Tsukiji's drivers and porters are remarkably tolerant of the unwary, but it is still your responsibility to be aware of traffic around you and to be ready to leap out of the way of the people who work at the marketplace.

·   Taking pictures is quite all right, with one important caveat: flash photography around the auctions themselves is prohibited, because the flash can momentarily blind an auctioneer to the bidding. This is one of the few market regulations that is prominently posted in English, and recently the point has been announced by loudspeaker in English before the auctions begin.

·   Do not block traffic in the aisles or in front of stalls while taking photographs or pausing to take your bearings; if you stop, try to tuck yourself into a corner or niche so that you don't hamper the flow of traffic.

·   Do not carry much with you. The aisles at Tsukiji are narrow and crowded with busy people. Backpacks, large handbags, and elaborate camera bags will get in other people's way and make it awkward for you to maneuver.

·   If you are coming to the marketplace with a large number of people, do not go through the inner market together: break into groups of three or four. The narrow aisles and the constant traffic make any group an impediment to the people who work there.

- Tsukiji is a working marketplace full of water, ice, and fish in the midst of being processed. Wear casual clothes that can be washed. The marketplace isn't dirty but it can be messy and you may get splattered. Wear long pants and solid shoes with good nonskid soles, not sandals or open-toed shoes. Puddles are everywhere!

- Do not touch or pick up seafood on display.

- Unless someone offers you a taste, do not sample seafood on display.

- Do not bring children. This is an environment with sharp edges, slippery surfaces, forklifts and motorized delivery carts, and the hustle and bustle of tens of thousands of hardworking people.

- In the inner market, stalls do not generally sell seafood in small amounts, and bargaining is not part of the market culture. In the outer market, small purchases are common, but haggling is not the norm (although merchants may spontaneously "throw in" a small amount or round the price down to a convenient figure). Aggressive bargaining is not part of the scene.

OTHER SITES IN THE VICINITY

The area around the marketplace includes several interesting possibilities for walks.

Just north of the outer market is the Tsukiji Hongan-ji temple. Its main hall is open to visitors. At the north edge of the parking lot, a row of old monuments includes one to the memory of Mori Magoemon, the fisher who accompanied Ieyasu to Edo in 1590 and founded the settlement on Tsukudajima (see chapter 3).

The streets behind Hongan-ji (to the east and north) are still slightly residential, and a few old houses give a sense of what mercantile Tokyo looked like in the early twentieth century.

From Kachidoki Bridge, a promenade extends up the western bank of the Sumida River. The modern glass skyscraper of St. Luke's Hospital has a riverfront plaza up a few steps from the promenade. A few carved stones—an American eagle and a shield of the Union—from the original building of the nineteenth-century American Legation are on display in this plaza, almost the only visible remnants of the Tsukiji Foreign Settlement. The St. Luke's tower has an observation deck and a restaurant on its uppermost floors that are open to the public. They offer spectacular views of central Tokyo (and of course of the Tsukiji marketplace). On the inland side of St. Luke's tower, a small park includes a monument commemorating Sugita

Genpaku, the eighteenth-century scholar of Dutch who pioneered the study of anatomy based on Western treatises, on this, the site of Japan's first autopsy.

On the opposite side of the Sumida, a walk through the back streets of Tsukishima provides a glimpse of an old-fashioned Tokyo neighborhood. And further north is the tiny neighborhood of Tsukuda, site of the original fishers' settlement, and the Sumiyoshi Shrine.

South of the marketplace is the Hama Rikyū, the Hama Detached Palace, now a park open to the public. It and a similar public park a bit further south, next to Hamamatsu-chō Station, are the only surviving examples of the estates that lined the banks of the Sumida River during the Tokugawa period.

GETTING THERE

On Foot

The Tsukiji marketplace is within walking distance of major hotels in the Ginza, Hibiya, and Higashi Ginza districts of central Tokyo. No matter where you are staying, your hotel's front desk or concierge can suggest the best means of transportation and provide you with a map.

In general, the easiest way to reach the Tsukiji marketplace on foot is to head east along Harumi-dōri (which extends roughly east-west through central Tokyo, one axis of the major Ginza intersection). The intersection of Harumi-dōri and Shin-Ōhashi-dōri, just south of the huge Hongan-ji temple, marks the northeast corner of the outer market. Anytime during the morning, the flow of pedestrian traffic from that intersection will point you unmistakably toward the market.

By Taxi

Taxi is the best way to get to Tsukiji early in the morning, before Tokyo's public transportation system begins running in earnest (around 5:30 A.M.). Tsukiji is the name of an entire neighborhood, not just the market. If you ask to be taken to Tsukiji, the driver will almost certainly understand you want to go to the marketplace; but to be absolutely certain, ask to be taken to "Tsukiji ichiba no seimon" ("the main gate of the Tsukiji market"), which is directly across the street from the headquarters of the *Asahi* newspaper ("Asahi Shimbun no mae"). If you are leaving Tsukiji and want to find a taxi, there is a taxi stand at the main gate (Seimon), though you may have to wait a few minutes for one to appear.

By Subway

Four subway lines—the Ō-Edo and Asakusa Lines of the Toei subway system and the Hibiya and Yurakuchō Lines of the Eidan subway system—
have stations within easy walking distance of the Tsukiji marketplace.
Because the Tokyo subways generally start around 5:00 or 5:30 A.M. in most
parts of the city, if you want to arrive at Tsukiji before the auctions begin a
subway is not your best bet.

The closest station is Tsukiji Shijō (Tsukiji Market) on the Ō-Edo Line of
the Toei subway system. The eastern exits of this station lead directly to the
main gate (Seimon) of the marketplace, across from the office building of
the *Asahi* newspaper.

Almost as convenient is the Tsukiji Station on the Hibiya Line (part of
the Eidan subway system). The station's exits are in front of the Hongan-ji
temple, just north of the outer market. Walk south one block along Shin-
Ōhashi-dōri to the intersection with Harumi-dōri. The outer marketplace
occupies the southeastern corner of this intersection, and further south on
the eastern side of Shin-Ōhashi-dōri is the Tsukiji marketplace.

Slightly further away is the Higashi Ginza Station served both by the
Hibiya Line and by the Asakusa Line (of the Toei subway system), which
intersect at this station. Several exits come out in front of the Kabuki-za
(Tokyo's major kabuki theater) on Harumi-dōri. Walk three blocks, less than
five minutes, east from the Kabuki-za to get to the intersection of Harumi-
dōri and Shin-Ōhashi-dōri.

The Yurakuchō Line (Eidan system) serves Shintomi-chō Station, which
is the furthest local station from the marketplace, located about ten blocks
north of Honganji. From the eastern exits of Shintomi-chō Station, walk
east to Shin-Ōhashi-dōri, and then turn south. You will walk past Hongan-
ji (on your left) on your way to the intersection of Shin-Ōhashi-dōri and
Harumi-dōri mentioned above.

By Rail

The closest railroad station is Shinbashi Station on the JR Yamanote Line
(Shinbashi is also a stop on several other JR commuter and intercity lines,
as well as on the Ginza Line of the Eidan subway, and is the terminus of the
Yuri Kamome monorail system that extends out to newly developed artificial islands in Tokyo Bay). Shinbashi Station is west of the marketplace,
about a twenty-minute walk.

If you are coming from Shinbashi Station, the municipal bus system
runs a shuttle from its eastern plaza to the center of the marketplace; the bus

is labeled (in Japanese) *Ichi Ichi* (Market 1). During the peak morning hours, the bus is crowded with Tsukiji traders and buyers; you can probably figure out which bus it is just by looking for the line of passengers wearing rubber boots and toting wicker baskets to carry home their purchases for the day.

The other railway option is to take the JR to Yurakuchō Station (the next station north of Shinbashi), where you can transfer to the Hibiya subway line; on the Hibiya Line, Tsukiji Station is the third from Yurakuchō Station. Tsukiji is about a twenty-minute walk from Yurakuchō Station, straight along Harumi-dōri through the heart of the Ginza district.

Video, Web, and Statistical Resources

VIDEOS ABOUT TSUKIJI

The Tsukiji marketplace is an inherently colorful and vivid place, and several excellent video documentaries capture its visual appeal.

Full Moon Lunch is a classic documentary of Tokyo life, produced and directed by John Nathan (1976); it focuses on a family-owned shop that produces box lunches (the *mangetsu bentō* or "full moon lunch" of the title) for Buddhist temples in a *shitamachi* neighborhood. Several scenes show the master chef shopping at Tsukiji; his cynical comments put Tsukiji into the larger context of mercantile culture. The video version of *Full Moon Lunch*, which runs about an hour, is distributed through the Asian Educational Media Service of the University of Illinois at Urbana-Champaign (homepage at www.aems.uiuc.edu/index.las).

Peregrine Beckman's documentary video *Fish Is Our Life!* (1994) focuses on the people who work at Tsukiji, through interviews with auctioneers and stall keepers. The 28-minute video is distributed by the University of California Extension Center for Media and Independent Learning (homepage at http://ucmedia.berkeley.edu).

"Giant Bluefin Tuna" (National Geographic 2001), a documentary originally broadcast on MSNBC's National Geographic *Explorer* on May 4, 2001, follows the international tuna trade from fishing vessels and docks in New England to the auctions at Tsukiji.

WEBSITES ABOUT TSUKIJI AND FISHERIES ISSUES

Many websites sponsored by Japanese organizations and agencies provide information about fisheries, foodstuffs, and the operations of the Tsukiji marketplace. The websites below, which were all active as of January 2004, are listed by the name of the organization (or website title). English versions of these websites often include less detailed information than the Japanese versions, and are less frequently updated. Some of the information on English websites is presented only in Japanese.

Governmental Agencies and Other Organizations

AFFRC (Agriculture, Forestry and Fisheries Research Council)—
Nōrinsui Gijitsu Kaigi
  in English: www.affrc.go.jp
  in Japanese: www.affrc.go.jp/index-j.html

JF-Net (website maintained by the National Federation of Fisheries Cooperative Associations)
  in Japanese: www.jf-net.ne.jp

Ministry of Agriculture, Forestry and Fisheries
  in English: www.maff.go.jp/eindex.html
  in Japanese: www.maff.go.jp

Tokyo Metropolitan Government, Central Wholesale Market
  in Japanese: www.shijou.metro.tokyo.jp

Tsukiji Jōgai Shijō (Tsukiji Outer Market)
  in Japanese: www.tsukiji.or.jp

Za Tsukiji Shijō (The Tsukiji Market)
  in English: www.tsukiji-market.or.jp/tukiji_e.htm
  in Japanese: www.tsukiji-market.or.jp

Tsukiji Auction Houses

Chiyoda Suisan K.K.
  in Japanese: www.marusen.co.jp

Chūō Gyorui K.K.
  in English: www.marunaka-net.co.jp/maruna_e/index.htm
  in Japanese: www.marunaka-net.co.jp

Daiichi Suisan, K.K.
  in English: www.daiichisuisan.co.jp/emain.html
  in Japanese: www.daiichisuisan.co.jp

Daito Gyorui, K.K.
  in English: www.daitogyorui.co.jp/indexe.htm
  in Japanese: www.daitogyorui.co.jp/indexe.htm

Tōto Suisan, K.K.
   in English: http://edi.tohsui.co.jp/Web/index_e.html
   in Japanese http://edi.tohsui.co.jp

Tsukiji Uoichiba K.K.
   in Japanese: www.tsukiji-uoichiba.co.jp

The websites sponsored by auction houses include a great deal of informa-tion about market trends in general, as well as the internal operations of the companies, the commodities they handle, and current market prices. How-ever, their websites are not always up-to-date, and they often use idiosyn-cratic translations of Japanese language market terms.

Although not specifically focused on the Tsukiji market, a great deal of economic information about the global fishing industry, including Japanese seafood markets and prices, is available from "Fish Information & Services" (www.fis.com).

Other websites provide information about the global conservation of marine resources, including the impact of Japanese markets for seafood on various fisheries around the world. The National Audubon Society maintains a website with extensive links to other sources of information ("National Audubon Society Living Oceans Program," www.audubon.org/campaign/lo).

TRAFFIC, jointly sponsored by WWF–World Wide Fund for Nature and IUCN–The World Conservation Union, monitors the international trade in endangered species—including many oceanic species—that are considered to be at risk of overexploitation or habitat degradation (see "Welcome to the TRAFFIC Network," www.traffic.org).

My own website for research on Tsukiji and related topics is www.people .fas.harvard.edu/~bestor/tsukiji.htm. This site includes additional photo-graphs, articles, news stories about Tsukiji and Japanese food culture, and updated links to other sources of information about the marketplace, Tokyo, and the larger world of Japanese seafood.

STATISTICAL SOURCES

Major sources of statistical data (published annually) relevant to this research include the following (each title is followed by the name of the organization that compiles and publishes it):

Gaishoku sangyō tōkei shiryō-shū (Collection of Statistical Material on the Restaurant Industry)—Gaishoku Sangyō Sōgō Chōsa Kenkyū Sentaa

Japan Statistical Yearbook—Nihon Tōkei Kyōkai

Shijō memo (Market Memo)—Tōkyō-to Chūō Oroshiuri Shijō

Shoku seikatsu deeta sōgō tōkei nenpō (Yearbook of General Food Consumption Statistics)—Shokuhin Ryūtsū Jōhō Sentaa

Suisan nenkan (Fisheries Yearbook)—Suisansha

Suisan tōkei (Fisheries Statistics)—Nōrinsuisanshō (Ministry of Agriculture, Forestry and Fisheries)

Tōkyō-to Chūō Oroshiuri Shijō gaiyō (Tokyo Central Wholesale Market Overview)—Tōkyō-to Chūō Oroshiuri Shijō

Tsukiji Shijō gaiyō (Tsukiji Market Overview)—Tōkyō-to Chūō Oroshiuri Shijō Tsukiji Shijō

Several of the websites mentioned above—particularly those maintained by Tōkyō-to Chūō Oroshiuri Shijō; the Ministry of Agriculture, Forestry and Fisheries; and the various auction houses at Tsukiji—contain a great deal of current statistical data on market activities.

The United States Department of Commerce, which administers American fisheries policy, issues many detailed reports on Japanese fishing and markets for selected seafood products (e.g., Asakawa 1997; Sonu 1993, 1994, 1995, 1996, 1997, 1998). These contain statistics on current market trends as well as on the structure of distribution channels and consumer demand.

Glossary

*Indicates a commodity category around which a customary trade group *(moyori gyōkai)* is organized at Tsukiji.

agari	a cup of tea (sushi slang)
*aimono	semiprocessed (dried, salted, smoked) seafood, often prepackaged
aitai-uri	sales through face-to-face negotiation or private agreement (compare *seri-uri*)
aji	horse mackerel, saurel
akagai	red clams
amadai	tilefish, sea bream
amimoto	fishing bosses, "net masters"
ankō	monkfish, angler fish
asaichi	morning market
awabi	abalone
ayu	sweetfish
baburu keizai	the "Bubble Economy" of the 1980s
baibaisankasha	"authorized traders" licensed to purchase at Tsukiji's auctions
baisan	see *baibaisankasha*
bantō	head clerk
budomari	yield; the proportion of seafood left after a fish has been gutted, boned, and trimmed into appropriate, salable portions
buri	yellowtail, amberjack

chaya	literally, "teahouses"; the loading docks (and the people who run them) where buyers have their daily purchases sent and watched over until they are ready to pick up them up; administratively known as *kainihokansho* (merchandise custodial places) (see *shiomachijaya*)
chihō oroshiuri shijō	regional wholesale markets; regulated as part of the national framework of markets, regional wholesale markets include "production region" markets, many of which are operated by local fisheries cooperatives, and "consumption region" markets (see also *sanchi* and *shōhichi*)
chikuyō	aquaculture of wild fish raised in captivity (compare *tennen* and *yōshoku*)
chirashi-zushi	a sushi dish of fish and vegetables over a bowl of rice
chōba	cashier's booth in a Tsukiji stall
chūō oroshiuri shijō	central wholesale markets; established in major urban centers by national and local governments to supply fresh seafood, meat, and produce
Chūō Oroshiuri Shijō-Hō	Central Wholesale Market Law
dangō	a price-fixing agreement
danna	a master of a shop
detchi	a shop apprentice
detchibōkō	long-term, live-in apprenticeship
dojō	loach
Doyō no ushi no hi	the "Day of the Ox," the occasion to eat eel to maintain one's stamina against the withering heat of midsummer
ebi	shrimp
Edo	the pre-1868 name of what is now Tokyo
Edokko	natives of *shitamachi*; literally, "children of Edo"
Edomae cuisine	"in front of Edo" cuisine; specialties made from seafood (supposedly) caught in Tokyo Bay; Tokyo-style sushi; *nigiri-zushi,* sometimes called *Edomae-zushi*
enkaimono	fresh fish from Japanese coastal waters distant from Tokyo, used primarily for sushi and seasonal cuisine
enkangyo	salted and dried seafood, including *niboshi* (dried sardines) and *surume* (dried squid)

*enyōmono	pelagic fish
fuchō	codes used for confidential pricing
fugu	blowfish, globefish, puffer
funa	crucian carp, freshwater carp from Lake Biwa
funa-zushi	sushi prepared with fermented fish and rice; a regional specialty of Shiga Prefecture, reminiscent of the oldest styles of sushi (compare *nigiri-zushi*)
furiitaa	"freeters" or "free-timers," young people who are not interested in long-term employment and who work on a semi-casual basis, moving frequently from one job to another
gaishoku	eating outside the home (a major market segment for the food industry)
gari	pickled ginger (sushi slang)
gashi	see *uogashi*
goyō ichiba	a marketplace "by appointment to the court"
gyogyōken	sea tenure rights to particular fishing grounds exercised collectively by fisheries cooperatives
gyogyō kyōdō kumiai	fisheries cooperative associations
gyōkai	see *moyori gyōkai*
haitatsunin	delivery workers at Tsukiji
hamachi	yellowtail
hamadai	snapper
hamaguri	clams
hamane	"beach price" paid to a producer; the ex vessel price
hatsugatsuo	the first bonito of the season
hatsumono	first products of a season
hatsuni	"first shipments," the first products of the season to arrive at auction
hatsuryō	first catch of a season
hikarimono	"shiny things," silver-scaled fish
himono	dried, smoked, and salted seafood
hirame	flounder, sole
hōjin	a legal entity, a corporation (see *kabushiki gaisha* and *yūgen gaisha*; compare *kojin*)
*hokuyōmono	"North Pacific things," salmon, salmon roe, crab, and other seafood from Hokkaidō
hon-maguro	"real tuna"—northern bluefin tuna (see *maguro*)

i, ro, ha, ni	a customary sequencing device, analogous to "A, B, C, D"
ichiba	market, marketplace (colloquial term) (compare *shijō*)
ika	squid
iki	the flamboyant aesthetic style of Edo's and Tokyo's *shitamachi* subculture
ikura	salmon roe
Indo maguro	southern bluefin tuna (Indian Ocean tuna) (see *maguro*)
ipponjime	a traditional round of rhythmic clapping that marks the conclusion *(shime* or *jime)* of a meeting, a ritual, or a transaction
*Ise ebi	Pacific spiny lobster
itafuneken	"board rights," rights to operate as an open-air dealer in the Nihonbashi fish market
itaku (itaku hanbai)	consignment (consignment sales) through Tsukiji's auction houses (compare *kaitsuke*)
itamae-san	a sushi chef
iwashi	sardine, anchovy
jan-ken	child's hand game of rock-paper-scissors, used to break ties in auctions
jōgai ryūtsū	distribution "outside the market," that is, distribution channels that do not pass through the central wholesale market system (compare *jōnai ryūtsū*)
jōgai shijō	literally, the "outer market." At Tsukiji this has two meanings. Specifically, the term refers to the outer marketplace, just to the north of the licensed inner market, which has a large retail sector. More generally, it can refer to trade channels outside the licensed wholesale market system and its auctions (compare *jōnai shijō*).
jōmono	top-quality seafood, for the restaurant trade
jōnai ryūtsū	distribution channels that pass through the central wholesale market system, especially through the Tsukiji auction system (compare *jōgai ryūtsū*)
jōnai shijō	literally, the "inner market," the official central wholesale market (compare *jōgai shijō*)
kabayaki	a style of preparing grilled eel
kabushiki gaisha	an incorporated, joint-stock company (abbreviated as K.K.) (see *hōjin*)

kaidashi	to purchase wholesale, to lay in stock
kaidashinin	a purchaser, a chef or fishmonger
kainihokansho	"merchandise custodial places," loading docks (see *chaya*)
kaiten-zushi	"rotary sushi," sushi served on a conveyer belt
kaitsuke	purchasing products for resale on an auction house's own account, rather than accepting goods on consignment (compare *itaku*)
kajiki	swordfish
kamaboko	fish pâté
kani	crab
kansatsu	the license of a *nakaoroshi gyōsha*
karei	flounder, sole
kashi	see *uogashi*
kata	form or shape; the outward appearance of a product (and its packaging); the form and style of a person's activity, such as a chef's perfected technique with a carving knife
katsugyo	live fish (sold alive)
katsuo	bonito, skipjack
katsuobushi	dried bonito flakes, a staple of Japanese cooking
kazunoko	herring roe
keiretsu	vertically integrated groups of firms
kigō	the registered name of a shop or company (see also *yagō*)
kihada (kiwada)	yellowfin tuna
kinkaimono	fresh fish from coastal waters near Tokyo, used primarily for sushi and seasonal cuisine
koage	unloading and arranging seafood for auctions
kohada	shad (also known as *konoshiro*)
koi	carp
kojin	an unincorporated individual proprietorship; a legal category of business organization (compare *hōjin*)
kouri	retail sales
kujira	whale
kurodai	black sea bream
kuromaguro	"black tuna," northern bluefin tuna (see *maguro*)
MAFF	the Ministry of Agriculture, Forestry and Fisheries; Nōrinsuisanshō

maguro	tuna (varieties include *hon-maguro, Indo maguro, kihada/kiwada, kuromaguro, mebachi, meji,* and *minami maguro*)
maru	circle, cycle, completion; suffix for the name of a vessel; round or whole (as in "round fish")
masu	trout
mebachi	big-eye tuna (see *maguro*)
meibutsu	famous local products, often foodstuffs
meisan	famous local products, often foodstuffs
meji	juvenile northern bluefin tuna (see *maguro*)
mikoshi	Shintō portable shrine
minami maguro	southern bluefin tuna (see *maguro*)
moyori gyōkai	"customary trade groups"of Tsukiji, intermediate wholesalers organized around commodity specializations
murasaki	soy sauce (sushi slang)
nabemono	seafood stew, bouillabaisse
nagamono	"long things," swordfish
nakagai or *nakagainin*	"middle traders," intermediate wholesalers or brokers; an old-fashioned term no longer used at Tsukiji, but still used in some other markets (compare *nakaoroshi gyōsha*)
nakaoroshi gyōsha	intermediate wholesalers, sometimes called secondary wholesalers or middlemen; at Tsukiji *nakaoroshi gyōsha* are licensed by market administrators and can purchase goods at auction and resell them in market stalls; *nakaoroshi gyōsha* is the official designation used in the central wholesale market system
namazu	catfish
neko	"cats," long, narrow, two-wheeled barrows
*neriseihin	fish paste and fish pâté products, including *kamaboko* and *surumi*
neta	market slang for sushi toppings (see *tane* and *sushidane*)
niboshi	dried sardines
nigiri-zushi	"squeezed" or "hand-molded" sushi, the standard Edo/Tokyo style of sushi (also known as *Edomae-zushi*)
Nihonbashi uogashi	the fish market at Nihonbashi
nimotsu	goods sent to market on consignment

ninushi	the consignor of goods to a market (a producer, a broker, or some other intermediary)
nishin	herring
niuke	the consignee for goods sent to auction
niuke gaisha	a company that acts as consignee, a Tsukiji auction house *(oroshi gyōsha)*
noren	curtainlike sign bearing a shop's trade name
norenwake	"dividing the curtain"; establishing a child or apprentice in a branch shop
Nōrinshō	abbreviation of Nōrinsuisanshō
Nōrinsuisanshō	Ministry of Agriculture, Forestry and Fisheries, which is responsible for regulating the fishing industry as well as licensing and supervising the operations of central wholesale markets
nyūka	incoming goods on consignment
nyūsatsu (nyūsatsu-uri)	a written bid (an auction conducted with written, secret bids; compare with *seri*)
o-bentō	box lunches
okonomiyaki	an omelet or frittata of eggs, vegetables, and meat or seafood, prepared on a griddle to one's own tastes
*ōmono	"big things," usually refers to tuna but may also include swordfish
oroshi gyōsha	literally, "wholesale dealer," sometimes translated as "primary wholesaler"; the licensed auction houses at Tsukiji (see also *niuke gaisha*)
oroshi-uri	wholesale sales
orosu	to sell at wholesale
o-sechi (o-sechi ryōri)	New Year's cuisine
reitōhin	frozen products
ryōtei	formal Japanese-style restaurant
saba	Pacific mackerel
sake (shake)	salmon
sakidori	"taking beforehand," taking merchandise away from auction site before sales begin and paying price set by competitors
*samé	shark
sanchi	production region; markets in fishing ports (compare *shōhichi*)
sanma	saury

sashine	a stop order, a designated minimum auction price (rarely used in fresh fish auctions)
sawara	Spanish mackerel
seikamono	fresh produce (fruits and vegetables)
seisansha	producer
sekku or *gosekku*	traditional dividing points between seasons, marked by customary foods
senjafudagaku	congratulatory plaques donated by a shopkeeper's friends and supporters
seri	auction, specifically with open bidding by voice or gesture (compare *nyūsatsu*)
seribō	a cap with an auction license clipped to it
serinin	licensed auctioneers
seri-uri	competitive sales through auctions (compare *aitai-uri*)
sharé	banter, wordplay, puns
shari	rice (sushi slang)
shiire	laying in stock, purchases
shiiresaki	a supplier
shijō	a market, in economic and legal terms (compare *ichiba*)
shiomachijaya	literally, "teahouses for awaiting the tides"; shops and inns in the Nihonbashi market that acted as freight agents for buyers and sellers (see *chaya*)
shirauo	whitebait, icefish
shitamachi	the subculture and neighborhoods of Edo's and Tokyo's mercantile "Low City"
shitami	buyers' inspection before auction
shōhichi	consumption region; markets in consuming rather than producing regions (compare *sanchi*)
shoku bunka	food culture
shoku seikatsu	culinary life
shokunin	artisan, journeyman worker
shujin	the master or head of a shop (or a family)
shūka	shipper, freight forwarder, consolidator
shun	season or seasonality; freshness; originally, one-third of a lunar month
sōgō shōsha	general trading companies, often affiliated with major Japanese conglomerates *(keiretsu),* which specialize in foreign trade ventures

suisan-bu	the seafood division of the Tsukiji market
suisanbutsu	marine products, seafood
surimi	fish paste, often sold as imitation crab made from white fish such as Alaskan pollack
surume	dried squid
sushidane	sushi toppings; the types of seafood that sushi chefs purchase, also known as *tokushumono* (see also *tane* and *neta*)
sushiya	sushi shop
suzuki	sea bass
tai	sea bream (also known as *madai*)
*tako	octopus
takohiki	the style of knife favored by sushi chefs in Osaka (compare *yanagiba*)
tane	literally, "seed" or "source"; sushi toppings (see *sushidane* and *neta*)
*tansuigyo	freshwater fish, including eel
tara	cod, pollack
tarako	cod roe
tāretto	"turrets," three-wheeled flatbed carts that swivel on the front motor "turret"
tegurimono	literally, "net-hauled things"; trawl catches of fish such as mackerel, sardines, or saury
tennen	natural species harvested in the wild, as in "free-range" fish, not cultivated (aquacultural) products (compare *chikuyō* and *yōshoku*)
tenpo	a shop, specifically a stall at Tsukiji
tesūryō	a commission
teyari	finger signals used in auction bidding
TMG	Tokyo Metropolitan Government, Tōkyō-to
tobiuo	flying fish
*tokushumono	top-grade fish for the restaurant trade, especially sushi toppings (*sushidane*)
Tōkyō-to	Tokyo Metropolitan Government, TMG
ton'ya	a wholesaler (in trade sectors outside the central wholesale market system)
Tō-Oroshi	Tōkyō Uoichiba Oroshi Kyōdō Kumiai—the Tokyo Fishmarket Wholesalers' Cooperative Federation
torihiki	transaction

torihikisaki	transactional partner
toro	fat tuna belly
*tsukudani	seafood and vegetables boiled in thick soy sauce
ukiyo	Edo's "floating world" of pleasure and sensuality
unagi	eel
uni	sea urchin roe
uogashi	the "fish wharf," "fish quay,"or "fish market"; an old-fashioned term for the marketplace
uoichiba	fish market
wakadanna	"young master," the heir or successor to a family-owned business
wa-shoku	cuisine and foodstuffs regarded as "traditionally" Japanese (compare *yō-shoku*)
-ya	this suffix converts a commodity *(cha,* tea; *maguro,* tuna) into a place of business (*chaya,* teahouse or tea shop; *maguroya,* a tuna shop), and the resulting term can be applied to the business or to its proprietor and people in the trade
yagō	shop name or trade symbol (see also *kigō*)
yake	"burn," damage to tuna caused by enormous buildup of body heat of the fish and improper chilling by fishers
yamai	"sickness," a whitish cloudiness that sometimes appears in the flesh of tuna
yanagiba	literally, "willow leaf"; a style of long tapered knife for slicing sashimi, characteristic of Tokyo's style of cutlery (compare *takohiki*)
yatchaba	colloquial term for the produce division of the marketplace
yoseba	labor markets for day laborers
yō-shoku	"Western" cuisine or foodstuffs (compare *wa-shoku*)
yōshoku	cultivated species, raised through aquaculture, bred in captivity (compare *chikuyō* and *tennen*)
yūgen or *yūgen gaisha*	a limited liability company (see *hōjin*)

Notes

1. *Shitamachi* (literally, "the low city") is the part of central Tokyo that traces its social ancestry—real or imagined—to the merchant neighborhoods of the preindustrial city. R. J. Smith (1960), Seidensticker (1983), T. Bestor (1989, 1990, 1992b), and Kondo (1990) offer accounts of shitamachi's history, the social meanings of shitamachi identity, and the recent shitamachi revival, an aspect of the nostalgic rediscovery of Japanese "tradition" (see also Kelly 1986, 1990; Robertson 1991; Ivy 1995).

2. The suffix -*ya,* meaning "shop" or "house," converts a commodity into a line of business: "sushi" into "sushi shop" *(sushiya);* "tuna" *(maguro)* into "tuna dealer" *(maguroya).* The resulting term can refer generically to a store or company, or to the occupation of its proprietor, in which case the additional suffix -*san* is often added: Sushiya-san is Mr. Sushi Chef, Maguroya-san is Mr. (or Ms.) Tuna Dealer. The suffix -*ya* also converts personal or geographic names into shop names. Thus, for example, the Tanaka family's shop might be known as Tanakaya, while the Kawamura family, hailing from the old province of Shinshū, might call their business Shinshūya.

3. The puzzle and its solution depend on a visual pun more cumbersome to explain than to accomplish. The character for autumn *(aki)* is written with nine strokes, arranged in two side-by-side clusters, one written with five strokes and the other with four; the latter, when used as an independent character, means "fire." The solution, therefore, is simple: lay out five unbroken matches to form the first cluster, then light the sixth match.

4. Wordplay is central to this slang. *Shari* means rice to a sushi chef, but originally it was a religious term for Buddha's white bones. *Murasaki* generally means "purple," in this case the deep dark color of soy sauce. And *agari* means the completion or end of something; tea concludes a meal. Omae and Tachibana (1981: 20) and Yoshino (1986: 95) offer more extensive glossaries of sushi vocabulary.

5. A team of anthropologists, including myself, conducted research on

coastal whaling villages in 1988 to assess the social impact of the moratorium on "small-type coastal whaling" imposed by the International Whaling Commission; see Akimichi et al. 1988; Freeman et al. 1989; Takahashi et al. 1989; Kalland and Moeran 1992.

6. Official marketplace sales figures report on roughly 450 major categories of seafood, but many of these include five or six distinct varieties recognized in the trade. Most traders, when asked about the total number of varieties, shake their heads and guess "over two thousand."

7. I use 1996 for comparison because during that year, under a court order related to federal racketeering charges, the Fulton Fish Market's operations were unusually open to public scrutiny. In 1996 Tsukiji's seven seafood auction houses sold a total of 629 million kilograms of seafood for ¥610,378 million, or roughly $5.7 billion at an exchange rate of ¥106 to $1.00 (*Tsukiji Shijō Gaiyō* 1997: 16–17). During the yearlong audit of the Fulton Fish Market, investigators estimated that it handled 183 million pounds of seafood (roughly 83.2 million kilograms) worth approximately $1 billion from September 1, 1995, to August 31, 1996 (Raab 1996).

8. In the mid-1990s, the faintly exotic communalism of the Tsukiji "village," the historical legacy of the fish trade, the distinctive rhythms of traditional shitamachi life, and the warm familiarity of old-fashioned cuisine were featured on NHK, the Japan Broadcasting Corporation, in a dramatic series *Watashi no kare wa uogashi no purinsu* (My guy is the prince of the fish market). Tsukiji was seen through the eyes of a woman who married into an intermediate wholesaler's family. The drama was based on a popular book (Hirano Fumi 1993) written by an NHK announcer whose husband is in fact the heir to a successful Tsukiji firm.

9. In Japanese cuisine, edibility is not an abstract concept. If a maritime species can be consumed by human beings, in Japan it almost certainly has been. Records from one whaling village in 1832, for example, name seventy edible parts of whales, as well as various kinds of edible barnacles and parasites for which whales are hosts (Takahashi et al. 1989: 130).

10. Throughout Japan, 705 regional wholesale markets and 54 central wholesale markets deal in seafood (1987 and 1988 figures respectively; Oroshiuri Shijō-hō Kenkyūkai 1989: 34, 41). Japan has 2,944 fishing ports (as of 1998), all but about 100 of them exclusively local; employment in fisheries stood at 478,000 in 1978, 392,000 in 1988, and 278,000 in 1997 (figures from the MAFF website, www.maff.go.jp).

11. The *New York Times* ("Fish Smugglers" 2001) reported the firebombing murder of a Russian general of the border security forces on Sakhalin Island. Those responsible were alleged to be fish smugglers extracting revenge for his efforts to crack down on their trade (see also Kattoulas 2002).

12. For example, at the height of international trade friction in the 1980s over Japanese barriers to North American and European imports, the *Economist* ("Japanese Distribution" 1989) argued that Japanese distribution is roughly half

as efficient as that in the United States or the United Kingdom, based on the ratio of wholesale to retail sales (4.2:1 in Japan versus 1.9:1 in the United States and the United Kingdom), and of retail stores to population (1.6 million shops for 125 million Japanese versus 1.5 million shops for 250 million Americans). Schoppa's study of the American negotiating position in the Structural Impediments Initiative reproduces many similar statistics that compare Japanese retail and wholesale trade to that of other nations (1997: 146–80).

13. *Naka* is written 仲, combining an element indicating person 亻 with middle 中. The character also appears in *nakōdo*, the ultimate go-between, the person who arranges a marriage.

14. The term *nakaoroshi gyōsha* has specific legal and administrative meaning within the wholesale market system; it is not used to refer to wholesalers outside the market system, who are by definition unlicensed. *Nakagainin* is a more colloquial term for wholesalers, no longer used at Tsukiji except to refer to traders outside the wholesale market system or, historically, Tsukiji or Nihonbashi traders before the present licensing system began.

15. Data in this and the following paragraphs are calculated from *Shijō Jigyō Gaiyō* (1995: 96; 1997: 86–88; 1999: 82) and *Tsukiji Shijō Gaiyō* (2000), and from the market's website (www.shijou.metro.tokyo.jp).

16. Because yen–dollar exchange rates fluctuated greatly during the 1990s, the dollar equivalents greatly exaggerate the extent of the market's decline. For example, in 1995 the dollar value of Tsukiji's trade was $6.4 billion, $5.7 billion in 1996, $5.1 billion in 1997, and $4.5 billion in 1998. In dollar terms this is a 30 percent drop from a period of an exceptionally strong yen to a comparatively weak one, against only a 2.2 percent drop in yen terms. The fluctuations in exchange rates throughout the 1990s also had an enormous impact on imports of seafood to Japan, resulting in unstable price levels for foreign products at Tsukiji's auctions.

17. Early on, I was a bit nervous that I would run into some code of silence, some Japanese version of the Sicilian *omertà*, and that sometime, somewhere, someone would emerge from the shadows, tap me on the shoulder and growl something like "The boss would like to talk with you." My fears, perhaps the product of typical New York paranoia, were entirely unfounded.

18. Nishimura Eiko is *not* a pseudonym.

19. In addition to conducting extensive fieldwork at Tsukiji, I have collected data at markets in Abashiri, Kushiro, Mombetsu, and Sapporo (Hokkaidō); Ayukawa, Ishinomaki, and Sendai (Miyagi); Iwaki (Fukushima); Funabashi (Chiba); Kyoto; Osaka; and Hakata (Fukuoka), as well as at Tokyo's new Ōta Market.

20. As I finish this manuscript about Tsukiji, I am working on a related book—tentatively titled *Global Sushi*—that examines the transnational tuna trade, based on my research at Tsukiji as well as my fieldwork in overseas fishing ports and among foreign producers, distributors, chefs, and consumers (see T. Bestor 1999a, 2000, 2001b, 2002c).

CHAPTER 2. GROOVED CHANNELS

1. In 1998, the marketplace employed about 15,500 people and about 36,500 people came to Tsukiji for trade or deliveries each day; the numbers have declined over the past decade, according to occasional TMG surveys that earlier reported roughly 17,000 and 41,500, respectively, in 1994 and 17,500 and 42,500, respectively, in 1989. Daily sales volumes in tonnage and value cited here are from 2000 (*Tsukiji Shijō Gaiyō* 1991, 1996, 2001).

2. In Tokyo homemakers typically shop for foodstuffs nearly every day, purchasing for immediate consumption rather than storing perishable groceries at home for several days. A survey by the TMG found that 14.2 percent of homemakers reported they purchased fresh seafood daily, 37.4 percent reported purchases two or three times a week, and 34.0 percent reported buying seafood twice a week (Tōkyō-to Chūō Oroshiuri Shijō 1999: 8–11). Cross-cultural perspectives on meal schedules and the social contexts of both meal times and shopping hours are discussed in Rotenberg's analysis (1992: 105–47) of contemporary Vienna.

3. I use the term "buyers" to refer collectively to the two categories of traders licensed to purchase at Tsukiji's auctions: intermediate wholesalers *(nakaoroshi gyōsha)* and authorized traders *(baibaisankasha).* In April 2003, there were 901 intermediate wholesalers (*Tō-Oroshi*, May 2003). Their numbers have shrunk dramatically over the past dozen years (from 1,075 in 1991, to 981 in 1996, and to 929 in 2001). During the same period, the numbers of authorized buyers have dropped as well (from 402 in 1991, to 388 in 1996, to 375 in 2001) (*Tsukiji Shijō Gaiyō* 1991, 1996, 2001). Reasons for these declines will be discussed later. The distinctions between the roles of intermediate wholesalers and authorized buyers will also become clearer later; in brief, intermediate wholesalers are licensed to operate one or more of the 1,677 stalls and sell products inside the marketplace; authorized traders must sell their products outside the marketplace. In many cases authorized traders are purchasing agents for large retail chains, restaurant supply houses, and food processors, whereas intermediate wholesalers deal largely with small-scale, independent fishmongers and restaurateurs.

4. The dramaturgical tone set by my references to casts and stages, of course, echoes Goffman's discussions (1959, 1974) of frontstage, backstage, and conventions of framing social life both spatially and temporally. Other related perspectives on the social significance of space, place, and time include Sorokin and Merton (1937), Lawrence and Low (1990), Rotenberg (1992), and McDonogh and Rotenberg (1992). The cultural connections between time, space, and economy have been explored by many scholars, including Simmel (1990), Thompson (1967), Hannerz (1980), and Harvey (1989).

5. Since the early 1990s, Tokyo's residents and urban planners have come to appreciate the waterfront anew. Today, attractive esplanades line the banks of the

lower Sumida River, starting from the Tsukiji marketplace; a decade earlier, the riverfront was blocked by bleak concrete flood walls. The fashionable, contemporary turn in the river's image is clear from the increasing recent use of the term *ribaafuranto* (riverfront) instead of the traditional term *kawazoi* (along the river banks) in real estate advertising for new condominiums.

6. The famous kabuki play *Sukeroku*, first performed in 1713, established the prototypical stage version of the Edokko—the native-born child of Edo—and was perennially popular among Nihonbashi fish dealers, reports Nishiyama (1997: 50).

7. These adjacent place-names—Tsukudajima, Tsukishima, and Tsukiji—may strike non-Japanese ears as similar, but this is an artifact of phonetic coincidence rather than etymology.

8. The perception (or illusion) that one *can* bargain (and that one is knowledgeable and skillful enough to do so) is, as de la Pradelle (1995) points out, a central aspect in the construction of a marketplace as a social space.

9. The prize honors Akutagawa Ryūnosuke (1892–1927), the celebrated author of short stories who was born in Tsukiji (near the site of St. Luke's Hospital). Tsukiji's other claim to modern literary fame stems from the Tsukiji Little Theater (Tsukiji Shōgekijō), which from 1924 until 1928 was a center of Japan's modern drama movement.

10. Not everyone is scared off, however. Beyond the large "wholesale only" signs, smaller ones remind visitors that shopping carts are prohibited. Especially toward the end of the market day, a small but noticeable flow of "civilian" shoppers rambles through the outermost sets of stalls. At lunchtime, sushi bars in the inner market attract sizable numbers of customers from outside.

Foreign visitors are ignorant of (or purposefully ignore) the Japanese-language signs that guard the entrances. They stream through the inner marketplace every morning, individually or in organized tours. In the past decade, a few signs in English have been posted around the tuna auctions banning flash photography, which might interfere with bidders and auctioneers as they signal and record split-second hand bids. Elsewhere, Tsukiji's workers are remarkably tolerant of foreign tourists and journalists despite the disruptions they cause. I once watched a German television film crew elbow their way into work spaces without asking anyone's permission and then set about rearranging fish to suit their camera angles. Several times I have seen the traffic of handcarts snarl to a halt as a group of middle-aged Americans or young Europeans blocked the passageway as they shot videos of each other mugging next to exotic-looking fish. Workers and proprietors view these transgressions by foreigners with resigned patience, although Japanese visitors pushing into a stall interior, handling the merchandise, or blocking traffic would provoke immediate, sharp reactions. (See appendix 1 for information about visiting the marketplace.)

11. The team of government architects responsible for designing the Tsukiji complex visited markets in Munich and Frankfurt (Nihon Kenchiku Gakkai

1987: 85). German functional design was adapted to the particular needs of the planned market: its huge daily volume of seafood and the large numbers of existing traders. The architectural style of the 1935 Tsukiji marketplace reflects many characteristics of the so-called *neue Sachlichkeit* or "new sobriety" of the International Style developing at that time (Ken Oshima, personal communication). The streamlined functionalist lines of the Tsukiji market, the ornate pan-Asian architecture of the neighboring Tsukiji Hongan-ji temple, and the art deco style of St. Luke's Hospital, completed at almost the same time during the post-earthquake rebuilding of Tokyo, vividly display the competing influences and interpretations of modernity and internationalism that characterized early Shōwa Tokyo in the late 1920s and early 1930s.

12. The numbers fluctuate from year to year, but generally fewer than two fishing vessels dock a day at Tsukiji: 568 in 2000, 360 in 1995, and 411 in 1990 (*Tsukiji Shijō Gaiyō* 1991, 1996, 2001).

13. Almost 32,000 vehicles passed through the market's gates each day, including long-distance trucks bringing products to market as well as local vans, buses, taxis, bicycles, delivery carts, and private cars, according to a TMG traffic survey in March 1998—down a bit from 1989, when almost 36,000 vehicles were recorded (*Tsukiji Shijō Gaiyō* 1991, 1996, 2001).

14. Four other auction houses operate in Tsukiji's produce division. Two handle fruits and vegetables, one deals in pickled vegetables, and one sells eggs.

15. It is a standing joke—but only partly a joke—at the office of Chūō Ward, within which Tsukiji is located, that if smoking ever falls out of fashion, the municipality will go broke. National excise taxes on cigarette sales are a major source of municipal revenue, as the central government returns a percentage of the cigarette excise tax to the localities where the cigarettes were sold. Between the Tsukiji marketplace and the smoky bars and nightspots of the Ginza, I was told, Chūō Ward has the highest per capita level of cigarette sales (and hence receives the highest subvention) in Japan.

16. Both the engine and steering wheel swivel in a turretlike vertical cylinder above the single front wheel, hence the vehicle's name. They are surprisingly fast and highly maneuverable.

17. Market administrators take pride in the plastic-recycling plants and facilities for water purification as hallmarks of the TMG's strenuous efforts since the late 1960s to reduce Tsukiji's impact on the environment and to contribute to the rebirth of the adjacent Sumida River.

18. Andō misunderstood—as the go-between probably intended—because personal pronouns marked by gender are rarely used in spoken Japanese.

19. Lindenfeld's study of language in French marketplaces (1990), de la Pradelle's analysis of marketplace and public space (1995), Boeck's folkloric description of Texas livestock auctions (1990), and Kuiper's linguistic analysis of auctioneers' performances (1996: 33–73) all point to the many close connections between language and marketplaces. Constantine (1994) includes a chapter on Tsukiji slang and jargon.

CHAPTER 3. FROM LANDFILL TO MARKETPLACE

1. Some Japanese festivals are held at long, sometimes irregular intervals, once a generation or so. Most likely the interval in this case is simply a historical coincidence. The first Uogashi Suijin-sai of the twentieth century (and the last at the old Nihonbashi fish market) was held in 1920. Another was planned for 1932, but because the fish trade reeked of scandal at the time, it was indefinitely postponed. A Suijin-sai was held in 1950—the year in which wholesalers were first relicensed after World War II—but because rationing and food controls were just ending, the festival that year was small and subdued. The first major Suijin-sai since 1920 was held in 1955 *(Uogashi hyakunen* 1968: 504–5). Another small festival was held in 1971.

2. The Suijin Shrine at the Kanda Myōjin is one of several sub-shrines there that are dedicated to markets, including one for the old Kanda Market for fruits and vegetables, which was located just north of Akihabara Station, down the hill from Kanda Myōjin, and another for the Ōta Market, near Haneda Airport, where the Kanda Market was relocated in the early 1990s.

3. *Tobi* are construction workers who specialize in scaffolding. *Tobi-gashira,* head tobi, historically were chiefs of local fire brigades, central community institutions in Edo (see Kelly 1994). Tobi characteristically have very specific geographical territories and are employed to recruit and organize crews of laborers on most if not all construction projects within those territories. They also customarily control the local production and sale of the twisted straw hawsers *(shimenawa)* and other ritual decorations for the New Year's celebrations. In many neighborhoods they are in charge of assembling *mikoshi* and other festival floats and they therefore have close ties to Shintō shrines and to their parishes. Their role in the rough-and-tumble construction world, as well as their traditionalistic social ethos, also loosely links them to the demimonde of the *yakuza.* I discuss these realms of Tokyo's social geography in greater detail elsewhere (see T. Bestor 1989, 1992a, 1992b; Plath 1992b).

4. In this chapter, I present a general account of the historical background and development of the marketplace drawn largely from secondary sources. In the interests of readability, I note sources only where specific figures are cited, when I have directly quoted from a work, or where accounts differ significantly from one another.

There are several extensive narrative histories of the Tsukiji marketplace and its predecessor, the Nihonbashi fish market. Institutional histories issued by government agencies include *Tōkyō-to Chūō Oroshiuri Shijō-shi* (Tōkyō-to Chūō Oroshiuri Shijō 1958–63, 2 vols.) and *Chūō-ku sanjūnen-shi* (Chūō-kuyakusho 1980, 2 vols.). Illustrations of the old fish market, maps, and documents (such as letters of transit for merchant vessels) are reproduced in an illustrated exhibition catalogue, *Ō-Edo happyaku hatchō* (Edo Tōkyō Hakubutsukan 2003: 92–121, 134–40, 172–87). Company histories include *Tōto Suisan Kabushiki Gaisha gojūnen-shi* (Tōto Suisan 1987, 2 vols.) and *Daito Gyorui Kabushiki Gaisha sanjūnen-shi* (Daito Gyorui 1980). A documentary history of the development of central wholesale markets throughout Japan appeared in 6 volumes (Oroshiuri Shijō Seido Gojūnen-shi Hensan Iinkai 1979). Nakamura Masaru, an economic historian, has published two studies that focus largely on labor issues: *Shijō no kataru Nihon no kindai* (1980) and *Uogashi wa ikiteiru* (1990). Other general histories of the market include *Uogashi hyakunen* (1968), compiled by an organization of Tsukiji wholesalers, and *Nihonbashi uogashi no rekishi* (Okamoto and Kido 1985), by journalists who specialize in the fishing industry. Autobiographies and reminiscences by market traders include *Nihonbashi monogatari* (Omura Kōzaburō 1984), by a tuna dealer; *Uogashi seisuiki* (Taguchi 1962), by the founder of one of the major auction houses at Tsukiji; and *Maguroya hanjōki* (Takarai 1991), also by a tuna dealer.

Mori Kazan Gashū: Nihonbashi Uogashi (Mori 1977) is a nostalgic collection of marketplace sketches. The artist, Mori Kazan (1880–1944), was born to a fishmonger's family in Nihonbashi and became a newspaper illustrator and commercial artist. Mori's drawings of the Nihonbashi marketplace during his lifetime, and his historical sketches of Nihonbashi as it was during the Tokugawa period, were posthumously published by a group of wholesalers at Tsukiji.

5. See Tōkyō-to Kyōiku-chō Shakai Kyōiku-bu Bunka-ka (1989: esp. maps 24 and 27) and Chūō-kuritsu Kyōbashi Toshokan (1996) for Edo-era maps of the Tsukiji area that are superimposed on maps of contemporary Tokyo.

6. Tokyo's contemporary place-names generally are not identical with those of the past. The larger area known as Tsukiji through the nineteenth century has now been divided into several smaller districts. The site of the Tsukiji foreign settlement is now called Akashi-chō, just to the north of the neighborhoods still called Tsukiji.

7. Between 1771 and 1774, Sugita Genpaku, a doctor attached to one of the feudal estates in the Tsukiji area, painstakingly translated a Dutch anatomy text into Japanese after comparing its illustrations with the autopsied remains of executed criminals and realizing that the European book's accuracy far surpassed that of any Japanese medical treatises (Sugita 1969). In 1858 Fukuzawa Yukichi, then a low-ranking samurai trained in Dutch studies, began to offer private lessons in Dutch language and Western sciences in his Tsukiji quarters (for a brief account of his Tsukiji days, see Fukuzawa 1972: 95–103). Monuments to Japan's first scientific autopsy, to Sugita's translation, and to Fukuzawa's academy stand in a tiny park across the street from St. Luke's Hospital, a few blocks north of the present-day Tsukiji market.

8. Several stones carved with the American eagle and the U.S. shield, from the original American legation in Tsukiji, are displayed on the patio of St. Luke's Hospital facing the Sumida River. General historical material on the Tsukiji Foreign Settlement is compiled in Tōkyō-to Kōbunshokan (1957).

9. Accounts of Mori Magoemon, his ties to Ieyasu, and the ancestral fishers from the villages of Tsukuda and Ōwada in the Kansai region are common. Almost every history of Tsukiji opens with a chapter on the subject. Typical versions appear in Kondō (1974: 3–9) and Okamoto and Kido (1985: pref., 15–40). Nishiyama et al. (1984: 134) flatly state there is no historical evidence to back

this account of Ieyasu's role in bringing the fishers to Edo. Okamoto and Kido themselves are openly skeptical of the historical accuracy of this version of the origins of Edo's fish market, but consider the "romance" to be central to the legendary traditions of Nihonbashi and its successor, Tsukiji. See also Tōkyō-to Kōbunshokan (1978).

10. Two small stone memorials to Magoemon, erected 200 years after his death, stand in the northwestern corner of Tsukiji Hongan-ji's compound.

11. Periodic markets—markets that are held at regular but not daily intervals—were common throughout late medieval Japan (Higuchi 1977; see also Skinner 1964–65). Many still-extant place-names reflect these origins, such as the towns and cities of Yokkaichi (Fourth-Day Market) in Mie Prefecture, Itsukaichi (Fifth-Day Market) in both Tokyo and Hiroshima, Muika (Sixth Day) and Muikaichi (Sixth-Day Market) in Niigata and Shimane respectively, Yokaichi (Eighth-Day Market) and Yokaichiba (Eighth-Day Marketplace) in Shiga and Chiba, Tokaichi (Tenth-Day Market) in Niigata, and Hatsukaichi (Twentieth-Day Market) in Hiroshima (Kokusai Chigaku Kyōkai 1974).

The character read *ichi* 市, meaning market, as used in these place-names and in the term *ichiba* (marketplace), is also used to designate cities *(shi)* in contemporary Japanese.

12. A *ryō* (also known as a *koban)* was roughly equivalent in value to one *koku* of rice, the conventional measure of value for the Tokugawa regime: the amount of rice generally reckoned to be a year's supply for an adult.

13. Local systems of sea tenure are enduring characteristics of Japanese fisheries. During the feudal period, villages routinely held rights to particular fishing locations or monopolies over catching particular species, rights granted (or taken away) by the local feudal lord. In the latter part of the nineteenth century, administration of sea tenure and the associated fishing rights *(gyogyōken)* was transferred from feudal authorities to local fishers. Today these rights are administered by local fisheries cooperative associations *(gyogyō kyōdō kumiai)* (Befu 1980b; Kalland 1981, 1995; Ruddle and Akimichi 1984, 1989; Marra 1986; Plath and Hill 1987).

14. Anjin-chō drew its name from "The Pilot" *(Anjin-san)*, Will Adams (1564–1620), the British sea captain who entered the service of the Tokugawa court and who lived in this neighborhood, just north of Nihonbashi; Blackthorne, the hero of James Clavell's 1975 novel, *Shōgun*, was closely modeled on Adams (see also Rogers 1965).

15. During the Tokugawa period, months were subdivided not into weeks but into three equal segments of roughly ten days apiece: upper, middle, and lower shun. The term *shun* is still widely used to indicate microseasonality, especially when applied to fresh foods.

16. An intricately realistic scroll, *Kidai Shōran* (The scroll of prospering Nihonbashi) by an unknown artist, ca. 1805, depicts street life around Nihonbashi in great detail, including crowds around the fish market (reproduced in Edo Tōkyō Hakubutsukan 2003: 92–121).

17. This glorious account is summarized from *Uogashi hyakunen* (1968:

135–40). The Meiji Restoration was far more a political struggle than it was a civil war. Aside from a few skirmishes, there was never much fighting in or around Edo.

18. The dominance of relatively large-scale capitalist distributors over scattered, small-scale peasant fishermen is discussed, from the perspective of fishing villages, in Kalland's account (1981) of the proto-capitalist development of fishing enterprises in Kyūshū, in Marra's analysis (1986) of the history of producer-distributor relations on the island of Iki off the Kyūshū coast, and in Howell's examination (1995) of the capitalist development of Hokkaidō's fisheries.

19. These figures are reported by Okamoto and Kido (1985: 463–64), who point out that the classifications apparently were somewhat inconsistent and that the numbers are not entirely reliable. The figures nonetheless demonstrate the fluidity of trade during the period. Combined sales volume for this twelve-month period totaled 1,001,096 yen, with monthly fluctuations from 48,000 yen during the summer to 152,000 yen in December. The December high is perhaps in part reflective of the then-common commercial practice of settling annual credit accounts on the last day of the year, *Ōmisoka*.

20. That both dried fish and fresh fish were now traded within the same market regime is a change worth noting; for the previous 350 or so years the two trades had existed next door to one another with few institutional links. On the other hand, not all dried fish are sold through the Tsukiji marketplace today. The Tokyo federation of dealers in *katsuobushi* (dried bonito, a staple ingredient for stocks, sauces, and condiments) maintains a privately run exchange for dried *katsuo* where auctions are held twice a month for its hundred-odd members. The trading floor is located in a complex of katsuo warehouses, drying rooms, offices, and traders' apartments in Harumi, a short distance from Tsukiji.

21. After World War I, Germany's possessions in the Pacific (including the Caroline Islands [today, the Federated States of Micronesia], the Marianas, and the Marshalls) were awarded to Japan under a League of Nations mandate. Japan heavily fortified these strategic islands and exploited them for labor, for plantation agriculture, and for their rich fishing grounds.

22. Factory ship whaling was dominated by three major fisheries companies, Taiyō Gyogyō, Nippon Suisan, and Kyokuyō, both before and after World War II. These are three of the so-called Big Six fisheries companies, which I discuss in chapter 5.

23. Licenses were reissued either to former proprietors or their heirs. The first round of relicensing in June 1950 was reserved for former license holders; and of 1,397 nakagainin licensed in 1941, 1,238 received licenses again in June 1950, including 1,166 licensed to trade at Tsukiji and 72 authorized at two other subsidiary markets (Tōkyō-to Chūō Oroshiuri Shijō 1958–63: 2.695–97).

24. Subsequently, the market authorities revoked one license of an intermediate wholesaler involved in flagrant financial fraud. For some reason, the license was not transferred to another intermediate wholesaler as usually happens when a trader is suspended; the position was permanently eliminated and the number of stalls and licenses reduced to its present 1,677.

25. Murky scandals surrounding the land transactions, real estate developers, a land company owned by the Mitsui group, and local and national politicians are outlined briefly by Raz (1999: 23–27).

CHAPTER 4. THE RAW AND THE COOKED

1. Although minute differences in the average body temperatures of males and females indeed are found in some human populations (Ralph Holloway, personal communication), there is no evidence that differences in skin temperature—whether between males and females, or among handlers of seafood of the same sex—have any effect on seafood or other food products.

2. My thanks to Alice Falk for pointing out the salience of feral cats.

3. Several Japanese works illuminate the "cultural biographies" of seafood in varying ways. Murai's *Ebi to Nihonjin* (Shrimp and the Japanese, 1988) examines shrimp production from the perspective of the political economy of Japanese relations with Southeast Asia. Watanabe Fumio's *Maguro o marugoto ajiwau hon* (The complete book of tuna tasting, 1991) is a celebration of tuna in Japanese life, while the volume *Sakana no Nihonshi* (Fish and Japanese history, Yano 1989)—a special issue of a mass-market illustrated history magazine—provides a similar overview of seafood throughout Japanese cultural history. In a different realm of commodities, Ohnuki-Tierney (1993) analyzes the cultural construction of rice as a symbolic core of the Japanese diet and agrarian economy.

4. A cuisine, in one definition (Messer 1984: 228), is distinguished by (1) its selection of sets of basic staple and secondary foods; (2) its characteristic forms of flavoring; (3) its characteristic methods of preparing ingredients; and (4) its rules that dictate acceptable foodstuffs, appropriate combinations of foods, festive and symbolic uses of foods, and the social context of eating. Although this definition of cuisine does, in its first and fourth clauses, consider the identification and classification of things as foodstuffs, it does not address the production and distribution—that is, the actual availability—of commodities.

5. Japanese do not find the wasteful use of food entertaining, as sometimes appears in American television, where, for example, pies are thrown, contestants wallow in vats of gelatin, or milk is poured on someone's head. Japanese television producers consciously avoid using food solely for play (Andrew Painter, personal communication).

6. The *Oishinbo* series includes (as of summer 2003) 84 volumes, some now in their sixtieth printing, each volume more than 200 pages long. Volume 2 in the series, titled *Maboroshi no sakana* (Phantom fish), is representative (Kariya and Hanasaki 1985).

7. Cuisine as an element of local identity is an important aspect of the recent *furusato* (hometown) boom that focused on recapturing or reinventing a mythic pastoral homeland. Kelly (1986), T. Bestor (1989, 1992), and Robertson (1991), among others, have examined nostalgia for hometown and the invention of tradition in contemporary Japan. Ivy (1995) analyzes the symbolic salience in par-

ticular of domestic tourism, its exoticization of the Japanese past (including the past-in-the-present qualities of remote travel destinations), and the creation of a distinctive sense of Japanese cultural identity.

8. This last dish, prepared by male members of a mountain community for the village's annual festival, was so repulsive to the young interviewer that she refused to even taste it; indeed, she was able to coax from one middle-aged man the on-camera admission that though his household had made the dish for generations he had never tasted it himself nor had any desire to do so (he had married into the community, he said, and was still something of an outsider). Challenged on the spot by the television crew, he tasted it and came close to spitting it out before smiling wanly and declaring it the most wretched stuff he had ever swallowed.

9. The term *shoku*, as used in the contrastive *wa-shoku* and *yō-shoku*, has the connotation of food or foodstuffs, and in a sense the distinction between *wa-shoku* and *yō-shoku* reflects a gross dichotomy between universes of basic ingredients: e.g., rice, fish, and extracts of soybeans, on the one hand, versus wheat, red meat, and dairy derivatives, on the other hand (see Mintz 1997). On a somewhat different conceptual level are cuisines (*ryōri*; literally, "logic of ingredients"), characterized by techniques of preparation, sauces and seasonings, typical flavors, and visual presentation. On the *yō-shoku* side of the equation are such concepts as *Furansu ryōri, Itaria ryōri,* or *Supein ryōri* (French, Italian, and Spanish cuisine); on the *wa-shoku* side, distinctions are drawn by region, style of preparation, or flavorings, such as *kaiseki ryōri* (the cuisine to accompany the tea ceremony) or *Kaga ryōri* (characteristic of the seacoast near the city of Kanazawa).

10. On this score, the United States has generally fared poorly, being regarded as an unreliable supplier of basic foodstuffs and likely to hold food supplies hostage to other political and trade issues. President Nixon's sudden embargo on soybean exports to Japan in the 1970s, for example, was viewed by most Japanese as an unwarranted assault. Similarly, the United States frequently links issues in fisheries to trade disputes. Not surprisingly, at Tsukiji and in the Japanese fishing and food industries more generally, such tactics are seen as cynical policy gambits that imperil Japanese food supplies for reasons having little or nothing to do with fisheries.

11. The whaling controversy is complex, and a full discussion is far beyond the scope of this book. There is an enormous literature on Japanese whaling, taking many different perspectives; a few examples include Akimichi et al. (1988), Earle (1995), Freeman et al. (1989), Friedheim (2001), Institute of Cetacean Research (1996, 1999), Japan Whaling Association (1988), Kalland and Moeran (1992), Mulvaney (2003), Schmidhauser and Totten (1978), Stoett (1997), Takahashi et al. (1989), United States (1996), and, of course, the Greenpeace Whales Site (http://whales.greenpeace.org/whales/index.html).

Japanese draw a distinction between what is called "small-type coastal whaling" *(kogata engan hōgei)* and pelagic whaling. The former refers to whaling carried out (until the 1980s) by relatively small vessels in pursuit of whales in

Japanese waters. Many of the small ports for these vessels have whaling histories that extend back to the early or middle Tokugawa period. The most famous such port, Taiji in Wakayama Prefecture, now has a tourist industry (and a large whale museum) focused on this history and the place of whaling and whale products in many aspects of Japanese life. Food, of course, was the primary use, but the range of other applications includes lubricants and spring mechanisms (made from baleen) in *bunraku* puppets. Japanese advocates have unsuccessfully sought international approval to resume coastal whaling under the rubric of subsistence whaling, arguing that it is critical to community survival in some cases.

Pelagic whaling is large-scale, industrial whaling involving fleets of catcher boats working with a large factory ship on which entire carcasses can be processed. The technology was largely developed in Europe, and in the 1920s and 1930s, Japanese companies—including Kyokuyō, Nippon Suisan, and Taiyō Gyogyō—began to send factory fleets into North Pacific and Antarctic waters. Pelagic whaling resumed after World War II with the encouragement of the American Occupation, which saw whaling as essential for the postwar Japanese food supply. The companies that pioneered the pelagic whaling industry became dominant more generally in the postwar fishing industry—members of the so-called Big Six—with large trawler fleets for distant water operations. Taiyō Gyogyō, in particular, also became a major player in domestic distribution through its ownership of auction houses in major markets throughout Japan, including Tsukiji's Daito Gyorui. The pelagic whaling industry was viable until the 1970s, when major companies began to scale back and then cease their whaling activities, in part because of international criticism.

Pelagic whaling continues (as of this writing, in 2003) with a small fleet of vessels under Japanese government auspices that catch minke whales off Antarctica, in what Japanese refer to as "research whaling," nominally rationalized as an effort to compile accurate population statistics. The question of whether minke whales are endangered is hotly debated; the Japanese position is that the minke population in Antarctic waters is large and sufficient to permit at least modest whaling activity. Japanese research whaling is routinely condemned by the International Whaling Commission and foreign critics as thinly veiled commercial whaling. Indeed, Japanese authorities allow the whale meat from these catches to be sold.

Whale is no longer a common item of cuisine, and at least in Tokyo it is generally available only in highly specialized restaurants or as an exotic item on the menu of a bar; whale is served as sashimi, grilled, or as *beekon* (bacon)—thinly sliced, salted blubber. Some whale meat from government-sanctioned Antarctic whaling, and allegedly some from other illicit whaling by unlicensed foreign vessels, reaches Tsukiji and other markets. In 2002, 665 kilograms of fresh and 233,820 kilograms of frozen whale meat were sold at Tsukiji, for 2.6 million and 664 million yen respectively; the much smaller Adachi Market in Tokyo sold 26,815 kilograms of fresh and 1,542 kilograms of frozen whale meat for 79 million and 3.4 million yen respectively (Tōkyō-to Chūō Oroshiuri Shijō website, www.shijou.metro.tokyo.jp).

12. Margaret Lock (personal communication) confirms the vast amount of Japanese culinary and medical lore on risk factors for cancer in the Japanese diet.

13. In the trade, all fish are presumptively *tennen* unless otherwise stated, so *yōshoku* constitutes the linguistically marked category, the one that requires special comment or labeling. The coincidental homonyms, *yōshoku* (cultivated) and *yō-shoku* (Western-style food), bear no etymological relationship, as the two terms are written with entirely different characters.

14. Between 1980 and 2000, marine aquaculture has been the only major segment of Japanese fisheries to increase its annual production. As a percentage of total marine fisheries production, marine aquaculture contributed 10 percent in both 1980 and 1985, 13 percent in 1990, 22 percent in 1995, and 25 percent in 2000. In 1980 Japanese marine fisheries as a whole produced 9.9 million metric tons, 10.9 million mt in 1985, 9.6 million mt in 1990, 6.0 million mt in 1995, and 5.0 million mt in 2000, a decline of more than 49 percent from 1980 production. Distant water fisheries (outside Japan's exclusive economic zone) in 1980 produced 2.2 million mt, 2.1 million mt in 1985, 1.5 million mt in 1990, 892,000 mt in 1995, and 855,000 mt in 2000, a decline of just about 61 percent from 1980. Coastal fishing (within Japanese waters) in 1980 produced 7.8 million mt, 8.8 million mt in 1985, 8.1 million mt in 1990, 5.1 million mt in 1995, and 4.2 million mt in 2000, a decline of 46 percent from 1980. In contrast, marine aquacultural production was 992,000 mt in 1980, 1.1 million mt in 1985, 1.3 million mt in both 1990 and 1995, and 1.2 million mt in 2000, an overall increase of 21 percent since 1980 (MAFF 2001: 44).

15. Tuna are an exception; cultivated tuna are now sold at auction alongside wild catches.

16. For many years cultivation of shrimp in Taiwan for sale to Japanese markets was a major industry. It was almost entirely wiped out by a virus that swept through Taiwanese shrimp compounds and rendered them unusable.

17. Mitsukan, a vinegar manufacturer based near Nagoya, provides another example of the successful early industrialization of culinary ingredients. In 1804, Nakano Matazaemon discovered a new method for cheaply making vinegar by using rice lees from saké brewing and was able to take advantage of his proximity to coastal shipping routes linking Edo and Osaka in order to supply urban markets; a century and a half later, the firm he founded remains the dominant national brand for vinegar products.

18. The commercial appeal of "Edomae" now extends to other products as well; the Asahi brewing company, for example, sells one of its popular brands as "Edomae Draft Beer."
   Despite the contemporary cachet of the term, people in the seafood business often point out to me that the rich fishing grounds in Edo Bay were a by-product of the city itself. Runoff waste from the city's many canals fed plankton growth in the bay's shallow waters, enriching the base of the coastal food chain—an ecological relationship that contemporary retailers and restaurateurs would be loathe to promote.

19. As a "new" sales technique, some supermarket chains in the Tokyo region have resurrected the stock-in-trade of the old-fashioned retail fishmonger: service. Employees at a service counter will clean, bone, fillet, or even cook fish that shoppers select from the supermarket's nearby refrigerated cases full of prepackaged fish. What a traditional fishmonger does as a matter of course, supermarkets advertise as special service (for which, not surprisingly, they charge modest fees).

20. Other changes in food and household technology took hold with equal or greater speed. The production of frozen food products for home consumption began rising in the late 1960s, from only about 20,000 metric tons in 1968, to about 150,000 mt in 1975, and then to 350,000 mt in 1995. Microwave ovens for the home were introduced in Japan in 1970; by 1980, 33 percent of homes had them; by 1995 microwaves were in 87 percent of households (Hirano Minase 1997: 65).

21. A survey by the House Food Industrial Co. (reported in the *Japan Digest,* July 25, 1991) found that only 11 percent of Tokyo elementary school children ate dinner with both their parents every evening. On average their fathers ate at home only three nights a week, and 12 percent of the children reported that they preferred meals without their father. Twenty-seven percent of the children reported that they sometimes missed family meals because of cram school classes.

22. The extensive literature on gendered differentiation of roles and responsibilities in contemporary Japanese society is surprisingly mute on the subject of cooking. Bernstein (1983: 72–74) gives a brief account of cooking in the context of the much larger repertory of domestic tasks in the daily life of a contemporary rural woman. R. J. Smith (1978: 143–47) outlines general changes in the domestic diet, also in a rural setting. *Makiko's Diary* (Nakano 1995), a journal kept by the wife of a merchant family in Kyoto in 1910, records in detail the elaborately differentiated cuisine and heavy cooking duties for women of the time. The emergence of cooking as an urban middle-class hobby and element of cultivated leisure during the first three decades of the twentieth century is briefly sketched by Cwiertka (1998). Bumiller (1995) offers passing comments on cooking and shopping in the daily life of Mariko, a middle-class Tokyo housewife. Other academic English-language works on Japanese women's roles in the domestic realm generally ignore cooking and meals (e.g., Bernstein 1991; Imamura 1987; J. Lebra et al. 1976; T. Lebra 1984; R. J. Smith and Wiswell 1982; E. Vogel 1991).

23. The title of Yagyū (2003) is itself an example of sushi wordplay: *Kaiten-zushi no sa-sushi-se-so,* which I translate as *The ABCs of Kaiten-zushi,* plays with the conventional order of syllables in Japanese: those starting with "s" would ordinarily be given as sa-shi-su-se-so (hence something like ABC), but the author has switched the order around to get *sushi* into the sequence.

24. In the early 1990s, one kaiten-zushi chain, Sushi Boy, sparked an international trade incident. It produced frozen sushi in the United States to ship to its Japanese restaurants because labor costs were lower in the United States.

Its imports were blocked by Japanese customs agents because the rice was American-grown. At the time, Japanese government regulations strictly banned the import of rice but took no position on the sushi toppings.

25. The 7-Eleven chain of convenience stores is owned—in both Japan and the United States—by the Japanese retailing giant Itō Yōkadō. In 1973, Itō Yōkadō opened its first convenience store under license from the Southland Corporation, the Texas-based originator of the 7-Eleven franchise, and began using the 7-Eleven name in Japan in 1978. In 1991, Itō Yōkadō acquired 70 percent of the shares of the Southland Corporation, and in 1993, the 5,000th Japanese 7-Eleven store was opened ("ItoYokado Company Profile," 2003, www.itoyokado.iyg.co.jp/iy/com/cm5_e.htm).

26. Sunday closings at Tsukiji are a fairly recent development, reflecting pressure on employers to adjust to the rhythms of the wider labor market and to give workers at least one day a week off. Historically, the market operated year-round, closing only for a few days around the New Year's holiday and around the midsummer O-Bon holiday, so workers could return to their ancestral villages and tend to the souls of deceased forebears.

27. Abalone also plays a role in the intricate symbolism of gift-giving (Befu 1968). Dried abalone *(awabi)* is a ritually significant decoration (called *noshi* or *noshi-awabi)* attached to the outer covering of a gift with auspiciously colored red-and-white cords. Originally, abalone was an offering to Shintō gods, and because one must be in a ritually purified state to make such offerings, the abalone accompanying a gift signifies that the recipient need not fear being ritually contaminated by the gift itself (Hendry 1990: 33–34).

Actual dried abalone is rarely if ever used today; instead, it is usually represented by an intricately folded piece of paper that vaguely resembles the stylized shape of the shellfish or by a folded-paper-and-cords motif printed on a piece of wrapping paper. Stationers, convenience stores, and supermarkets sell appropriate sets of pre-folded and pre-tied paper-and-cord, or, for gifts of cash, envelopes printed with the appropriate design.

28. One set of seasonal festivals, *sekku* or *gosekku*, revolves around offerings of food made on days traditionally considered as marking seasonal changes. During the Tokugawa period, five sekku were officially designated by the shōgunate; in their modern versions they fall on January 7 (known as *ko-shōgatsu*, "little New Year's," or *nanakusa*, "seven herbs," for a dish traditionally associated with the day); March 3 (Momo no Sekku, "Peach Festival," commonly known as the Doll Festival, Hina Matsuri, or Girl's Day); May 5 (Shōbu no Sekku, "Iris Festival," or Boy's Day, now celebrated as a national holiday called Children's Day); July 7 (Tanabata, "Star Festival"); and September 9 (Kiku no Sekku, "Chrysanthemum Festival"). The *sekku* follow the numerological pattern 1–1, 3–3, 5–5, 7–7, 9–9, with the exception of "little New Year's" (although, of course, the "real" New Year's on January 1 fills out the set). Each sekku is marked by its own complement of special foods, most notably New Year's. The characteristic cuisine for New Year's is called *o-sechi*, a term etymologically related to *sekku*.

29. The six days of *rokuyō* follow a set order, but the sequence starts over at the beginning of each "micro-season" *(sekki)* and secular month.

30. In contrast to the lunar calendar used officially in premodern Japan, the traditional solar calendar used to calculate planting seasons divided the natural year into twelve months *(setsu)* of precisely 30.44 days each. Each setsu was further divided into two parts, known as *sekki*. This solar calendar was highly accurate for marking the meteorological changes of Japan's predictable climate, and the date on which a given sekki begins each year is quite stable, always falling on one of two adjacent days as determined by the Western Gregorian calendar (Webb with Ryan 1965: 15–25). These twenty-four divisions of the year remain widely known and used.

31. In addition to the twenty-four micro-seasons or sekki explained in the previous note, the four seasons of the year are each divided into five phases of roughly eighteen days that each correspond to one of the five primal elements of Chinese cosmology: wood, fire, earth, metal, and water (see Lock 1980: 27–49, for a discussion of these five elements and their relationship to health and nutrition). The earth phase *(doyō)* occurs in the final eighteen days of each of the four major seasons, but best-known is the summer doyō. The summer doyō begins around July 20 each year and spans parts of two fifteen-day sekki or micro-seasons: the last few days of Shōsho (Little Heat) and the entirety of Taisho (Great Heat). In the old calendar, days occur in a sequence calculated from the ancient East Asian sexagenary cycle (known in Japanese as *jikkan jūnishi,* sometimes glossed as "the Chinese zodiac") that designated years, days, times of day, and directions (especially for purposes of geomancy). The twelve elements in this system bear the names of animals; Ushi no hi, the Day of the Ox, occurs every twelfth day. Since doyō lasts eighteen days, in any given year the midsummer Day of the Ox can occur either once or twice, sometime between July 20 and August 7.

32. Eating eel during doyō was recorded in an eighth-century poetry collection, the *Man'yōshū,* but the specific association with the Day of the Ox apparently began during the Edo period (1603–1867), perhaps because of the linguistic correspondence between *ushi* (ox) and *unagi* (eel) (Ōtsuka Minzoku Gakkai 1972: 69, 507–8). Another possibility starts from fundamentals of Chinese cosmology. Each of the five elements of Chinese cosmology corresponds to or is represented by one or another item from each of several general categories (domestic animals, organs of the body, colors, etc.). Items linked to the earth phase point toward the associations among doyō, the Day of the Ox, and the consumption of broiled eels; the correspondences for doyō include domestic animal—ox; human senses—taste; organ of body—stomach; fragrance— sweet; flavor—sweet (Lock 1980: 32).

33. Unexpectedly, eel dealers say that years with only one midsummer Day of the Ox are better for business than those with two such days. Apparently, consumers lose interest after the first day, suppliers are uncertain how to time their shipments, and the extra work of preparing eels for two bursts of sales is not worth the effort.

34. The traditional Japanese calendar did not include "weeks." Months were simply divided into early, middle, and late segments of roughly ten days apiece, called *shun*. In old-fashioned mercantile practice, recurring dates—those of regular holidays, for example—would be chosen on the same day in each of the three segments; some retail shops in Tokyo still follow this calendar, closing on, say, the 5th, the 15th, and the 25th rather than on a specific day of the week.

CHAPTER 5. VISIBLE HANDS

1. The impelling hegemony of economic principles in contemporary life—what de la Pradelle (1995) refers to as "economism"—renders markets (and auctions) as culturally *normal,* and hence sets them *outside* the expected scope of social and cultural analysis. Such "normality," however, makes the phenomena themselves no less cultural or social. Her argument about the cultural embeddedness of economic activity parallels Granovetter's analysis (1985) of social embeddedness.

2. Analysts of auctions, ranging from mainstream neoclassical economists (e.g., V. Smith 2000; V. Smith and Williams 1992) to sociological theorists of structuration (e.g., C. Smith 1989), operating from very different theoretical starting points, provide extensive examples and typologies of the social and institutional constraints affecting the operations and outcomes of auctions. See also Vickrey 1961; Cassady 1967; Milgrom 1989; McAfee and McMillan 1987.

3. The generic Japanese term for "auction" *(seri)* usually is written in the phonetic katakana script often reserved for non-Japanese words セリ, so some Japanese assume that both the word and the practice are foreign imports. But *seri* can also be written with a standard kanji that denotes competition 競リ and with a complicated and nowadays very obscure character 糶 that originally referred to rice markets.

4. Except in professional business circles, competitive bidding and auctions are uncommon in Japan. There are, to my knowledge, only a few counterexamples, including *tanomoshi-kō*, rotating credit associations once common in rural Japan (Embree's description of their workings is still apt; 1939: 138–47). In these groups, participants each contribute a fixed sum of money to a communal kitty and then submit written bids of how much they will pay each other over time—in effect, proposing an interest rate and an amortization schedule—to "win" the entire pot now.

Outside Tsukiji and other seafood and produce markets, I have encountered only two other instances of auctions or public competitive bidding in Japan. Peddlers at shrine fairs and street markets sometimes offer inexpensive clothing or foodstuffs at a fixed price and add additional items to the lot until someone steps forward to pay the asked-for price for the now greatly increased pile of goods. Thus, a peddler may start out offering two shirts for ¥2,000 and end up selling five shirts for that amount. (Economists refer to this as a "Dutch auction," a type of "falling bid" auction. See Cassady 1967.) My other auction encounter came by a chance invitation from a friend, an avid gardener, to accompany him to an orchid sale held at a community hall near his home in Tokyo. It turned out to be a public auction of individual plants and cuttings among about three dozen men—some devoted hobbyists, others professionals (including, I was told, some from as far away as Shikoku); they bid in an "English auction," in which bids are made vocally (and for increasing amounts) in response to the auctioneer's cry.

5. The logic of capitalism, as a *cultural* system (Bell 1976; Herzfeld 1992; de la Pradelle 1995), is perhaps most readily apparent in societies not (yet) entirely or officially capitalist (see, e.g., Hertz 1998; Ruble 1995; Ikels 1996; Janelli with Yim 1993; Yang 1994).

6. Daily trade figures for 1995 are calculated from data provided in *Tsukiji Shijō Gaiyō* (1996: 16–17). In 1994, of all seafood passing through central wholesale markets throughout the country, Tsukiji handled 17.6 percent of the tonnage and 20.0 percent of the total value (*Shijō Memo* 1995: 70, 112). Figures for the national trade in seafood as a whole show that in 1993, the total tonnage of seafood commercially distributed in Japan was 8.05 million metric tons; of this, 5.0 million metric tons (or 61.7 percent) passed through central wholesale markets, and 808,000 metric tons (or 10.0 percent of the national total) passed through the entire TMG central wholesale market system (*Shijō Jigyō Gaiyō* 1995: 1).

7. Regional wholesale markets, chartered and licensed by prefectural governments, are owned and managed by municipalities, fisheries cooperatives, and private businesses. The substantial difference in structure is illustrated by a 1987 survey of regional markets (Suisansha 1989: 229). Of 335 production region markets, 292 (87.2 percent) were operated by fisheries cooperatives, 32 (9.6 percent) by local governments, and 11 (3.3 percent) by private corporations. In contrast, of 222 consumption region markets that deal exclusively in seafood, 167 (75.2 percent) were operated by private corporations, 47 (21.2 percent) by fisheries and other cooperatives, and only 8 (3.6 percent) by local governments.

8. In the Kantō region surrounding the Tokyo megalopolis, there are ten central wholesale markets that handle seafood (including Tsukiji and two other TMG markets at Ōta and Adachi), two markets each in the cities of Yokohama and Kawasaki, and one apiece in the cities of Chiba, Funabashi, and Utsunomiya. A bit beyond the Kantō Plain, there are also central wholesale markets for seafood in provincial centers such as Kōfu, Shizuoka, Hamamatsu, and Iwaki. These central wholesale markets cap a marketing system that also includes 130 smaller regional wholesale markets scattered throughout the Kantō region, 52 of which are located in fishing ports (hence classified as production or *sanchi* markets), and the remainder classified as consumption or *shōhichi* markets (Oroshiuri Shijō-hō Kenkyūkai 1989).

9. Whether their licenses are from MAFF or the TMG, the business activities of Tsukiji firms are carefully defined and regulated. These licensing regulations—which restrict market entry by holding the number of licenses constant—define the scope of activities that a firm may engage in within the

marketplace; they also constrain its activities in related or unrelated fields of business outside the marketplace.

10. "His" is used advisedly here; since the early 1990s, a number of women have passed the TMG examinations to become serinin, but apparently none have become active auctioneers on the market floor.

11. John Nathan's documentary film *Full Moon Lunch* (1976) follows a family of box-lunch makers in Tokyo and, in passing, observes their up-and-down dealings with Tsukiji traders.

12. Direct purchases by the auction houses are regulated by the marketplace's authorities and are allowed only for certain categories of commodities, or under specified market conditions.

Overall, consignments and direct purchases are about equally frequent: in 1994 consignments represented 53 percent of the value and 51 percent of the quantity of the seafood handled at Tsukiji, and these proportions have held relatively steady in recent years. However, consignments are much more common for sales of fresh seafood than for frozen or processed seafood: consignments accounted for 79 percent of the total value and 81 percent of the total quantity of all fresh seafood sold, while for frozen and processed seafood, the corresponding percentages were 39 percent and 36 percent (of total value) and 26 percent and 45 percent (of total quantity) (Tōkyō-to Chūō Oroshiuri Shijō 1995: 96).

13. The TMG's regulations classify several hundred commodity categories according to whether products must be sold at auction or can be sold through negotiated sales. Most frozen and processed seafood and aquacultural products can be sold by negotiated sale, but some high-value products, such as frozen tuna, are sold at auction like their fresh counterparts: one fish at a time. Negotiated sales are also allowed if surpluses remain for any commodity after traders have ceased to bid on the day's offerings. In addition, marketplace administrators may waive auction requirements if they determine that supplies or prices must be stabilized in the wake of extraordinary circumstances (e.g., major typhoons or catastrophic transportation disruptions). Such special waivers are rare.

14. In theory, by way of contrast, governance by hierarchy can deal with uncertainty over time through managerial fiat; and market governance need not take account of change "over time," because each new transaction is approached independently of its predecessor.

15. Rumors of under-the-table rebates to suppliers surface from time to time, but illegal payments appear to be uncommon, or at least seldom brought to light. Transaction records for all auction houses are audited on a continuing basis by the TMG and annually by the MAFF. Roger Janelli (personal communications) has pointed out to me, however, that the audits are rarely aimed at uncovering these particular kinds of irregularities.

16. Indeed, intermediate wholesalers at Tsukiji can also participate in out-of-market channels. Market regulations permit them to make a certain portion of

their purchases directly from producers or other shippers, thereby bypassing the auctions. And some intermediate wholesalers establish separate companies, outside the market system, to actively participate in out-of-market transactions, occasionally even purchasing shipments that they in turn consign to an auction house and put up for sale to their competitors.

17. Figures on stock holding are from company reports and filings with the Ministry of Finance.

CHAPTER 6. FAMILY FIRM

1. Of course, family and kinship are used strategically for business ends (as Hamabata 1990 makes clear), and as moral ideals to ensure the hegemony of small business proprietors over their workers (as Kondo 1990 discusses). Some real-life rough edges of family as business (or business as family) are vividly shown in John Nathan's documentary film *Full Moon Lunch* (1976).

2. *Yagō* refers, in Japanese mercantile culture, to the "house name" of a shop or business. It implies a traditional, familial enterprise, passed down from generation to generation. Modern corporate-sounding names (e.g., "Tokyo Frozen Foods, Inc.") are not yagō, although some huge corporations use old mercantile yagō as their formal names: Mitsubishi (literally, "Three Diamonds") is an internationally known example. As explained in chapter 5, the Japanese fisheries company Maruha recently adopted its old yagō as its formal corporate name. At Tsukiji, in the licensed world of intermediate wholesalers, shop names are known officially as *kigō* (registered names); many kigō are yagō in the old-fashioned vein, some are corporate names, and some combine a yagō with a corporate form (e.g., "Kanemaru Frozen Fish Products, Inc.").

3. The Urayasu land reclamation project, various financial scandals surrounding it, and the ultimate construction of Disneyland on part of this landfill are briefly discussed by Raz (1999: 23–28).

4. Among a sample of seventy-two firms whose owners listed Urayasu addresses, 56 percent were members of the *tokushumono* group that supplies shellfish and other sushi specialties, and 29 percent were members of the *ōmono* group of tuna dealers.

5. The legal forms for Tsukiji's intermediate wholesale firms include unincorporated individual proprietorships *(kojin)* and four types of incorporated status (known collectively as *hōjin,* or juridical persons): limited liability firms *(yūgen gaisha),* joint-stock corporations *(kabushiki gaisha),* and two forms of partnership known as *dōshi* and *dōgo.* The majority of incorporated wholesalers at Tsukiji are limited liability firms, a much simpler legal structure than a joint-stock corporation.

6. The traditional kinship pattern of the Japanese household *(ie)* is known in anthropological and sociological terms as a "stem family." Its most salient characteristic is preserving family assets across the generations by designating a single heir and successor in each generation, and by sharply demarcating family members who will stay with the household and those (noninheriting) chil-

dren who will be expected to make their way in the world on their own. Often the heir, in the Japanese case, is the eldest son, but Japanese kinship and inheritance allow families considerable flexibility to select the most well-qualified successor in the next generation; sometimes eldest sons are skipped over in favor of a younger son, a daughter, an adopted child, or a son-in-law who is adopted in to carry on the family line. The legal structure of the stem family was largely disestablished after World War II, but these kinds of households remain common in modified form in urban Japanese mercantile life as well as in rural sectors of Japan.

7. Eight months' worth of records were unavailable from the period (unpublished records in the files of Tō-Oroshi).

8. On the basis of straight salary alone (leaving aside bonuses and allowances), the market staff job paid slightly over ¥1,600 per hour, or about ¥14,500 for an nine-hour day. Another ad for a fish slicer and delivery person working outside the marketplace (from 2:30 to 10:00 A.M., one or two days off a week) offered ¥1,350 per hour, along with transportation and clothing allowances, plus the possibility of overtime. On the same page of *AN*, advertised hourly wages ranged from ¥900 to ¥1,500, mostly around ¥1,100 to ¥1,200 for delivery people; daily wages ranged from ¥7,000 to ¥12,600 (the latter for a night-shift truck driver); and monthly wages ranged from ¥160,000 to ¥250,000 (for a window washer).

9. Unions and others have successfully promoted the term *haitatsunin* to replace—at least in public—the older, pejorative term "coolie" *(karuko)*.

10. In 1990, according to a survey conducted on November 1 of that year, 451 foreign workers were employed at Tsukiji: 306 worked in the seafood division, 70 in the produce division, and 75 in related enterprises *(kanren jigyō)*, which include shipping, unloading, and service businesses (unpublished data from TMG files). Of the 306 foreign workers in the seafood division, one worked for an auction house and the other 305 worked for intermediate wholesalers. Their nations of origin (including workers in both the seafood and the produce divisions) were the People's Republic of China, 404; Bangladesh, 15; Taiwan, 3; Brazil, 2; the Republic of Korea, 1; Malaysia, 1; and unidentified, 25. Many such foreign workers enter Japan on student visas that generally allow part-time employment.

11. Chinese and Japanese belong to entirely different language families. However, the Chinese writing system was introduced into Japan in the sixth century, via Korea, and grafted onto the spoken Japanese language. Along with the writing, innumerable loanwords entered Japanese from Chinese, so the two languages share broad similarities in fundamental vocabularies, though not in grammar, syntax, or phonetics. Over the centuries, the writing systems used in China, Japan, and Korea diverged, particularly in the twentieth century when language reformers in each country launched separate and uncoordinated programs to simplify ideographs. Nevertheless, it is quite easy for Chinese to recognize and learn to pronounce contemporary Japanese ideographs, even without great fluency in spoken Japanese.

12. It is easy to interpret this notion of "stealing the secrets" as evidence that masters regard their apprentices as future economic competitors. John Singleton, however, suggests instead that it reflects core attitudes toward apprenticeship and the educational process: "If you haven't struggled to figure out for yourself how to accomplish specific craft techniques, you haven't really learned them. Amateurs will be told how to do something; serious apprentices must discover the same things on their own—because their learning is important" (Singleton, personal communication; see also Singleton 1998).

13. *Norenwake* is only metaphorical at Tsukiji, where wholesalers' stalls do not actually have shop curtains.

14. Sometimes the connection is signified by including the character *bun* (meaning "divided," also read as *wake*, as in *norenwake*) in a shop name, such as Isebun. Or, more prosaically, the apprentice's shop may simply be known as a *shiten*, or branch store. Of course, some "branches" long outlive their roots.

CHAPTER 7. TRADING PLACES

1. There is a large, and in some cases Nobel Prize–winning, economic literature on auctions and the ways in which different sets of rules for conducting an auction—rising bids or falling bids, simultaneous or sequential bidding, secret or open bidding—create very different patterns of market power among participants. Economists' analyses of auctions and behavior include Cassady (1967), Kirman (2001), McAfee and McMillan (1987), McMillan (2002), Milgrom (1987, 1989), Milgrom and Weber (1982), V. Smith (2000), V. Smith and A. Williams (1992), and Vickrey (1961). Much of the theoretical interest surrounding auctions has to do with information asymmetries (see Akerlof 1984). A few anthropologists and sociologists have focused on the social structures surrounding auctions (see Errington 1987; Garcia 1986; Peterson 1973; Peterson and Georgianna 1988; C. Smith 1989). More generally, anthropologists have focused on flows of information within markets, types of bargaining behavior, the social mechanisms that surround price-setting, and what Plattner refers to as "equilibrating relationships" among trade partners (see Acheson 1994, 2003; Alexander and Alexander 1991; Byrne 1985; Geertz 1978; Khuri 1968; Plattner 1982, 1983, 1984, 1985, 1989a, 1989b; Radford 1968; Wilson 1980).

2. The systematic use of chaya as agents for transactions—or, put another way, the practice of referring to agents as chaya—dates to the mercantile culture of the Edo period. Other examples of chaya include booking agents for geisha and those who handle tickets for sumo matches (Dalby 1983; Cuyler 1979: 123, 162–63; Kenrick 1969: 20–22).

3. This aim parallels the model of group decision making proposed by Robert Marshall (1984). For group decisions to be feasible, the outcomes of a potential decision must be seen not to jeopardize the individual positions of the parties to the decision. If the probable outcomes do not ensure parity, Marshall argues, either the group will not make the decision or individual defections or group fissioning will occur.

4. The first lottery to assign stalls was held after intermediate wholesalers were reauthorized to operate in the market in July 1950. Throughout the 1950s, stall rotations occurred every one or two years. From the 1960s until the middle 1990s, they have taken place every three to five years, most recently in 1981, 1985, 1990, and 1995 (unpublished records of Tō-Oroshi). Another lottery is planned for spring 2004.

5. The TMG's ongoing efforts to encourage kojin to convert to incorporated status also reflect administrators' concerns that small-scale individual proprietorships are less able to provide health and disability insurance for workers than are incorporated firms.

6. In addition to the major blocks of stalls, four other "special blocks" that include only twenty-seven stalls exist for largely technical reasons—mostly plumbing problems. The largest special block, containing sixteen stalls, lost its access to running water during a remodeling of the marketplace in the early 1960s; since then it has been reserved for dealers in dried fish. A second block (with six stalls) has been reserved for wholesalers who process shark products using an ammonia solution and who therefore were segregated off in a corner by themselves so that the smell of ammonia would not contaminate other stalls' goods. The two remaining special blocks contain a total of five stalls between them; structural difficulties in the design of the market sheds made these stalls very oddly shaped, preventing their occupants from installing modern equipment—large coolers, for example—that are now standard in other stalls. Stallholders in the special blocks were for many years virtually assured permanent tenancy, and in the 1990 lotteries occupants of the first two special blocks mentioned were unopposed by any other wholesalers seeking their space.

7. In 1990, the ratio of applicants to stalls ranged from 1.7:1 for the most popular section (the north block) to 0.4:1 for the least popular (the inner block) (calculated from unpublished Tō-Oroshi data).

8. Although these divisions may seem to be arbitrary administrative devices, koma reflect physical features of the sheds—the placement of pillars and of water connections—that create basic spatial units. These units are now divided into two stalls, but in the past some of the same spaces were divided into three stalls apiece.

9. In 1990, the monthly surcharges collected by the federation totaled ¥6,830,000 (roughly $46,000, at the average 1990 exchange rate of ¥150 to $1.00), an average of ¥7,100 ($47) collected from each favorably located stall; the rebates for disadvantaged stallholders totaled ¥7,030,000 (roughly $47,000) per month, an average of ¥24,240 ($162) for each stall rated below average. Surcharges are collected monthly and rebates are disbursed semiannually, so interest covers the difference between income and payments.

10. The ratings for the lotteries in 1981, 1985, and 1990 changed very little from one cycle to the next. In those three years, 886, 964, and 964 stalls, respectively, were rated as advantaged, with points (against which surcharges are assessed) averaging 6.03, 7.12, and 7.09. Figures are not available for 1981, but in 1985 the average surcharge was ¥7,122; in 1990, ¥7,085. On the other side of

the equation, during the same years 216, 280, and 280 stalls, respectively, were ranked below average and assigned points (from which rebates are calculated) that averaged −3.46, −2.89, and −2.89. Again, figures for 1981 are not available, and in both 1985 and 1990 the average rebate per below average stall remained the same: ¥24,240. In the 1981 rankings, 595 stalls were considered average, with neither a surcharge imposed nor a rebate granted, and the number of points separating the best and worst locations was 25. In both the 1985 and the 1990 rankings, the number of average stalls decreased to 433, and the total possible point spread increased to 26. The monthly value of the "points" in 1985 and 1990 was the same: ¥1,000 per positive point and ¥8,400 per negative point. Taken together, these data (calculated from unpublished information in the files of Tō-Oroshi) suggest that the system is moving toward increasingly more minute gradations in the perception of locational advantage and disadvantage.

11. Several other kō—focused on the Narita temple, on the Asakusa Kannon, or on other major religious sites in the Kantō region—are also active at Tsukiji, although their members are not necessarily all from the same occupational specialties. And, of course, many traders individually belong to kō that have no particular connection to the marketplace.

CHAPTER 8. FULL CIRCLE

1. In the past couple of decades, supermarkets and department stores have increasingly supplied the bulk of Tokyo's consumers with fresh foodstuffs. Unlike old-fashioned fishmongers, these retailers take only one or two days' holiday at the New Year. Supermarkets and department stores are more likely to use "out-of-market" *(jōgai)* channels. In fact, one supermarket executive told me his chain developed its own channels to suppliers primarily to deal with holidays when the market is closed, rather than to try to bypass the market on a regular basis.

2. See Plattner 1989a for an overview of anthropological debates—sometimes sharp disputes—between those who see economic behavior in formalist or substantivist terms. LeClair and Schneider (1968) reprint key papers representing both sides.

3. In Japanese lore, the "firsts" of the New Year—the first bath of the year, the first person one greets, the first dream, the first visit to a shrine—all foretell one's fortunes for the coming year.

4. Some Tsukiji traders have mentioned to me their amused embarrassment, at social events outside the marketplace at which such clapping is also a closing element, when they have fallen silent after one round as everyone around them roars into a second refrain.

Bibliography

Acheson, James. 1985. "Social Organization of the Maine Lobster Market." In *Markets and Marketing,* edited by Stuart Plattner, pp. 105–30. Monographs in Economic Anthropology, no. 4. Lanham, Md.: Society for Economic Anthropology.

———. 1994. "Welcome to Nobel Country: A Review of Institutional Economics." In *Anthropology and Institutional Economics,* edited by James Acheson, pp. 3–42. Monographs in Economic Anthropology, no. 12. Lanham, Md.: Society for Economic Anthropology.

———. 2003. *Capturing the Commons: Devising Institutions to Manage the Maine Lobster Industry.* Hanover, N.H.: University Press of New England.

Akamoto, Mariko. 2002. "New, Improved *Kaiten* Shops Herald a Revolution in Dining." *Asahi Shimbun,* September 14–15, p. 36.

Akerlof, George A. 1984. *An Economic Theorist's Book of Tales: Essays That Entertain the Consequences of New Assumptions in Economic Theory.* Cambridge: Cambridge University Press.

Akimichi, Tomoya, et al. 1988. *Small-Type Coastal Whaling in Japan: Report of an International Workshop.* Occasional Publication, no. 27. Edmonton: Boreal Institute for Northern Studies, University of Alberta.

Akiya Shigeo and Shokuhin Ryūtsū Kenkyūkai, eds. 1996. *Oroshiuri shijō ni mirai wa aru ka* (Is there a future for wholesale markets?). Tokyo: Nihon Keizai Shinbunsha.

Akiyoshi Shigeru. 1975. *Ekiben no machi: Nishi Nihon-hen* (Towns with box lunches: Western Japan). Tokyo: Asahi Sonorama.

Alexander, Jennifer, and Paul Alexander. 1991. "What's a Fair Price? Price-Setting and Trading Partnerships in Javanese Markets." *Man,* n.s., 26 (3): 493–512.

Allison, Anne. 1991. "Japanese Mothers and Obentos: The Lunch-Box as Ideological State Apparatus." *Anthropological Quarterly* 64 (4): 195–208.

Anderson, Benedict. 1983. *Imagined Communities: Reflections on the Origin and Spread of Nationalism.* London: Verso.

Andoh, Elizabeth. 1988. *An Ocean of Flavor: The Japanese Way with Fish and Seafood.* New York: William Morrow.

Appadurai, Arjun, ed. 1986a. "On Culinary Authenticity." *Anthropology Today* 2 (4): 25.

———. 1986b. *The Social Life of Things: Commodities in Cultural Perspective.* Cambridge: Cambridge University Press.

———. 1990. "Disjuncture and Difference in the Global Cultural Economy." *Public Culture* 2 (2): 1–24.

———. 1996. *Modernity at Large: Cultural Dimensions of Globalization.* Minneapolis: University of Minnesota Press.

Asakawa, Tomohiro. 1997. "Japan's Eel Market." Unpublished report issued by the Commercial Section, U.S. Embassy, Tokyo. October 21.

Ashkenazi, Michael, and Jeanne Jacob. 2000. *The Essence of Japanese Cuisine: An Essay on Food and Culture.* Philadelphia: University of Pennsylvania Press.

Beckman, Peregrine, dir. 1994. *Fish Is Our Life!* Video submitted as thesis for M.F.A. in film, San Francisco State University. Distributed by University of California Extension Center for Media and Independent Learning, Berkeley.

Befu, Harumi. 1968. "Gift-Giving in a Modernizing Japan." *Monumenta Nipponica* 23: 445–56.

———. 1980a. "The Group Model of Japanese Society and an Alternative." *Rice University Studies* 66 (1): 169–87.

———. 1980b. "Political Ecology of Fishing in Japan." *Reseach in Economic Anthropology* 3: 323–47.

———. 1998. "Globalization of Japan: Its Implications for the Globalization Model." Paper presented at conference at the International Center for Japanese Studies, Kyoto, January 12–16.

Bell, Daniel. 1976. *The Cultural Contradictions of Capitalism.* New York: Basic Books.

Ben-Ari, Eyal. 1997. *Body Projects in Japanese Childcare.* Richmond, Surrey: Curzon.

Beretta P-03. 2003. *Tōkyō Tsukiji* (Tokyo Tsukiji). Tokyo: Raichō-sha.

Bernstein, Gail Lee. 1983. *Haruko's World.* Stanford: Stanford University Press.

———, ed. 1991. *Recreating Japanese Women, 1600–1945.* Berkeley: University of California Press.

Bestor, Theodore C. 1985. "Tradition and Japanese Social Organization: Institutional Development in a Tokyo Neighborhood." *Ethnology* 24 (2): 121–35.

———. 1989. *Neighborhood Tokyo.* Stanford: Stanford University Press.

———. 1990. "Tokyo Mom-and-Pop." *Wilson Quarterly* 14 (4): 27–33.

———. 1990–91. "Daidokoro kara haireru machi" (Entering from the pantry). *Tsukiji monogatari,* no. 7 (autumn 1990): 26–28; no. 8 (winter 1991): 28–30.

———. 1991. "On the Waterfront: An Anthropologist Visits the Tokyo Fish Market," *Columbia,* fall, pp. 30–34.

———. 1992a. "Conflict, Legitimacy, and Tradition in a Tokyo Neighborhood." In *Japanese Social Organization,* edited by Takie S. Lebra, pp. 23–47. Honolulu: University of Hawai'i Press.

————. 1992b. "Rediscovering *Shitamachi:* Subculture, Class, and Tokyo's 'Traditional' Urbanism." In *The Cultural Meaning of Urban Space,* edited by Gary McDonogh and Robert Rotenberg, pp. 47–60. North Hadley, Mass.: Bergen and Garvey.

————. 1995. "What Shape's Your Seafood In? Food Culture and Trade at the Tsukiji Market." *American Seafood Institute Report.* September.

————. 1996. "Forging Tradition: Social Life and Identity in a Tokyo Neighborhood." In *Urban Life: Readings in Urban Anthropology,* edited by George Gmelch and Walter P. Zenner, pp. 524–47. 3rd ed. Prospect Heights, Ill.: Waveland Press.

————. 1999a. "Constructing Sushi: Food Culture, Trade, and Commodification in a Japanese Market." In *Lives in Motion,* edited by Susan O. Long, pp. 151–90. Cornell East Asia Series, no. 106. Ithaca, N.Y.: East Asia Program, Cornell University.

————. 1999b. "Wholesale Sushi: Culture and Commodity in Tokyo's Tsukiji Market." In *Theorizing the City: The New Urban Anthropology Reader,* edited by Setha M. Low, pp. 201–42. New Brunswick, N.J.: Rutgers University Press.

————. 2000. "How Sushi Went Global." *Foreign Policy,* November/December, pp. 54–63.

————. 2001a. "Markets, Anthropological Aspects." In *International Encyclopedia of the Social and Behavioral Sciences,* edited by Neil J. Smelser and Paul B. Baltes, pp. 9227–31. Pergamon: Oxford.

————. 2001b. "Supply-Side Sushi: Commodity, Market, and the Global City." *American Anthropologist* 102 (1): 76–95.

————. 2002a. *"Konbini"* (Convenience stores). In *Encyclopedia of Japanese Business and Management,* edited by Allan Bird, 268–70. London: Routledge.

————. 2002b. "Networks, Neighborhoods, and Markets: Field Research in Tokyo." In *Urban Life: Readings in the Anthropology of the City,* edited by George Gmelch and Walter P. Zenner, pp. 146–61. 4th ed. Prospect Heights, Ill.: Waveland Press.

————. 2002c. "What Shape's Your Seafood In? Trade and Food Culture in the Tsukiji Seafood Market." *Foods and Food Ingredients Journal of Japan* 197: 34–45.

————. 2003a. "Inquisitive Observation: Following Networks in Urban Fieldwork." In *Doing Fieldwork in Japan,* edited by Theodore C. Bestor, Patricia G. Steinhoff, and Victoria Lyon Bestor, pp. 315–34. Honolulu: University of Hawai'i Press.

————. 2003b. "Markets and Places: Tokyo and the Global Tuna Trade." In *The Anthropology of Space and Place: Locating Culture,* edited by Setha Low and Denise Lawrence-Zúñiga, pp. 301–20. Oxford: Blackwell.

————. In preparation. "Global Sushi." Book manuscript.

Bestor, Victoria Lyon. 1998. "Who's Cooking, Whose Kitchen?" Paper presented at the New York Asian Studies Conference, New Paltz, N.Y., October.

Boeck, George A., Jr. 1990. *Texas Livestock Auctions: A Folklife Ethnography.* New York: AMS Press.

Bonacich, Edna. 1973. "A Theory of Middleman Minorities." *American Sociological Review* 38 (5): 583–94.

Borgstrom, Georg. 1964. *Japan's World Success in Fishing.* London: Fishing News.

Bourdain, Anthony. 2001. *A Cook's Tour: Global Adventures in Extreme Cuisines.* New York: HarperCollins.

Bourdieu, Pierre. 1984. *Distinction: A Social Critique of the Judgement of Taste.* Translated by Richard Nice. Cambridge, Mass.: Harvard University Press.

Bourgois, François. 1950. *Japanese Offshore Trawling.* Report Number 138, Natural Resources Section, General Headquarters, Supreme Commander for the Allied Powers. December. [Tokyo.]

Bumiller, Elisabeth. 1995. *The Secrets of Mariko.* New York: Times Books.

Byrne, Daniel. 1985. "Economic Rationality in a Competitive Marketplace." In *Markets and Marketing,* edited by Stuart Plattner, pp. 153–69. Monographs in Economic Anthropology, no. 4. Lanham, Md.: Society for Economic Anthropology.

Cassady, Ralph, Jr. 1967. *Auctions and Auctioneering.* Berkeley: University of California Press.

Chandler, Alfred D., Jr. 1977. *The Visible Hand: The Managerial Revolution in American Business.* Cambridge, Mass.: Harvard University Press.

Chūō-kuritsu Kyōbashi Toshokan, comp. 1996. *Chūō-ku enkakuzu-shū: Kyōbashi-hen* (Collection of historical maps of Chūō-ku: Kyōbashi). Tokyo: Chūō-ku Kyōiku Iinkai.

Chūō-kuyakusho. 1980. *Chūō-ku sanjūnen-shi* (Thirty-year history of Chūō Ward). 2 vols. Tokyo: Chūō-kuyakusho.

Clammer, John. 1997. *Contemporary Urban Japan: A Sociology of Consumption.* Oxford: Blackwell.

Clark, Gracia. 1994. *Onions Are My Husband.* Chicago: University of Chicago Press.

Clark, Rodney. 1979. *The Japanese Company.* New Haven: Yale University Press.

Coaldrake, William H. 1996. *Architecture and Authority in Japan.* London: Routledge.

Coase, Ronald H. 1988. "The Nature of the Firm" (1937). In *The Firm, the Market, and the Law,* pp. 33–55. Chicago: University of Chicago Press.

Cohen, Abner. 1969. *Custom and Politics in Urban Africa.* Berkeley: University of California Press.

Condon, Camy, and Sumiko Ashizawa. 1978. *The Japanese Guide to Fish Cooking.* Tokyo: Shufunotomo.

Constantine, Peter. 1994. *Japanese Slang Uncensored.* Tokyo: Yenbooks.

Cronon, William. 1991. *Nature's Metropolis: Chicago and the Great West.* New York: W. W. Norton.

Cuyler, P. L. 1979. *Sumo: From Rite to Sport.* New York: Weatherhill.

Cwiertka, Katarzyna. 1998. "How Cooking Became a Hobby: Changing Attitudes toward Cooking in Early Twentieth-Century Japan." In *The Culture of Japan as Seen through Its Leisure,* edited by Sepp Linhart and Sabine Frühstück, pp. 41–58. Albany: State University of New York Press.

———. 1999a. "Culinary Globalization and Japan." *Japan Echo* (June), pp. 52–58.

———. 1999b. "The Making of Modern Culinary Tradition in Japan." Ph.D. diss., Center for Japanese Studies, University of Leiden.

———. 2002. "Popularising a Military Diet in Wartime and Postwar Japan." *Asian Anthropology* 1: 1–30.

———. 2003. "Eating the World: Restaurant Culture in Early Twentieth Century Japan." *European Journal of East Asian Studies* 2 (1): 89–116.

Cybriwsky, Roman. 1998. *Tokyo: The Shogun's City at the Twenty-first Century.* New York: John Wiley and Sons.

Dahlmann, Joseph. 1924. *The Great Tokyo Earthquake, September 1, 1923: Experiences and Impressions of an Eye-witness.* New York: America Press.

Dai-matsuri Jujiin. n.d. *Suijin aireiki* (Chronicle of the Suijin festival). Tokyo: privately published.

Daito Gyorui. 1980. *Daito Gyorui Kabushiki Gaisha sanjūnen-shi* (Thirty-year history of Daito Gyorui K.K.). Tokyo: Daito Gyorui.

Dalby, Liza. 1983. *Geisha.* Berkeley: University of California Press.

Daniels, Gordon. 1975. "The Great Tokyo Air Raid, 9–10 March 1945." In *Modern Japan: Aspects of History, Literature, and Society,* edited by W. G. Beasley, pp. 113–31. Berkeley: University of California Press.

de la Pradelle, Michèle. 1995. "Market Exchange and the Social Construction of a Public Space." *French Cultural Studies* 6: 359–71.

Dobbs, David. 2000. *The Great Gulf: Fisherman, Scientists, and the Struggle to Revive the World's Greatest Fishery.* Washington, D.C.: Island Press.

Dore, R. P. 1958. *City Life in Japan.* Berkeley: University of California Press.

———. 1987. "Goodwill and the Spirit of Market Capitalism." In *Taking Japan Seriously: A Confucian Perspective on Leading Economic Issues,* pp. 169–92. Stanford: Stanford University Press.

Douglas, Mary. 1966. *Purity and Danger: An Analysis of the Concepts of Pollution and Taboo.* London: Routledge and Kegan Paul.

———. 1971. "Deciphering a Meal." In *Myth, Symbol, and Culture,* edited by Clifford Geertz, pp. 61–81. New York: W. W. Norton.

———, ed. 1984. *Food in the Social Order: Studies of Food and Festivities in Three American Communities.* New York: Russell Sage Foundation.

Douglas, Mary, and Baron Isherwood. 1971. *The World of Goods: Towards an Anthropology of Consumption.* Harmondsworth: Penguin.

Earle, Sylvia A. 1995. *Sea Change.* New York: Fawcett Columbine.

Ebisawa Shirō. 1996. *Katsuo maguro to Nihonjin* (Bonito, tuna, and the Japanese). Tokyo: Seisando Shoten.

Edo Tōkyō Hakubutsukan, comp. 2003. *Ō-Edo happyaku hatchō* (Great Edo's 808 towns). Tokyo: Edo Tōkyō Hakubutsukan.

Egawa Kōichi. 1990. "Idensei no matsuri chūdoku-tachi" (The guys intoxicated by the festival in their blood). *Tsukiji monogatari,* no. 6 (autumn): 23–29.

Embree, John F. 1939. *Suye Mura: A Japanese Village.* Chicago: University of Chicago Press.

Errington, Frederick. 1987. "The Rock Creek Auction: Contradiction between Competition and Community in Rural Montana." *Ethnology* 26 (4): 297–311.

FAO. n.d. "UN Food and Agriculture Organization, "FAOSTAT Nutrition Data: Food Balance Sheets." http://apps.fao.org/page/collections?subset=nutrition. Data for 1999.

Fields, George. 1983. *From Bonsai to Levi's: When West Meets East, an Insider's Surprising Account of How the Japanese Live.* New York: Macmillan.

"Fish Smugglers Seem to Reap Grim Revenge on Russian General." 2001. *New York Times,* May 29, p. 11.

Flath, David. 1988. "The Economic Rationality of the Japanese Distribution System." Working Paper no. 29. Center on Japanese Economy and Business, Graduate School of Business, Columbia University.

———. 1989a. "Vertical Restraints in Japan." *Japan and the World Economy* 1: 187–203.

———. 1989b. "Why Are There So Many Retail Stores in Japan?" Unpublished paper.

———. 2000. *The Japanese Economy.* Oxford: Oxford University Press.

Fowler, Edward. 1996. *San'ya Blues: Laboring Life in Contemporary Tokyo.* Ithaca, N.Y.: Cornell University Press.

Freeman, Milton M. R., et al. 1989. *Kujira no bunkajinruigaku* (The cultural anthropology of whales). Tokyo: Kaimeisha.

Friedheim, Robert L., ed. 2001. *Toward a Sustainable Whaling Regime.* Seattle: University of Washington Press; Edmonton: Canadian Circumpolar Institute Press.

Fruin, Mark W. 1983. *Kikkoman: Company, Clan, and Community.* Cambridge, Mass.: Harvard University Press.

Fukuzawa Yukichi. 1972. *The Autobiography of Yukichi Fukuzawa.* Revised translation by Eiichi Kiyooka. New York: Schocken Books.

Furushima Toshio. 1996. *Daidokoro yōgu no kindaishi* (The modern history of kitchen utensils). Tokyo: Yūhikaku.

Gaishoku Sangyō Sōgō Chōsa Kenkyū Sentaa, comp. 1998. *Gaishoku sangyō tōkei shiryō-shū* (Collection of statistical material on the restaurant industry). Tokyo: Gaishoku Sangyō Sōgō Chōsa Kenkyū Sentaa. [Annual.]

Garcia, Marie-France. 1986. "La construction sociale d'un marché parfait: le marché au cadran de Fontaines-en-Sologne." *Actes de la recherche en sciences sociales,* no. 65: 2–13.

Geertz, Clifford. 1973. *The Interpretation of Cultures.* New York: Basic Books.

———. 1978. "The Bazaar Economy: Information and Search in Peasant Marketing." *American Economic Review* 68 (2): 28–32.

———. 1979. "Suq: The Bazaar Economy of Sefrou." In *Meaning and Order in Moroccan Society,* by Clifford Geertz, Hildred Geertz, and Lawrence Rosen, pp. 123–314. Cambridge: Cambridge University Press.

Gereffi, Gary, and Miguel Korzeniewicz, eds. 1994. *Commodity Chains and Global Capitalism.* Westport, Conn.: Praeger.

Gerlach, Michael L. 1992a. *Alliance Capitalism: The Social Organization of Japanese Business.* Berkeley: University of California Press.

———. 1992b. *The Keiretsu: A Primer.* New York: Japan Society.

Gill, Tom. 2001. *Men of Uncertainty: The Social Organization of Day Laborers in Contemporary Japan.* Albany: State University of New York Press.

Ginrin (Silver scales). 1951–. Occasional publication of Tōkyō-to Chūō Oroshi-uri Shijō Ginrinkai. No. 1.

Gluck, Carol, and Stephen R. Graubard, eds. 1992. *Shōwa: The Japan of Hiro-hito.* New York: W. W. Norton.

Go, Minoru. 1963. "A Linguistic Analysis of Oyabun-Kobun Slang Terms." Appendix D in *Paternalism in the Japanese Economy: Anthropological Studies of Oyabun-Kobun Patterns,* by John W. Bennett and Iwao Ishino, pp. 273–77. Minneapolis: University of Minnesota Press.

Goffman, Erving. 1959. *The Presentation of Self in Everyday Life.* Garden City, N.Y.: Doubleday.

———. 1974. *Frame Analysis: An Essay on the Organization of Experience.* Cambridge, Mass.: Harvard University Press.

Goldfrank, Walter L. 1994. "Fresh Demand: The Consumption of Chilean Produce in the United States." In *Commodity Chains and Global Capitalism,* edited by Gary Gereffi and Miguel Korzeniewicz, pp. 267–79. Westport, Conn.: Praeger.

Goody, Jack. 1982. *Cooking, Cuisine, and Class: A Study in Comparative Sociology.* Cambridge: Cambridge University Press.

Granovetter, Mark. 1985. "Economic Action and Social Structure: The Problem of Embeddedness." *American Journal of Sociology* 91 (3): 481–510.

Hall, Stuart. 1992. "The Question of Cultural Identity." In *Modernity and Its Futures,* edited by Stuart Hall, David Held, and Tony McGrew, 274–316. London: Polity Press.

Hamabata, Matthews M. 1990. *Crested Kimono: Power and Love in the Japanese Business Family.* Ithaca, N.Y.: Cornell University Press.

Hamilton, Gary G., and Nicole Woolsey Biggart. 1988. "Market, Culture, and Authority: A Comparative Analysis of Management and Organization in the Far East." *American Journal of Sociology* 94 (suppl.): s52–s94.

Hanley, Susan B. 1997. *Everyday Things in Premodern Japan.* Berkeley: University of California Press.

Hannerz, Ulf. 1980. *Exploring the City.* New York: Columbia University Press.

———. 1996. "The Cultural Role of World Cities." In *Transnational Connections,* 127–39. London: Routledge.

Hansen, Karen Tranberg. 2000. *Salaula: The World of Secondhand Clothing and Zambia.* Chicago: University of Chicago Press.

Hardacre, Helen. 1997. *Marketing the Menacing Fetus in Japan.* Berkeley: University of California Press.

Harris, Marvin. 1985. *The Sacred Cow and the Abominable Pig: Riddles of Food and Culture.* New York: Simon and Schuster.

Harvey, David. 1989. *The Urban Experience*. Baltimore: Johns Hopkins University Press.

Hashimoto Mitsuo and Nabeshima Masaharu. 2003. *Tsukiji uogashi sandaime, 8, Amadai no ude* (Third-generation Tsukiji Uogashi, vol. 8, The arm for tilefish). Tokyo: Shōgakkan.

Hayashi Junshin. 1998. *Edo-Tōkyō gurume saijiki* (The gourmet gazetteer of Edo-Tokyo). Tokyo: Yūhikaku.

Hayden, Thomas. 2003. "Empty Oceans: Why the World's Seafood Supply Is Disappearing." *U.S. News and World Report*, June 9, pp. 38–45.

Hendry, Joy. 1986. *Becoming Japanese: The World of the Pre-School Child*. Honolulu: University of Hawai'i Press.

———. 1990. "Humidity, Hygiene, or Ritual Care: Some Thoughts on Wrapping as a Social Phenomenon." In *Unwrapping Japan*, edited by Eyal Ben-Ari, Brian Moeran, and James Valentine, pp. 18–35. Manchester: Manchester University Press.

———. 1993. *Wrapping Culture: Politeness, Presentation, and Power in Japan and Other Societies*. Oxford: Oxford University Press.

Hertz, Ellen. 1998. *The Trading Crowd: An Ethnography of the Shanghai Stock Market*. Cambridge: Cambridge University Press.

Herzfeld, Michael. 1992. *The Social Production of Indifference: Exploring the Symbolic Roots of Western Bureaucracy*. New York: Berg.

Hibbett, Howard. 2002. *The Chrysanthemum and the Fish: Japanese Humor since the Age of the Shoguns*. Tokyo: Kodansha International.

Higuchi Setsuo. 1977. *Teikiichi* (Periodic markets). Tokyo: Gakuseisha.

Hill, Jacquetta F., and David W. Plath. 1998. "Moneyed Knowledge: How Women Become Commercial Shellfish Divers." In *Learning in Likely Places*, edited by John Singleton, pp. 211–25. Cambridge: Cambridge University Press.

Hirano Fumi. 1993. *Omiai aite wa Tsukiji no purinsu* (My fiancé is the prince of Tsukiji). Tokyo: NHK Shuppankai.

———. 1999. *Tsukiji ichiba no sakana ka na?* (Is this a Tsukiji fish?). Tokyo: Asahi Bunko.

Hirano Minase. 1997. "Sengo gojūnen ni okeru chōriyō katei denki seihin hensen" (Changes in home electrical kitchen appliances during the fifty years since World War II). *Vesta* 28: 60–65.

Honda Yukiko. 1997. *Sushi neta zukan* (The illustrated book of sushi toppings). Tokyo: Shōgakkan.

Hori, Takeaki. 1996. *Tuna and the Japanese: In Search of a Sustainable Ecosystem*. Tokyo: Japan External Trade Organization.

———. 2001. *Sashimi bunka ga sekai o ugokasu* (Sashimi culture stirs the world). Tokyo: Shinchōsha.

Hoshino Eiki and Dōshō Takeda. 1993. "*Mizuko kuyō* and Abortion in Contemporary Japan." In *Religion and Society in Modern Japan*, edited by Mark R. Mullins, Shimazono Susumu, and Paul L. Swanson, pp. 171–90. Berkeley: Asian Humanities Press.

Hosking, Richard. 1996. *A Dictionary of Japanese Food: Ingredients and Culture.* Tokyo: Charles E. Tuttle.

Howell, David L. 1995. *Capitalism from Within: Economy, Society, and the State in a Japanese Fishery.* Berkeley: University of California Press.

Huddle, Norie, and Michael Reich, with Nahum Stiskin. 1975. *Island of Dreams: Environmental Crisis in Japan.* New York: Autumn Press.

Iijima Masao. 1972. *Suisan seika shijō yōgo-shū* (Lexicon of terms for seafood and vegetable markets). Tokyo: Sōgō Kenkyūjō.

———. 1989. *Shijō yōgo-shū* (Lexicon of market terminology). 7th rev. ed. Tokyo: Sōgō Chōsa Kenkyūjō.

Ikels, Charlotte. 1996. *The Return of the God of Wealth: The Transition to a Market Economy in Urban China.* Stanford: Stanford University Press.

Imamura, Anne E. 1987. *Urban Japanese Housewives: At Home and in the Community.* Honolulu: University of Hawai'i Press.

———, ed. 1996. *Re-imagining Japanese Women.* Berkeley: University of California Press.

Institute of Cetacean Research. 1996. *Whaling for the Twenty-first Century.* Tokyo: Institute of Cetacean Research.

———. 1999. *Whaling and Anti-whaling Movement.* Tokyo: Institute of Cetacean Research.

Irie, Hiroshi. 1988. "Apprenticeship Training in Tokugawa Japan." *Acta Asiatica* 54: 1–23.

Ishige Naomichi. 1991. *Bunka menruigaku koto hajime* (Beginning cultural noodle studies). Tokyo: Fūdeiamu Komyunikēshon.

———. 1992. *Shoku bunka: Shinsen ichiba* (Food culture: Market of freshness). Tokyo: Mainichi Shinbunsha.

———. 1995. *Shoku no bunka chiri* (Cultural geography of food). Tokyo: Asahi Sensho.

———. 1997. *Shokuzen: Shokugo* (Before the meal: After the meal). Tokyo: Heibonsha.

———, ed. 1999. *Koza: Shoku no bunka: Dai-ni-kan, Nihon no shokuji bunka.* (Series on food culture, vol. 2, The culture of Japanese meals). Tokyo: Ajinomoto Shoku no Bunka Sentaa.

———. 2001. *The History and Culture of Japanese Food.* London: Kegan Paul.

———. n.d. "The Way We Eat." Privately published collection of essays that originally appeared in *AjiCommunications* between 1979 and 1983.

Ishige Naomichi, Koyama Shūzō, Yamaguchi Masatomo, and Ekuan Shōji. 1985. *Rosu Anjerusu no Nihon ryōriten: Sono bunka jinruigakuteki kenkyū* (Japanese restaurants in Los Angeles: Cultural anthropological research). Tokyo: Domesu Shuppan.

Ishiguro Kaoru. 1988. *Maguro ga tonda* (The tuna flew). Tokyo: Tōkyō Tsukiji Uoichiba Ōmono Gyōkai.

Ishiguro Masakichi. 1978. *Kurashi no naka no sakana* (Fish in daily life). Tokyo: Mainichi Shinbunsha.

Ishii Izuo. 1975. *Ekiben ryokō* (Box-lunch travels). Tokyo: Hoikusha.

Ishii Kinza. 1989. *Sono mukashi Tsukushima ryōshi yobanashi* (Tales of the Tsukushima fishers from the old days). Tokyo: privately published.

Ivy, Marilyn. 1995. *Discourses of the Vanishing: Modernity, Phantasm, Japan.* Chicago: University of Chicago Press.

———. 1996. "Tracking the Mystery Man with the 21 Faces." *Critical Inquiry* 23 (1) (autumn): 11–36.

Iwai Hiromi, ed. 1998. *Mingu no seiyōshi* (The living history of folk utensils). Rev. ed. Tokyo: Kawade Shobō.

Iwanami Shoten, comp. 1950. *Uo no ichiba* (The fish market). Iwanami Shashin Bunko 4. Tokyo: Iwanami Shoten.

Janelli, Roger, with Dawnhee Yim. 1993. *Making Capitalism: The Social and Cultural Construction of a South Korean Conglomerate.* Stanford: Stanford University Press.

"Japanese Distribution: Too Many Shopkeepers." 1989. *Economist*, January 28, p. 70.

Japan Whaling Association. 1988. *Subsistence Whaling and Research Whaling.* Tokyo: Japan Whaling Association.

Jinnai, Hidenobu. 1995. *Tokyo: A Spatial Anthropology.* Berkeley: University of California Press.

Jussaume, Raymond A., Jr., Nobuhiro Suzuki, and Dean H. Judson. 1989. *Japanese Wholesale Auction Markets for Fresh Fruits and Vegetables.* Information Series no. 34. [Pullman]: Washington State University, College of Agriculture and Home Economics, IMPACT Center.

Jussaume, Raymond A., Jr., and Patriya Tansuhaj. 1991. "Asian Variations in the Importance of Personal Attributes for Wholesaler Selection: Japanese and Thai Marketing Channels." *Journal of International Consumer Marketing* 3 (3): 127–40.

"Kaiten-zushi dake! 1200-kan!" (Rotary sushi only! 1200 servings!). 2001. *Tōkyō Isshūkan*, December 25.

Kalat, David. 1997. *A Critical History and Filmography of Toho's Godzilla Series.* Jefferson, N.C.: McFarland and Company.

Kalland, Arne. 1981. *Shingū: A Study of a Japanese Fishing Community.* London: Curzon.

———. 1995. *Fishing Villages in Tokugawa Japan.* Honolulu: University of Hawai'i Press.

Kalland, Arne, and Brian Moeran. 1992. *Japanese Whaling: End of an Era?* London: Curzon.

Kariya Tetsu and Hanasaki Akira. 1985. *Oishinbo: Maboroshi no sakana* (Oishinbo: The phantom fish). Tokyo: Shōgakkan.

Kattoulas, Velisarios. 2002. "The Death of Sushi?" *Far Eastern Economic Review*, August 15, pp. 48–51.

Kelly, William W. 1986. "Rationalization and Nostalgia: Cultural Dynamics of New Middle-Class Japan." *American Ethnologist* 13 (4): 603–18.

———. 1990. "Japanese No-Noh: The Crosstalk of Public Culture in a Rural Festivity." *Public Culture* 2 (2): 65–81.

———. 1992. "Regional Japan: The Price of Prosperity and the Benefits of Dependency." In *Shōwa: The Japan of Hirohito,* edited by Carol Gluck and Stephen R. Graubard, pp. 209–27. New York: W. W. Norton.

———. 1994. "Incendiary Actions: Fires and Firefighting in the Shōgun's Capital and the People's City." In *Edo and Paris: Urban Life and the State in the Early Modern Era,* edited by James L. McClain, John M. Merriman, and Ugawa Kaoru, pp. 310–31. Ithaca, N.Y.: Cornell University Press.

Kemf, Elizabeth, Michael Sutton, and Alison Wilson. 1996. *Wanted Alive: Marine Fishes in the Wild.* Gland, Switzerland: WWF—World Wide Fund for Nature.

Kenrick, Doug. 1969. *The Book of Sumo: Sport, Spectacle, and Ritual.* New York: Walker/Weatherhill.

Kerr, Alex. 1996. *Lost Japan.* Oakland, Calif.: Lonely Planet.

Khuri, Fuad I. 1968. "The Etiquette of Bargaining in the Middle East." *American Anthropologist* 70 (4): 698–706.

Kikkawa Takos, ed. 1997. *Japan's Distribution System.* Special issue of *Social Science Japan,* no. 11.

Kingston, Anthony, et al. 1991. *Changes in the Japanese Seafood Market.* Canberra: Australian Bureau of Agricultural and Resource Economics.

Kirman, Alan. 2001. "Market Organization and Individual Behavior: Evidence from Fish Markets." In *Networks and Markets,* edited by James E. Rauch and Alessandra Casella, pp. 155–95. New York: Russell Sage Foundation.

Kodama Setsurō and Otome Masakazu. 1990. *Nihon no ichiba* (Japan's markets). Tokyo: Yōzensha.

Kojima Kazuaki and Edward Gaw. 1990. *A Guide to Grading Tunas and Understanding the Japanese Market.* Lighthouse Point, Fla.: SE Research Publications.

Kōjiro, Yūichiro. 1986. "Edo: The City on the Plain." In *Tokyo: Form and Spirit,* edited by Mildred Friedman, pp. 37–53. Minneapolis: Walker Art Center; New York: Harry N. Abrams.

Kokusai Chigaku Kyōkai. 1974. *Nihon chizu-chō* (Atlas of Japan). Tokyo: Kokusai Chigaku Kyōkai.

Kollock, Peter. 1994. "The Emergence of Exchange Structures: An Experimental Study of Uncertainty, Commitment, and Trust." *American Journal of Sociology* 100 (2): 313–45.

Kondo, Dorinne K. 1990. *Crafting Selves: Power, Gender, and Discourses of Identity in a Japanese Workplace.* Chicago: University of Chicago Press.

———. 1992. "The Aesthetics and Politics of Japanese Identity in the Fashion Industry." In *Re-made in Japan: Everyday Life and Consumer Taste in a Changing Society,* edited by Joseph J. Tobin, pp. 176–203. New Haven: Yale University Press.

Kondō Masaya. 1974. *Uogashi no ki* (Chronicle of the fish market). Tokyo: Tōkyō Shobō-sha.

Kopytoff, Igor. 1986. "The Cultural Biography of Things: Commoditization as Process." In *The Social Life of Things: Commodities in Cultural Perspective,* edited by Arjun Appadurai, pp. 64–91. Cambridge: Cambridge University Press.

Kuiper, Koenraad. 1996. *Smooth Talkers: The Linguistic Performance of Auctioneers and Sportscasters.* Mahwah, N.J.: L. Erlbaum Associates.

LaFleur, William R. 1992. *Liquid Life: Abortion and Buddhism in Japan.* Princeton: Princeton University Press.

Lapp, Ralph E. 1957. *The Voyage of the Lucky Dragon.* New York: Harper.

Lave, Jean, and Etienne Wenger. 1991. *Situated Learning: Legitimate Peripheral Participation.* Cambridge: Cambridge University Press.

Lawrence, Denise L., and Setha M. Low. 1990. "The Built Environment and Spatial Form." *Annual Review of Anthropology* 19: 453–505.

Lebra, Joyce, et al., eds. 1976. *Women in Changing Japan.* Boulder, Colo.: Westview Press.

Lebra, Takie Sugiyama. 1984. *Japanese Women: Constraint and Fulfillment.* Honolulu: University of Hawai'i Press.

LeClair, Edward E., Jr., and Harold K. Schneider, eds. 1968. *Economic Anthropology.* New York: Holt, Rinehart, and Winston.

Lefebvre, Henri. 1991. *The Production of Space.* Translated by Donald Nicholson-Smith. Oxford: Blackwell.

Leshkowich, Ann Marie. 2000. "Tightly Woven Threads: Gender, Kinship, and 'Secret Agency' among Cloth and Clothing Traders in Ho Chi Minh City's Ben Thanh Market." Ph.D. diss., Harvard University.

Lévi-Strauss, Claude. 1966. "The Culinary Triangle." *Partisan Review* 33: 586–95.

———. 1970. *The Raw and the Cooked.* Translated by John and Doreen Weightman. New York: Harper and Row.

Lewis, Michael L. 1990. *Rioters and Citizens: Mass Protest in Imperial Japan.* Berkeley: University of California Press.

Lie, John. 1997. "Sociology of Markets." *Annual Review of Sociology* 23: 341–60.

Lincoln, Edward J. 1990. *Japan's Unequal Trade.* Washington, D.C.: Brookings Institution.

———. 2001. *Arthritic Japan: The Slow Pace of Economic Reform.* Washington, D.C.: Brookings Institution Press.

Lindenfeld, Jacqueline. 1990. *Speech and Sociability at French Urban Marketplaces.* Amsterdam: J. Benjamins Publishing.

Linhart, Sepp. 1998. "From *Kendō* to *Jan-ken:* The Deterioration of a Game from Exoticism into Ordinariness." In *The Culture of Japan as Seen through Its Leisure,* edited by Sepp Linhart and Sabine Frühstück, pp. 319–44. Albany: State University of New York Press.

Lock, Margaret. 1980. *East Asian Medicine in Urban Japan.* Berkeley: University of California Press.

Longworth, John W. 1983. *Beef in Japan: Politics, Production, Marketing and Trade.* St. Lucia: University of Queensland Press.

Macneil, Ian R. 2001. *The Relational Theory of Contract: Selected Works of Ian Macneil.* Edited by David Campbell. London: Sweet and Maxwell.

MAFF. See Nōrinsuisanshō and Ministry of Agriculture, Forestry and Fisheries for publications in Japanese and English, respectively.

Marra, Robert J. 1986. "The Katsumoto-ura Fishing Cooperative: A Lesson in the Autonomous Control of a Fishing Economy." Ph.D. diss., University of Pittsburgh.

Marshall, Robert. 1984. *Collective Decision-Making in Rural Japan*. Ann Arbor: Center for Japanese Studies, University of Michigan.

Maruha. 1996. *Maruha: Kaisha annai* (Maruha: Company guide). Tokyo: Maruha.

Masai Yasuo. 1975. *Edo no toshiteki tochi riyō-zu, 1860-nen goro* (Urban land use map of Edo, ca. 1860). Tokyo: privately published.

McAfee, R. Preston, and John McMillan. 1987. "Auctions and Bidding." *Journal of Economic Literature* 25: 699–738.

McClain, James L. 1994. "Edobashi: Power, Space, and Popular Culture in Edo." In *Edo and Paris: Urban Life and the State in the Early Modern Era*, edited by James L. McClain, John M. Merriman, and Ugawa Kaoru, pp. 105–31. Ithaca, N.Y.: Cornell University Press.

———. 1999. "Space, Power, Wealth, and Status in Seventeenth-Century Osaka." In *Osaka: The Merchants' Capital of Early Modern Japan*, edited by James L. McClain and Wakita Osamu, pp. 44–79. Ithaca, N.Y.: Cornell University Press.

McClain, James L., and Wakita Osamu, eds. 1999. *Osaka: The Merchants' Capital of Early Modern Japan*. Ithaca, N.Y.: Cornell University Press.

McClellan, Edwin. 1985. *Woman in the Crested Kimono: The Life of Shibue Io and Her Family*. New Haven: Yale University Press.

McCloskey, William. 1998. *Their Fathers' Work: Casting Nets with the World's Fishermen*. Camden, Me.: International Marine/McGraw Hill.

McDonogh, Gary, and Robert Rotenberg, eds. 1992. *The Cultural Meaning of Urban Space*. North Hadley, Mass.: Bergen and Garvey.

McMillan, John. 1991. "*Dango*: Japan's Price-Fixing Conspiracies." *Economics and Politics* 3 (3): 201–17.

———. 2002. *Reinventing the Bazaar: A Natural History of Markets*. New York: W. W. Norton.

Messer, Ellen. 1984. "Anthropological Perspectives on Diet." *Annual Review of Anthropology* 13: 205–49.

Milgrom, Paul. 1987. "Auction Theory." In *Advances in Economic Theory*, edited by Truman Bewley, pp. 1–32. Cambridge: Cambridge University Press.

———. 1989. "Auctions and Bidding: A Primer." *Journal of Economic Perspectives* 3 (3): 3–22.

Milgrom, P. R., and R. J. Weber. 1982. "A Theory of Auctions and Competitive Bidding." *Econometrica* 50: 1089–1122.

Ministry of Agriculture, Forestry and Fisheries (MAFF). 2001. *Abstract of Statistics on Agriculture Forestry and Fisheries in Japan*. Tokyo: MAFF Statistics and Information Department.

[Ministry of Agriculture, Forestry and Fisheries (MAFF). *See also* Nōrinsuisanshō for Japanese-language publications by the same agency.]

Mintz, Sidney. 1985. *Sweetness and Power: The Place of Sugar in Modern History.* New York: Viking.

—. 1996a. "Fish, Food Habits, and Material Culture." *Hong Kong Anthropologist,* no. 9: 2–9.

—. 1996b. *Tasting Food, Tasting Freedom: Excursions into Eating, Culture, and the Past.* Boston: Beacon Press.

—. 1997. "Swallowing Modernity." In *Golden Arches East: McDonald's in East Asia,* edited by J. L. Watson, pp. 183–200. Stanford: Stanford University Press.

Mochizuki Kenji, ed. 1997. *Sakana to kai no daijiten* (The encyclopedia of fish and shellfish). Tokyo: Kashiwa Shobō.

Mori Kazan. 1977. *Mori Kazan gashū: Nihonbashi uogashi* (Collected sketches of Mori Kazan: Nihonbashi fish market). Tokyo: Tōkyō Uoichiba Oroshi Kyōdō Kumiai.

Morooka Yukio. 1986. *Kanda Tsuruhachi sushibanashi* (Sushi stories from Kanda Tsuruhachi). Tokyo: Sōshisha.

Motohashi Seiichi. 1988. *Uogashi—hito no machi* (Uogashi—a neighborhood of people). Tokyo: Shōbunsha.

Mulvaney, Kieran. 2003. *The Whaling Season: An Inside Account of the Struggle to Stop Commercial Whaling.* Washington, D.C.: Island Press/Shearwater Books.

Murai Yoshinori. 1988. *Ebi to Nihonjin* (Shrimp and the Japanese). Tokyo: Iwanami Shoten.

Myers, Ransom A., and Boris Worm. 2003. "Rapid Worldwide Depletion of Predatory Fish Communities." *Nature* 423 (May 15): 280–83.

Nakagawa Hiroshi. 1995. *Shoku no sengo-shi* (The postwar history of food). Tokyo: Akashi Shoten.

Nakamura Masaru. 1980. *Shijō no kataru Nihon no kindai* (Markets and Japan's modern times). Tokyo: Soshiete.

—. 1990. *Uogashi wa ikiteiru* (The fish market lives). Tokyo: Soshiete.

Nakane, Chie. 1970. *Japanese Society.* Berkeley: University of California Press.

Nakano Makiko. 1995. *Makiko's Diary.* Translated by Kazuko Smith. Stanford: Stanford University Press.

Nathan, John, prod. and dir. 1976. *Full Moon Lunch.* Japan Society Films. Distributed in video format by Asian Educational Media Service, University of Illinois at Urbana-Champaign.

—, prod. and dir. 1981. *The Colonel Comes to Japan.* WGBH-TV, Boston, Mass.

National Geographic. 2001. "Giant Bluefin Tuna." Broadcast on MSNBC's *National Geographic Explorer,* May 4.

Ng, Wai-ming. 2001. "Popularization and Localization of Sushi in Singapore: An Ethnographic Survey." *New Zealand Journal of Asian Studies* 3 (1): 7–19.

Nihon Kenchiku Gakkai, comp. 1987. *Sōran Nihon no kenchiku: Dai-san-kan,*

Tōkyō (Catalogue of Japanese architecture, vol. 3, Tokyo). Tokyo: Shinken-chiku.

Nihon Tōkei Kyōkai, comp. 2003. *Nihon tōkei nenkan* (Japan statistical year-book). Tokyo: Nihon Tōkei Kyōkai. [Annual.]

Nikkan Shokuryō Shinbunsha, comp. 1990. *Tōkyō-to Chūō Oroshiuri Shijō suisanbutsu-bu nakaoroshi gyōsha meibō 1990-nenpan* (TMG Central Wholesale Market, seafood division intermediate wholesalers' directory, 1990 edition). Tokyo: Nikkan Shokuryō Shinbunsha.

Nishiyama Matsunosuke. 1997. *Edo Culture: Daily Life and Diversions in Urban Japan, 1600–1868.* Translated and edited by Gerald Groemer. Honolulu: University of Hawai'i Press.

Nishiyama Matsunosuke et al., eds. 1984. *Edogaku jiten* (Encyclopedia of Edo studies). Tokyo: Kōbundō.

Noguchi, Paul H. 1994. "*Ekiben:* The Fast Food of High-Speed Japan." *Ethnology* 33 (4): 317–30.

Norbeck, Edward. 1954. *Takashima, a Japanese Fishing Community.* Salt Lake City: University of Utah Press.

Nōrinsuisanshō. 1989. *Suisan tōkei* (Fisheries statistics). Tokyo: Nōrinsuisanshō Tōkei Jōhō-bu. [Annual.]

———. 1997. *Poketto suisan tōkei: Heisei kyūnendo-ban* (Pocket fisheries statistics: 1997 fiscal year). Tokyo: Nōrinsuisanshō Tōkeijōhōbu. [Annual.]

———. 2002. *Suisanbutsu yushutsunyū jisseki: 1997-nen 2001-nen* (Actual exports and imports of marine products: 1997–2001). Tokyo: Nōrinsuisanshō Suisanchō.

[Nōrinsuisanshō. *See also* Ministry of Agriculture, Forestry and Fisheries for English-language publications by the same agency.]

Ohnuki-Tierney, Emiko. 1990. "The Ambivalent Self of the Contemporary Japanese." *Cultural Anthropology* 5 (2): 197–216.

———. 1993. *Rice as Self: Japanese Identities through Time.* Princeton: Princeton University Press.

———. 1997. "McDonald's in Japan: Changing Manners and Etiquette." In *Golden Arches East: McDonald's in East Asia,* edited by J. L. Watson, pp. 161–82. Stanford: Stanford University Press.

Okamoto Makoto and Kido Tokunari. 1985. *Nihonbashi uogashi no rekishi* (The history of the Nihonbashi fish market). Tokyo: Suisansha.

Omae, Kinjiro, and Yuzuru Tachibana. 1981. *The Book of Sushi.* Tokyo: Kodansha International.

Omura Bajin. 1990. *Kushū: Ichiba-shō—maguro haiku nōto* (Anthology: Market excerpts—tuna haiku notes). Tokyo: Tōkyō Shiki Shuppan.

Omura Kōzaburō. 1984. *Nihonbashi monogatari* (The tale of Nihonbashi). Tokyo: Seiabō.

Oroshiuri Shijō-hō Kenkyūkai. 1989. *Shijō ryūtsū yōran* (Handbook of market distribution). Tokyo: Taisei Shuppansha.

Oroshiuri Shijō Seido Gojūnen-shi Hensan Iinkai, comp. 1979. *Oroshiuri shijō seido gojūnen-shi* (Fifty-year history of the wholesale market system). 6 vols. Tokyo: Shokuhin Jūkyū Kenkyū Sentaa.

Ōtsuka Minzoku Gakkai, comp. 1972. *Nihon minzoku jiten* (Japan folklore dictionary). Tokyo: Kōbundō.

Patrick, Hugh T., and Thomas P. Rohlen. 1987. "Small-Scale Family Enterprises." In *The Political Economy of Japan*, vol. 1, *The Domestic Transformation*, edited by Kozo Yamamura and Yasukichi Yasuba, pp. 331–84. Stanford: Stanford University Press.

Peterson, Susan B. 1973. "Decisions in a Market: A Study of the Honolulu Fish Auction." Ph.D. diss., University of Hawai'i.

Peterson, Susan, and Daniel Georgianna. 1988. "New Bedford's Fish Auction: A Study in Auction Method and Market Power." *Human Organization* 47 (3): 235–41.

Plath, David W. 1992a. "My-Car-isma: Motorizing the Showa Self." In *Shōwa: The Japan of Hirohito*, edited by Carol Gluck and Stephen R. Graubard, pp. 229–44. New York: W. W. Norton.

———, prod. 1992b. *Neighborhood Tokyo*. Video distributed by DER, Watertown, Mass.

———, dir. 1994. *Fit Surroundings*. Video distributed by DER, Watertown, Mass.

———. 1998. "Calluses: When Culture Gets under Your Skin." In *Learning in Likely Places: Varieties of Apprenticeship in Japan*, edited by John Singleton, pp. 341–51. Cambridge: Cambridge University Press.

Plath, David W., and Jacquetta Hill. 1987. "The Reefs of Rivalry: Expertness and Competition among Japanese Shellfish Divers." *Ethnology* 26 (3): 151–63.

———. 1988. "'Fit Surroundings'—Japanese Shellfish Divers and the Artisan Option." *Social Behaviour* 3: 149–59.

Plattner, Stuart. 1982. "Economic Decision Making in a Public Marketplace." *American Ethnologist* 9 (2): 399–420.

———. 1983. "Economic Custom in a Competitive Market Place." *American Anthropologist* 85: 848–58.

———. 1984. "Economic Decision Making of Marketplace Merchants: An Ethnographic Model." *Human Organization* 43 (3): 252–64.

———. 1985. "Equilibrating Market Relationships." In *Markets and Marketing*, edited by Stuart Plattner, pp. 133–52. Monographs in Economic Anthropology, no. 4. Lanham, Md.: Society for Economic Anthropology.

———. 1989a. "Economic Behavior in Markets." In *Economic Anthropology*, edited by Stuart Plattner, pp. 209–21. Stanford: Stanford University Press.

———. 1989b. "Markets and Marketplaces." In *Economic Anthropology*, edited by Stuart Plattner, pp. 171–208. Stanford: Stanford University Press.

Price, John. 1967. "The Japanese Market System: Retailing in a Dual Economy." Ph.D. diss., University of Michigan.

Prindle, Tamae. 1996. "Globally Yours: *Tampopo* as a Postmodern Film." In *Japan Engaging the World: A Century of International Encounter*, edited by Harumi Befu, pp. 61–71. Denver, Colo.: Center for Japanese Studies, Teikyo Loretto Heights University.

Raab, Selwyn. 1996. "Gains Seen in Fish Market Crackdown; Mayor's Office

Asserts Prices Are Lower, but Some Doubt Findings." *New York Times,* November 11, p. B3.

Radford, R. A. 1968. "The Economic Organisation of a P.O.W. Camp." In *Economic Anthropology,* edited by Edward E. LeClair, Jr., and Harold K. Schneider, pp. 403–14. New York: Holt, Rinehart, and Winston. [Originally published in *Economica,* November 1945.]

Rakugakisha, comp. 1988. *Zukai: Yo no naka kō natte iru: Ryūtsūhen* (It's this way in the world, diagrammed: Distribution). Tokyo: Rakugakisha. [English edition published in 1989 as *What's What in Japan's Distribution System* (Tokyo: Japan Times).]

Rakugo Shin'ichi. 1990. "Sushidane saijiki" (Annual chronicle of sushi toppings). *Taiyō: Sushi dokuhon* (The sushi reader), no. 343 (February): 38–51.

Raz, Aviad E. 1999. *Riding the Black Ship: Japan and Tokyo Disneyland.* Cambridge, Mass.: Harvard University Asia Center.

Redfield, Robert, and Milton Singer. 1954. "The Cultural Role of Cities." *Economic Development and Cultural Change* 3 (October): 53–77.

Reich, Michael. 1991. *Toxic Politics: Responding to Chemical Disasters.* Ithaca, N.Y.: Cornell University Press.

Reid, T. R. 1995. "The Great Tokyo Fish Market." *National Geographic* 188 (5): 38–55.

Richie, Donald. 1985. *A Taste of Japan.* Tokyo: Kodansha International.

Richie, Donald, and Ian Buruma. 1980. *The Japanese Tattoo.* Tokyo: Weatherhill.

Robertson, Jennifer. 1991. *Native and Newcomer.* Berkeley: University of California Press.

Rogers, Philip G. 1956. *The First Englishman in Japan: The Story of Will Adams.* London: Harvill Press.

Rohlen, Thomas. 1974. *For Harmony and Strength.* Berkeley: University of California Press.

Roseberry, William. 1996. "The Rise of Yuppie Coffees and the Reimagination of Class in the United States." *American Anthropologist* 98 (4): 762–775.

Rotenberg, Robert. 1992. *Time and Order in Metropolitan Vienna: A Seizure of Schedules.* Washington, D.C.: Smithsonian Institution Press.

Ruble, Blair. 1995. *Money Sings: The Changing Politics of Urban Space in Post-Soviet Yaroslavl.* Washington, D.C.: Woodrow Wilson Center Press; Cambridge: Cambridge University Press.

Ruddle, Kenneth, and Tomoya Akimichi, eds. 1984. *Maritime Institutions in the Western Pacific.* Osaka: National Museum of Ethnology.

———. 1989. "Sea Tenure in Japan and the Southwestern Ryukyus." In *A Sea of Small Boats,* edited by John Cordell, pp. 337–70. Cambridge, Mass.: Cultural Survival.

Safina, Carl. 1995. "The World's Imperiled Fish." *Scientific American* 273 (5): 46–53.

———. 1997. *Song for the Blue Ocean.* New York: Henry Holt.

Sahlins, Marshall. 1972. *Stone Age Economics.* Chicago: Aldine-Atherton.

———. 1976. *Culture and Practical Reason.* Chicago: University of Chicago Press.

Sanger, David E. 1990. "For a Job Well Done, Japanese Enshrine the Chip." *New York Times,* December 11.

Sato, Kazuo. 1990. "The Paradox of Japan's Distribution System." Paper presented to the Japan Economic Seminar, East Asian Institute, Columbia University.

Satomi Shinzō. 1997. *Sukiyabashi Jirō: Shun o nigiru* (Sukiyabashi Jirō: Grasping the season). Tokyo: Bungei Shunjū.

Sawada Shigetaka. 1985. *Uoichiba* (The fish market). Tokyo: Hyōronsha.

Schaede, Ulrike. 1991. "The Development of Organized Futures Trading: The Osaka Rice Bill Market of 1730." In *Japanese Financial Market Research,* edited by W. T. Ziemba, W. Bailey, and Y. Hamao, pp. 339–66. Amsterdam: North-Holland.

Schmidhauser, John R., and George O. Totten III, eds. 1978. *The Whaling Issue in U.S.-Japan Relations.* Boulder, Colo.: Westview Press.

Schoppa, Leonard J. 1997. *Bargaining with Japan: What American Pressure Can and Cannot Do.* New York: Columbia University Press.

Seabrook, John. 1994. "Death of a Giant: Stalking the Disappearing Bluefin Tuna." *Harper's Magazine,* June, 48–56.

Seibidō Mook, comp. 1998. *Ryōrinin ga oshieru hōchōzukai to sakana no sabakikata* (Chefs teach using a knife and handling fish). Tokyo: Seibidō Shuppan.

Seidensticker, Edward. 1983. *Low City, High City.* New York: Knopf.

———. 1990. *Tokyo Rising.* New York: Knopf.

Seligmann, Linda J., ed. 2001. *Women Traders in Cross-Cultural Perspective.* Stanford: Stanford University Press.

Shaw, John. 2002. "Australia Casts Net for Fish Poachers." *New York Times,* September 8, p. 10.

Shield, Renée Rose. 2002. *Diamond Stories: Enduring Change on 47th Street.* Ithaca, N.Y.: Cornell University Press.

Shijō jigyō gaiyō (Overview of market operations). 1989–2003. Tokyo: Tōkyō-to Chūō Oroshiuri Shijō. [Annual.]

Shijō memo (Market memo). 1988–2003. Tokyo: Tōkyō-to Chūō Oroshiuri Shijō. [Annual.]

Shimoda Tōru. 2001. *Itamae shūgyō* (Chefs' training). Tokyo: Shūeisha.

Shokuhin Ryūtsū Jōhō Sentaa, comp. 1989–99. *Shoku seikatsu deeta sōgō tōkei nenpō* (Yearbook of general food consumption statistics). Tokyo: Shokuhin Ryūtsū Jōhō Sentaa. [Annual.]

Simmel, Georg. 1990. *The Philosophy of Money.* Edited by David Frisby, translated by Tom Bottomore and David Frisby. 2nd ed. London: Routledge.

Singleton, John. 1993. " 'Stealing the Secrets': Cultural Acquisition in Folk Craft Practice." Paper presented at the annual meetings of the American Anthropological Association, Washington, D.C., November.

———, ed. 1998. *Learning in Likely Places: Varieties of Apprenticeship in Japan.* Cambridge: Cambridge University Press.

Skinner, G. William. 1964–65. "Marketing and Social Structure in Rural China." Parts 1 and 2. *Journal of Asian Studies* 24 (1): 3–43; (2): 195–228.

Smith, Charles W. 1989. *Auctions: The Social Construction of Value.* New York: Free Press.

Smith, Henry D., II. 1979. "Tokyo and London: Comparative Conceptions of the City." In *Japan: A Comparative View,* edited by Albert M. Craig, pp. 49–99. Princeton: Princeton University Press.

———. 1986. "Sky and Water: The Deep Structures of Tokyo." In *Tokyo: Form and Spirit,* edited by Mildred Friedman, pp. 21–35. Minneapolis: Walker Art Center; New York: Harry N. Abrams.

Smith, Robert J. 1960. "Pre-industrial Urbanism in Japan." *Economic Development and Cultural Change* 9 (1, part 2): 241–57.

———. 1978. *Kurusu: The Price of Progress in a Japanese Village.* Stanford: Stanford University Press.

———. 1992a. "The Cultural Context of the Japanese Political Economy." In *The Political Economy of Japan,* vol. 3, *Cultural and Social Dynamics,* edited by Shumpei Kumon and Henry Rosovsky, pp. 13–31. Stanford: Stanford University Press.

———. 1992b. "The Living and the Dead in Japanese Popular Religion." Paper presented to the Columbia University Modern Japan Seminar.

Smith, Robert J., and Ella Lury Wiswell. 1982. *The Women of Suye Mura.* Chicago: University of Chicago Press.

Smith, Vernon L. 2000. *Bargaining and Market Behavior: Essays in Experimental Economics.* Cambridge: Cambridge University Press.

Smith, Vernon L., and Arlington W. Williams. 1992. "Experimental Market Economics." *Scientific American* 267 (6): 116–21.

Smith, W. Eugene, and Aileen M. Smith. 1981. *Minamata.* Tucson: Center for Creative Photography, University of Arizona.

Sonu, Sunee C. 1993. *Japan's Squid Market.* Technical Memorandum NOAA-TM-NMFS-SWR-028. Long Beach, Calif.: U.S. Department of Commerce, National Oceanic and Atmospheric Administration, National Marine Fisheries Service, Southwest Region.

———. 1994. *The Japanese Market for U.S. Tuna Products.* Technical Memorandum NOAA-TM-NMFS-SWR-029. Long Beach, Calif.: U.S. Department of Commerce, National Oceanic and Atmospheric Administration, National Marine Fisheries Service, Southwest Region.

———. 1995. *The Japanese Sea Urchin Market.* Technical Memorandum NOAA-TM-NMFS-SWR-030. Long Beach, Calif.: U.S. Department of Commerce, National Oceanic and Atmospheric Administration, National Marine Fisheries Service, Southwest Region.

———. 1996. *The Japanese Sablefish Market.* Technical Memorandum NOAA-TM-NMFS-SWR-031. Long Beach, Calif.: U.S. Department of Commerce, National Oceanic and Atmospheric Administration, National Marine Fisheries Service, Southwest Fisheries Science Center.

———. 1997. *The Japanese Swordfish Market.* Technical Memorandum NOAA-TM-NMFS-SWR-032. Long Beach, Calif.: U.S. Department of Commerce, National Oceanic and Atmospheric Administration, National Marine Fisheries Service, Southwest Fisheries Science Center.

————. 1998. *Shark Fisheries, Trade, and Market of Japan*. Technical Memorandum NOAA-TM-NMFS-SWR-033. Long Beach, Calif.: U.S. Department of Commerce, National Oceanic and Atmospheric Administration, National Marine Fisheries Service, Southwest Region.

Sorokin, Pitirm A., and Robert K. Merton. 1937. "Social Time: A Methodological and Functional Analysis." *American Journal of Sociology* 42 (5): 615–29.

Stevens, Carolyn S. 1997. *On the Margins of Japanese Society*. London: Routledge.

Stoett, Peter J. 1997. *The International Politics of Whaling*. Vancouver: University of British Columbia Press.

Suehiro Yasuo. 1997. *Sushibanashi, uobanashi* (Sushi talk, fish talk). Rev. ed. Tokyo: Heibonsha.

Sugita Genpaku. 1969. *Dawn of Western Science in Japan*. Translated by Matsumoto Ryōzō and Eiichi Kiyōka. Tokyo: Hokuseido Press.

Suisansha. 1989–2002. *Suisan nenkan* (Fisheries yearbook).Tokyo: Suisansha. [Annual.]

Sunada, Toshiko. 1980. "Fresh Green Leaves to See . . . " *AjiCommunications* 3.

Suzuki Masao, ed. 1999. *Tōkyō no chiri ga wakaru jiten* (Handbook for understanding Tokyo's geography). Tokyo: Nihon Jitsugyō Shuppansha.

Swedberg, Richard, and Mark Granovetter. 1992. Introduction to *The Sociology of Economic Life*, edited by Mark Granovetter and Richard Swedberg, pp. 1–26. Boulder, Colo.: Westview Press.

Taguchi Tatsuzō. 1962. *Uogashi seisuiki* (Ups-and-downs of the Uogashi). Tokyo: Isana Shobō.

Taiyō. 1990. Special issue, *Sushi dokuhon* (The sushi reader), no. 343 (February).

Takahashi, Jun'ichi, et al. 1989. "Japanese Whaling Culture: Continuities and Diversities." *Maritime Anthropological Studies* 2 (2): 105–33.

Takarai Zenjirō. 1991. *Maguroya hanjōki* (Chronicle of a tuna merchant's good times). Tokyo: Shufunotomosha.

Tamamura Toyō. 2000. *Kaiten-zushi sekai hitomeguri* (Rotary sushi around the world). Tokyo: Sekaibunkasha.

Tanizaki, Jun'ichirō. 1988. *Childhood Years: A Memoir*. Translated by Paul McCarthy. Tokyo: Kodansha International.

Terasawa Daisuke. 1992. *Shōta no sushi* (Shōta's sushi). Vol. 1. Tokyo: Kōdansha.

Thompson, E. P. 1967. "Time, Work-Discipline, and Industrial Capitalism." *Past and Present*, no. 38 (December): 56–97.

Tilton, Mark. 1996. *Restrained Trade: Cartels in Japan's Basic Materials Industries*. Ithaca, N.Y.: Cornell University Press.

Tobin, Jeffrey. 1992. "A Japanese-French Restaurant in Hawai'i." In *Re-made in Japan: Everyday Life and Consumer Taste in a Changing Society*, edited by Joseph J. Tobin, pp. 159–75. New Haven: Yale University Press.

Tōkyōjin. 2001. Special issue, *Nenmatsu no Tsukiji Shijō annai* (Guide to the Tsukiji market at year's end), no. 161 (January).

Tokyo Metropolitan Government. 1988. *The Tokyo Central Wholesale Market:*

In Brief Outline. Tokyo: Tokyo Metropolitan Government Central Whole-sale Market.

———. 1995. *Wholesale Market Guide.* Tokyo: Tokyo Metropolitan Government Central Wholesale Market.

[Tokyo Metropolitan Government. *See also* Tōkyō-to (for Japanese language publications).]

Tōkyō-shiyakusho. 1935. *Tōkyō-shi Chūō Oroshiuri Shijō Tsukiji honjō: Kenchiku zushū* (City of Tokyo Central Wholesale Market Tsukiji main market: Album of architectural illustrations). Tokyo: Tōkyō-shiyakusho.

[Tōkyō-to. *See also* Tokyo Metropolitan Government (for English language publications).]

Tōkyō-to Chūō Oroshiuri Shijō. 1958–63. *Tōkyō-to Chūō Oroshiuri Shijō-shi* (History of the Tokyo Central Wholesale Market). 2 vols. Tokyo: Tōkyō-to.

———. 1985. *Tokyo-to Chūō Oroshiuri Shijō gojūnen no ayumi* (Fifty years of the Tokyo Metropolitan Government's Central Wholesale Market). Tokyo: Tōkyō-to Chūō Oroshiuri Shijō.

———. 1988. *Shijō nenpō* (Market yearbook). Tokyo: Tōkyō-to. [Annual.]

———. 1990–2000. *Tōkyō-to Chūō Oroshiuri Shijō gaiyō* (Tokyo Central Wholesale Market overview). Tokyo: Tōkyō-to Chūō Oroshiuri Shijō. [Annual.]

———. 1991. *Suisanbutsu budomari chōsa gaiyō* (Overview of survey on yields of marine products). Tokyo: Tōkyō-to Chūō Oroshiuri Shijō.

———. 1996. *Dai jūrokkai seisen shokuryōhin oyobi kaki shōhi-kanbai dōkō: Chōsa kekka* (Results of the sixteenth survey of consumption and sales trends for perishable foodstuffs and flowers). Tokyo: Tōkyō-to Chūō Oroshiuri Shijō.

———. 1999. *Dai jūkyūkai seisen shokuryōhin oyobi kaki shōhi-kanbai dōkō: Chōsa kekka* (Results of the nineteenth survey of consumption and sales trends for perishable foodstuffs and flowers). Tokyo: Tōkyō-to Chūō Oroshiuri Shijō.

———. 2003. *Deeta de miru nakaoroshi gyōsha no keiei jōkyō 2002* (Looking at data on intermediate wholesalers' management conditions, 2002). Tokyo: Tōkyō-to Chūō Oroshiuri Shijō.

Tōkyō-to Kōbunshokan, comp. 1957. *Tsukiji iryūchi* (The Tsukiji foreign settlement). *Toshi Kiyō* (Metropolitan history memoirs) vol. 4. Tokyo: Tōkyō-to.

———, comp. 1978. *Tsukudajima to shirauo gyogyō* (Tsukudajima and whitebait fisheries). *Toshi Kiyō* (Metropolitan history memoirs) vol. 26. Tokyo: Tōkyō-to.

Tōkyō-to Kyōiku-chō Shakai Kyōiku-bu Bunka-ka, comp. 1989. *Edo fukugen-zu* (Recreated maps of Edo). Tokyo: Tōkyō-to.

Tōkyō Uoichiba Oroshi Kyōdō Kumiai, comp. 2002. *Tōkyō Uoichiba Oroshi Kyōdō Kumiai gojūnen-shi* (Fifty-year history of the Tokyo Fish Market Wholesalers' Cooperative Federation). Tokyo: Tōkyō Uoichiba Oroshi Kyōdō Kumiai.

Tō-Oroshi. Monthly publication of Tōkyō Uoichiba Oroshi Kyōdō Kumiai.

Tōto Suisan. 1987. *Tōto Suisan Kabushiki Gaisha gojūnen-shi* (Fifty-year history of Tōto Suisan K.K.). 2 vols. Tokyo: Tōto Suisan.

Tōyō Keizai Shinpōsha, comp. 1987–2002. *Japan Company Handbook (First Section).* Tokyo: Tōyō Keizai Shinpōsha. [Semi-annual.]

Trewartha, Glenn T. 1965. *Japan: A Geography.* Madison: University of Wisconsin Press.

"Tsukiji jōnai katsuyō hakka" (A practical encyclopedia of Tsukiji's inner market). 1982. *Senmon Ryōri,* December, pp. 66–81.

Tsukiji monogatari (Tales of Tsukiji). Quarterly publication sponsored by merchants in the outer marketplace.

Tsukiji Shijō gaiyō (Tsukiji Market overview). 1990–2003. Tokyo: Tōkyō-to Oroshiuri Shijō Tsukiji Shijō. [Annual.]

Tsutsui, William. 2002. "Landscapes in the Dark Valley: Toward an Environmental History of Wartime Japan." Paper presented at the Reischauer Institute of Japanese Studies, Harvard University, Cambridge, Mass., May 3.

Uchida Eiichi. 1990. *Asakusa sushiya banashi* (Tales of an Asakusa sushi shop). Tokyo: Chikuma Bunko.

Ueda Takeshi. 2003. *Uogashi maguro keizaigaku* (The market economics of tuna). Tokyo: Shūeisha.

United States. 1996. *Whaling Activities of Japan: Message from the President of the United States Transmitting a Report Regarding Certification by the Secretary of Commerce Concerning Japan's Research Whaling Activities That Diminish the Effectiveness of the International Whaling Commission (IWC) Conservation Program, Pursuant to 22 U.S.C. 1978(b).* Washington: U.S. Government Printing Office.

Uogashi hyakunen (The fish market's hundred years). 1968. Tokyo: Uogashi Hyakunen Hensan Iinkai.

Uogashi Suijin-sai Iinkai. 1989. *Suijin-sha mikoshi dashi shūfuku kinen kiroku* (Commemorative record of the restoration of Suijin Festival's *mikoshi* and cart). Privately distributed videotape.

———. 1990. *Uogashi Suijin-sai: Heisei ninen aki* (The Uogashi's Suijin Festival: Autumn 1990). Privately distributed videotape.

Utsukushii Nihon no Jōshiki o Saihakken suru Kai, comp. 2003. *Nihonjin wa sushi no koto o nani mo shiranai* (Japanese know nothing about sushi). Tokyo: Gakken.

Vickrey, William. 1961. "Counterspeculation, Auctions, and Competitive Sealed Tenders." *Journal of Finance* 16: 8–37.

Vogel, Ezra F. 1991. *Japan's New Middle Class.* 3rd ed. Berkeley: University of California Press.

Vogel, Suzanne H. 1978. "Professional Housewife: The Career of Urban Middle Class Japanese Women." *Japan Interpreter* 12 (1): 16–43.

Wagatsuma, Hiroshi, and George A. DeVos. 1984. *Heritage of Endurance.* Berkeley: University of California Press.

Watanabe Fumio, ed. 1991. *Maguro o marugoto ajiwau hon* (The complete book of tuna tasting). Tokyo: Kōbunsha.

Watanabe Yonehide. 2002. *Kaiten-zushi no keizaigaku* (The economics of kaiten-zushi). Tokyo: Besuto Shinsho.

Watanabe Zenjirō, ed. 1988. *Kyōdai toshi Edo ga washoku o tsukutta* (Metro-politan Edo created Japanese cuisine). Tokyo: Nobunkyō.

Watson, James L. 1997. "Transnationalism, Localization, and Fast Foods in East Asia." In *Golden Arches East: McDonald's in East Asia*, edited by James L. Watson, pp. 1–38. Stanford: Stanford University Press.

Webb, Herschel, with Marleigh Ryan. 1965. *Research in Japanese Sources: A Guide*. New York: Columbia University Press.

White, Merry I. 2002. *Perfectly Japanese: Making Families in an Era of Upheaval*. Berkeley: University of California Press.

Whitney, Clara. 1979. *Clara's Diary: An American Girl in Meiji Japan*. Tokyo: Kodansha International.

Whynott, Douglass. 1995. *Giant Bluefin*. New York: Farrar Straus Giroux.

Williams, S. C. 1988. *Marketing Chilled Fish in Japan*. Brisbane: Queensland Department of Primary Industries.

Williamson, Oliver E. 1985. *The Economic Institutions of Capitalism: Firms, Markets, Relational Contracting*. New York: Free Press.

Williamson, Oliver E., and Scott E. Masten, eds. 1999. *The Economics of Trans-action Costs*. Cheltenham: E. Elgar.

Wilson, James. 1980. "Adaptation to Uncertainty and Small Numbers Exchange: The New England Fresh Fish Market." *Bell Journal of Economics* 11: 491–504.

Woodard, Colin. 2000. *Ocean's End*. New York: Basic Books.

Yagyū Kyūbe'e. 2003. *Kaiten-zushi no sa-sushi-se-so* (The ABCs of kaiten-zushi). Tokyo: Ekusunoreji.

Yamagishi Toshio. 1999. *Anshin shakai kara shinrai shakai e* (From safe society toward trust society). Tokyo: Chūō Shinsho.

Yamagishi, Toshio, and Yamagishi Midori. 1994. "Trust and Commitment in the United States and Japan." *Motivation and Emotion* 18 (2): 129–66.

————. 1998. "Trust and Commitment as Alternative Responses to Social Uncertainty." In *Networks, Markets, and the Pacific Rim: Studies in Strategy*, edited by W. Mark Fruin, pp. 109–23. New York: Oxford University Press.

Yamashita Machiko. 1998. *From Kitchen: Katei no Shokuji*. Osaka: Gasu Enerugi Bunka Kenkyūjo.

Yang, Mayfair Mei-hui. 1994. *Gifts, Favors, and Banquets: The Art of Social Relationships in China*. Ithaca, N.Y.: Cornell University Press.

Yano Ken'ichi, ed. 1989. *Sakana no Nihonshi: Shiriizu shizen to ningen no Nihonshi 1* (Fish and Japanese history: Series on nature, humans, and Japan-ese history 1). Tokyo: Shinjinbutsu Oraisha.

Yonemoto, Marcia. 1999. "Nihonbashi: Edo's Contested Center." *East Asian History*, nos. 17/18: 49–70.

Yoshino Masuo. 1986. *Sushi*. Tokyo: Gakken.

Young, Louise. 1998. *Japan's Total Empire: Manchuria and the Culture of Wartime Imperialism*. Berkeley: University of California Press.

Zenner, Walter P. 1991. *Minorities in the Middle*. Albany: State University of New York Press.

Zukin, Sharon. 1991. *Landscapes of Power*. Berkeley: University of California Press.

Index

Page numbers in *italics* refer to figures, illustrations, maps, or tables.

New Year's holidays *(continued)*
Shrine, *296,* 296; Tsukiji closing for,
225, 314
NHK (Nippon Hōsō Kyōkai) (television network), 134, 218, 336n8.
See also Mass Media; Television
Nichiro Gyogyō K.K. (fisheries company), *203*
Nigiri-zushi (variety of sushi), 141,
154, 326, 330. See also *Edomae-zushi*
Nihonbashi fish market, 24, 93, *99,*
103, 215, 218, 330; bidding at, *191;*
cheating at to evade taxes, 108, *109;*
dealers' land-use rights *(itafune-ken),* 112, 114–15, 269, 303, 328;
and defense of Tokugawa shōgunate,
110, 307; destroyed by Kantō earthquake (1923), 24, 100–101, 112–13,
113; feudal tribute system, 106–7,
108, 109; fish wholesalers' guilds
in, 106; location of, *59, 94,* 98–99;
New Year's at, *298;* origins of, 60,
101–3; relocation of, 95, 97, 112–
13, 115; shōgun authorities and,
103, 104, 105, 108–10; as shōgun
court supplier, 102, 103, 105, 106–7,
109; teahouses *(chaya)* at, 87–88;
under Meiji government, 110–12;
vertical control in, 201; wholesalers
at, 105–6. *See also* Edo; Tsukiji
market
Nihonbashi uogashi. *See* Nihonbashi
fish market
Nimotsu. See Consignment goods
Ninushi. See Consignors
Nippon Suisan K.K. (fisheries
company), 120, *203,* 344n22, 347n
Nishimura Eiko, xx, 44, 337n18
Nishin. See Herring
Niuke. See Consignees
Niuke gaisha. See Auction houses: as
consignee firms
Noren. See Shop curtain
Norenwake. See Shop division
Nōrinshō, Nōrinsuisanshō. *See* Ministry of Agriculture, Forestry and
Fisheries (MAFF)

Northern bluefin tuna. *See* Tuna:
northern bluefin
Norway, seafood imported from, *33*
Nyūka. See Consignment goods:
incoming
Nyūsatsu (written bidding). *See* Auctions; Bidding

"O.B." *See* Affiliations; "Old boys"
network
O-bentō. See Box lunches
Obligatory contracting. *See*
Relational contracting
O-Bon (holiday season, August), 224–
25
Octopus *(tako), 5, 11, 32,* 150, *248,* 333
Ohnuki-Tierney, Emiko, 140
Oishinbo: manga series, 135, *136,*
345n6; television program, 135
Okonomiyaki (egg omelet or frittata),
144, *321*
O-kure (end-of-year season), 295,
296–97
"Old boys" network, 221, 243. *See
also* Affiliations
Ōmono. See Swordfish; Tuna
Ōmono Gyōkai (Large Products Trade
Group), 223, *261,* 262, 266–67,
355n4. *See also* Swordfish; Tuna
Ōmori Market, 269, 270
Open bidding *(seri). See* Auctions;
Bidding
Organized crime. *See* Gangsters
Oroshi gyōsha. See Auction houses
Oroshi-uri. See Wholesale sales
Orosu. See Wholesale selling
Osaka, 93, 101; food preferences, 139,
140, 197; and *E. coli* outbreak, 144;
during Tokugawa period, 104
O-sechi ryōri. See New Year's cuisine
Ōta Dōkan, 102
Ōta Market, 74, 183, 269–71; proposed
Tsukiji relocation to, 271, 303; TMG
and, 269–70, 293, 303; Tō-Oroshi
at, 270–71; Tsukiji wholesalers relocated to, 269–70, 271
Outer market *(jōgai shijō),* 21–22, *58,*

United States *(continued)*
seafood trade with Japan, 31, *33,*
166, 349n24; trade negotiations 6-7,
336n12. *See also* Allied Occupation
of Japan; World War II
Unloading. *See* Seafood handling and
arranging
Uogashi. See Fish quay
Uogashi (children's book), 234
Uogashi-kai (Uogashi Suijin Festival
committee), 93, 96
Uogashi Suijin Festival (Uogashi Suijin-sai), 91–95, 96, 341n1. *See also*
Suijin Shrine
Uoichiba. See Fish market
Urayasu, 221, 222; compensation for
fishing rights, 120, 223, 269; Disneyland's impact on, 222; historical ties
to Tsukiji, 120; land reclamation,
120; real estate values in, 222
Urayasu firms, as Tsukiji traders, 120–
21, 221–23, 355n4

Vertical integration, 192, 200; of central wholesale markets, 184–86;
licenses and, 201; to limit market
power, 201; of Maruha group, 204–
5; of Tsukiji auctions, 182, 201–6,
210–11, 219, 247. *See also* Distribution channels; *Keiretsu*
Vertically integrated conglomerates.
See *Keiretsu*
Vickrey, William. *See* Auctions:
economic theory of
Videotapes, about Tsukiji, 321
Vietnam, seafood imported from, *33*
Vinegar, 348n17

Wakadanna. See Family firms: heirs
to
Wa-shoku. See Japanese cuisine
Watanabe (sushi shop owner) (pseud.),
1–2, 47–49; sushi shop of, 1–4, 48;
at Tsukiji, 4–6
Water pollution: in Tokyo Bay, 55, 120,
348n18; from Tsukiji wastes, 121,
340n17

Websites on Tsukiji, fisheries, and
environmental issues, 321–23
"Western" cuisine *(yō-shoku),* 141,
150–52, 157–58, 334, 346n9,
348n13; canned goods, use in, 152;
"Franco-Japonaise" style, 157
Whale *(kujira),* 171, *248,* 329, 347n;
Japanese vs. American cultural perceptions, 131
Whaling, 119, 143, 344n22, 346n11;
International Whaling Commission ,
34; ritual practices, 171
Whitebait *(shirauo),* 332
Wholesale markets, 7, 183–84;
categories, 184–86; hierarchies
of traders, 186; legal aspects, 182,
184, 187; in Tokyo, *184;* vertical
organization of, 184–86. *See also*
Central wholesale markets; Regional
wholesale markets
Wholesale merchant firms *(ton'ya),*
107–8, 111, 115, 201, 333; Central
Wholesale Market Law and, 114;
control of fishing grounds, 105–6,
111; origins of, 105–6
Wholesale purchasers *(kaidashinin).*
See Fishmongers; Intermediate
wholesalers; Retail shops; Supermarkets; Sushi chefs; Trade buyers
Wholesale purchasing *(kaidashi),* 329
Wholesalers. *See* Auction houses;
Guilds; Intermediate wholesalers;
Wholesale merchant firms
Wholesale sales *(oroshi-uri),* 331
Wholesale selling *(orosu),* 331
Williamson, Oliver, 182, 192
Women: as auctioneers, 83, 354n10; as
cashiers, 83; clerical workers, 83, 84;
culinary expertise, 83, 158, 159,
349n22; jobs at Tsukiji, 233; mothering skills, social pressures on, 159;
roles in family firms, 84; seafood
sellers, 83; as sushi chefs, 83–84,
126–27; temperature of hands, 83,
126, 345n1
Wordplay *(sharé),* 311, 332; counting
slang, 86–87, *87;* pricing codes, 85–

Compositor: BookMatters, Berkeley
Text: 10/13 Aldus
Display: Franklin Gothic
Indexer: Jeanne Moody
Cartographer: Bill Nelson
Printer and binder: Sheridan Books, Inc.

CALIFORNIA STUDIES IN FOOD AND CULTURE

Darra Goldstein, Editor